Critique Book

PROLOG

Gynecologic Oncology and Surgery

Third Edition

acog
The American College of Obstetricians and Gynecologists

ISBN 0-915473-28-3

The American College of Obstetricians and Gynecologists
409 12th Street, SW
Washington, DC 20024-2188

Contributors

PROLOG Editorial and Advisory Committee

Leo J. Dunn, MD, Chairman
Chairman, Department of Obstetrics and Gynecology
Medical College of Virginia
Virginia Commonwealth University

Sharon L. Dooley, MD
Professor, Obstetrics and Gynecology
Section of Maternal–Fetal Medicine
Department of Obstetrics and Gynecology
Northwestern University Medical School

Gerald B. Holzman, MD
Director
Division of Education
The American College of Obstetricians and Gynecologists

PROLOG Task Force for *Gynecologic Oncology and Surgery,* Third Edition

William J. Hoskins, MD, Chairman
Chief, Gynecology Service
Department of Surgery
Avon Chair in Gynecologic Oncology Research
Memorial Sloan–Kettering Cancer Center
Professor of Obstetrics and Gynecology
Cornell University Medical College

Carolyn D. Runowicz, MD
Vice Chairman
Professor and Director
Division of Gynecologic Oncology
Department of Obstetrics and Gynecology
Albert Einstein College of Medicine and Montefiore Medical Center

Vicki V. Baker, MD
George W. Morley Professor of Obstetrics and Gynecology
Director, Division of Gynecologic Oncology
University of Michigan Medical Center

David L. Hemsell, MD
Professor and Director
Division of Gynecology
Department of Obstetrics and Gynecology
University of Texas Southwestern Medical Center

William H. Hindle, MD
Professor of Clinical Obstetrics and Gynecology
Division of Gynecology
Department of Obstetrics and Gynecology
University of Southern California

Robert J. Kurman, MD
Professor of Gynecology, Obstetrics, and Pathology
Director of Gynecologic Pathology
Department of Gynecology, Obstetrics, and Pathology
The Johns Hopkins School of Medicine

John R. Lurain, MD
John and Ruth Brewer Professor of Gynecology and Cancer Research
Head, Section of Gynecologic Oncology
Department of Obstetrics and Gynecology
Northwestern University Medical School

Peter F. McComb, MD
Professor
Division of Reproductive Endocrinology and Infertility
Department of Obstetrics and Gynaecology
University of British Columbia

Steven J. Ory, MD
Northwest Center for Infertility and Reproductive Endocrinology
Margate, Florida

ACOG Staff

Sallye B. Shaw, RN, MN
Associate Director
Division of Education
Willa Houtwed Cleary
Editor

Preface

Purpose

PROLOG, Personal Review of Learning in Obstetrics and Gynecology, is a voluntary, strictly confidential self-evaluation program. PROLOG is designed to enable physicians to assess their current knowledge and to review current concepts within the specialty. The content is carefully selected and presented in clinically oriented multiple-choice questions. The questions are designed to stimulate and challenge physicians in areas of medical care that they confront in their practice or as consultant obstetrician–gynecologists.

PROLOG also provides the American College of Obstetricians and Gynecologists with a means of identifying the educational needs of the Fellowship. Individual scores are reported only to the participant; however, cumulative performance data obtained for each PROLOG unit help determine the direction for future educational programs offered by the College.

Continuing medical education credits may be earned by participation in the PROLOG self-evaluation process. In addition, PROLOG serves as a valuable study tool, reference guide, and means of attaining up-to-date knowledge in the specialty.

Process

PROLOG offers the most advanced knowledge available in five areas of the specialty—obstetrics, gynecology, reproductive endocrinology and infertility, gynecologic oncology and surgery, and patient management in the office. A new PROLOG unit is produced annually, addressing one of these subject areas. *Gynecologic Oncology and Surgery,* Third Edition, is part of the third 5-year series of PROLOG.

Each unit of PROLOG represents the efforts of a special task force of subject experts under the supervision of an editorial and advisory committee. PROLOG sets forth current information as viewed by recognized authorities in the field of women's health. This educational resource does not define a standard of care, nor is it intended to dictate an exclusive course of management. It presents recognized methods and techniques of clinical practice for consideration by obstetrician–gynecologists for incorporation into their practices. Variations of practice taking into account the needs of the individual patient, resources, and limitations unique to the institution or type of practice may be appropriate.

Each unit of PROLOG is presented as a two-part set, with performance information and cognate credit available to those who choose to send their answer sheets for confidential scoring.

A. The first part of the PROLOG set is the Question Book, which contains educational objectives for the unit, multiple-choice questions, and a computer-scored answer sheet. Participants can work through the book at their own pace, choosing to use PROLOG as a closed- or open-book assessment. Return of the answer sheet for scoring is encouraged, but is voluntary.

B. The Critique Book completes the PROLOG set. The Critique Book reviews the educational objectives and questions set forth in the Question Book and contains a discussion, or critique, of each question. The critique provides the rationale for correct and incorrect options. Current, accessible references are listed for each question. ACOG Fellows may request additional literature searches as well as information about ACOG publications by contacting the Resource Center, 409 12th Street SW, Washington, DC 20024, telephone (202) 863-2518.

C. Participants who return their answer sheets for credit will receive a Performance Report indicating their answers and their percentage correct score. A data package will be sent offering participants a means of comparing their scores with the scores of a sample group of other participants. *Please allow 2 months to process answer sheets.*

D. Fellows who submit their answer sheets for scoring will be credited automatically with 25 cognate hours of Formal Learning in the ACOG Program for Continuing

Professional Development. Twenty-five category 1 credit hours may be reported for the Physician's Recognition Award of the American Medical Association.

Credit for *Gynecologic Oncology and Surgery,* Third Edition, is initially available through December 1998. During that year, the unit will be reevaluated. If it is determined that content in the unit remains current, credit will be extended for an additional 3 years. This change in policy has been made to ensure that the College is in compliance with the Standards for Enduring Materials of the Accreditation Council for Continuing Medical Education. This continuing medical education activity was planned and produced in accordance with the *Accreditation Council for Continuing Medical Education Essentials.*

Conclusion

PROLOG was developed specifically as a personal study resource for the practicing obstetrician–gynecologist. It is presented as a self-assessment mechanism, which—with its accompanying performance information—should assist the physician in designing a personal, self-directed learning program. The many quality resources developed by the College, as detailed each year in the ACOG *Publications and Educational Materials* catalog, are available to help fulfill the educational interests and needs that have been identified.

PROLOG is not intended as a substitute for the certification or recertification programs of the American Board of Obstetrics and Gynecology.

PROLOG Objectives

PROLOG is a voluntary, strictly confidential, personal continuing education resource designed to be both stimulating and enjoyable. By participating in PROLOG, obstetrician–gynecologists will be able to:

- Review and update clinical knowledge
- Recognize areas of knowledge and practice in which they excel, be stimulated to explore other areas of the specialty, and identify areas requiring further study
- Plan continuing education activities in light of identified strengths and deficiencies
- Compare and relate present knowledge and skills to those of other participants
- Obtain continuing medical education credit, if desired
- Have complete personal control of the setting and pace of the experience

***Gynecologic Oncology and Surgery,* Third Edition**

Obstetrician–gynecologists who complete *Gynecologic Oncology and Surgery,* Third Edition, will be able to:

- Identify epidemiologic factors that contribute to the risk of various malignancies and determine appropriate screening tests
- Analyze the pathophysiology and evaluate the histopathology of various malignancies
- Associate symptoms with early onset of specific malignancies, determine appropriate diagnostic tests, and select the diagnosis
- Identify physical and surgical findings related to specific stages of malignant disease
- Determine appropriate surgical or nonsurgical management for various types of cancer and identify common complications of therapy
- Determine approaches for preoperative assessment, select surgical techniques for gynecologic disorders, and identify common complications of surgery
- Apply knowledge of anatomy, wound healing, and appropriate surgical techniques in the surgical therapy of gynecologic disease
- Counsel patients regarding therapy and expected outcome of management of gynecologic malignancies

***Gynecologic Oncology and Surgery,* Third Edition, includes the following topics:**

SCREENING
Breast cancer
Cervical cancer
Colorectal cancer
Skin cancer

PHYSIOLOGY AND PATHOPHYSIOLOGY
Endometrial hyperplasia and cancer risk
Epithelial ovarian cancer
Estrogen and progesterone receptors and breast cancer
Intraductal breast carcinoma
Malignant mixed mesodermal tumor
Microinvasive carcinoma of the cervix
Partial and complete mole
Tumor markers in ovarian germ cell tumor
Uterine papillary serous carcinoma
Vulvar intraepithelial neoplasia

Color plates and a subject matter index appear at the end of the book.

PROLOG

Gynecologic Oncology and Surgery

Third Edition

1

Conservative therapy of stage I ovarian tumor

A 27-year-old woman, gravida 1, para 0, abortus 1, underwent exploratory laparotomy for an 8-cm complex ovarian mass. A unilateral salpingo-oophorectomy and full surgical staging procedure were performed. The final pathologic examination reveals International Federation of Gynecology and Obstetrics (FIGO) stage IA1 serous cystadenocarcinoma of the ovary. The patient wishes to maintain her reproductive capacity. The best postsurgical management is

* (A) no further treatment
(B) total abdominal hysterectomy and removal of the remaining fallopian tube and ovary
(C) cisplatin (Platinol) and cyclophosphamide
(D) intraperitoneal ^{32}P
(E) paclitaxel (Taxol) and cisplatin

Therapy in a young woman with ovarian cancer is determined by 1) FIGO stage, 2) histologic cell type, 3) histologic grade, and 4) the reproductive desires of the patient. This patient has undergone a full surgical staging procedure, which by definition includes partial omentectomy; biopsies of the pelvic peritoneum, bladder, rectal serosa, lateral pericolic gutters, and hemidiaphragms; and sampling of the pelvic and paraaortic lymph nodes. The diagnosis of stage IA carcinoma indicates that the tumor is confined to the ovary with no rupture or tumor on the surface of the ovary and that all of the biopsies were negative. Histologic grade 1 serous, mucinous, or endometrioid carcinoma may be treated conservatively. Clear cell or small cell carcinomas should not be treated conservatively. The histologic grade in this patient is 1.

The most appropriate therapy for this patient is follow-up with no further therapy. The Gynecologic Oncology Group (GOG) data have shown that such patients have a 95% survival rate with no additional treatment (Table 1-1, Fig. 1-1). Similar survival was noted in patients receiving melphalan (Alkeran) chemo-

TABLE 1-1. Tumor Recurrences and Deaths Among Patients with Stage I or Stage II Ovarian Cancer

Characteristic	First Trial: Observation Group	First Trial: Melphalan Group	Second Trial: ^{32}P Group	Second Trial: Melphalan Group
No. of patients with follow-up	38	43	73	68
No. (%) of recurrences	4 (11)	1 (2)	14 (19)	13 (19)
Time to recurrence (mo)	23, 29, 57, 65	18	Median: 16; range: 4–78	Median: 12; range 3–84
Site of recurrence				
Pelvis only	1	0	5	3
Pelvis and abdomen	1	1	3	7
Distant	1	0	6	3
Unknown	1	0	0	0
No. of deaths	4	2	16	15
Ovarian cancer primary cause	3	1	12	10
Ovarian cancer secondary cause	1	0	2	0
Late therapy-related complication	0	1*	0	2
Other	0	0	2	3
Time to death (mo)	28, 57, 65, 71	35, 38	Median: 37; range: 3–90	Median: 36; range: 10–94

* This patient died of aplastic anemia that was possibly related to treatment.

Reprinted by permission of The New England Journal of Medicine from Young RC, Walton LA, Ellenberg SS, Homesley HD, Wilbanks GD, Decker DG, et al. Adjuvant therapy in stage I and stage II epithelial ovarian cancer: results of two prospective randomized trials. N Engl J Med 1990;322:1025; copyright 1990, Massachusetts Medical Society

* Indicates correct answer.

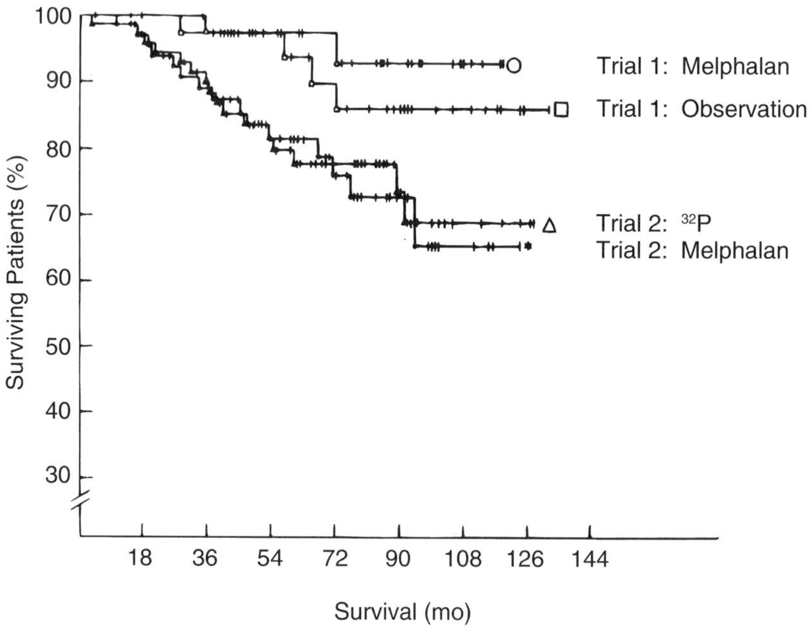

FIG. 1-1. Overall survival of patients with stage I or stage II epithelial ovarian cancer, according to protocol and treatment. Of the 81 patients in the first trial, 4 of 38 in the observation group and 2 of 43 in the melphalan group died. Of the 141 patients in the second trial, 16 of 73 in the ^{32}P group and 15 of 68 in the melphalan group died. (Reprinted by permission of The New England Journal of Medicine from Young RC, Walton LA, Ellenberg SS, Homesley HD, Wilbanks GD, Decker DG, et al. Adjuvant therapy in stage I and stage II epithelial ovarian cancer: results of two prospective randomized trials. N Engl J Med 1990;322:1025; copyright 1990, Massachusetts Medical Society)

therapy. To be monitored without additional therapy, however, these patients must have had a full surgical staging procedure. The GOG investigators found that 31% of patients referred to participating institutions who were diagnosed with stage I or II disease without a full surgical staging procedure were up-staged (most to stage III) when a full surgical staging procedure was performed (Table 1-2).

Immediate reoperation to remove the uterus and remaining fallopian tube and ovary is not indicated for this patient, who wants further childbearing. Although there may be a small risk of developing a cancer in the remaining ovary, the risk is considered sufficiently low to allow the patient to retain the remaining ovary. Follow-up, however, is indicated.

TABLE 1-2. Results of Repeat Staging in Apparent Stage I and II Ovarian Cancer

Initial Stage	No. of Patients	Percentage Up-Staged
IA	37	16
IB	10	30
IC	2	0
IIA	4	100
IIB	38	39
IIC	9	33
Total	100	31

Young RC, Decker DG, Wharton JT, Piver MS, Sindelar WF, Edwards BK, et al. Staging laparotomy in early ovarian cancer. JAMA 1983;250:3072–3076; copyright 1983, American Medical Association

The GOG data showed no benefit for the administration of chemotherapy in patients with stage IA1 cancers. For patients at higher risk (stage IA3 or IB3; stage IC; and stage IIA, IIB, and IIC), most authorities recommend some type of adjunctive therapy. The optimal choice of such therapy is less clear. The GOG is evaluating a short course (three cycles) of cisplatin and cyclophosphamide versus intraperitoneal ^{32}P, and one European study indicated improved progression-free survival but not improved overall survival for five courses of cisplatin and cyclophosphamide compared with intraperitoneal ^{32}P. Combination therapy with paclitaxel and cisplatin has not been tested in early-stage disease.

Buchsbaum HJ, Brady MF, Delgado G, Miller A, Hoskins WJ, Manetta A, et al. Surgical staging of carcinoma of the ovaries. Surg Gynecol Obstet 1989;169:226–232

Pecorelli S, Bolis G, Colombo N, Favalli G, Giardina G, Landoni F, et al. Adjuvant therapy in early ovarian cancer: results of two randomized trials (abstract). Gynecol Oncol 1994;52:103

Young RC, Decker DG, Wharton JT, Piver MS, Sindelar WF, Edwards BK, et al. Staging laparotomy in early ovarian cancer. JAMA 1983;250:3072–3076

Young RC, Walton LA, Ellenberg SS, Homesley HD, Wilbanks GD, Decker DG, et al. Adjuvant therapy in stage I and stage II epithelial ovarian cancer: results of two prospective randomized trials. N Engl J Med 1990;322:1021–1027

2

Risk of lymph node metastasis in cervical cancer

A 36-year-old woman, gravida 5, para 5, reports postcoital bleeding of 6 months' duration. A pelvic examination reveals a 5-cm lesion replacing the cervix. Rectovaginal examination fails to disclose parametrial invasion. A cervical biopsy is reported to show a poorly differentiated squamous cell cancer with no lymph-vascular invasion and a high nuclear grade. A chest X-ray, intravenous pyelogram, cystoscopy, and sigmoidoscopy are normal. You inform the patient that her risk of lymph node metastasis is

* (A) approximately 15% based on her stage of disease
(B) not correlated with tumor size
(C) not correlated with cervical stromal invasion
(D) related to tumor grade
(E) predicated by the presence or absence of lymph-vascular invasion in the cervical biopsy

The 5-year survival rate for patients with stage IB cervical carcinoma is 85%. Survival is influenced by the histopathological variables of tumor size, lymph node metastasis, and stage.

The clinical staging of cervical cancer is determined by inspection and palpation of the cervix, vagina, and pelvis and by examination of extrapelvic areas, chiefly the abdomen and supraclavicular lymph nodes. The extent of the disease should be further evaluated by chest X-ray, intravenous urography, and if indicated by the location or extent of disease, cystoscopy and sigmoidoscopy. Lymphangiography, computed tomography, ultrasonography, and pretherapy extraperitoneal surgical staging by pelvic and/or paraaortic lymph node biopsy are not currently used for clinical staging; however, these may assist in individualized therapy. Based on the above information, this patient has clinical stage IB disease. Approximately 15% of women with stage IB carcinoma of the uterine cervix have metastasis to the pelvic lymph nodes.

Increased tumor size and depth of cervical stromal invasion are associated with an increased probability of pelvic nodal disease and are inversely correlated with progression-free interval and survival. In most studies, histologic grade does not correlate with lymph node metastasis or overall survival. Grading by the histopathologist is often not reproducible. Multivariate analysis in several studies has failed to identify grading as an important prognostic indicator.

Lymph-vascular invasion on a cervical biopsy or in a hysterectomy specimen is an important biologic marker and predictor of survival and may be predictive of metastasis to pelvic or paraaortic lymph nodes.

Alvarez RD, Potter ME, Soong S-J, Gay FL, Hatch KD, Patridge EE, et al. Rationale for using pathologic tumor dimensions and nodal status to subclassify surgically treated stage IB cervical cancer patients. Gynecol Oncol 1991;43:108–112

American College of Obstetricians and Gynecologists. Diagnosis and management of invasive cervical carcinomas. ACOG Technical Bulletin 138. Washington, DC: ACOG, 1989

Stehman FB, Bundy BN, DiSaia PJ, Keys HM, Larson JE, Fowler WC. Carcinoma of the cervix treated with radiation therapy, I: a multi-variate analysis of prognostic variables in the Gynecologic Oncology Group. Cancer 1991;67:2776–2785

Zaino RJ, Ward S, Delgado G, Bundy B, Gore H, Fetter G, et al. Histopathologic predictors of the behavior of surgically treated stage IB squamous cell carcinoma of the cervix: a Gynecologic Oncology Group study. Cancer 1992;69:1750–1758

3

Breast cancer screening

A 50-year-old woman, on her first visit to your office for an annual physical examination, asks your advice about breast cancer screening. A mammogram 5 years ago indicated that her breasts were dense. She has taught herself to do breast self-examination (BSE), which she does monthly. Your clinical breast examination reveals prominent, diffuse, and tender nodules throughout both her breasts with no dominant mass. You advise her that with her findings, the single most effective breast cancer screening method is

(A) annual clinical breast examinations by a physician
(B) annual breast thermography
(C) annual breast ultrasound examination with color flow Doppler
* (D) annual mammography
(E) monthly BSE after instruction

Annual screening mammography is the most effective technique for early breast cancer detection for all women. Annual clinical breast examination is an essential component of breast cancer screening because at least 10% of palpable breast cancers are not seen on mammograms.

Breast thermography has low specificity for cancer, with an unacceptable level of false-positive and false-negative responses. Ultrasonography has not proven to be a reliable screening technique for breast cancer. It does not have the degree of resolution of X-rays. It is useful, however, for distinguishing between solids and liquids and thus is helpful in identifying benign cysts. Although color flow Doppler may increase the sensitivity of sonographic diagnosis in a focused ultrasound breast examination, the technique is investigational and not appropriate for breast cancer screening.

Compared with no self-examination, monthly BSE results in earlier detection of breast cancer at the time of diagnosis, but it has not been demonstrated to increase overall survival. The most effective method of teaching BSE is to provide verbal instruction, demonstrate the procedure on the patient, and finally reinforce the patient's learning by having her demonstrate the procedure on herself.

American College of Radiology. Policy statement on sonography for the detection and diagnosis of breast disease. Reston, Virginia: American College of Radiology, 1984

Baines CJ, Wall C, Risch HA, Kuin JK, Fan IJ. Changes in breast self-examination behaviour in a cohort of 8214 women in the Canadian National Breast Screening Study. Cancer 1986;57:1209–1216

Baker LH. Breast cancer detection demonstration project: five-year summary report. CA Cancer J Clin 1982;32:194–225

Foster RS Jr, Lang SP, Costanza MC, Worden JK, Haines CR, Yates JW. Breast self-examination practices and breast-cancer stage. N Engl J Med 1978;299:265–270

Greenwald P, Nasca PC, Lawrence CE, Horton J, McGarrah RP, Gabriele T, et al. Estimated effect of breast self-examination and routine physician examinations on breast-cancer mortality. N Engl J Med 1978;299:271–273

Kopans DB, Meyer JE, Sadowsky N. Breast imaging. N Engl J Med 1984; 310:960–967

Wertheimer MD, Costanza ME, Dodson TF, D'Orsi C, Pastides H, Zapka JG. Increasing the effort toward breast cancer detection. JAMA 1986;255:1311–1315

4
Chemotherapy for germ cell tumor

A 17-year-old woman is diagnosed with stage IA endodermal sinus tumor of the ovary after right salpingo-oophorectomy and surgical staging. The optimal management after surgery is

(A) surveillance at 4-month intervals including pelvic examination and serum alpha-fetoprotein determination
(B) combination chemotherapy with vincristine sulfate (Oncovin), dactinomycin (Cosmegen), and cyclophosphamide (the VAC regimen)
* (C) combination chemotherapy with bleomycin sulfate (Blenoxane), etoposide (VePesid), and cisplatin (Platinol) (the BEP regimen)
(D) adjunctive whole-pelvis radiation therapy

This patient should be treated with bleomycin, etoposide, and cisplatin (BEP). In the absence of combination chemotherapy, the survival of patients with stage I endodermal sinus tumor is poor. Surveillance with pelvic examination and tumor marker measurements is unacceptable, because the recurrence rate for stage I endodermal sinus tumor is as great as 85%.

The BEP regimen is associated with sustained disease-free intervals. In one series of 35 patients, 34 remained free of disease with a median follow-up of 10 to 54 months. In another series of 52 patients with stage I, II, or III disease, 50 patients with completely resected disease were disease-free after three cycles of BEP. Short-term toxicity associated with the BEP regimen includes alopecia, nausea, vomiting of variable severity, and occasional interim neutropenia.

Before introduction of the BEP regimen, patients with nondysgerminomatous germ cell neoplasms of the ovary were treated with vincristine, dactinomycin, and cyclophosphamide (VAC). This regimen demonstrates greater short-term toxicity, such as interim febrile neutropenia requiring hospitalization (15%) and reversible neurotoxicity. In view of the more favorable short-term toxicity profile and improved efficacy, BEP has replaced VAC in this country.

Long-term toxicities associated with cisplatin-based regimens originally used in men treated for testicular neoplasms included neurotoxicity, ischemic heart disease, leukemia, Raynaud phenomenon, nephrotoxicity, high-tone hearing loss, skin changes, and pulmonary dysfunction. There are no data concerning the frequency of these adverse effects in women with nondysgerminomatous ovarian neoplasms treated with BEP.

Interestingly, ovarian function usually appears to be preserved in young women who are treated with cisplatin-based regimens. One series reported 40 patients who were diagnosed with malignant ovarian germ cell tumors at a median age of 15 years, were treated with cisplatin-based therapy, and subsequently were interviewed at a median age of 25.5 years. Twenty-seven patients maintained regular menses. Sixteen patients attempted conception and 11 were successful, delivering 22 healthy infants, none of whom exhibited major birth defects.

Adjuvant radiation therapy does not play a role in the initial postsurgical management of germ cell neoplasms of the ovary.

Gershenson DM. Menstrual and reproductive function after treatment with combination chemotherapy for malignant ovarian germ cell tumors. J Clin Oncol 1988;6:270–275

Gershenson DM. Update on malignant ovarian germ cell tumors. Cancer 1993; 71:1581–1590

Gershenson DM, Kavanagh JJ, Copeland LJ, del Junco G, Cangir A, Saul PB, et al. Treatment of malignant nondysgerminomatous germ cell tumors of the ovary with vinblastine, bleomycin, and cisplatin. Cancer 1986;57:1731–1737

Gershenson DM, Morris M, Cangir A, Kavanagh JJ, Stringer CA, Edwards CL, et al. Treatment of malignant germ cell tumors of the ovary with bleomycin, etoposide, and cisplatin. J Clin Oncol 1990;8:715–720

5
Melanoma of the vulva

A 47-year-old white woman presents for annual examination. At physical examination, a 1.1 × 1.5-cm scaly, slightly raised area of hyperpigmentation with irregular, curved borders is noted along the inferior lateral aspect of the right labium minus. The patient states that it has been present for many years. Speculum and bimanual examinations are normal. The appropriate next step in the management of this patient is

(A) schedule return in 1 year
(B) steroid cream to the lesion
* (C) punch biopsy of the lesion
(D) wide local excision of the lesion

This patient probably has superficially spreading melanoma, which may be confused with several benign conditions such as seborrheic keratosis, benign nevus, lentigo, or freckle. Superficially spreading melanoma is preceded by lentigo maligna (in situ melanoma) for up to 20 years. Simple excisional biopsy of a benign nevus or lentigo will eliminate concern about future melanoma.

Because biopsy is indicated for a pigmented vulvar lesion, continued observation of this patient would be inappropriate. A therapeutic trial of steroid cream would also be inappropriate, as it could delay diagnosis and suggest to the patient that the finding is insignificant and that follow-up is unnecessary.

Biopsy will allow accurate diagnoses of the lesion and guide any further definitive therapy. Biopsy should be taken in a manner that allows depth measurement, because depth is the most important prognostic variable. Wide local excision would provide definitive therapy but would be a more extensive procedure than that needed for diagnosis.

The International Federation of Gynecology and Obstetrics staging for squamous vulvar malignancy does not apply to vulvar melanoma because melanomas are smaller, and prognosis is influenced more by depth of penetration than by lesion diameter. Prognosis worsens and recurrence increases with increased tumor volume, however. Patients with lesions having a volume less than 100 mm^3 have an excellent prognosis. Microstaging classifications for vulvar melanoma, which have been proposed by Clark, Chung, and Breslow (Table 5-1), allow individualized therapy and a decrease in mutilating vulvar surgery without compromising survival.

The overall survival rate of women with vulvar melanoma is similar to that of women with cutaneous melanomas elsewhere. The survival rate at 10 years for women treated for lateral vulvar lesions (61%) is better than that observed for women with medial lesions (37%).

Breslow A. Thickness, cross-sectional areas and depth of invasion in the prognosis of cutaneous melanoma. Ann Surg 1970;172:902–908

Chung AF, Woodruff JM, Lewis JL Jr. Malignant melanoma of the vulva: a report of 44 cases. Obstet Gynecol 1975;45:638–646

Clark WH Jr, From L, Bernardino EA, Mihm MC. The histogenesis and biologic behavior of primary human malignant melanomas of the skin. Cancer Res 1969;29:705–726

Look KY, Roth LM, Sutton GP. Vulvar melanoma reconsidered. Cancer 1993;72:143–146

TABLE 5-1. Microstaging for Vulvar Melanoma Based on Depth of Invasion with Survival Rates

	Depth of Invasion (% Survival)*		
Stage	**Clark†**	**Chung‡**	**Breslow§**
I	Intraepithelial	Intraepithelial	<0.76 mm
II	Into papillary dermis (92)	<1 mm from granular layer (100)	0.76–1.50 mm (97)
III	Filling dermal papillae (45)	1–2 mm from granular layer (40)	1.51–2.25 mm (76)
IV	Into reticular dermis (30)	>2 mm from granular layer (40)	2.26–3.0 mm (43)
V	Into subcutaneous fat (10)	Into subcutaneous fat (20)	>3 mm (34)

* Classifications are described in the references found in the reference list.
† Survival rate shown is at 2 years.
‡ Corrected 5-year survival rate is at 5 years.
§ Data are for those free of disease at 5+ years.
Adapted from Hacker NF, Eifel P, McGuire W, Wilkinson EJ. Vulva. In: Hoskins WJ, Perez CA, Young RC, eds. Principles and practice of gynecologic oncology. Philadelphia: JB Lippincott, 1992:559

6

Cervical cancer risk with human immunodeficiency virus infection

A 24-year-old woman, gravida 4, para 2, who recently tested positive for the human immunodeficiency virus (HIV) presents for her annual gynecologic examination. Three consecutive annual Pap tests have been satisfactory and negative. Her pelvic examination reveals no abnormalities. The patient is anxious because her mother died of cervical cancer 1 year ago. The strongest risk factor for the development of cervical cancer in this patient is

(A) a family history of cervical cancer
(B) her Pap test history
(C) her positive HIV status
* (D) her CD4 lymphocyte count

Risk factors for cervical neoplasia include the age at onset of sexual activity, cigarette smoking, the number of sexual partners, Pap test history, and a history of sexually transmitted infections. The American College of Obstetricians and Gynecologists has suggested that after three annual negative, satisfactory Pap tests, subsequent screening is at the discretion of the physician. Recommendations concerning subsequent screening should take into account the individual patient's risk factors.

At this time, there is no evidence to suggest a heritable component for cervix cancer. A positive family history is not considered a risk factor for this disease.

Three annual satisfactory Pap tests are reassuring with respect to a patient's risk of future cervical neoplasia. However, other risk factors must be considered. Infection with HIV has emerged as a potential risk factor for cervical neoplasia. This risk is related to the degree of immunosuppression that is present, predicted by the absolute mean CD4 lymphocyte count. CD4 lymphocytes are helper–inducer T cells, and CD8 lymphocytes are suppressor–cytotoxic T cells. CD4 cells and CD8 cells are differentiated by the expression of T-cell surface markers, which can be detected by immunohistochemical methods. An absolute mean CD4 count of less than 360/mm^3 is associated with increased risk of cervical cancer and more rapid progression of disease.

Women who are HIV positive and have a normal CD4 cell count (>600/mm^3) do not appear to be at increased risk of cervical neoplasia, compared with a population that has a similar risk profile. HIV-infected women diagnosed with invasive cervical cancer are considered to have the acquired immunodeficiency syndrome (AIDS), based on the expanded case definition proposed by the Centers for Disease Control and Prevention in 1993.

Because HIV-infected patients are at risk for numerous medical problems, they should be followed closely. It has been recommended that HIV-infected women whose CD4 count is below normal have Pap tests at 6-month intervals.

Adachi A, Fleming I, Burk RD, Ho GYF, Klein RS. Women with human immunodeficiency virus infection and abnormal Papanicolaou smears: a prospective study of colposcopy and clinical outcome. Obstet Gynecol 1993;81:372–377

American College of Obstetricians and Gynecologists. Cervical cytology: evaluation and management of abnormalities. ACOG Technical Bulletin 183. Washington, DC: ACOG, 1993

Maiman M. Cervical neoplasia in women with HIV infection. Oncology 1994;8:83–89

Maiman M, Fruchter RG, Guy L, Cuthill S, Levine P, Serur E. Human immunodeficiency virus infection and invasive cervical carcinoma. Cancer 1993;71:402–406

Mandelblatt JS, Fahs M, Garibaldi K, Senie RT, Peterson HB. Association between HIV infection and cervical neoplasia: implications for clinical care of women at risk for both conditions. AIDS 1992;6:173–178

Smith JR, Kitchen VS, Botcherby M, Hepburn M, Wells C, Gor D, et al. Is HIV infection associated with an increase in the prevalence of cervical neoplasia? Br J Obstet Gynaecol 1993;100:149–153

7
Histopathology of uterine sarcomas

Examination of a 47-year-old woman with lower abdominal discomfort and regular, heavy menstrual bleeding reveals a symmetrically enlarged uterus. Your diagnosis is uterine leiomyomata, and you perform a total abdominal hysterectomy and bilateral salpingo-oophorectomy. When the 12-week-size uterus is cut, a soft, yellow-gray tumor mass without an apparent capsule is noted to protrude from the cut surface. In some areas, pale yellow, worm-like tumor extensions are noted within the vessels of the broad ligament. On the basis of the surgical findings, your diagnosis is

(A) uterine leiomyosarcoma
(B) cystic degeneration of a uterine leiomyoma
(C) malignant mixed mesodermal tumor of the uterus
* (D) low-grade endometrial stromal sarcoma
(E) endometrial stromal nodule

The gross examination of the uterus, revealing worm-like protrusions of yellow-gray cords of tumor that fill the blood vessels in the broad ligament, suggests the diagnosis of a low-grade endometrial stromal sarcoma. In the past, this tumor was termed endolymphatic stromal myosis or stromatosis.

In contrast to high-grade stromal sarcomas, low-grade stromal sarcomas have a characteristic pattern of myometrial invasion manifested by masses of endometrial stromal cells with minimal cytologic atypia that diffusely infiltrate the myometrium, penetrating vascular and lymphatic channels (Fig. 7-1; see color plates). High-grade stromal sarcomas completely destroy and replace the myometrium rather than infiltrating through the uterine wall in discrete masses and nests. Although mitotic activity is usually low (less than 5 mitotic figures per 10 high-power fields), this feature does not provide the basis for distinguishing low-grade from high-grade stromal sarcomas. It is the overall growth pattern on microscopic examination that provides the basis for the diagnosis.

In contrast to low-grade stromal sarcoma, uterine leiomyosarcoma lacks specific characteristics that distinguish it on gross examination. On occasion, areas of softening in an otherwise typical leiomyoma may raise concern about sarcomatous change, but in general the diagnosis is rarely suspected on gross examination. Microscopically, the tumor is composed of neoplastic smooth muscle cells.

The classic appearance of cystic degeneration within a preexisting leiomyoma is quite distinctive. The myoma, with its well-circumscribed capsule, is unchanged; however, a central area of softening and necrosis is apparent on cut section.

Patients with mixed mesodermal tumor and carcinosarcoma present with exophytic polypoid masses that often prolapse through the cervix. Both of these neoplasms display a characteristic biphasic appearance consisting of both carcinoma and sarcoma. Heterologous elements such as rhabdomyosarcoma, osteosarcoma, or chondrosarcoma are found in mixed mesodermal tumors.

An endometrial stromal nodule on gross examination is typically a well-circumscribed mass. Its cut surface is homogeneous and yellow and lacks the whorled appearance of a leiomyoma. The appearance of the cells in a benign endometrial stromal nodule is similar to that of a low-grade endometrial stromal sarcoma. In contrast to the irregular infiltrating margin of the latter, the endometrial stromal nodule has an expansive margin.

Baggish MS, Woodruff JD. Uterine stromatosis. Clinical pathologic features in hormone dependency. Obstet Gynecol 1972;40:487–498

Baker VV, Walton LA, Fowler WD Jr, Currie JL. Steroid receptors in endolymphatic stromal myosis. Obstet Gynecol 1984;63(3 suppl):72S–74S

Hart WR, Yoonessi M. Endometrial stromatosis of the uterus. Obstet Gynecol 1976;49:393–403

Zaloudek C, Norris HJ. Mesenchymal tumors of the uterus. In: Kurman RJ, ed. Blaustein's pathology of the female genital tract. 4th ed. New York: Springer-Verlag, 1994:487–528

8

Therapy for endometrial adenocarcinoma

A 65-year-old woman presents with postmenopausal bleeding. Physical examination is significant only for an enlarged, mobile, anteverted uterus. Endometrial curettage reveals a grade 3 endometrial adenocarcinoma; the endocervical curettage is negative for malignancy. Chest X-ray does not reveal any abnormalities.

The patient undergoes a total abdominal hysterectomy and bilateral salpingo-oophorectomy, as well as pelvic and paraaortic lymph node sampling. Histologic examination reveals a grade 3 endometrial adenocarcinoma, 90% myometrial invasion with lymph-vascular space invasion, negative lymph nodes, and negative peritoneal cytology. The most commonly used treatment plan for a patient with this diagnosis is

(A) careful follow-up
(B) vaginal cuff radiation therapy
* (C) irradiation of the pelvis and upper vagina
(D) whole-abdomen radiation therapy
(E) chemotherapy with doxorubicin hydrochloride

Endometrial carcinoma is the most common tumor of the female genital tract. In approximately 75% of patients with endometrial cancer, the disease appears to be confined to the uterus at the time of diagnosis, yet 15% of such patients will develop recurrence after hysterectomy. Many of these recurrences are in the pelvis. The potential for endometrial carcinoma to recur locally despite apparent surgical removal of the tumor, as well as the proven effectiveness of radiotherapy in this disease, has led to the practice of combining hysterectomy with radiotherapy for certain groups of patients with endometrial cancer.

In recent years, preoperative radiotherapy has given way to postoperative radiotherapy based on accurate surgical staging and pathologic findings. Postoperative irradiation may involve irradiation of the vaginal apex alone (brachytherapy), treatment of the entire pelvis with or without paraaortic or whole-abdomen irradiation by using external-beam techniques (teletherapy), or a combination of these techniques.

Postoperative vaginal irradiation alone can be given with a vaginal cylinder or colpostats to deliver a surface dose of 6,000–7,000 cGy to the upper vagina. More recently, after-loading outpatient techniques with a high dose rate have been used at some centers. Numerous studies have demonstrated that the frequency of vaginal recurrence in stage I endometrial cancer can be reduced from 3–8% to approximately 1% by the administration of postoperative vaginal irradiation. Patients most likely to benefit from vaginal irradiation are those with grade 1 and 2 tumors with superficial (less than one half the thickness of the myometrium) myometrial invasion.

Postoperative whole-pelvis external-beam irradiation usually involves the delivery of 4,500–5,000 cGy in 180-cGy daily fractions over 5–6 weeks to a field encompassing the upper one half of the vagina inferiorly, the lower border of the L4 vertebral body superiorly, and 1 cm lateral to the margins of the bony pelvis (Fig. 8-1). The dose of irradiation at the surface of the vaginal apex is often boosted to 6,000–7,000 cGy by a variety of techniques. Whole-pelvis irradiation is often preferred to vaginal cuff irradiation because the radiation field (whole pelvis) includes both the pelvis and the upper vagina.

Patients found to benefit most from adjuvant postoperative whole-pelvis irradiation are those with clinical stage I disease who are at significant risk for nodal metastases because of any of the following tumor characteristics:

- Grade 3 tumor with any degree of myometrial invasion
- Grade 1 tumor or tumor with deep (at least one half the thickness of the myometrium) myometrial invasion
- Large (>2 cm) grade 2 tumor with superficial myometrial invasion

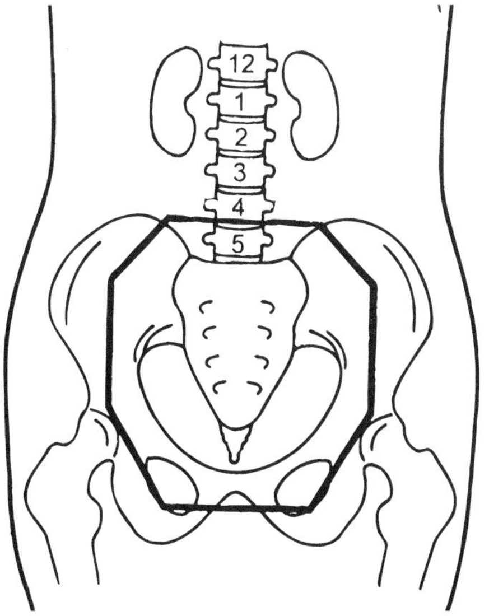

FIG. 8-1. The field for whole-pelvis and upper vagina irradiation.

- Any grade tumor with lymph-vascular space invasion or cervical involvement

The rate of recurrence in the pelvis is reduced by giving postoperative pelvic irradiation to these groups of high-risk patients. At least in patients with grade 3 tumors and deep myometrial invasion, such as the patient described, survival may also be improved.

Whole-abdomen radiation therapy is usually reserved for patients with stage III and IV endometrial cancer. It may also be considered for patients who have papillary serous or mixed müllerian tumors, which have a propensity for recurrence in the upper abdomen. The recommended dose to the whole abdomen is 3,000 cGy in 20 daily fractions of 150 cGy with kidney shielding at 1,500–2,000 cGy, along with an additional 1,500 cGy to the paraaortic lymph nodes and 2,000 cGy to the pelvis.

Patients with metastatic endometrial carcinoma not amenable to cure by surgery or radiotherapy, or both, are candidates for hormone therapy or chemotherapy. For patients with well-differentiated advanced or late recurrent disease, hormone therapy with progestins or antiestrogens should be considered first. For patients with poorly differentiated recurrent or advanced endometrial cancer, initial cytotoxic therapy may be best. Doxorubicin hydrochloride, the most effective single-agent therapy, yields response rates up to 37%. The combination of doxorubicin and cisplatin (Platinol) has produced a response rate of 69%. Based on current data, there is no apparent benefit to the use of adjuvant chemotherapy in combination with or in place of radiation therapy in patients at high risk for recurrence or metastasis.

Aalders J, Abeler V, Kolstad P, Onsrud M. Postoperative external irradiation and prognostic parameters in stage I endometrial carcinoma. Obstet Gynecol 1980;56:419–426

Kadar N, Malfetano JH, Homesley HD. Determinants of survival of surgically staged patients with endometrial carcinoma histologically confined to the uterus: implications for therapy. Obstet Gynecol 1992;80:655–659

Morrow CP, Bundy BN, Kurman RJ, Creasman WT, Heller P, Homesley HD, et al. Relationship between surgical-pathological risk factors and outcome in clinical stage I and II carcinoma of the endometrium: a Gynecologic Oncology Group study. Gynecol Oncol 1991;40:55–65

Schink JC, Rademaker AW, Miller DS, Lurain JR. Tumor size in endometrial cancer. Cancer 1991;67:2791–2794

9

Surgical staging of ovarian carcinoma

A 52-year-old woman underwent a laparotomy 10 days ago for an abdominal mass (Fig. 9-1; see color plate). A grade 1 serous cystadenocarcinoma was diagnosed and confirmed by histology after the procedure. The operative report describes the tumor as confined to one ovary. A total abdominal hysterectomy and bilateral salpingo-oophorectomy were performed; no other surgical procedures were described. The optimal management for this woman is

(A) no further treatment
* (B) repeat laparotomy
(C) abdominopelvic radiotherapy
(D) chemotherapy
(E) abdominopelvic radiotherapy and chemotherapy

The accurate staging of ovarian cancer (Appendix, Table 1) reduces the possibility of residual tumor being unrecognized and untreated and results in improved survival in women who otherwise might not be selected for further therapy. One third of women who are referred with apparent stage I or II ovarian cancer will have a change in stage with further investigation, including laparotomy. Frequently unrecognized sites of the disease are pelvic and paraaortic lymph nodes, omentum, cul-de-sac peritoneum, and diaphragm. Comprehensive staging to discover metastasis has decreased the number of reported early-stage cancers.

Comprehensive staging is performed as follows. The peritoneal cavity is entered through a midline incision, and ascitic fluid or washings are obtained and sent for cytologic evaluation. The tumor capsule is examined for adhesions, rupture, or excrescences. Complete abdominal exploration is performed, with particular attention to pelvic peritoneum, paracolic gutters, surface of the diaphragm, and serosal surfaces of the intestines. In addition to resection of the primary tumor, infracolic omentectomy and pelvic and paraaortic lymph node sampling are completed.

In the clinical example presented, the patient's disease has been inadequately staged. Despite an understandable reluctance to reoperate, it is imperative that surgery be performed to allow correct staging and treatment of the cancer. Conversely, to provide no further therapy, radiotherapy, chemotherapy, or a combination of radiotherapy and chemotherapy cannot be justified.

Friedlander ML, Dembo AJ. Prognostic factors in ovarian cancer. Semin Oncol 1991;18:205–212

Parker RT, Parker CH, Wilbanks GD. Cancer of the ovary: survival studies based upon operative therapy, chemotherapy, and radiotherapy. Am J Obstet Gynecol 1970;108:878–887

Richardson GS, Scully RE, Nikrui N, Nelson JH. Common epithelial cancer of the ovary (first of two parts). N Engl J Med 1985;312:417–424

Rubin SC, Jones WB, Curtain JP, Barakat RR, Hakes TB, Hoskins WJ. Second-look laparotomy in stage I ovarian cancer following comprehensive surgical staging. Obstet Gynecol 1993;82:139–142

Young RC, Walton LA, Ellenberg SS, Homesley HD, Wilbanks GD, Decker DJ, et al. Adjuvant therapy in stage I and stage II epithelial ovarian cancer. N Engl J Med 1990;322:1021–1027

10

Factors affecting breast cancer risk

A 32-year-old woman who underwent a total abdominal hysterectomy and bilateral salpingo-oophorectomy for tuboovarian abscess wishes to discuss estrogen replacement therapy. She is particularly concerned about her risk of breast cancer, because her 60-year-old mother was diagnosed as having the disease 1 month ago. The patient had a breast biopsy for a fibroadenoma earlier, but her history is otherwise unremarkable. Which of the following statements is correct to use when counseling this patient?

(A) Breast cancer is the most common cause of death from cancer in women in the United States.

* (B) Oophorectomy in premenopausal women is associated with a decreased risk of breast cancer.

(C) Her risk of breast cancer can be significantly reduced by the addition of progestin to the estrogen replacement therapy regimen.

(D) Estrogen replacement therapy is contraindicated by her history of fibroadenoma.

Breast cancer, the most common type of cancer in women, is second only to lung cancer as a cause of death among women. The American Cancer Society estimated that there were 182,000 new cases and 46,300 deaths from breast cancer in 1994. The risk of breast cancer continues to increase proportional to age, and by age 85 the lifetime risk is 1 in 9 (Table 10-1). Despite the frequency with which breast cancer occurs, a clear understanding of etiologic factors is still forthcoming.

The following observations are cited as circumstantial evidence that suggest a relationship between estrogen and breast cancer. Bilateral oophorectomy in premenopausal women reduces the risk of subsequent breast cancer by 40–70%, and this effect is most dramatic for women losing ovarian function before age 35. Early menarche and late menopause are associated with increased risk. There is an inverse relationship between parity and breast cancer, but the age at first birth is an even more important factor. Compared with women having their first child at age 35 or later, women having their first child before 18 years of age have one third the risk of developing breast cancer. Breast cancer occurs only after puberty, and the risk of developing breast cancer increases with age. Although breast cancer does occur in men, it is 182 times more common in women. Untreated women with gonadal dysgenesis do not develop breast cancer. There is an association between breast cancer and endometrial cancer, which has a well-established estrogen link. Breast tumors usually contain estrogen receptors.

TABLE 10-1. Women's Lifetime Risk of Developing Invasive Breast Cancer*

Age (y)	Risk
25	1 in 17,637
30	1 in 2,261
35	1 in 218
40	1 in 96
45	1 in 51
50	1 in 34
55	1 in 24
60	1 in 18
65	1 in 18
70	1 in 14
75	1 in 12
80	1 in 10
85	1 in 9
Ever	1 in 8

* Data are from 1989–1991, all races.

DEVCAN: Probability of Developing cancer software, version 3.1. Feuer EJ, Wun LM. National Cancer Institute, 1994

Despite a large body of evidence suggesting increased risk of breast cancer with protracted *endogenous* estrogen exposure, there is no clear evidence confirming increased risk as a consequence of exogenous estrogen exposure. To establish cause and effect, the relative risk established in one study should be confirmed by other centers and correlated with increased duration and dosage of therapy. The data should be consistent with current medical knowledge, as well as with clinical, laboratory, and animal data establishing such a link, and the data should be internally consistent. The current body of clinical data does not satisfy all these criteria.

Over 40 epidemiologic studies have addressed the relationship between estrogen therapy and breast cancer since 1970. Their conclusions are not consistent. Five recently published metaanalyses of these data, commonly based on no more than 5 years of use, found no increased risk of breast cancer in women who ever took estrogen compared with nonusers. Most studies failed to demonstrate a relationship between increasing dose or different treatment regimens and risk of breast cancer. Metaanalyses have been even less consistent in establishing a relationship between the duration of therapy and risk of breast cancer. Two recent metaanalyses described a summary risk estimate of 1.3 (confidence interval, 1.2–1.6) for women using estrogen for at least 15 years compared with nonusers. An additional recent study, which addressed pooled estimates from case–control and cohort studies in women using estrogen for 8 years or more, calculated a summary relative risk of 1.25 (confidence interval, 1.04–1.51). These estimates may be high because of surveillance biases in women receiving estrogen or low if estrogen therapy is selectively withheld from women at higher risk for breast cancer. These studies effectively exclude estrogen therapy as a major risk factor for breast cancer but do not exclude a possible low risk with long-term therapy.

A family history of breast cancer in a first-degree relative increases the risk of breast cancer two to three times over that of the general population. It is uncertain whether this risk is further modified by estrogen use. The recently identified *BRCA* breast cancer genes may allow this risk to be estimated more precisely in some women.

Several studies have evaluated the effect of estrogen with the addition of progestin on breast cancer, and their conclusions are inconsistent. Only one of these studies suggested a statistically significant decrease in breast cancer in women receiving estrogen plus progestin, and that study contained significant methodologic flaws and potential confounding variables. Currently there is no compelling evidence that progestin therapy reduces the risk of developing breast cancer. The value of including a progestin in a hormone replacement therapy (HRT) regimen in women who have had a hysterectomy is not supported by the current literature.

A history of benign breast disease has been suggested as a risk factor in the past. Fibrocystic change and fibroadenoma per se are not considered risk factors for breast carcinoma except in women with a previous biopsy showing atypia as part of fibrocystic change.

In all patients considering HRT, the potential benefits of reduced risk of cardiovascular disease and osteoporosis must be weighed against the potential risks. There is no reason to withhold HRT in the patient described, and she may experience statistically significant benefits in reduced risk of cardiovascular disease and osteoporosis.

Colditz GA, Egan KM, Stampfer MJ. Hormone replacement therapy and risk of breast cancer: results from epidemiologic studies. Am J Obstet Gynecol 1993;168:1473–1480

Dupont WD, Page DL, Rogers LW, Parl FF. Influence of exogenous estrogens, proliferative breast disease, and other variables on breast cancer risk. Cancer 1989;63:948–957

Gambrell RD Jr. Role of progestogens in the prevention of breast cancer. Maturitas 1986;8:169–176

Grady D, Rubin SM, Petitti DB, Fox CS, Black D, Ettinger B, et al. Hormone therapy to prevent disease and prolong life in postmenopausal women. Ann Intern Med 1992;117:1016–1037

Henderson BE, Ross RK, Pike MC. Breast neoplasia. In: Mishell DR Jr, ed. Menopause: physiology and pharmacology. Chicago: Year Book Medical Publishers, 1987:261–274

Lyle KC. Female breast cancer: distribution, risk factors, and effect of steroid contraception. Obstet Gynecol Surv 1980;35:413–427

Steinberg KK, Thacker SB, Smith SJ, Stroup DF, Zack MM, Flanders WD, et al. A meta-analysis of the effect of estrogen replacement therapy on the risk of breast cancer. JAMA 1991;265:1985–1990; errata JAMA 1991:266:1362

11

Vulvar surgery and its effect on sexual function

A 51-year-old woman presents with a 1.5-cm squamous cell carcinoma of the vulva, which is located 3 cm lateral to the midportion of the right labium majus. No other vulvar lesions are visible, and there are no palpable groin lymph nodes.

A radical wide excision is performed in the operating room, and 2-cm free margins are achieved on all sides. Frozen section diagnosis confirms that the patient has invasive squamous cell carcinoma of the vulva, with 4 mm of tumor invasion into the stroma. Which of the following options is most likely to achieve adequate treatment and preservation of sexual function?

(A) No additional therapy
* (B) Ipsilateral inguinal–femoral lymphadenectomy
(C) Simple vulvectomy and bilateral inguinal–femoral lymphadenectomy
(D) Radical vulvectomy
(E) Radical vulvectomy and bilateral inguinal–femoral lymphadenectomy

Carcinoma of the vulva is a relatively uncommon gynecologic malignancy, representing 4–5% of all gynecologic tumors and resulting in approximately 0.3% of all cancer deaths in women. Survival has been positively affected by extirpative surgical procedures, specifically radical vulvectomy and bilateral groin dissection. However, significant morbidity has been described with these procedures. Wound infection, wound necrosis, serous fluid collection, wound separation, and chronic lymphedema have been reported in up to 50% of patients in some series.

Adverse psychosexual consequences of radical vulvectomy have been recognized more recently. In one study, women who had undergone vulvectomy were compared with age-matched controls by using standard psychometric indices. Patients undergoing vulvectomy were noted to be in the third percentile for current sexual activity, the eighth percentile for sexual arousal, and the fourth percentile for positive body image. All patients who had undergone vulvectomy described a major disruption in their sexuality. The incision required for radical vulvectomy and bilateral groin dissection is shown in Fig. 11-1.

Over the past two decades there has been a well-established trend toward conservative surgical treatment of vulvar carcinoma in an effort to avoid immediate and long-term postoperative morbidity. Radical wide excision (defined as a dissection to the deep perineal fascia) of early vulvar carcinomas is safe and adequate treatment for many patients with unifocal T1 disease (≤2 cm) and in selected patients with T2 or T3 (≥2 cm) lesions. Surgical margins of at least 2 cm are desirable, and the dissection should be extended to the deep perineal fascia. Radical wide excision with separate inguinal–femoral lymphadenectomy has been documented to be an effective alternative to simple or radical vulvectomy and bilateral inguinal–femoral lymphadenectomy in selected patients. It offers more rapid recovery, fewer complications, and better functional results. A more extensive operation, removing the entire vulva with the clitoris, does not contribute to survival and would severely compromise this patient's sexual function. A simple vulvectomy would not adequately treat this lesion.

Lymph node dissection is the single most important factor in reducing mortality from early recurrence of vulvar cancer. Patients presenting with recurrent disease with lymph node involvement after initial treatment limited to vulvectomy usually do not survive, so whether or not to perform a lymphadenectomy is a critical decision.

Although most patients with early vulvar carcinomas do not have lymph node involvement, a consistent, small percentage of patients present with early inguinal node metastases. Their subsequent treatment and survival are influenced by an inguinal–femoral lymphadenectomy being performed initially. Several different techniques have been described for evaluating and man-

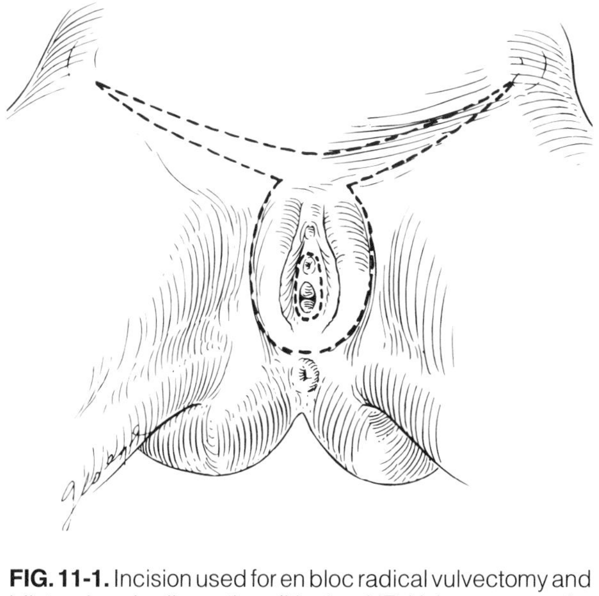

FIG. 11-1. Incision used for en bloc radical vulvectomy and bilateral groin dissection. (Hacker NF. Vulvar cancer. In: Berek JS, Hacker NF, eds. Practical gynecologic oncology. 2nd ed. Baltimore: Williams & Wilkins, 1994:419; copyright Williams & Wilkins)

aging these patients. There has also been debate over how depth of invasion is measured and which depth constitutes a significant risk for regional nodal involvement.

The World Health Organization and the International Society of Gynecologic Pathologists recommend that depth of invasion be measured from the most superficial dermal papilla adjacent to the tumor, to the deepest focus of invasion. It is recommended that a lymph node dissection be performed if the depth of invasion is greater than 1 mm. Lateral lesions may be adequately treated with a unilateral inguinal–femoral lymphadenectomy because the risk of positive contralateral nodes is less than 1% if there is no involvement of the ipsilateral nodes. Bilateral groin dissection would be indicated in this patient if the ipsilateral nodes were positive. A bilateral groin dissection should be performed in patients with midline lesions and lesions extending to adjacent tissues (T3 lesions).

Triple-incision radical vulvectomy (performing a vulvectomy with separate incisions for each inguinal–femoral lymphadenectomy) (Fig. 11-2) provides satisfactory survival results with less morbidity than en bloc radical vulvectomy, but either operation is much more extensive than that required for the patient described, who has early vulvar carcinoma. Loss of the vulva by either of these techniques is associated with impaired sexual function and altered body image.

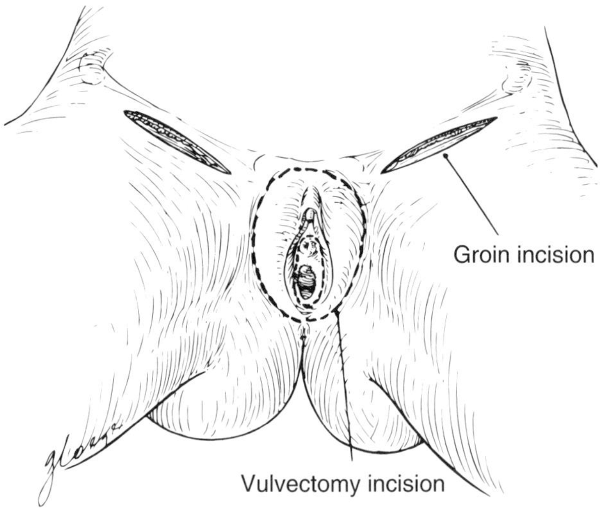

FIG. 11-2. Triple-incision vulvectomy. (Hacker NF. Vulvar cancer. In: Berek JS, Hacker NF, eds. Practical gynecologic oncology. 2nd ed. Baltimore: Williams & Wilkins, 1994:418; copyright Williams & Wilkins)

Anderson BL, Hacker NF. Psychosexual adjustment after vulvar surgery. Obstet Gynecol 1983;62:457–462

Burke TW, Stringer CA, Gershenson DM, Edwards CL, Morris M, Wharton JT. Radical wide excision and selective inguinal node dissection for squamous cell carcinoma of the vulva. Gynecol Oncol 1990; 38:328–332

Cavanagh D, Fiorica JV, Hoffman MS, Roberts WS, Bryson SCP, LaPolla JP, et al. Invasive carcinoma of the vulva: changing trends in surgical management. Am J Obstet Gynecol 1990;163:1007–1015

Hacker NF. Vulvar cancer. In: Berek JS, Hacker NF, eds. Practical gynecologic oncology. Baltimore: Williams & Wilkins, 1994:417–419

Hacker NF, Van der Velden J. Conservative management of early vulvar cancer. Cancer 1993;71:1673–1677

Hopkins MP, Reid GC, Morley GW. Radical vulvectomy: the decision for the incision. Cancer 1993;72:799–803

Kelley JL III, Burke TW, Tornos C, Morris M, Gershenson DM, Silva EG, et al. Minimally invasive vulvar carcinoma: an indication for conservative surgical therapy. Gynecol Oncol 1992;44:240–244

12

Atypical endometrial hyperplasia and cancer risk

A 62-year-old woman presents with postmenopausal bleeding. An endometrial biopsy shows complex, atypical endometrial hyperplasia. You explain to the patient that this condition

* (A) is a precursor of endometrial cancer
(B) has the same risk of progression to cancer as complex hyperplasia without atypia
(C) is rarely associated with abnormal vaginal bleeding
(D) cannot reliably be diagnosed by endometrial biopsy

Endometrial cancer may be prevented by the recognition and treatment of precursor lesions (hyperplasia) of the endometrium. Endometrial hyperplasias are classified as simple or complex based on the architectural pattern or glandular complexity. They are further classified by the presence or absence of cytologic atypia. The World Health Organization classification of endometrial hyperplasia is shown in the box. Architectural complexity without atypia in a postmenopausal woman

Classification of Endometrial Hyperplasia

Simple hyperplasia
Complex hyperplasia (adenomatous)
Simple atypical hyperplasia
Complex atypical hyperplasia (adenomatous with atypia)

Reproduced with permission of World Health Organization, from: Scully RE, et al. Histologic typing of female genital tract tumours. 2nd ed. Berlin: Springer-Verlag, 1994

TABLE 12-1. Relationship Between Type of Endometrial Hyperplasia and Risk of Progression to Carcinoma

Type of Hyperplasia	No. of Patients	Percentage Progressed to Cancer	Mean Years of Follow-up
No cytologic atypia			
Simple	93	1	15.2
Complex	29	3	13.5
Atypical			
Simple	13	8	11.4
Complex	35	29	11.4

Adapted from Kurman RJ, Kaminski PF, Norris HJ. The behavior of endometrial hyperplasia. A long-term study of "untreated" hyperplasia in 170 patients. Cancer 1985;56:410

may indicate abnormal stimulation of the endometrium, as occurs with anovulation at the perimenopause.

Table 12-1 shows the potential of endometrial hyperplasia to progress to carcinoma of the endometrium. As can be seen, hyperplasia on the basis of architectural complexity alone is not related to increased risk of developing endometrial carcinoma, but any cytologic atypia does carry increased risk.

There is little or no risk of progression to endometrial carcinoma in simple or complex endometrial hyperplasia without atypia. However, simple hyperplasia with atypia progresses to carcinoma in 8% of cases, and complex (adenomatous) hyperplasia with atypia progresses to carcinoma in 29% of cases.

Most patients with complex atypical hyperplasia have abnormal vaginal bleeding, and prompt endometrial biopsy or dilation and curettage will result in a correct diagnosis. Endometrial hyperplasia that is not associated with atypia may be treated by the administration of oral progestins. In patients with atypical hyperplasia who have no medical contraindications, hysterectomy should be considered. In selected patients who desire further childbearing, atypical hyperplasia may be treated with progestin. Follow-up of such patients with periodic endometrial biopsies is indicated.

Kurman RJ, Kaminski PF, Norris HJ. The behavior of endometrial hyperplasias. A long-term study of "untreated" hyperplasia in 170 patients. Cancer 1985;56:403–412

Park RC, Grigsby PW, Muss HB, Norris HJ. Corpus: epithelial tumors. In: Hoskins WJ, Perez CA, Young RC, eds. Principles and practice of gynecologic oncology. Philadelphia: JB Lippincott, 1992:663–665

Silverberg SG. Hyperplasia and carcinoma of the endometrium. Semin Diagn Pathol 1988;5:135–153

Tumors of the endometrium. In: Morrow CP, Curtin JP, Townsend DE, eds. Synopsis of gynecologic oncology. 4th ed. New York: Churchill Livingstone, 1993:153–188

13
Diagnosis of postsurgical urinary fistula

A 46-year-old woman returns to your office complaining of urine leakage from her vagina 10 days after a total abdominal hysterectomy and bilateral salpingo-oophorectomy. On examination, you note excoriated external genitalia and perineum. Speculum examination reveals urine pooled in the vaginal vault. The next step in evaluating the site of the fistula is

(A) cystoscopy
* (B) instillation of methylene blue by urethral catheter into the bladder
(C) injection of intravenous indigo carmine into a peripheral vein
(D) intravenous pyelogram

Urinary fistulas usually occur within 2 weeks of the causative injury. It has been estimated that serious injury to the urinary tract occurs in more than 8,000 of the 700,000 patients (1.1%) who have hysterectomies performed each year. In large reported series, more than 50% of the fistulas resulted from a simple abdominal hysterectomy. Injury to the bladder most commonly occurs at the time of dissection of the bladder off of the lower uterine segment and cervix, especially in patients with scarring from previous surgery or inflammatory processes. Ureteral injuries during laparoscopically assisted hysterectomy have been linked to the use of an endoscopic stapler and to extensive laparoscopic dissection of the bladder off of the cervix and vagina.

Ureteral injury may also occur with other laparoscopic procedures such as ablation of endometriosis or uterosacral nerve ablation.

When a fistula is suspected because of a watery or profuse vaginal discharge during the postoperative period, it is frequently possible to diagnose the problem without cystoscopic examination. An early step consists of the instillation of a solution of 1 ml of methylene blue per 100 ml of saline into the bladder and the insertion of a tampon into the vagina. If the tampon becomes stained with the dye, a vesicovaginal fistula is diagnosed. If the tampon is not stained, 5 ml of 0.8% indigo carmine is intravenously injected into a peripheral vein. If the tampon becomes stained with the dye, a ureterovaginal fistula may be present.

Immediate additional diagnostic measures may not be necessary for a vesicovaginal fistula. The bladder should be drained by a large-caliber transurethral Foley catheter. Definitive therapy should be delayed to allow for resolution of the associated edema. Spontaneous healing may occur in small fistulas not associated with malignancy or radiation therapy. Catheter drainage beyond 30 days rarely results in spontaneous closure. A cystourethroscopic study should eventually be performed to determine the position of the fistula in relation to the trigone, bladder neck, and ureteral orifices and to exclude multiple fistulas, which occur in 15% of patients.

If a ureterovaginal fistula has been detected, intravenous or retrograde urography should be performed to demonstrate the fistula site. Cystoscopy may allow retrograde insertion of a ureteral stent. If this insertion is successful, the stent can be left in place for 4–6 weeks and operative repair may be avoided. If retrograde insertion is unsuccessful, a percutaneous nephrostomy is left in place to drain the kidney. In a few days, an antegrade stent can be placed through the percutaneous nephrostomy.

Fistula repair should be deferred until the surrounding tissues are in optimal condition. Depending on the type and location of the fistula, the type of initial operation, and the conditions for which the operation was performed, a delay of 2–4 months may be required.

American College of Obstetricians and Gynecologists. Genitourinary fistulas. ACOG Technical Bulletin 83. Washington, DC: ACOG, 1985

Kadar N, Lemmerling L. Urinary tract injuries during laparoscopically assisted hysterectomy: causes and prevention. Am J Obstet Gynecol 1994;170: 47–48

Mandal AK, Sharma SK, Vaidyanathan S, Goswami AK. Ureterovaginal fistula: summary of 18 years' experience. Br J Urol 1990;65:453–456

Woodland MB. Ureter injury during laparoscopy-assisted vaginal hysterectomy with the endoscopic linear stapler. Am J Obstet Gynecol 1992;167:756–757

14

Diagnosis of vulvar Paget disease

A 65-year-old woman who was diagnosed with Duke stage C colon cancer 2 years ago presents with vulvar itching and pain of several months' duration. She has been prescribed a variety of topical ointments and creams with little improvement in her symptoms. Inspection of the vulva reveals an eczematoid, erythematous lesion of the labia majora (Fig. 14-1; see color plate).

A punch biopsy of the lesion is performed in the office. Immunohistochemical stains are positive for carcinoembryonic antigen and negative for the S-100 antigen. The diagnosis is

* (A) extramammary Paget disease
(B) melanoma
(C) vulvar intraepithelial neoplasia
(D) squamous hyperplasia
(E) colon cancer metastatic to the vulva

Paget disease of the vulva (Fig. 14-1) is often misdiagnosed clinically as eczema, contact dermatitis, squamous hyperplasia, vulvar intraepithelial neoplasia, or melanoma. A history of prior unsuccessful treatment of symptoms with a variety of topical antibiotics and antifungal agents is common. In this patient, who has been treated for colon cancer, metastatic disease to the vulva is included in the differential diagnosis.

Accurate diagnosis of a vulvar lesion is established by biopsy. Inspection of the photomicrograph from this patient's biopsy (Fig. 14-2; see color plate) reveals Paget cells, which have prominent nucleoli and coarse chromatin, clustered near the basement membrane. The cytoplasm of these cells is pale with a vacuolated or foamy appearance.

Histologically, extramammary Paget disease of the vulva may be confused with melanoma and vulvar intraepithelial dysplasia. Melanoma may also exhibit large, irregular, vacuolated cells. Vulvar intraepithelial neoplasia can exhibit large, pale intraepithelial cells.

TABLE 14-1. Immunohistochemical Stains Diagnostic of Vulvar Disease

Disease	Carcinoembryonic Antigen	S-100	Melanoma Antigen	Cytokeratin
Paget cells	Positive	Negative	Negative	Negative
Melanoma	Negative	Positive	Positive	Negative
Vulvar intraepithelial neoplasia	Negative	Negative	Negative	Positive

When the histopathologic diagnosis is not clear, these conditions can be differentiated by the results of special immunohistochemical stains (Table 14-1).

Squamous hyperplasia and colon cancer metastatic to the vulva exhibit distinct histologic appearances and are not confused with Paget disease of the vulva, vulvar intraepithelial neoplasia, or melanoma.

Bacchi CE, Goldfogel GA, Greer BE, Gown AM. Paget's disease and melanoma of the vulva: use of a panel of monoclonal antibodies to identify cell type and to microscopically define adequacy of surgical margins. Gynecol Oncol 1992;46:216–221

Olson DJ, Fujimura M, Swanson P, Okagaki T. Immunohistochemical features of Paget's disease of the vulva with and without adenocarcinoma. Int J Gynecol Pathol 1991;10:285–295

Shah KD, Tabibzadeh SS, Gerber MA. Immunohistochemical distinction of Paget's disease from Bowen's disease and superficial spreading melanoma with the use of monoclonal cytokeratin antibodies. Am J Clin Pathol 1987;88: 689–695

15

Control of postoperative hemorrhage

A difficult vaginal hysterectomy with bilateral salpingo-oophorectomy was performed on a healthy 47-year-old woman, gravida 3, para 3. Her preoperative hemoglobin was 12.0 g/dl. Estimated blood loss during the operation was 350 ml. Six hours after surgery, her hemoglobin was 11.5 g/dl and her urine output was 50 ml/h.

On the first postoperative day, the patient is nervous and restless and reports back pain. Her pulse rate is 110 beats per minute; blood pressure is 100/70 mm Hg, which is maintained when upright; and her urine output is 40 ml/h. Her hemoglobin is 10 g/dl. Abdominal examination reveals no masses, rebound tenderness, or shifting dullness. Speculum examination reveals an intact vaginal cuff without bulging and no blood in the vault.

Several hours later, her pulse rate and blood pressure have not significantly changed, her urine output has decreased to 15 ml/h, and her hemoglobin is 8 g/dl. Of the following management options, the most appropriate for this patient is

* (A) transfusion and observation
(B) serial pelvic examinations
(C) pelvic ultrasound examination
(D) angiography with embolization
(E) exploratory laparotomy

The diagnosis for this patient is continued postoperative bleeding. The initial decrease in hemoglobin from 12 g/dl to 10 g/dl can be explained by the combination of blood loss at the time of surgery and hemodilution after vigorous intravenous hydration. However, further decrease in hemoglobin from 10 g/dl to 8 g/dl during a 24-hour period along with a decrease in urine output indicates continued slow blood loss from a venous source, a reduction in intravascular volume, and renal hypoperfusion. The absence of worsening tachycardia and hypotension illustrate that a healthy individual can tolerate significant loss of blood volume before hemodynamic instability occurs.

Transfusing this patient and managing her expectantly is the most appropriate option. It is probable that bleeding has stopped or will stop shortly, and reoperation or embolization is unnecessary. Transfusion is necessary to restore her intravascular volume and to stay ahead of the loss.

Serial pelvic examinations and pelvic ultrasonography

will not aid in the management of this patient, even though the ultrasound examination may identify whether bleeding is intraperitoneal or extraperitoneal.

Angiography with embolization would be appropriate management if the patient had more rapid blood loss. Angiography to identify the site of bleeding followed by embolization has been used in the management of posthysterectomy hemorrhage, postpartum hemorrhage, and bleeding secondary to unresectable cancer. Even when a bleeding site cannot be identified, embolization of the anterior division of the hypogastric arteries has been effective. Advantages of angiography with embolization versus exploratory laparotomy include the avoidance of a second major surgical procedure and the difficulty of localizing the site of bleeding in tissues that are edematous after surgery, as well as the improved likelihood of achieving hemostasis when bleeding originates from the obturator, iliolumbar, and deep circumflex iliac arteries. If a skilled interventional radiologist is not readily available and if blood loss is rapid, a patient should undergo immediate exploratory laparotomy to identify and control the site of bleeding.

O'Hanlan KA, Trambert J, Rodriguez-Rodriguez L, Goldberg GL, Runowicz CD. Arterial embolization in the management of abdominal and retroperitoneal hemorrhage. Gynecol Oncol 1989;34:131–135

Yamashita Y, Harada M, Yamamoto H, Miyazaki T, Takahashi M, Miyazaki K, et al. Transcatheter arterial embolization of obstetric and gynaecological bleeding: efficacy and clinical outcome. Br J Radiol 1994;67:530–534

Yamashita Y, Takahashi M, Ito M, Okamura H. Transcatheter arterial embolization in the management of postpartum hemorrhage due to genital tract injury. Obstet Gynecol 1991;77:160–163

16

Risk factors for breast cancer

A patient whose sister has just been diagnosed with invasive ductal carcinoma seeks consultation about her own risk of developing breast cancer. Which of the following findings in this patient's history and physical examination adds the most to her breast cancer risk?

(A) Obesity
(B) Menarche at age 10
(C) Dysplasia on mammography
(D) Nulliparity
* (E) Another sister with breast cancer

Relative risk is the ratio of the incidence of disease in a population exposed to a specific risk factor to the incidence in an unexposed population. Because incidence is the number of new cases of disease in a population at risk observed over a defined period of time, relative risk is calculated on the basis of prospective epidemiologic studies. Relative risk cannot be determined by retrospective studies. A relative risk of up to 2.0 is considered a weak association (low risk). A relative risk of any amount is statistically significant only if the 95% confidence interval does not include 1.0. For example, a relative risk of 1.9 (95% confidence interval, 1.1–3.2) is statistically significant, whereas a relative risk of 2.4 (95% confidence interval, 0.9–6.1) is not. Relative risk can be estimated by an odds ratio, which is a ratio of the odds of disease in exposed versus unexposed populations.

A woman who has two sisters with breast cancer has a fivefold increased risk of the disease and is considered to be at high risk. Other examples of clinically significant relative risk are the fourfold to eightfold increased relative risk of endometrial carcinoma in women receiving unopposed estrogen therapy and the more than tenfold increased relative risk of invasive ductal carcinoma for women with ductal carcinoma in situ.

Obesity in postmenopausal women is a moderate epidemiologic risk factor for breast cancer but is not a significant clinical risk factor. In contrast, obese premenopausal women have a lower breast cancer risk compared with thin premenopausal women.

Menarche before age 12 is associated with a slight increase in breast cancer risk, which may relate to the greater number of ovulatory cycles. It is estimated that each year of delay in the onset of menarche beyond age 12 decreases the risk by 20%.

In 1976 Wolfe attempted to define mammographic patterns that would identify a subset of women at high risk for developing breast cancer. The assignment of patterns proved to be subjective and difficult to duplicate in other studies. Furthermore, many breast cancers occurred in women classified as being at low risk by their mammographic patterns. The Wolfe classification of DY (dysplasia) mammographic pattern is correlated with moderately increased breast cancer risk. Dysplasia is a histologic diagnosis, however, and is not an appropriate mammographic diagnosis.

TABLE 16-1. Recognized Risk Factors for Breast Cancer in Women

Relative Risk	Risk Factors
>4.0	Older age Country of birth (North America or Northern Europe) Personal history of breast cancer, in situ or invasive Strong family history* Biopsy showing proliferative lesion with atypia
2.0–4.0	Upper socioeconomic class Obesity, postmenopausal DY or P2 mammographic pattern† Any first-degree relative with a history of breast cancer Personal history of primary cancer of the ovary or endometrium Significant irradiation to the chest Age at first term pregnancy >30 years Nulliparity
1.1–1.9	Moderate alcohol intake Menarche before age 12 years Menopause after age 55 years
Not yet reliably quantified	Oral contraceptives Hormone replacement therapy

* Family history of bilateral premenopausal breast cancer or a familial cancer syndrome (Li-Fraumeni, breast–ovarian).

† The Wolfe classification is used. DY indicates highest risk. Severe involvement with dysplasia, often obscuring an underlying prominent duct pattern. P2 indicates high risk. Severe involvement with prominent duct pattern occupying more than one fourth of the volume of breast.

Harris JR, Hellman S, Henderson IC, Kinne DW, eds. Breast diseases. 2nd ed. Philadelphia: JB Lippincott, 1991:155

Nulliparity is associated with a moderately increased epidemiologic risk of breast cancer. It is estimated that each year of delay of first full-term birth after age 30 increases the risk by 3.5%. Table 16-1 lists the risk factors for breast cancer.

American College of Radiology. BIRADS: Breast Imaging Reporting and Data System. Reston, Virginia: American College of Radiology, 1993

Bain C, Speizer FE, Rosner B, Belanger C, Hennekens CH. Family history of breast cancer as a risk indicator for the disease. Am J Epidemiol 1980;111: 301–308

Harris JR, Hellman S, Henderson IC, Kinne DW, eds. Breast diseases. 2nd ed. Philadelphia: JB Lippincott, 1991

Henderson BE. Endogenous and exogenous endocrine factors. Hematol Oncol Clin North Am 1989;3:577–598

Kvåle G, Heuch I, Eide GE. A prospective study of reproductive factors and breast cancer, I: parity. Am J Epidemiol 1987;126:831–841

Le Marchand L, Kolonel LN, Earle ME, Mi M-P. Body size at different periods of life and breast cancer risk. Am J Epidemiol 1988;128:137–152

Trichopoulos D, Hsieh C-C, MacMahon B, Lin T-M, Lowe CR, Mirra AP, et al. Age at any birth and breast cancer risk. Int J Cancer 1983;31:701–704

Wolfe JN. Breast patterns as an index of risk for developing breast cancer. AJR Am J Roentgenol 1976;126:1130–1139

17
Clear cell adenocarcinoma of the vagina

A 35-year-old woman presents with vaginal spotting. On pelvic examination, a small nodule is palpable on the anterior wall of the vagina near the cervix. You perform a biopsy, and the pathologist advises you that the lesion is malignant. Microscopic sections of the tumor are shown in Fig. 17-1 (see color plates). The diagnosis is

(A) sarcoma botryoides
(B) leiomyosarcoma
* (C) clear cell adenocarcinoma
(D) squamous cell carcinoma
(E) melanoma

Clear cell adenocarcinoma should always be considered in the differential diagnosis of vaginal tumors in young women, although it is much less common than squamous cell carcinoma. Most cases of clear cell carcinoma of the vagina have been diagnosed in women in their late teens and early 20s. The oldest woman thus far reported at diagnosis was 42 years of age. According to data from the Registry on Hormonal Transplacental Carcinogenesis, 60–65% of patients with this diagnosis have a documented history of in utero diethylstilbestrol, hexestrol, or dienestrol exposure; another 10% were exposed in utero to an unknown form of medication usually administered for high-risk pregnancy.

Although large clear cell adenocarcinoma tumors are typically associated with vaginal bleeding or discharge, small tumors may be asymptomatic. On gross examination, most of these tumors are polypoid and nodular, but some are flat and some are ulcerated. They range in size from barely visible to 10 cm in greatest dimension. Tumors of less than 1 cm are usually palpable but may be difficult to identify on colposcopic examination. Some of these tumors penetrate deeply, extending beyond the apparent limits of the lesion on gross examination.

On microscopic examination, several histologic patterns including solid, tubulocystic, and papillary patterns may be observed in these tumors. The characteristic cell is the clear cell, but hobnail cells, characterized by bulbous nuclei protruding into the lumen of the glandular space, are also frequently found. Flat cells, lining cystic spaces, may be deceptively innocuous in their appearance. Neoplasms with a tubulocystic pattern appear to have a somewhat better prognosis than the other types. Benign glands, designated adenosis, are found immediately adjacent to the tumor in over 90% of cases. As shown in Fig. 17-1, this patient's tumor is composed of glands, tubules, and cysts lined by flat and clear cells, confirming the diagnosis of clear cell adenocarcinoma.

In contrast to clear cell carcinoma, sarcoma botryoides typically presents in children under the age of 5 years. This neoplasm tends to be papillary, forming grape-like masses that are evident on gross examination. Microscopically, the tumor is composed of rhabdomyoblasts, rounded or strap-like cells with cross striations. Consequently, this tumor is often termed embryonal rhabdomyosarcoma.

Vaginal leiomyosarcomas are bulky lesions that usually arise in the rectovaginal septum. Microscopically, leiomyosarcoma is composed of fascicles of spindle-shaped, smooth muscle cells with hyperchromatic and pleomorphic nuclei and frequent mitoses.

Squamous cell carcinoma of the vagina is characteristically a disease of older women. Seventy percent of the cases occur in women more than 50 years old, with a peak incidence between 60 and 70 years. The microscopic appearance of vaginal squamous carcinoma is similar to that of cervical squamous carcinoma, being composed of solid masses of squamous cells with pleomorphic nuclei and usually abundant cytoplasm. Keratinization is often evident.

Melanoma may occur in women of any age. This tumor is almost uniformly pigmented and microscopically is composed of large epithelioid cells containing melanin granules.

Herbst AL, Norusis MJ, Rosenow PJ, Welch WR, Scully RE. An analysis of 346 cases of clear cell adenocarcinoma of the vagina and cervix with emphasis on recurrence and survival. Gynecol Oncol 1979;7:111–122

Herbst AL, Ulfelder H, Poskanzer DC. Adenocarcinoma of the vagina: association of maternal stilbestrol therapy with tumor appearance in young women. N Engl J Med 1971;284:878–881

Robboy SJ, Welch WR, Young RH, Truslow GY, Herbst AL, Scully RE. Topographic relation of cervical ectropion and vaginal adenosis to clear cell adenocarcinoma. Obstet Gynecol 1982;60:546–551

Zaino RJ, Robboy SJ, Bentley R, Kurman RJ. Diseases of the vagina. In: Kurman RJ, ed. Blaustein's pathology of the female genital tract. 4th ed. New York: Springer-Verlag, 1994:131–183

18
Staging of endometrial cancer

A 75-year-old woman presents with postmenopausal bleeding of 6 months' duration. On physical examination she is obese and has a moderately enlarged, mobile uterus; no adnexal masses are noted. She has a 2-cm left inguinal mass. The chest X-ray is normal. An endometrial biopsy reveals a grade 3 endometrial adenocarcinoma, and the endocervical curettage is negative for malignancy.

The patient undergoes a total abdominal hysterectomy, bilateral salpingo-oophorectomy, and pelvic, paraaortic, and left inguinal lymph node sampling. Results of the abdominal exploration are negative. Surgical pathology demonstrates full-thickness myometrial invasion of a grade 3 endometrial adenocarcinoma and positive pelvic and inguinal lymph nodes. Peritoneal cytology is negative for malignancy.

According to the International Federation of Gynecology and Obstetrics (FIGO) criteria, this patient's endometrial cancer is classified as

(A) stage IIIA, grade 3
(B) stage IIIC, grade 3
(C) stage IVA, grade 3
* (D) stage IVB, grade 3

The 1971 FIGO staging system for carcinoma of the endometrium was based on clinical parameters determined by the results of physical examination, fractional dilation and curettage, uterine sounding, chest X-ray, and other radiologic tests. This system was simple, could be universally applied even when surgical intervention was contraindicated, and included some known prognostic factors such as tumor grade, cervical involvement, and clinically detectable metastatic disease.

On the other hand, many other important prognostic factors that are inaccessible to clinical examination, such as depth of myometrial invasion, tumor size, adnexal spread, peritoneal cytology, and lymph node status, could not be incorporated into this staging system. Clinical staging was also notoriously inaccurate. For instance, the predictive value of endocervical curettage for differentiating between stage I and stage II disease is poor, with a false-negative rate of approximately 10% and a false-positive rate of 50%. Of women undergoing surgery for clinical stage I endometrial cancer, 3–7% had adnexal metastases, 10% had pelvic lymph node metastases, 6% had paraaortic lymph node metastases, and 8% had occult peritoneal spread of disease. Overall, preoperative clinical staging was incorrect approximately 50% of the time.

In 1988 the FIGO clinical staging system for endometrial carcinoma was replaced by a surgical staging system, based on initial surgical therapy and evaluation of potential metastatic sites (Appendix, Table 2). Comprehensive surgical staging of endometrial cancer involves total hysterectomy, bilateral salpingo-oophorectomy, peritoneal washings for cytology, pelvic and paraaortic lymph node sampling, abdominal exploration, and biopsy of any suspicious lesions. In this system, tumor grade, myometrial invasion, cervical extension, peritoneal cytology, adnexal status, and lymph node metastases are emphasized. Preoperative assessment in this system need only focus on perioperative care and areas of concern based on symptoms or physical findings.

Surgical staging is not suitable for some patients who have coexisting medical conditions or clinically detectable spread of disease. It is also apparent that not all patients require lymph node sampling, because the incidence of lymph node metastasis is exceedingly low for small grade 1 and 2 endometrial cancers with superficial myometrial invasion. Several studies have demonstrated, however, that extended surgical staging can be performed safely without significant increases in perioperative morbidity or mortality. It is hoped that the information gained about the true extent of disease at surgery will allow better planning and individualization of postoperative therapy to improve survival.

This patient has inguinal lymph node metastasis, and her disease is, therefore, staged as FIGO IVB, grade 3. Stage IVA connotes bladder or bowel invasion. Metastases to pelvic or paraaortic lymph nodes or both indicates stage IIIC disease, whereas positive peritoneal cytology, adnexal spread, or uterine serosal extension is classified as stage IIIA disease.

Boronow RC, Morrow CP, Creasman WT, DiSaia PJ, Silverberg SG, Miller A, et al. Surgical staging in endometrial cancer: clinical-pathologic findings of a prospective study. Obstet Gynecol 1984;63:825–832

Cowles TA, Magrina JF, Masterson BJ, Capen CV. Comparison of clinical and surgical staging in patients with endometrial carcinoma. Obstet Gynecol 1985; 66:413–416

Creasman WT, Morrow CP, Bundy BN, Homesley HD, Graham JE, Heller PB. Surgical pathologic spread patterns of endometrial cancer: a Gynecologic Oncology Group study. Cancer 1987;60:2035–2041

Lurain JR, Rice BL, Rademaker AW, Poggensee LE, Schink JC, Miller DS. Prognostic factors associated with recurrence in clinical stage I adenocarcinoma of the endometrium. Obstet Gynecol 1991;78:63–69

19

Cervical cancer in pregnancy

A primigravid woman is diagnosed with stage IB nonbulky cervical carcinoma at 20 weeks of gestation. She wishes to continue the pregnancy and seeks advice. Which statement best reflects current knowledge pertaining to this clinical situation?

(A) Delay in therapy is acceptable in bulky stage IB disease.
(B) The histologic type is likely to be adenosquamous cell carcinoma.
* (C) Delay of therapy from 20 weeks of gestation until after delivery will not affect prognosis in nonbulky stage IB disease.
(D) Immediate therapy is the only acceptable option.

Cervical carcinoma is the most common malignancy in women worldwide. In the United States, it is estimated that 15,800 cases of invasive cervical cancer are diagnosed annually; the incidence of invasive cervical cancer is 1.6 to 10.6 cases per 10,000 pregnancies. This wide range reflects population difference. When cervical carcinoma complicates pregnancy, both the mother and the fetus must be considered.

In advising pregnant patients who have cervical carcinoma, one considers the stage of the disease, size of the lesion, number of weeks to optimal fetal maturity, and the mother's desire for the pregnancy. It is intuitive to believe that delay in therapy may carry an increased risk of disease progression, although there are limited data to support this view. Any risk of progression in the mother must be weighed against improved fetal outcome.

Of 26 women with stage IA cervical carcinoma who delayed therapy, 20 had 2 years of follow-up and all were reported disease-free. Similarly, 16 of 20 women with stage IB cervical cancer were disease-free with up to 2 years of follow-up. These data suggest that there is no apparent increase in maternal risk or risk at delivery incurred by delay of therapy for stage IA or nonbulky stage IB cervical carcinoma. Immediate therapy is advised for women who have bulky (lesion greater than 4 cm) stage IB cervical carcinoma or more advanced disease at any time during pregnancy.

The predominant histologic type of cervical cancer that complicates pregnancy is squamous cell (93% of cases); adenosquamous carcinoma accounts for only 1.1% of cases.

The treatment options for cervical cancer are radical hysterectomy or irradiation. Both are uniformly lethal to the fetus, as is delivery at this gestational age.

Boring CC, Squires TS, Tong T, Montgomery S. Cancer statistics, 1994. CA Cancer J Clin 1994;44:7–26

Duggan B, Muderspach LI, Roman LD, Curtain JP, d'Ablaing G III, Morrow CP. Cervical cancer in pregnancy: reporting on planned delay in therapy. Obstet Gynecol 1993;82:598–602

Hacker NF, Berek JS, Lagasse LD, Charles EH, Savage EW, Moore JG. Carcinoma of the cervix associated with pregnancy. Obstet Gynecol 1982;59:735–747

Hopkins MP, Morley GW. The prognosis and management of cervical cancer associated with pregnancy. Obstet Gynecol 1992;80:9–13

Lee RB, Neglia W, Park RC. Cervical carcinoma in pregnancy. Obstet Gynecol 1981;58:584–589

Monk BJ, Montz FJ. Invasive cervical cancer complicating intrauterine pregnancy: treatment with radical hysterectomy. Obstet Gynecol 1992;80:199–203

20
Incisional hernia repair

A 32-year-old woman presents with a ventral hernia at the superior aspect of a lower midline incision performed 6 months ago at cesarean delivery. After the delivery she developed a wound infection, which was treated with incision and drainage. She is otherwise healthy and not overweight. On examination the incisional hernia is 3 cm in diameter, with adherent bowel palpable below the skin. Surgical repair is elected. Of the following options, the most appropriate option for closure is

* (A) modified Smead–Jones (far-near, near-far) closure with nonabsorbable suture
(B) simple interrupted closure of the fascia with polyglycolic acid (Dexon) or polyglactin 910 (Vicryl) suture
(C) closure with polypropylene prosthetic mesh (Prolene)
(D) through-and-through closure with steel wire

Incisional or ventral hernia is a result of incomplete healing of a prior surgical incision. With this condition the peritoneum remains intact and the fascial margins and adjacent muscles separate, producing a hernial defect into the subcutaneous fat. Postoperative wound infection is a common antecedent of incisional hernia. Infection impairs fibroblastic activity and collagen synthesis during the active phase of wound healing. Coughing, vomiting, and other causes of increased intraabdominal pressure may lead to necrosis along the fascial margins, and a suture may pull through the edges. Incisional hernia occurs as a complication of lower midline incision in 0.5–1% of gynecologic surgical cases; the incidence increases 10- to 20-fold after a wound infection.

The key principles of repair of an incisional hernia include exposure and dissection of the hernial sac from the peritoneal margins, rectus fascia, and subcutaneous fat; excision of the redundant peritoneal hernia sac; and attention to the repair of the rectus fascia. After excision of the incisional scar and mobilization of the underlying subcutaneous fat, the margins of the hernia are identified. This may be facilitated by opening the hernia sac and releasing any adherent bowel and omentum.

If adequate fascial support can be identified and the defect is not large, the anterior rectus fascia is closed with a nonabsorbable suture by using the modified Smead–Jones closure (Fig. 20-1). In this closure, interrupted far-near, near-far sutures are placed to incorporate the inner margins of the rectus musculature. Future pull-through of the suture from the incision edge is unlikely. The sutures function as internal stays to increase the tensile strength of the closure. Alternatively, a "vest-over-pants" closure can be used, creating a double layer of fascia. With this closure the peritoneum is closed separately, and the rectus fascia of the hernia margins are widely separated on each side. Permanent horizontal mattress sutures are placed 3–4 cm from the fascial edge, passed through the free margin of the underlying surface, and brought out through the distal edge of the anterior fascia. The sutures are secured after all have been placed. The free fascial margin is then secured to the underlying opposite fascial layer, creating a double support for the hernia closure.

Simple interrupted fascial closure with polyglycolic acid (Dexon) or polyglactin 910 (Vicryl) suture may be adequate in many cases, but both simple closure and use of absorbable suture increase the risk of a failed repair over time. Either the modified Smead–Jones or vest-over-pants closure is stronger.

When the fascial defect is large and fascial margins cannot be reapproximated or initial hernial repair has failed, polypropylene prosthetic mesh (Prolene) or other synthetic material should be considered. Use of synthetic mesh is not favored for smaller primary repairs because of the increased risk of infection and foreign body reaction.

Through-and-through closure is appropriate for the acute repair of complete wound dehiscence with evisceration. Steel wire was used for this procedure in the past but has largely been replaced by nonabsorbable permanent suture. Through-and-through closure would provide a secure retention stitch to hold the wound together but would not permit precise anatomic reapproximation of the fascial edges, as is needed in this case.

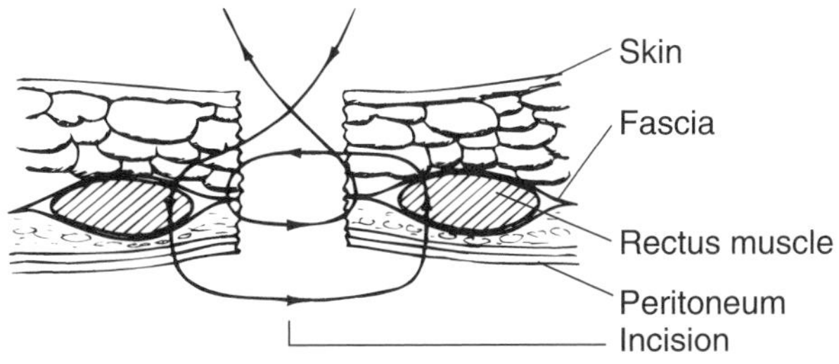

FIG. 20-1. Smead–Jones hidden retention suture. (Reprinted with permission from Morrow CP, Hernandez WL, Townsend DE, DiSaia PJ. Pelvic celiotomy in the obese patient. Am J Obstet Gynecol 1977;127:337)

Keill RH, Keitzer WF, Nichols WK, Henzel J, De Weese MS. Abdominal wound dehiscence. Arch Surg 1973;106:573–577

Thompson JD. Incisions for gynecologic surgery. In: Thompson JD, Rock JA, eds. Te Linde's operative gynecology. 7th ed. Philadelphia: JB Lippincott, 1992:239–277

Usher FC. The repair of incisional and inguinal hernias. Surg Gynecol Obstet 1970;131:525–530

21

Physical findings of vulvar intraepithelial neoplasia

A 29-year-old woman presents with vulvar pruritus and "burning pain" of several months' duration. Physical examination reveals several 1–2-cm lesions on the posterior fourchette and both labia majora. Some of the lesions are flat and red in color and others are brown (Fig. 21-1A; see color plates). The next step in this patient's management is

(A) biopsy of a red lesion
(B) biopsy of a brown lesion
* (C) biopsy of each type of lesion
(D) culture of the lesions
(E) trial of 0.05% hydrocortisone cream

Vulvar intraepithelial neoplasia (VIN) occurs in women under the age of 35 in 50% of cases. In younger patients, the disease is often multifocal and appears to progress slowly and with a lower subsequent incidence of invasive carcinoma than in older patients, who are more likely to have unifocal disease. The lesions are asymptomatic in 30–40% of patients, but when symptoms occur, pruritus is most common. Pain (often described as a burning sensation) is the second most common symptom. In older patients, invasive carcinoma may occur without associated VIN.

The appearance of VIN is extremely variable. Lesions may be flat, raised, or verrucous in appearance and red, white, gray, or brown in color. The thickness of a lesion is determined by the thickness of the keratin layer. Flat lesions have little keratin buildup, whereas wart-like, verrucous lesions, which are usually white or gray, have a large amount of keratin. Red lesions are associated with an abundance of blood vessels beneath the surface. With red lesions, one must also consider the diagnosis of Paget disease. The appearance of the lesions varies to some extent depending on their location on the vulva (mucosal versus keratinized areas) and on the degree of natural pigmentation of the patient. Figure 21-1 (A and B) shows the varied appearance of VIN. The lesions described in this patient are characteristic of VIN, and biopsy is indicated. Biopsies should be taken of representative lesions.

Human papillomavirus DNA is present in approximately 80–90% of cases of VIN in young women. In contrast to VIN lesions, infectious lesions of the vulva usually have a less varied appearance and are more confluent. The most common vulvitis is due to yeast and has a characteristic diffuse red appearance. Bacterial infections are characterized by folliculitis, and herpetic lesions usually manifest as ulcers or vesicles. The appearance of this patient's vulva does not suggest an infectious etiology; therefore, culture would not be warranted.

Squamous hyperplasia without atypia can be diagnosed only by biopsy, and the gross appearance is similar to VIN. Although patients with squamous hyperplasia may benefit from a short course (7–10 days) of hydrocortisone cream, such medication should be used only after the diagnosis has been established by biopsy.

Crum CP, Liskow A, Petras P, Keng WC, Frick HC II. Vulvar intraepithelial neoplasia (severe atypia and carcinoma in situ). A clinicopathologic analysis of 41 cases. Cancer 1984;54:1429–1434

Kaufman RH, Friedrich EG Jr, Faro S, Gardner HL. Benign diseases of the vulva and vagina. St Louis: Mosby, 1994:135–146

Morrow CP, Curtin JP, Townsend DE. Synopsis of gynecologic oncology. 4th ed. New York: Churchill Livingstone, 1993:23–35

Wilkinson EJ, Stone IK. Atlas of vulvar disease. Baltimore: Williams & Wilkins, 1995:101–103

22

Hereditary breast–ovarian cancer syndrome

A 50-year-old postmenopausal woman, para 0, is seen for the first time for a routine checkup. In taking her family history, you learn that the patient's mother and older sister both died of ovarian cancer in their early sixties. A maternal aunt was diagnosed with breast cancer at age 52, and her aunt's daughter (the patient's first cousin) developed breast cancer and died at age 35. In view of the patient's family pedigree (Fig. 22-1), you inform her that:

(A) She is at increased risk for hereditary nonpolyposis colorectal cancer, ovarian cancer, and endometrial cancer (Lynch syndrome II).
(B) If she develops ovarian cancer, the onset is likely to be when she is 10–15 years older than her relatives were when they developed the disease.
* (C) She has a lifetime probability of developing ovarian cancer as high as 50%.
(D) She should have a linkage analysis to determine whether she carries the *BRCA1* gene.

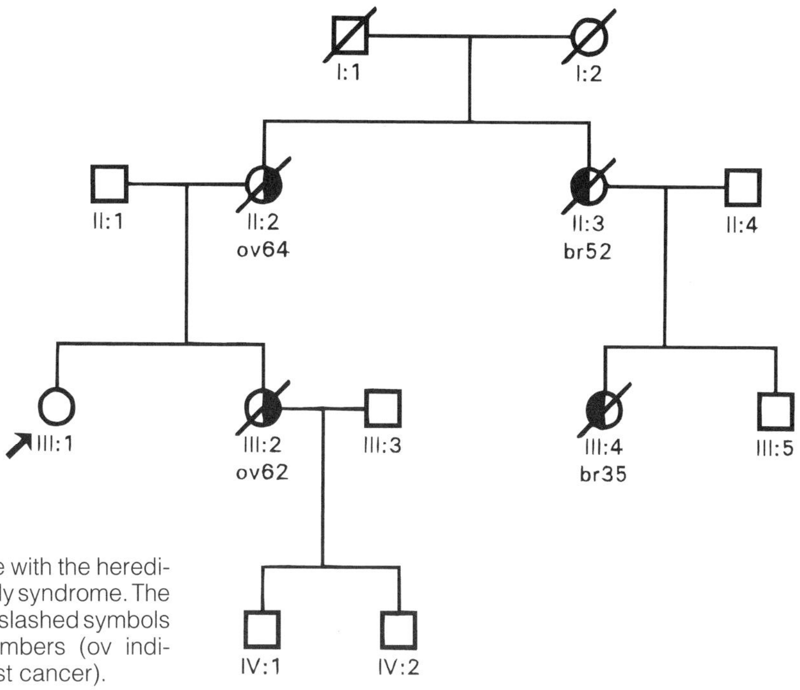

FIG. 22-1. Pedigree compatible with the hereditary breast–ovarian cancer family syndrome. The arrow identifies the patient, and slashed symbols indicate deceased family members (ov indicates ovarian cancer; br, breast cancer).

The term familial ovarian cancer is not clearly defined in the medical literature. It is used to describe ovarian cancer in a woman with a hereditary ovarian cancer syndrome as well as ovarian cancer in a woman who has one or more relatives with ovarian cancer. The term hereditary ovarian cancer syndrome refers to three cancer syndromes: 1) hereditary breast–ovarian cancer syndrome, 2) site-specific ovarian cancer syndrome, and 3) hereditary nonpolyposis colorectal cancer syndrome (Lynch syndrome II). Breast–ovarian cancer syndrome occurs in families with clusters of women with ovarian cancer and/or breast cancer, whereas site-specific ovarian cancer syndrome occurs in families with clusters of women with ovarian cancer. Lynch syndrome II occurs in families with a high incidence of nonpolyposis colorectal cancer with proximal colonic predominance, endometrial carcinoma, and ovarian carcinoma. This patient's pedigree (Fig. 22-1) is compatible with hereditary breast–ovarian cancer syndrome.

The average age at diagnosis of ovarian cancer for the population in general is 59 years. Women with one of the hereditary ovarian cancer syndromes tend to be 7–14 years younger at diagnosis. Hereditary ovarian cancer syndromes *may* involve an autosomal dominant inheritance pattern. A woman from a family with an ovarian cancer syndrome with autosomal dominant gene has a 50% lifetime probability of developing ovarian cancer. However, of all cases of breast cancer and ovarian cancer, only 5–7% can be attributed to inheritance of a gene conferring high risk.

The *BRCA1* (breast cancer) gene may be inherited in altered form, leading to a greatly increased risk of breast and/or ovarian cancer. Researchers estimate that about 5% of all breast cancer cases, or about 9,000 new cases in the United States annually, are due to inherited susceptibilities. The *BRCA1* gene is believed to account for about half of these cases. The gene is located on chromosome 17.

The sequence of the *BRCA1* gene is now known. Before the gene was sequenced, linkage analysis identified those patients inheriting the *BRCA1* gene. Linkage analysis, however, is limited to the research setting. The isolation of *BRCA1* has no immediate implications for the detection or prevention of breast cancer. When a test for *BRCA1* mutation becomes available, women with a family history of breast cancer will be able to find out whether they carry a mutated gene. It is estimated that 1 in 200 women in the United States may have an inherited mutation in the gene.

The risk of ovarian cancer in women from families with one of the hereditary ovarian cancer syndromes may be sufficiently high to warrant prophylactic oophorectomy. However, they should be counseled that even after removal of histologically healthy ovaries, about 5–10% of patients from affected families develop peritoneal adenocarcinoma, which is histologically indistinguishable from ovarian cancer.

Some experts have recommended yearly or twice yearly screening of patients from families with hereditary ovarian cancer syndrome with serum CA 125 determination, vaginal ultrasonography, and color flow Doppler imaging of the ovarian vascular tree. These screening strategies are expensive, and their efficacy is unproven.

Kerlikowske K, Brown JS, Grady DG. Should women with familial ovarian cancer undergo prophylactic oophorectomy? Obstet Gynecol 1992;80:700–707

King M-C, Rowell S, Love SM. Inherited breast and ovarian cancer. What are the risks? What are the choices? JAMA 1993;269:1975–1980

Runowicz CD, Goldberg GL, Smith HO. Cancer screening for women older than 40 years of age. Obstet Gynecol Clin North Am 1993;20:391–408

23
Deep vein thrombosis

A 72-year-old woman underwent a total abdominal hysterectomy and bilateral salpingo-oophorectomy for bilateral ovarian tumors. No evidence of malignancy was found in the abdomen during surgical staging.

Postoperatively the patient has a low-grade fever, persistent tachycardia, and intermittent pain in her right leg. Physical examination reveals tenderness in the calf. You are concerned about the possibility of a deep vein thrombosis. The most appropriate next step in this patient's management is

(A) check for Homans sign
(B) ^{125}I fibrinogen scan
(C) venography
(D) impedance plethysmography
* (E) duplex Doppler sonography

Deep vein thrombosis is a significant complication of surgery, including pelvic gynecologic surgery. The lethal potential of pulmonary embolization justifies this concern. Deep vein thrombosis during surgery occurs more often than either the postoperative frequency of clinically apparent disease or the frequency of pulmonary embolus would indicate. Risk factors for development of deep vein thrombosis (see box and Table 23-1) include the duration and complexity of the surgical procedure. Tests used in the diagnosis of deep vein thrombosis are shown in Table 23-2.

A careful preoperative history of patients will reveal conditions that may predispose to deep vein thrombosis, especially any previous deep vein thrombosis or the presence of malignancy. Although emphasis has been placed on physical examination, the reliability of physical findings in the diagnosis of deep vein thrombosis is low. Half of the patients who have proven deep vein thrombosis show none of the typical physical findings for the disorder, and about 50% of patients without deep vein thrombosis manifest physical findings that would lead to an erroneous clinical diagnosis.

One of the physical findings that has been relied on as an indicator of deep vein thrombosis is the Homans sign: When deep vein thrombosis is present, dorsiflexion of the foot is said to intensify the pain in that leg. Studies of the reliability of this physical finding yield disappointing results. When deep vein thrombosis is definitely present, only 30% of patients have a positive Homans sign. On the other hand, 50% of patients for whom deep vein thrombosis has been excluded have a positive Homans sign.

Investigative screening studies with ^{125}I fibrinogen show that asymptomatic thrombosis is a relatively common event that is rarely manifested by clinical complications. Although ^{125}I fibrinogen scanning has been useful in investigations of the pathophysiology of thrombosis, this technique is no longer clinically used,

Risk Factors for Deep Vein Thrombosis

Low Risk
Age <40 y
Operative time <30 min
No immobilization

Moderate Risk
Age >40 y
Exogenous estrogen use
Operative time >30 min
Varicose veins
Obesity
Postoperative infection

High Risk
History of thromboembolism
Surgery for malignancy
Immobilization

Adapted from Bonnar J. Venous thromboembolism and gynecologic surgery. Clin Obstet Gynecol 1985;28:435

TABLE 23-1. Incidence of Thromboembolic Events by Risk Category

Complication	Low Risk	Moderate Risk	High Risk
Calf vein thrombosis	<3%	10–30%	30–60%
Proximal vein thrombosis	<1%	2–8%	6–12%
Pulmonary embolization	<0.01	0.1–0.7%	1–2%

Adapted from Bonnar J. Venous thromboembolism and gynecologic surgery. Clin Obstet Gynecol 1985;28:435

because a delay of 24–36 hours is required to block the thyroid with iodine before the isotope is administered. The use of heparin during this delay interferes with the test by blocking the formation of fibrin. Furthermore, ^{125}I fibrinogen scanning is not accurate in diagnosing proximal venous occlusion, the most hazardous condition from the standpoint of risk of embolization. It is more accurate in diagnosing thrombosis in the calf, which is rarely hazardous from the standpoint of embolization but which may extend to become a proximal thrombosis.

Venography is considered the most accurate test (the gold standard) for deep vein thrombosis currently available. This technique is available in most hospitals and has a very low level of morbidity. Pulmonary embolization is not a major complication resulting from the use of venography. The presence of suspected venous thrombosis is not a contraindication to its use, and the patient undergoing the test does not have to receive anticoagulation therapy. Because venography is an invasive technique, it is reserved for patients in whom noninvasive techniques such as duplex Doppler ultrasonography are inconclusive.

Impedance plethysmography, a complex and expensive test, was previously relied on as a first-line method of diagnosis of deep vein thrombosis. The introduction of real-time B-mode ultrasonography has provided a promising alternative to impedance plethysmography, with a sensitivity for proximal thrombi that approaches 100% in patients with symptomatic deep vein thrombosis. Visualization of a venous thrombus is often possible but is not essential for diagnosis.

In duplex scanning, real-time B-mode ultrasonography is supplemented by Doppler flow-detection ultrasound imaging, which allows detection of blood flow in any vessel seen. In symptomatic patients with proximal deep vein thrombosis, its overall sensitivity in a meta-analysis of four well-designed studies was 93%, with a specificity of 98%. The sensitivity of duplex scanning for detection of distal thrombi is far less satisfactory because of poor visualization of the calf veins. Greater accuracy for color Doppler ultrasonography is claimed but may only be achievable in technically uncompromised studies.

Initial evaluation of symptomatic patients by duplex ultrasonography alone (ie, without supplementary phlebography) is enough to confirm or disprove suspected cases of deep vein thrombosis, as long as a negative examination is followed by repeated noninvasive testing to detect proximal extension. Duplex scanning is noninvasive and relatively inexpensive, and it can be used to follow the course of a patient receiving therapy over a long period of time. It is also more accurate than impedance plethysmography in the diagnosis of potentially lethal asymptomatic proximal thrombosis. Therefore, thrombi that pose the greatest threat of pulmonary embolus are more likely to be detected by this technique. Duplex scanning has become the first line of study for most patients with suspected deep vein thrombosis.

These findings make it clear that early clinical detection of most deep vein thromboses and early treatment are problematic because clinical findings are unreliable and laboratory tests are only used when there is a reasonable clinical suspicion. Therefore, prevention of deep vein thrombosis becomes a more important issue than early postoperative detection.

Bonnar J. Venous thromboembolism and gynecologic surgery. Clin Obstet Gynecol 1985;28:432–446

Weinmann EE, Salzman EW. Deep-vein thrombosis. N Engl J Med 1994; 331:1630–1641

TABLE 23-2. Tests Used in the Diagnosis of Deep Vein Thrombosis*

Test	Symptomatic Deep Vein Thrombosis†		Asymptomatic Deep Vein Thrombosis‡		Anatomical Area	Comment
	Sensitivity (%)	Specificity (%)	Sensitivity (%)	Specificity (%)		
Phlebography	Standard for comparison		Standard for comparison		Pelvis, thigh, popliteal area, calf	Invasive; provides equivocal results in cases of recurrent deep vein thrombosis; not easily repeated
Impedance plethysmography	92§	95	22	98	Thigh, popliteal area	For provisional diagnosis of primary or recurrent proximal deep vein thrombosis; insensitive to calf thrombi and to nonocclusive proximal thrombi
Ultrasonography						
Real-time B-mode or duplex	97	97	59	98	Thigh, popliteal area	Most sensitive confirmatory test for symptomatic deep vein thrombosis
Doppler flow velocity	88	88	—	—	Thigh, popliteal area	Can be used on limbs in traction or plaster; interpretation is subjective, requires skill
Magnetic resonance venography¶	96	100	—	—	Inferior vena cava, pelvis, thigh	Can distinguish between acute and chronic occlusion; can identify associated abnormalities; noninvasive; expensive; limited availability

* No data on ^{125}I-labeled fibrinogen are included because the test is no longer available.

† Testing is mostly used to verify clinical suspicion of deep vein thrombosis.

‡ Testing is mostly used to screen high-risk patients.

§ Recent studies have reported lower sensitivity.

¶ Magnetic resonance venography has only been evaluated in small clinical trials.

Reprinted by permission of The New England Journal of Medicine from Weinmann EE, Salzman EW. Deep-vein thrombosis. N Engl J Med 1994;331:1631; copyright 1994, Massachusetts Medical Society. Data derived from Lensing AWA, Hirsh J, Büller HR. Diagnosis of venous thrombosis. In: Colman RW, Hirsh J, Marder VJ, Salzman EW, eds. Hemostasis and thrombosis: basic principles and clinical practice. 3rd ed. Philadelphia: JB Lippincott, 1994:1297–1321

24

Preoperative evaluation of obstructive lung disease

A 62-year-old woman with recurrent ovarian cancer requires surgery for a transverse colon obstruction. Her medical history is significant for a 50-pack-per-year history of cigarette smoking and a diagnosis of chronic obstructive pulmonary disease (COPD).

The best predictor of an increased risk of postoperative pneumonia, prolonged hospitalization, and death from surgical complications in this patient is

(A) chest X-ray
(B) arterial blood gas
(C) pulmonary function tests
* (D) history and physical examination

Chest X-ray, arterial blood gas, and pulmonary function tests would all be expected to show abnormalities in a patient with known chronic obstructive pulmonary disease (COPD) and a 50-pack-per-year history of cigarette smoking. The chest X-ray of a patient with COPD typically indicates hyperaeration, flattened diaphragms, and pleural bullae (Fig. 24-1). Hypoxemia and hypercapnia, which parallel the clinical severity of the COPD, are detected on arterial blood gas studies. Pulmonary function tests typically reveal increased lung volumes and a decrease in the forced expiratory volume at one second. These abnormalities found on chest X-ray, arterial blood gas studies, and pulmonary function tests are not, however, predictive of postoperative complications for an individual patient.

The value of routine preoperative pulmonary tests to predict the risk of postoperative complications was the subject of a recent metaanalysis. With respect to upper abdominal surgery, seven studies that included a total of 739 patients were reviewed. The value of preoperative pulmonary function testing and arterial blood gas results was not consistently demonstrated. Other reviews have reported similar conclusions.

The best preoperative assessment of patients with COPD and a significant smoking history is a careful history and physical examination. Patients with COPD who do not have a superimposed respiratory infection and who are at their baseline condition generally do not experience an increased risk of pulmonary complications after abdominal surgery. In patients with dyspnea or a productive cough, pulmonary function should be optimized preoperatively with the administration of bronchodilators and steroids as indicated. Patients should ideally stop smoking cigarettes 8 weeks before surgery, but at least 48–72 hours before surgery.

Williams-Russo P, Charlson ME, MacKenzie CR, Gold JP, Shires GT. Predicting postoperative pulmonary complications: is it a real problem? Arch Intern Med 1992;152:1209–1213

Zibrak JD, O'Donnell CR, Marton K. Indications for pulmonary function testing. Ann Intern Med 1990;112:763–771

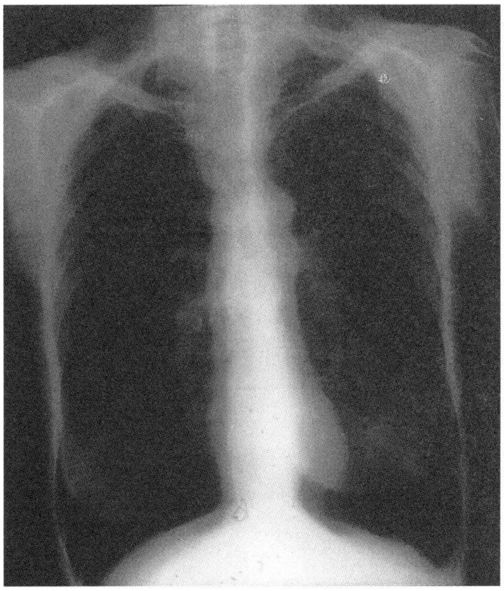

(A)

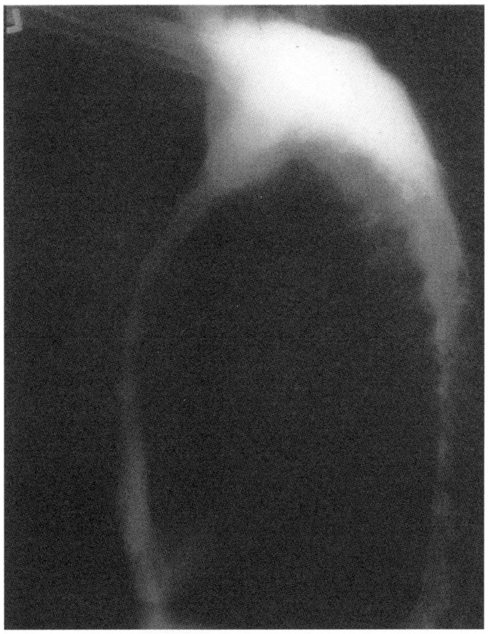

(B)

FIG. 24-1. Chest X-ray in a patient with chronic obstructive pulmonary disease. (A) Frontal view showing hyperaeration. (B) Side view showing flattening diaphragm.

25

Bladder injury at abdominal surgery

In planning abdominal hysterectomy for benign gynecologic disease, you routinely discuss risk factors for bladder injury with your patients. A history of which of the following circumstances poses the greatest risk of bladder injury during surgery?

* (A) Cervical myomectomy
(B) Cervical laser vaporization
(C) Ovarian cystectomy
(D) Tubal ligation

Injury to the bladder, with subsequent risk of vesicovaginal fistula formation, is most often a consequence of obstetric and gynecologic surgery. The factors that predispose to bladder injury are 1) previous uterine operation, especially cesarean delivery; 2) endometriosis; 3) recent cold-knife conization; 4) previous cervical myomectomy; and 5) previous pelvic irradiation. Common features to these conditions that predispose to bladder injury are scarring and ischemia.

In a large reported series, more than 50% of the fistulas resulted from a simple abdominal hysterectomy. Cervical laser vaporization, ovarian cystectomy, and tubal ligation are procedures that do not involve the bladder and are anatomically separate. Therefore, they do not pose the risk of bladder injury.

To prevent bladder injury in high-risk patients during abdominal surgery, incisions that yield maximum exposure and allow recognition of the vesicocervical and vesicovaginal spaces are necessary. The surgeon can then join these spaces with sharp dissection. The use of blunt dissection with a sponge stick or gauze should be avoided. A valuable adjunct to the surgery is the use of a three-way indwelling catheter intraoperatively. Inflation of the bladder allows identification of the bladder boundaries. Thinning of the muscularis will lead to ballooning of the mucosa, whereas frank leakage will confirm the loss of integrity of the bladder wall in the case of an unrecognized injury.

The most common site of bladder injury is immediately above the fixed bladder base. To repair the bladder, wide dissection of the tissue planes with mobilization is the first step. Healthy tissues are then sutured, without tension, in at least two layers. Omental grafts can provide added blood supply to the area of repair and also add some strength to the tissue closure.

Awareness of the conditions that can cause bladder injury, coupled with the measures described to prevent bladder injury and to recognize an injury if it does occur, will minimize the risk of formation of a vesicovaginal fistula.

Elkins TE, DeLancey JOL, McGuire EJ. The use of modified Martius graft as an adjunctive technique in vesicovaginal and rectovaginal fistula repair. Obstet Gynecol 1990;75:727–733

Lee RA, Symmonds RE, Williams TJ. Current status of genitourinary fistula. Obstet Gynecol 1988;72:313–319

Tancer ML. Observations on prevention and management of vesicovaginal fistula after total hysterectomy. Surg Gynecol Obstet 1992;175:501–506

Walters MD. Vesicovaginal fistula. American Uro-gynecologic Society Quarterly Report 1993;11:1–3

26 Management of enterocele

A 35-year-old woman, gravida 5, para 5, who delivered all of her children vaginally without complication, presents to your office with the complaint of a persistent progressive vaginal bulge and pelvic pressure. Six months ago she had a vaginal hysterectomy with anterior and posterior vaginal repair for symptomatic pelvic relaxation.

At bimanual pelvic examination, the posterior vaginal wall is noted to bulge from the apex of the vagina more than halfway down to the introitus. The remainder of the posterior vaginal wall is intact. With a Valsalva maneuver, a loop of bowel can be felt in the bulge. This condition probably resulted from

(A) failure to suspend the vaginal vault correctly at initial surgery
* (B) failure to close a deep cul-de-sac at initial surgery
(C) failure of the rectocele repair
(D) the patient's poor tissue integrity

This patient, who recently had a vaginal hysterectomy with anterior and posterior vaginal repair, presents with posthysterectomy enterocele formation.

The incidence of enterocele formation is as high as 18% in patients who have undergone major gynecologic procedures. Such a defect can result from failure to ligate a deep cul-de-sac or from failure to recognize an existing enterocele at the time of hysterectomy, as in this patient.

Several techniques have been described for obliterating potential and apparent enterocele sacs. The surgical objectives to repair or prevent an enterocele are the same: 1) to restore normal function and anatomy, 2) to prevent enterocele development or recurrence, and 3) to use the optimal surgical reconstructive procedure. For this patient, the optimal procedure is to open the posterior vaginal wall over the enterocele, dissect the enterocele sac free, remove the bowel from the sac, place a purse-string ligature high in the sac, and excise the excess sac below the ligature.

A repeat posterior repair is indicated for a patient who has a rectocele or symptoms such as constipation or the need to splint the vaginal wall to evacuate the bowels. Sacrospinous ligament fixation of the vaginal apex is indicated when the vaginal vault is prolapsed. This woman does not have vaginal vault prolapse.

On examination, the patient's previous posterior repair was intact; therefore, her posterior endopelvic fascia is intact. A posterior repair with levator plication is unnecessary, because she does not have a recurrent rectocele. Plication of the levator muscles is reserved for rectocele repair in a patient whose endopelvic fascia is too weak to support the rectal wall.

Because the lower portion of the posterior vaginal wall is supported, lack of tissue integrity is probably not the major reason that this complication occurred. It is more likely that an enterocele was missed.

Cruikshank SH. Preventing posthysterectomy vaginal vault prolapse and enterocele during vaginal hysterectomy. Am J Obstet Gynecol 1987;156:1433–1440

Holland JB. Enterocele and prolapse of the vaginal vault. Clin Obstet Gynecol 1972;15:1145–1154

McCall ML. Posterior culdoplasty: surgical correction of enterocele during vaginal hysterectomy. Obstet Gynecol 1957;10:595–602

Ranney B. Enterocele, vaginal prolapse, pelvic hernia: recognition and treatment. Am J Obstet Gynecol 1981;140:53–61

27
Diagnosis of endometrial cancer

A 68-year-old nulligravid woman presents with a 2-week history of light vaginal bleeding. She has been menopausal for 16 years and has been on hormone replacement therapy for 12 years. Four years ago she had some uterine bleeding, and her hormone replacement therapy was changed to continuous conjugated estrogens 0.625 mg and medroxyprogesterone acetate 2.5 mg daily. Since then, she had no further bleeding until recently. Her physical examination is within normal limits. She is 157 cm (62 in) tall and weighs 68 kg (150 lb). Her blood pressure is 160/90 mm Hg. As the initial step in management you recommend

(A) Pap test
* (B) office endometrial aspiration biopsy
(C) dilation and curettage (D&C)
(D) hysteroscopy
(E) transvaginal ultrasonography

Postmenopausal vaginal bleeding should always be taken seriously and properly investigated, no matter how minimal or nonpersistent it is. Approximately 10% of patients with postmenopausal bleeding have endometrial cancer; however, over 90% of patients with endometrial carcinoma have uterine bleeding as their only complaint. Other possible uterine causes of postmenopausal bleeding include estrogen replacement therapy, endometrial atrophy, endometrial polyps, and hyperplasia.

Physical examination seldom reveals any evidence of endometrial carcinoma. Only 30–50% of patients with endometrial cancer have an abnormal Pap test, making this an unreliable diagnostic test.

Office endometrial aspiration biopsy is the accepted first step in evaluating a patient with abnormal uterine bleeding or suspected endometrial pathology. The diagnostic accuracy of office-based endometrial biopsy is 90–98% when compared with subsequent findings at D&C or hysterectomy. The narrow plastic cannulas now available for use are relatively inexpensive and can often be used without a tenaculum. They cause less uterine cramping, resulting in increased patient acceptance. They are successful in obtaining adequate tissue samples in over 95% of patients. If cervical stenosis is encountered, a paracervical block can be performed and the cervix dilated. Premedication with an antiprostaglandin agent can reduce uterine cramping. Complications after endometrial biopsy are exceedingly rare; uterine perforation occurs in only 1–2 of 1,000 patients. An endocervical curettage may be performed at the time of endometrial biopsy if cervical pathology is suspected.

Dilation and curettage with or without hysteroscopy is indicated if cervical stenosis or patient tolerance does not permit adequate evaluation by office aspiration biopsy, if bleeding recurs after a negative endometrial biopsy, or if the specimen obtained is inadequate to explain the abnormal bleeding. Hysteroscopy as an adjunct is more accurate than endometrial biopsy or D&C alone in identifying focal lesions such as polyps, submucous myomas, and small carcinomas.

Transvaginal ultrasonography may be a useful adjunct to endometrial biopsy for evaluating abnormal bleeding and selecting patients for additional testing. The finding of an endometrial thickness greater than 5 mm, a polypoid endometrial mass, or a collection of fluid within the uterus demands further evaluation. Although most studies agree that an endometrial thickness of ≤5 mm in a postmenopausal woman is consistent with atrophy, more data are needed before ultrasound findings can be considered to eliminate the need for endometrial biopsy in a symptomatic patient.

Chambers JT, Chambers SK. Endometrial sampling: When? Where? Why? With what? Clin Obstet Gynecol 1992;35:28–39

Grimes DA. Diagnostic dilation and curettage: a reappraisal. Am J Obstet Gynecol 1982;142:1–6

Kaunitz AM, Masciello A, Ostrowski M, Rovira EZ. Comparison of endometrial biopsy with the endometrial Pipelle and Vabra aspirator. J Reprod Med 1988;33:427–431

Varner RE, Sparks JM, Cameron CD, Roberts LL, Soong S-J. Transvaginal sonography of the endometrium in postmenopausal women. Obstet Gynecol 1991;78:195–199

28

Prevention of deep vein thrombosis

A 47-year-old African–American woman, gravida 3, para 3, with adult-onset diabetes and anemia is evaluated for menometrorrhagia. She weighs 130 kg (287 lb) and has arthritis in her knees that requires her to use a cane. Her physical examination is normal except for a 26-week, nontender, irregular abdominal–pelvic mass. Her hemoglobin is 9.5 g/dl. A Pap test is normal, and secretory endometrium is identified at endometrial biopsy. Ultrasonography reveals a 16 × 18 × 20-cm irregular uterus with multiple inhomogeneous masses consistent with leiomyomas.

She is scheduled for a total abdominal hysterectomy and bilateral salpingo-oophorectomy. The most appropriate regimen for the prevention of leg vessel thrombosis and subsequent embolization in this patient is

(A) subcutaneous heparin sodium, beginning before surgery
(B) subcutaneous low-molecular-weight heparin beginning before surgery
(C) intravenous dextran during surgery
* (D) graded elastic stockings with intermittent pneumatic compression devices
(E) early ambulation

Thromboembolism, the most clinically important venous system disorder, develops in over 600,000 Americans yearly and results in 50,000 deaths. It is an infrequent but life-threatening complication of pelvic surgery. The incidence of fatal postoperative pulmonary embolism varies between 0.01% and 0.87%. In surgical patients, fatal pulmonary embolism is not usually preceded by recognized symptoms or signs of venous thrombosis. For that reason, it is important to identify risk factors for thromboembolism (see box) and initiate preventive measures.

From the operating table until ambulation begins after surgery, venous return from the legs is decreased with resultant blood pooling. Almost half of thrombi that develop do so on the day of surgery.

The lowest incidence of thrombosis of leg veins (7%) is found in women undergoing vaginal hysterectomy. Of women undergoing abdominal hysterectomy for benign diagnoses, 14% develop leg vein thrombi, as do 25% of women undergoing radical hysterectomy for cervical cancer. Almost 50% of women undergoing pelvic surgery for gynecologic carcinoma other than cervical cancer develop leg vein thromboses. Asymptomatic thromboses are also associated with asymptomatic pulmonary emboli as demonstrated by lung scanning studies.

Preoperative Risk Factors Associated with Postoperative Deep Vein Thrombosis*

Age >45 y
African–American race
Lower-extremity edema
Varicose veins
Prior deep vein thrombosis
Prior pelvic irradiation
Plan for radical surgery†

* Factors are significantly associated in stepwise logistic regression analysis.

† Options are radical vulvectomy or exenteration.

Clarke-Pearson DL, DeLong ER, Synan IS, Coleman RE, Creasman WT. Variables associated with postoperative deep venous thrombosis: a prospective study of 411 gynecology patients and creation of a prognostic model. Reprinted with permission from The American College of Obstetricians and Gynecologists (Obstetrics and Gynecology 1987;69:149)

Unfractionated heparin sodium may be associated with complications such as bleeding, hematoma formation, and thrombocytopenia, which may result in the need for transfusion. These complications have been observed more frequently with an 8-hour subcutaneous dosing regimen than with a 12-hour regimen. Low-molecular-weight fraction heparin has increased bioavailability and a longer half-life, requiring dosing only once daily. Its cost is almost 20 times that of unfractionated heparin sodium. It does not cause thrombocytopenia, but it is associated with bleeding and hematoma formation. Because of these complications, most pelvic surgeons select other preventive measures.

Intravenous dextran causes hemodilution by increasing the blood volume and thereby decreasing blood viscosity, increasing the lysis of thrombi, interfering with platelet function, and increasing the clotting time. Anaphylactic reactions and excessive bleeding have been reported with intravenous dextran. It offers few, if any, advantages over heparin and poses problems in older patients, who may be hypertensive or who may have decreased cardiovascular reserve.

Physical methods have been proven equivalent or superior to subcutaneous heparin in preventing pulmonary emboli, and they avoid the complications associated with pharmacologic methods. Elastic compression stockings reduce venous pooling and thrombosis if they are accurately fitted and pressure graduated. They have been shown to reduce the incidence of ^{125}I-detected thrombi by as much as 50%. Sequential, intermittent, pneumatic compression devices significantly increase venous blood return from the legs and increase endogenous fibrinolytic activity. Although pneumatic compression is the most effective way to reduce proximal vein thrombosis, the devices are cumbersome and cause leg sweating and itching when applied directly. Application over elastic compression stockings increases patient acceptance and enhances protection against the development of lower-extremity thrombosis and pulmonary embolism.

This patient is at increased risk for lower-extremity thrombosis and subsequent embolization because of her age, race, weight, and difficulty in ambulation. Her large pelvic abdominal mass may impede lower-extremity venous return. Prevention of thrombus formation and potential embolization is indicated, and mechanical methods are the most appropriate. Early ambulation is always important, but it is not as effective as other measures and will be difficult for this patient.

Clarke-Pearson DL, DeLong ER, Synan IS, Coleman RE, Creasman WT. Variables associated with postoperative deep venous thrombosis: a prospective study of 411 gynecology patients and creation of a prognostic model. Obstet Gynecol 1987;69:146–150

Clarke-Pearson DL, Synan IS, Dodge R, Soper JT, Berchuck A, Coleman RE. A randomized trial of low-dose heparin and intermittent pneumatic calf compression for the prevention of deep venous thrombosis after gynecologic oncology surgery. Am J Obstet Gynecol 1993;168:1146–1154

Imperiale TF, Speroff T. A meta-analysis of methods to prevent venous thromboembolism following total hip replacement. JAMA 1994;271:1780–1785

29
Repair of bowel injury

A 30-year-old woman undergoing diagnostic laparoscopy sustains a trochar injury to the rectosigmoid colon. She did not receive any bowel preparation. The injury is approximately 1 cm long, and there is no visible fecal contamination. The most appropriate treatment option is

(A) observation
(B) primary closure through the laparoscope
* (C) primary closure at laparotomy
(D) diverting loop colostomy
(E) segmental resection and end-to-end anastomosis

Surgical injuries to the large intestine are uncommon, but when they occur, they most often affect the sigmoid colon and rectum. Although primary repair of bowel injuries has been performed successfully through the laparoscope, this approach has not been validated and is not recommended. Immediate laparotomy should be performed after identification of a bowel injury to assess the extent of the injury and proceed with repair. Observation alone is not an acceptable option.

If the injury is confined to the serosa, simple interrupted closure of the serosa will suffice. If full-thickness injury has occurred, the affected area should be thoroughly cleansed, and the bowel wound edges should be trimmed if they are irregular. If the injury is small, primary closure can be accomplished with two layers of interrupted stitches (Fig. 29-1). The first layer should be a through-and-through suture. A second interrupted layer of suture is placed through the serosa and muscularis to reinforce the mucosal closure. Through-and-through lacerations of the intestine can also be repaired by using a stapling device. The wound should be closed transverse to the longitudinal axis of the intestine to avoid reducing the caliber of the bowel lumen.

A diverting loop colostomy is not necessary for a small, uncontaminated laceration of the colon, but may be appropriate if the defect is large, if significant fecal contamination has occurred, or if the bowel wall is unhealthy or previously irradiated. A diverting colostomy would be indicated if the primary repair does not heal and the patient develops peritonitis secondary to leakage.

Resection and anastomosis are indicated if the blood supply to the damaged segment has been compromised. This extensive procedure is unnecessary for the patient described. The procedure, which can be performed either with sutures or an automatic stapling device, is associated with a higher complication rate in patients who have not undergone preoperative bowel preparation. The abdomen should be irrigated thoroughly before closure, and antibiotics should be continued postoperatively.

Burch JM, Brock JC, Gevirtzman L, Feliciano DV, Mattox KL, Jordan GL, et al. The injured colon. In: Transactions of the Southern Surgical Association ninety-seventh annual meeting. Vol 97. Philadelphia: JB Lippincott, 1986:253

Monaghan JM. Complications of surgery. In: Burghardt E, Webb MJ, Monaghan JM, Kindermann G, eds. Surgical gynecologic oncology. Stuttgart: Georg Thieme Verlag, 1993:620–623

Wheeless CR Jr. Tubal sterilization. In: Thompson JD, Rock JA, eds. Te Linde's operative gynecology. 7th ed. Philadelphia: JB Lippincott Company, 1992:343–359

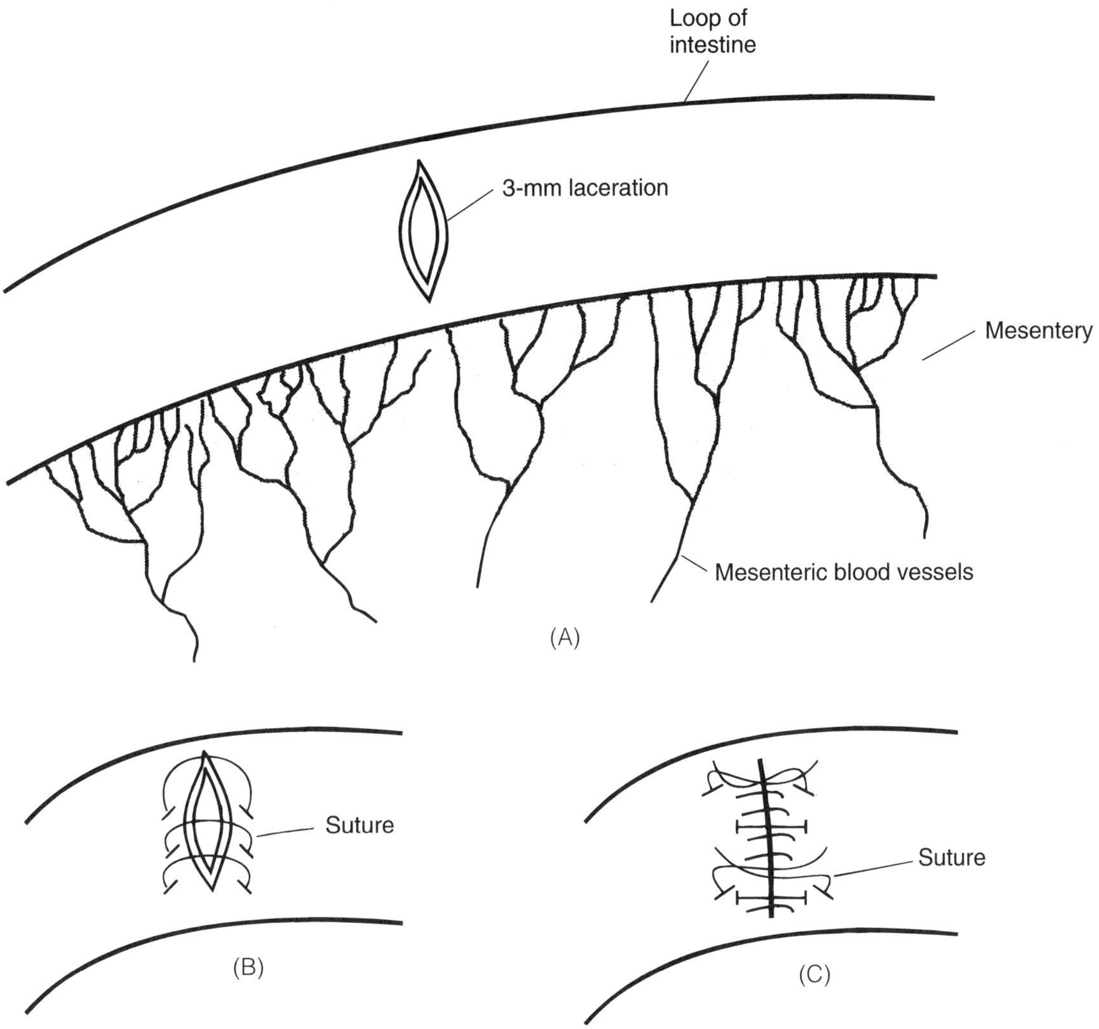

FIG. 29-1. Two-layer closure of bowel laceration. (A) A 3-mm laceration of intestine. (B) The first row of sutures is placed in the direction of the long axis of the bowel loop. Knots are tied so that they end up on the mucosal side of the bowel. (C) A second row of sutures overlaps the first row. Knots are tied so that they end up on the serosal side of the bowel.

30
Therapy for stage I vulvar cancer

A 71-year-old woman has a 1.5-cm squamous cell cancer of the vulva. The lesion is located on the mid left labium majus. The depth of invasion is 6 mm. The appropriate therapy is

(A) radical local excision of the lesion
* (B) radical local excision of the lesion and ipsilateral inguinofemoral lymphadenectomy
(C) radical local excision of the lesion and bilateral inguinofemoral lymphadenectomy
(D) radical vulvectomy and bilateral inguinofemoral lymphadenectomy (through separate inguinal incisions)
(E) radical vulvectomy and bilateral inguinofemoral lymphadenectomy (en bloc resection of vulva and lymph nodes)

Radical vulvectomy and en bloc bilateral inguinofemoral lymphadenectomy for the treatment of vulvar cancer result in significant destruction of the normal vulvar anatomy and have been associated with wound complications in up to 85% of patients. This operation distorts body image and leads to sexual dysfunction.

The cure rate for stage I vulvar cancer is high. In the past decade several reports of conservative management of early vulvar cancer have appeared. According to these reports, the frequency of local recurrence appears no greater when the primary tumor is treated by radical local excision (excision to the level of the deep perineal fascia with adequate lateral margins) compared with radical vulvectomy. Most authorities recommend a 2-cm lateral margin; some investigators have shown good results with a 1-cm lateral margin. Because of the significant improvement in quality of life with radical local excision and the lack of improved local control with the more mutilating radical vulvectomy, there is rarely a place for radical vulvectomy in the management of early vulvar cancer.

Table 30-1 shows the frequency of positive lymph nodes in stage I vulvar cancer stratified by depth of invasion. The frequency of metastasis to lymph nodes is negligible for tumors that invade less than 1 mm. However, for invasion greater than 1 mm, the frequency of metastases is significant. For invasion of 6 mm, as in this patient, the frequency of lymph node metastases is greater than 25%. It has been shown that the risk of nodal metastases for stage I vulvar cancers that do not involve the midline of the vulva is primarily to the ipsilateral inguinofemoral lymph nodes. The risk of contralateral nodal metastases for a unilateral stage I vulvar cancer with no metastases to ipsilateral lymph nodes is less than 1%. For stage I, II, and selected stage III lesions, most authorities recommend separate inguinal incisions. En bloc resection of the vulva and inguinofemoral nodes is rarely indicated.

TABLE 30-1. Incidence of Lymph Node Metastases Correlated with Depth of Invasion in Stage I Vulvar Cancer

Depth of Invasion (mm)	No. of Patients	No. with Positive Nodes (%)
≤1	120	0 (0)
1.1–2	121	8 (6.6)
2.1–3	97	8 (8.2)
3.1–4	50	11 (22.0)
4.1–5	40	10 (25.0)
>5	32	12 (37.5)
Total	460	49 (10.7)

Berek JS, Hacker NF, eds. Practical gynecologic oncology. Baltimore: Williams & Wilkins, 1989:397; copyright Williams & Wilkins

The treatment of choice for the patient described is radical local excision of the cancer with a 2-cm lateral margin of normal tissue and an ipsilateral inguinofemoral lymphadenectomy. In the absence of ipsilateral nodal metastases, contralateral inguinofemoral lymphadenectomy is not indicated.

Burke TW, Stringer CA, Gershenson DM, Edwards CL, Morris M, Wharton JT. Radical wide local excision and selective inguinal node dissection for squamous cell carcinoma of the vulva. Gynecol Oncol 1990;38:328–332

Hacker NF. Vulvar cancer. In: Berek JS, Hacker NF, eds. Practical gynecologic oncology. Baltimore: Williams & Wilkins, 1989:403–439

Hacker NF, Eifel P, McGuire W, Wilkinson EJ. Vulva. In: Hoskins WJ, Perez CA, Young RC, eds. Principles and practice of gynecologic oncology. Philadelphia: JB Lippincott, 1992:537–566

Heaps JM, Fu YS, Montz FJ, Hacker NF, Berek JS. Surgical-pathologic variables predictive of local recurrence in squamous cell carcinoma of the vulva. Gynecol Oncol 1990;38:309–314

31

Estrogen therapy and adenocarcinoma

A 56-year-old postmenopausal woman who is obese, hypertensive, and diabetic underwent a total abdominal hysterectomy and bilateral salpingo-oophorectomy 2 years ago for a stage IA, grade 1 endometrial cancer. She has remained in clinical remission and is currently symptomatic with vaginal dryness and dyspareunia. She wishes to discuss starting hormone replacement therapy (HRT). In addition to diet and exercise, you recommend

* (A) oral unopposed estrogen
(B) combination oral estrogen and progestin
(C) oral unopposed progestin
(D) clonidine (Catapres-TTS)
(E) Bellergal-S (phenobarbital, ergotamine tartrate, belladonna)

The use of estrogen replacement therapy in patients with endometrial carcinoma is being reevaluated. There are no definitive data to support specific recommendations regarding the use of estrogen in women previously treated for endometrial carcinoma. The Committee on Gynecologic Practice of the American College of Obstetricians and Gynecologists has concluded that for a woman with a history of endometrial carcinoma, estrogen can be used for the same indications as for any other woman, except that the selection of appropriate candidates should be based on prognostic indicators (depth of invasion, degree of differentiation, and cell type) and the risk the patient is willing to assume.

Because the consequences of estrogen deficiency are significant and estrogen administration is not without side effects, women need to be given complete information, including counseling about alternative therapies, to enable them to make an informed decision. For some women, the theoretical risk of stimulating tumor growth with estrogen therapy may be outweighed by the sense of well-being afforded by amelioration of menopausal symptoms or by the need to treat atrophic vaginitis, provide cardiovascular protection, and reduce the risk of osteoporosis. Life expectancy is increased by 2 years on average among women who use hormone replacement.

In this patient, the initial recommendation should include weight reduction and an exercise program. Patient counseling should include recommendations for adequate intake of calcium and vitamin D and reduction in the use of caffeine, alcohol, and tobacco. Although balanced calcium metabolism is important for healthy bones, calcium supplementation alone does not seem to be effective in preventing osteoporosis. Proper weight-bearing exercise is important in the prevention of osteoporosis and heart disease. A brisk 45–60-minute walk three to four times a week will accomplish aerobic fitness for almost everyone.

Patients with endometrial cancer share several epidemiologic risks factors with breast cancer patients. There is an increased risk of breast cancer in patients who have had endometrial cancer. The results of some epidemiologic studies have been interpreted as evidence that estrogen replacement therapy increases the risk of breast cancer (relative risk = 1.3–1.6). A relative risk up to 2.0 is considered a low risk. However, in view of the incidence of breast cancer, even a small increased risk may result in a significant public health issue. The issue of potential stimulation of an estrogen-dependent neoplasm (breast or uterus) needs to be reviewed with patients who have had endometrial cancer.

The published data supporting HRT in patients with endometrial cancer have been based on retrospective analyses of 142 patients. Selection bias may well have influenced the reported findings. The published data appear to argue against the pervasive clinical practice of withholding HRT in these patients. These studies are, however, limited by methodologic errors. Clearly, the definitive prospective study has not been done.

Present data suggest that when HRT is provided to patients who have had a hysterectomy, estrogen alone should be prescribed. Theoretically, progestin may increase the risk of breast cancer and heart disease. Progestin is the most effective treatment other than estrogen for the relief of vasomotor symptoms, and it may also be beneficial in preventing osteoporosis.

Clonidine, an antihypertensive agent, has been used in postmenopausal women to treat hot flushes with mixed results. It is not useful for vaginal atrophic changes. Bellergal-S, a combination of phenobarbital, ergotamine, and belladonna, has been reported to be useful in the treatment of hot flushes but is not useful for vaginal atrophic changes. It may be habit forming.

American College of Obstetricians and Gynecologists. Estrogen replacement therapy and endometrial cancer. ACOG Committee Opinion 126. Washington, DC: ACOG, 1993

Belchetz PE. Hormonal treatment of postmenopausal women. N Engl J Med 1994;330:1062–1071

Creasman WT, Henderson D, Hinshaw W, Clarke-Pearson DL. Estrogen replacement therapy in the patient treated for endometrial cancer. Obstet Gynecol 1986;67:326–330

Hutchinson-Williams KA, Gutmann JN. Estrogen replacement therapy (ERT) in high-risk cancer patients. Yale J Biol Med 1991;64:607–626

Lee RB, Burke TW, Park RC. Estrogen replacement therapy following treatment for stage I endometrial carcinoma. Gynecol Oncol 1990;36:189–191

32

Staging of cervical cancer

A 45-year-old woman, gravida 4, para 4, is diagnosed with squamous cell carcinoma of the cervix. She has a 16-week-size fibroid uterus that is deviated toward the right sidewall and is immobile. There is no inguinal or supraclavicular adenopathy. The cervix measures 5 × 4 cm with an exophytic, friable lesion that extends laterally to involve the right vaginal fornix mucosa. The parametria and uterosacral ligaments reveal no induration, thickening, or asymmetry.

Barium enema and chest X-ray are normal. Intravenous pyelography (IVP) reveals moderate right hydroureter arising at the level of the pelvic brim. Proctosigmoidoscopy reveals no abnormalities. Cystoscopy reveals bullous edema of the base of the bladder.

A lymphangiogram is consistent with metastatic disease in the left common iliac and left paraaortic nodes. Biopsy of the left paraaortic nodes by fine-needle aspiration reveals metastatic squamous cell carcinoma.

The International Federation of Gynecology and Obstetrics (FIGO) stage of disease for this patient is

* (A) IIA
(B) IIB
(C) IIIB
(D) IVA
(E) IVB

The current staging of cervical cancer is based on physical examination in conjunction with chest radiograph, IVP, barium enema, cystoscopy, and proctoscopy (Appendix, Table 3). Although other diagnostic tests including surgical staging, computed tomography of the pelvis and abdomen, magnetic resonance imaging, and lymphangiography may further define the extent of disease and allow the refinement of treatment plans, documentation of metastatic disease with these tests does not influence the FIGO-assigned stage of disease.

The patient described has FIGO stage IIA disease based on extension of disease onto the vaginal mucosa of the right vaginal fornix. Although IVP reveals moderate hydroureter, a 16-week-size immobile, fibroid uterus that is deviated to the right with ureteral compromise at the pelvic brim suggests extrinsic compression by the fibroid uterus. In addition, the fact that lymphangiography showed no suspicious lymph nodes on the side of the ureteral obstruction suggests that the hydroureter is due to a nonneoplastic process. Most patients with ureteral obstruction secondary to stage IIIB cervical cancer exhibit distal ureteral obstruction rather than obstruction at the pelvic brim. Furthermore, evidence of stage IIIB disease based on the results of IVP requires hydronephrosis, not hydroureter, according to FIGO.

The finding of bullous edema of the base of the bladder is nonspecific and does not indicate stage IVA disease. To assign stage IVA disease, biopsy confirmation of neoplastic involvement of the bladder or rectum must be obtained.

Retroperitoneal nodal metastasis to the pelvic and paraaortic nodes is a poor prognostic finding. It does not, however, influence the stage of disease.

American College of Obstetricians and Gynecologists. Classification and staging of gynecologic malignancies. ACOG Technical Bulletin 155. Washington, DC: ACOG, 1991

Lovecchio JL, Gal D. Diagnostic techniques in gynecologic oncology. In: Hoskins WJ, Perez CA, Young RC, eds. Principles and practice of gynecologic oncology. Philadelphia: JB Lippincott, 1992:431–441

33

Differential diagnosis of postcoital bleeding

A 24-year-old woman, gravida 3, para 2, with a long history of recurrent vaginal condyloma completed treatment with vaginal 5-fluorouracil (5-FU) cream 2 months ago. Her evaluation before treatment included a negative Pap test. She has been using oral contraceptives for 2 years and has been in a monogamous relationship for 5 years. Evaluation after 5-FU treatment showed no evidence of condyloma, but the patient now complains of vaginal discharge, dyspareunia, and postcoital bleeding. The most likely cause of her symptoms is

(A) cervical cancer
(B) oral contraceptives
(C) cervicovaginitis
(D) prolapsing submucous myoma
* (E) vaginal ulcers

An association has been increasingly observed between vaginal or cervical ulcer formation and previous 5-FU use. The incidence is higher in women who have used 5-FU for longer than 10 weeks. Ulcer size ranges from 0.5 to 0.7 cm, and ulcers may persist for 6 months after use. Vaginal ulcers are associated with vaginal discharge, dyspareunia, and postcoital bleeding. Because this patient was recently treated for vaginal condyloma with 5-FU cream, vaginal ulcers are the most likely cause of her symptoms.

It is no longer rare for a woman in her 20s to have cervical carcinoma. Although cervical cancer may cause postcoital bleeding, most women with postcoital bleeding do not have cancer. Careful inspection and palpation are necessary, with biopsy of any visible lesions. The Pap test is also required, and if the Pap test is abnormal, colposcopy with directed biopsy is required. Although vaginal discharge may be present with cervical cancer, dyspareunia is rare. A recent gynecologic examination with negative findings makes this possibility less likely.

Intermenstrual or postcoital bleeding occurs in up to 45% of women using oral contraceptives. Increased vascularity and eversion of the cervix associated with fragility and hyperplasia of the glands and trauma are one mechanism. However, vaginal discharge and dyspareunia are not associated with oral contraceptive use, and most occurrences of breakthrough bleeding are in the first months of use. Women with an intrauterine device, with or without progesterone, have intermenstrual or postcoital bleeding more frequently than women without the device.

Cervical infection can cause postcoital bleeding. Mucopurulent secretions associated with either chlamydia or gonococci are clinically apparent. This patient's monogamous relationship makes cervical infection less likely. Also, although discharge is common with cervical infection, dyspareunia is not. The guidelines of the Centers for Disease Control and Prevention suggest that culture investigation under these circumstances is not cost-effective. With vaginitis, postcoital bleeding is seen more commonly with bacterial vaginosis (10%) than with *Trichomonas vaginalis* (3%) or candidal infections (2%). Wet mount will confirm the clinical impression.

Uncommon causes of ulcers that bleed after intercourse include *Treponema pallidum*, *Haemophilus ducreyi*, or rarely *Mycobacterium tuberculosis*. Although there may be vaginal discharge, dyspareunia is uncommon. Culture, serology, or biopsy is required for accurate diagnosis. Ulceration also is observed with retained tampons, after trauma, and with Behçet syndrome.

Postcoital spotting in the absence of cancer or a specific cause is more frequently observed midcycle and late in the secretory phase of an ovulatory cycle and is due to changes in estrogen and progesterone production. Prolapsing endometrial or endocervical polyps or myomas may also be responsible. Vaginal discharge and dyspareunia are uncommon with these diagnoses.

Krebs H-B, Helmkamp BF. Chronic ulcerations following topical therapy with 5-fluorouracil for vaginal human papillomavirus-associated lesions. Obstet Gynecol 1991;78:205–208

Lindner LE, Geerling S, Nettum JA, Miller SL, Altman KH. Clinical characteristics of women with chlamydial cervicitis. J Reprod Med 1988;33:684–690

Morgan ED, Laszlo JD, Stumpf PG. Incomplete Behcet's syndrome in the differential diagnosis of genital ulceration and postcoital bleeding: a case report. J Reprod Med 1988;33:844–846

34

Fibrocystic change and risk of breast cancer

A 42-year-old woman had a biopsy of her left breast 4 years ago, which showed fibrocystic changes. Her former physician told her, on physical examination, that she had fibrocystic changes in her breasts. The present mammogram has been read as follows: "Moderately dense breasts, consistent with fibrocystic changes, no mass or signs of malignancy noted."

In a patient with fibrocystic changes of the breast, which of the following specific histopathologic diagnoses increases the risk of breast cancer most?

(A) Apocrine metaplasia
(B) Florid solid epithelial hyperplasia
(C) Papilloma with a fibrovascular core
(D) Sclerosing adenosis
* (E) Atypical lobular or ductal hyperplasia

Histologically confirmed atypical lobular or ductal hyperplasia on breast biopsy increases the relative risk of breast cancer fourfold to fivefold.

The histopathologic diagnosis of apocrine metaplasia does not increase a patient's relative risk of breast cancer. The histologic diagnoses of florid solid epithelial hyperplasia, papilloma with a fibrovascular core, and sclerosing adenosis are associated with slightly increased relative risk (1.5–2.0) for invasive breast cancer.

Although mammography and physical examination can be suggestive of fibrocystic changes, the definitive diagnosis is made only by tissue histology. Therefore, assigning that diagnosis to a patient on the basis of physical examination is an error. Women with a histopathologic diagnosis of atypical hyperplasia (lobular or ductal) should be followed with annual mammograms and breast examinations, regardless of their age.

Carter CL, Corle DK, Micozzi MS, Schatzkin A, Taylor PR. A prospective study of the development of breast cancer in 16,692 women with benign breast disease. Am J Epidemiol 1988;128:467–477

Dupont WD, Page RL. Risk factors for breast cancer in women with proliferative breast disease. N Engl J Med 1985;312:146–151

Is "fibrocystic disease" of the breast precancerous? Arch Pathol Lab Med 1986;110:171–173

Jensen RA, Page DL, Dupont WD, Rogers LW. Invasive breast cancer risk in women with sclerosing adenosis. Cancer 1989;64:1977–1983

London SJ, Connolly JL, Schnitt SJ, Colditz GA. A prospective study of benign breast disease and the risk of breast cancer. JAMA 1992;267:941–944

Love SM, Gelman RS, Silen W. Fibrocystic "disease" of the breast—a nondisease? N Engl J Med 1982;307:1010–1014

Page DL, Dupont WD, Rogers LW, Rados MS. Atypical hyperplastic lesions of the female breast: a long-term follow-up study. Cancer 1985;55:2698–2708

35 Screening for endometrial cancer

A 57-year-old nulliparous obese woman with diabetes consults you regarding her risk of endometrial cancer. Her last menstrual period was 3 years ago. She has not had any vaginal bleeding since then, and she is not on hormone replacement therapy. Her physical examination is normal with the exception of a weight of 110 kg (243 lb) and blood pressure of 160/96 mm Hg. You indicate to her that she is at increased risk for endometrial cancer. In addition to annual physical examination and Pap test, you recommend

(A) tamoxifen citrate (Nolvadex) prophylaxis
(B) annual transvaginal ultrasonography
(C) annual endometrial biopsy
(D) progesterone challenge test
* (E) evaluation of the endometrium only if uterine bleeding or discharge occurs

Endometrial carcinoma is the most common invasive malignancy of the female genital tract in the United States. Approximately 33,000 new cases are diagnosed annually, resulting in over 5,500 deaths. Overall, about 1% of women will develop endometrial cancer during their lifetime.

Endometrial cancer affects women primarily in the perimenopausal and postmenopausal years. Several risk factors for endometrial cancer have been identified. Most of these are associated with prolonged, unopposed estrogen stimulation of the endometrium. Nulliparous women have a two- to threefold increased risk compared with parous women. Infertility and a history of irregular menses, suggesting anovulation, increase the risk. In women who experience natural menopause after age 52, the risk of endometrial cancer is increased 2.4 times compared with the risk in women whose menopause occurred before age 49. The risk of endometrial cancer is increased threefold for women who are 21–50 pounds overweight and tenfold for those more than 50 pounds overweight. The increased risk with obesity is a result of excess estrone from peripheral conversion of androstenedione by aromatization in fat.

Other factors leading to long-term estrogen exposure, such as polycystic ovary syndrome and functioning ovarian tumors, are also associated with an increased risk of endometrial cancer. Menopausal estrogen replacement therapy without progestins increases the risk of endometrial cancer up to eightfold. This risk is greater with higher doses and more prolonged use and can be reduced to essentially baseline levels by the addition of progestin. Recently, an association between use of the antiestrogen tamoxifen for treatment of breast cancer and the development of endometrial hyperplasia and cancer has been noted. Therefore, tamoxifen use is associated with an increase in endometrial cancer, rather than protection against the disease.

Diabetes mellitus increases a woman's risk of endometrial cancer by 1.3–2.8 times. Other medical conditions such as hypertension and hypothyroidism have been associated with endometrial cancer, but a causal relationship has not been confirmed.

There is currently no screening test for endometrial cancer that is appropriate, cost-effective, and acceptable and that reduces mortality. Transvaginal ultrasonography of the uterus and endometrial biopsy are both too expensive to use as screening tests. A progesterone challenge test will tell the clinician if the endometrium has been primed by estrogen, but will not reliably identify the presence of cancer. Routine cervical cytology is too insensitive and nonspecific, and endometrial cytology is too difficult to interpret.

Although many risk factors for endometrial cancer have been identified, screening of high-risk individuals would detect only 50% of all cases of endometrial cancer. Furthermore, no controlled trials have been carried out to evaluate the effect of screening on mortality from this disease.

Fortunately, most patients who have endometrial cancer present with abnormal perimenopausal or postmenopausal uterine bleeding early in the development of the disease. Adequate sampling of the endometrium in this situation usually results in early diagnosis, timely treatment, and a high probability of cure.

Koss LG, Schreiber K, Oberlander SG, Moussouris HP, Lesser M. Detection of endometrial carcinoma and hyperplasia in asymptomatic women. Obstet Gynecol 1984;64:1–11

Mettlin C, Jones G, Averette H, Gusberg SB, Murphy GP. Defining and updating the American Cancer Society guidelines for the cancer-related checkup: prostate and endometrial cancers. CA Cancer J Clin 1993;43:42–46

Parazzini F, La Vecchia C, Bocciolone L, Franceschi S. The epidemiology of endometrial cancer. Gynecol Oncol 1991;41:1–16

36

Evaluation for androgen-secreting tumor

A 58-year-old woman is referred by her family physician because of her appearance (Fig. 36-1). She comments that she has a diminished sense of smell. On examination, the vagina and cervix are normal; bimanual palpation discloses a mobile, anteverted uterus and normal adnexa. The clitoris is enlarged (Fig. 36-2). The first step in the management of this patient is

(A) review of the family history and chromosomal analysis
* (B) assay of serum androgens
(C) computed tomography (CT) scan of the pituitary fossa
(D) biopsy of the vulva for testosterone receptor analysis
(E) cranial nerve testing with particular reference to the olfactory and optic nerves

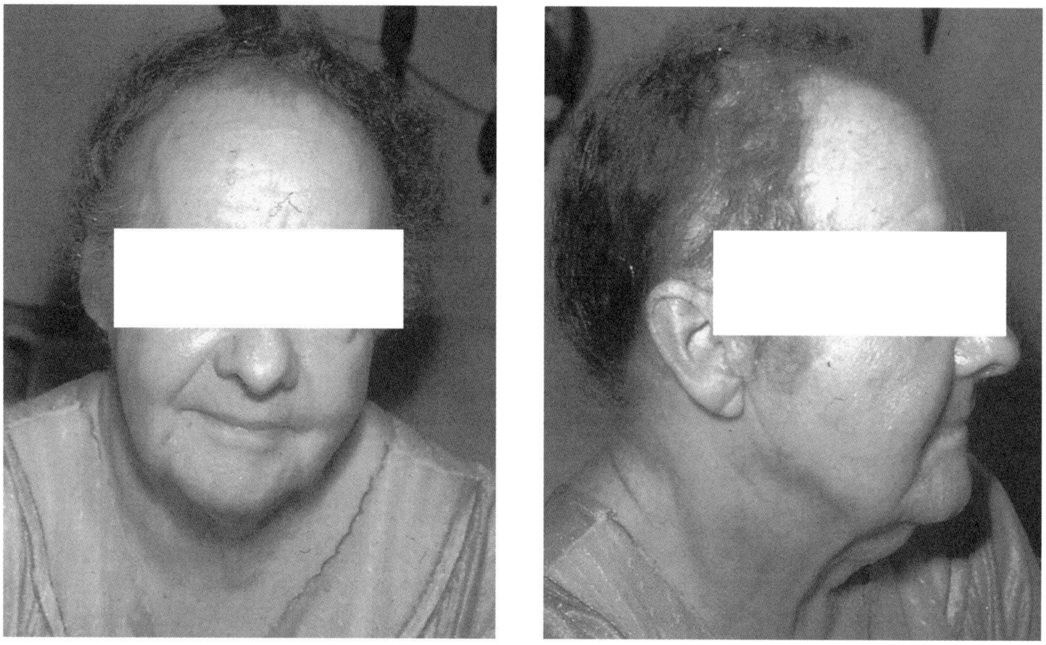

(A) (B)

FIG. 36-1. Facial appearance of a patient with Sertoli–Leydig cell tumor. (A) Front view showing prefrontal balding. (B) Right side view.

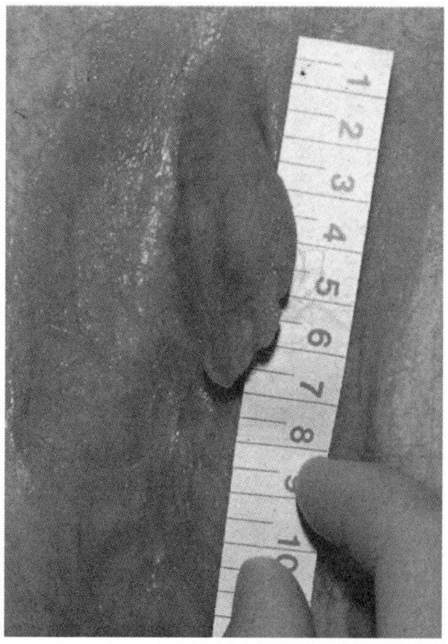

FIG. 36-2. Clitorimegaly. Centimeter rule is adjacent.

This patient's extensive prefrontal balding and marked clitorimegaly (Figs. 36-1 and 36-2) are consistent with high levels of androgen, which are, in turn, indicative of a tumor. The differential diagnosis includes Sertoli–Leydig cell tumor (arrhenoblastoma) and other rare androgen-secreting ovarian and adrenal tumors. The first investigation is measurement of serum androgen levels including dehydroepiandrosterone sulfate, testosterone, and androstenedione. Other steroids such as estrone may be elevated, depending on the tumor activity.

After confirmation of the elevated androgens, radiologic study of the adrenal glands and ovaries is undertaken. Typically, the tumors are small, measuring a few millimeters to a few centimeters. Computed tomography scanning has proven accuracy in assessing adrenal tissue, but not ovarian tissue. The finding of normal adrenal glands at CT scan is presumptive evidence that the source of the androgens is ovarian. Magnetic resonance imaging has advantages and limitations similar to those of CT scanning.

Other investigative techniques have been advocated. Pelvic ultrasonography may identify an ovarian tumor and differentiate it from normal ovarian tissue, especially with color Doppler to detect tumor-associated neovascularization. Transvaginal ultrasonography may assist in making the diagnosis, but not as effectively as the combination of serum androgen assay and CT scan of the adrenal glands.

Selective angiographic catheterization of the ovarian and adrenal veins can determine the source of the elevated androgens and localize the site of the tumor. However, this procedure is technically difficult. Instead of differential adrenal and ovarian venous catheterization, the CT scan can be accepted as evidence of adrenal involvement or, by exclusion, ovarian involvement. Even after successful identification of the source of the androgens, catheterization may not differentiate between hyperthecosis and tumor. In skilled hands, selective catheterization of the left and right ovarian veins may determine which ovary is the source of the increased androgen secretion. In view of the characteristic small size of these tumors, this procedure may help the surgeon decide on which ovary to operate in the case of a premenopausal woman. The definitive diagnosis of a virilizing tumor is made at laparotomy.

Family history, chromosomal analysis, pituitary imaging, thyroid testing, vulvar androgen receptor status, and cranial nerve testing are all unlikely to contribute directly to the diagnosis.

Case records of the Massachusetts General Hospital. Case 24-1993. N Engl J Med 1993;328:1770–1776

Cruikshank DP, Chapler FK. Arrhenoblastomas and associated ovarian pathology. Obstet Gynecol 1974;43:539–543

Fonseca ME, Carballo O, Gonzalez C, Aguilar-Parada E, Villegas A, Zárate A. Steroid secretion by a lipoid cell tumor causing virilization and its diagnosis with computerized tomography. Am J Obstet Gynecol 1985;153:797–798

Surrey ES, de Ziegler D, Gambone JC, Judd HL. Preoperative localization of androgen-secreting tumors: clinical, endocrinologic, and radiologic evaluation of ten patients. Am J Obstet Gynecol 1988;158:1313–1322

Young RH, Scully RE. Ovarian Sertoli-Leydig cell tumors: a clinicopathological analysis of 207 cases. Am J Surg Pathol 1985;9:543–569

37

Management of bowel obstruction

A 48-year-old woman is admitted to the hospital 10 days after undergoing total abdominal hysterectomy and bilateral salpingo-oophorectomy for severe endometriosis with extensive pelvic adhesions. She has had persistent nausea and vomiting for 5 days and mid-abdominal tenderness for 2 days. On examination her pulse is 120 beats per minute, temperature is 38.8°C (101.8°F), blood pressure is 100/60 mm Hg, and respirations are 18 per minute. The patient has increasing abdominal pain and rebound tenderness. Intermittent, high-pitched bowel sounds are present. The abdominal incision is dry and healing well.

Her hemoglobin is 18.5 g/dl, hematocrit is 57%, and leukocyte count is 34,000/mm^3 with a shift to the left. Platelet count is 90,000; clinical chemistries are consistent with hyponatremia (Na, 120 meq/L), hypokalemia (K, 3.1 meq/L), and mild metabolic acidosis. Urinalysis is normal except for increased osmolality. Abdominal roentgenograms are shown in Fig. 37-1. A nasogastric tube was placed on admission, and 1,200 ml of gastric fluid has been recovered. In addition to correction of the electrolyte imbalance, the most appropriate next step is

(A) reevaluation in 24 hours
(B) replacement of the nasogastric tube with a long tube (Miller–Abbott or Cantor tube), advancing it into the small intestine
(C) upper gastrointestinal series with a radiopaque water-soluble solution
(D) upper gastrointestinal series with barium suspension
* (E) laparotomy

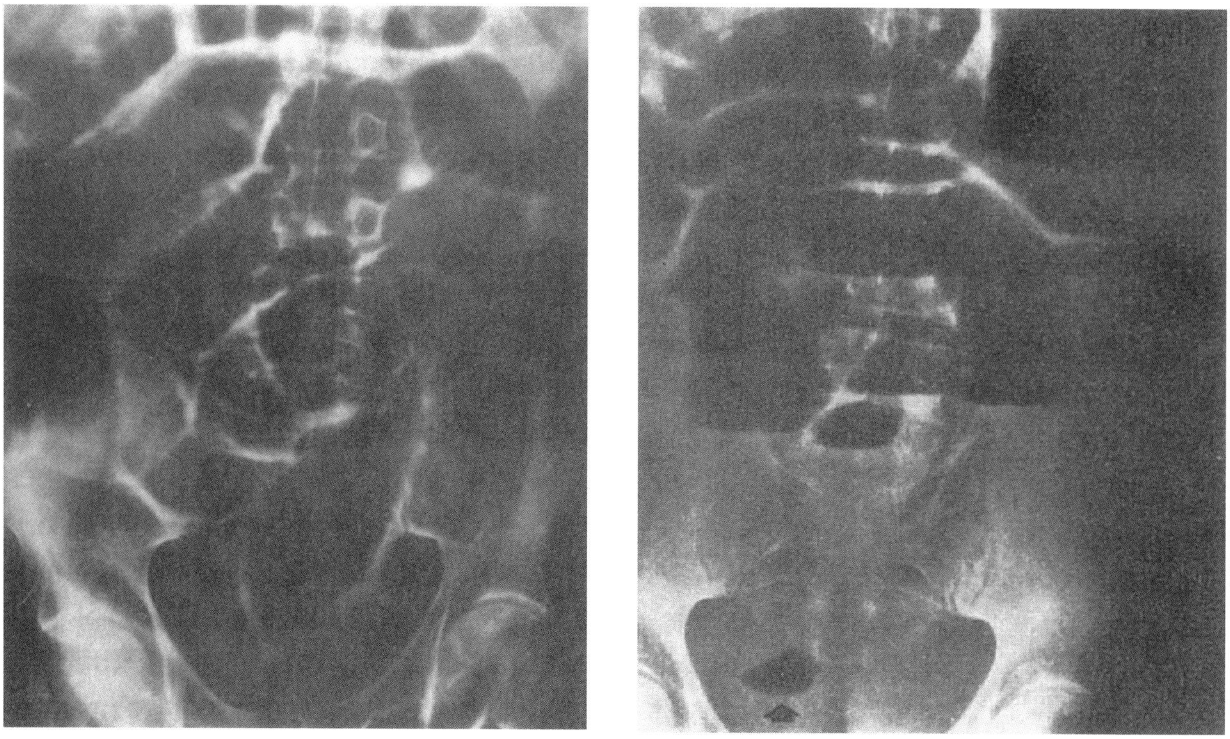

(A) (B)

FIG. 37-1. Abdominal roentgenograms revealing dilated loops of bowel without obvious air/fluid levels. (A) Supine view. (B) Upright view. Only a single, small collection of gas (arrow) is evident in the colon. (Eisenberg RL. Gastrointestinal radiology. Philadelphia: JB Lippincott, 1983: 420)

Small bowel obstruction occurs as a complication of major gynecologic surgery in approximately 1–2% of patients. The most common cause of bowel obstruction is adhesion to the operative site. Small bowel obstruction can also occur as a consequence of tumor, intussusception, and internal or external hernia. Complete small bowel obstruction, as suggested by the patient's history, carries a mortality rate of 10–20% and represents a surgical emergency. A 12-hour delay may mean the difference between simply finding and dividing an adhesive band versus finding gangrenous, perforated ileum with extensive peritonitis.

Small bowel obstruction produces distention, which is a result of intestinal secretions collecting proximal to the site of obstruction. Swallowed air, an inevitable accompaniment, contributes significantly to further bowel enlargement. The distention ultimately impairs perfusion of the small bowel. Venous return is impaired first, because the intraluminal pressure of veins is lower than arteries. The bowel becomes edematous, and a protein- and electrolyte-rich exudate accumulates in the bowel lumen, contributing further secretions and impairing absorption. Later, blood accumulates in the bowel wall and lumen. When intestinal integrity is compromised, bacteria penetrate the mucosa, and gangrene and later peritonitis result.

Although ileus is a more common postoperative complication, several features in the patient's history, including the presence of pain and high-pitched bowel sounds, suggest that she has an advanced mechanical small bowel obstruction. The laboratory report indicating decreased plasma volume and increased urine osmolality is consistent with acute small bowel obstruction. Rebound tenderness, an ominous finding in a patient with suspected small bowel obstruction, suggests impending peritonitis. Leukocytosis, metabolic acidosis, thrombocytopenia, and hyponatremia are all consistent with ischemic bowel and suggest the need for immediate operative intervention.

A long tube (Miller–Abbott or Cantor tube) correctly placed into the small intestine may be useful for treatment of prolonged ileus or incomplete small bowel obstruction. Correct placement of the tube frequently requires considerable time or may not be possible because of the lack of peristalsis. The use of a long tube would result in an inappropriate delay, because surgery is unequivocally indicated for this patient. An upper gastrointestinal radiographic series with either water-soluble or thin barium suspension may be helpful in distinguishing ileus from obstruction and in identifying the location and degree of obstruction, but this procedure would also cause an unnecessary delay in surgery. The characteristic differential air/fluid levels (Figs. 37-1 and 37-2) present on abdominal upright or lateral decubitus X-rays may be few or absent late in the course of intestinal obstruction.

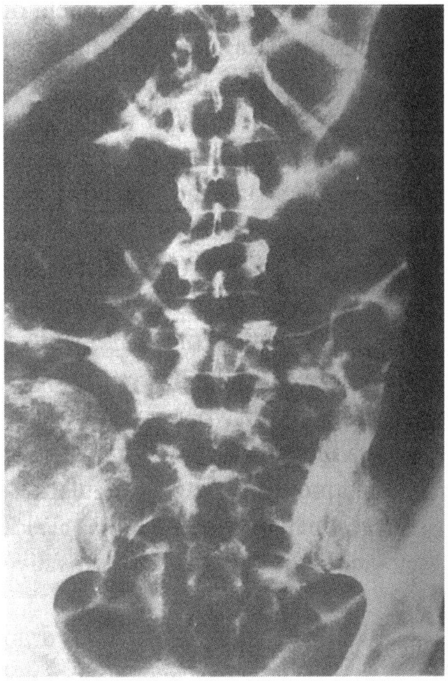

FIG. 37-2. Abdominal roentgenogram revealing air/fluid levels. (Eisenberg RL. Gastrointestinal radiology. Philadelphia: JB Lippincott, 1983:420)

Ileus may be produced by hypokalemia, and it is desirable to correct all electrolyte imbalances, replace whole blood, and restore normal urine output before proceeding to surgery. However, this critically ill patient is unlikely to be significantly improved by electrolyte correction alone.

Carey LC, Fabri PJ. The intestinal tract in relation to gynecology. In: Thompson JD, Rock JA, eds. Te Linde's operative gynecology. 7th ed. Philadelphia: JB Lippincott, 1992:1017–1047

Clarke-Pearson DL, Olt GJ, Rodriguez G, Boente M. Preoperative and postoperative care. In: Gershenson DM, DeCherney AH, Curry SL, eds. Operative gynecology. Philadelphia: WB Saunders, 1993:29–86

Ratcliff JB, Kapernick P, Brooks GG, Dunnihoo DR. Small bowel obstruction and previous gynecologic surgery. South Med J 1983;76:1349–1350

Wolfson PJ, Bauer JJ, Gelernt IM, Kreel I, Aufses AH Jr. Use of the long tube in the management of patients with small-intestinal obstruction due to adhesions. Arch Surg 1985;120:1001–1006

38

Therapy and outcome expectations with stage IIIC suboptimal ovarian cancer

A 65-year-old woman underwent surgical exploration, total abdominal hysterectomy, bilateral salpingo-oophorectomy, omentectomy, and tumor debulking for a stage IIIC, grade 3 serous cystadenocarcinoma of the ovary. Residual disease remaining included two 3-cm nodules on the right diaphragm, a 4-cm mass in the mesentery of the small intestine, and multiple 1-cm nodules in the abdomen and pelvis. The best next step in therapy is

* (A) a combination of cisplatin (Platinol) and paclitaxel (Taxol)
(B) an oral alkylating agent (melphalan [Alkeran] or chlorambucil [Leukeran])
(C) altretamine (Hexalen)
(D) intraperitoneal ^{32}P
(E) whole-abdomen irradiation and concurrent weekly cisplatin

Ovarian cancer is diagnosed in approximately 26,600 women in the United States annually and causes an estimated 14,500 deaths. This disease is the leading cause of death from gynecologic cancer in the United States.

The International Federation of Gynecology and Obstetrics staging system for ovarian cancer is shown in Table 1 of the Appendix. This patient's disease is classified as stage IIIC. The term *suboptimal disease* is used to describe residual disease of greater than 1–2 cm. Patients with suboptimal disease have a poor prognosis, with 5-year survival rates of 10–15%.

Treatment of ovarian cancer with single alkylating agents was the standard treatment in the 1960s and early 1970s. With this therapy, response rates of 40–45% were seen, and median survival for patients with suboptimal disease was about 13 months. Cisplatin-based combination therapy resulted in response rates of 70–80% and median survival of over 2 years.

The combination of paclitaxel and cisplatin has resulted in further improvement in overall survival in patients with ovarian cancer. In a recent Gynecologic Oncology Group study, the combination of paclitaxel and cisplatin resulted in a statistically significant improvement in progression-free and overall survival (Table 38-1). Median survival exceeded 3 years. When compared with the previous standard therapy of cisplatin and cyclophosphamide, a reduction to 0.6 of the relative risk of dying from ovarian cancer was seen. This decrease in the relative risk with the addition of paclitaxel is similar to the decrease in risk of dying that was seen with the addition of cisplatin to the therapy of ovarian cancer.

TABLE 38-1. Survival of Patients with Suboptimal Advanced Epithelial Ovarian Cancer Treated with Cisplatin and Either Cyclophosphamide or Paclitaxel*

	Survival (mo)		
Chemotherapy	Progression Free	Overall	*P*
Cisplatin and cyclophosphamide	12.9	24.4	0.002
Cisplatin and paclitaxel	17.9	37.5	0.001

* Data are from the Gynecologic Oncology Group randomized trial of cisplatin and cyclophosphamide versus cisplatin and paclitaxel.

Whole-abdomen irradiation was standard therapy for ovarian cancer in the 1950s and early 1960s. Several studies in the late 1960s and early 1970s demonstrated an equal survival rate and lower complication rate with alkylating-agent chemotherapy. In recent years, it has been shown that whole-abdomen irradiation is acceptable therapy only for patients with no gross residual disease. This patient with suboptimal residual disease should not receive irradiation. Intraperitoneal ^{32}P has been used as adjuvant therapy in early-stage disease. It is not appropriate therapy for patients with advanced disease. Several drugs such as ifosfamide, altretamine, and doxorubicin hydrochloride are active in ovarian cancer. They are not indicated as primary therapy, however, because cisplatin and paclitaxel result in better survival.

Although there are several experimental trials of concurrent chemotherapy and irradiation in squamous cell cancers of the vulva, cervix, head, and neck, this therapy has not been evaluated in ovarian cancer. The need to irradiate the entire abdomen in patients with ovarian cancer and the failure of irradiation to control large-volume disease in ovarian cancer makes this approach unlikely to be of benefit.

McGuire WP, Hoskins WJ, Brady MF, Kucera PR, Partridge EE, Look KY, et al. Cyclophosphamide and cisplatin compared with paclitaxel and cisplatin in patients with stage III and stage IV ovarian cancer. N Engl J Med, 1996;334:1–6

Omura GA, Bundy BN, Berek JS, Curry S, Delgado G, Mortel R. Randomized trial of cyclophosphamide plus cisplatin with or without doxorubicin in ovarian carcinoma: a Gynecologic Oncology Group Study. J Clin Oncol 1989;7:457–465

Ozols RF, Rubin SC, Dembo AJ, Robboy S. Epithelial ovarian cancer. In: Hoskins WJ, Perez CA, Young RC, eds. Principles and practice of gynecologic oncology. Philadelphia: JB Lippincott, 1992:731–781

Thigpen JT, Blessing JA, Vance RB, Lambuth BW. Chemotherapy in ovarian carcinoma: present role and future prospects. Semin Oncol 1989;16(4 suppl 6):58–65

39

Surgical management of hydatidiform mole

A 23-year-old woman, gravida 2, para 0, whose last menstrual period was 13 weeks ago, presents with vaginal spotting. Physical examination is normal except for an enlarged uterus with a fundal height 6 cm above the umbilicus and a small amount of blood coming from a closed cervical os. No fetal heart sounds are detected by Doppler. The pelvic ultrasonogram is shown in Fig. 39-1. A human chorionic gonadotropin level is 280,000 mIU/ml. A complete blood count and chest X-ray are normal. The preferred management is

* (A) suction curettage
(B) chemotherapy and suction curettage
(C) induction of labor
(D) hysterotomy
(E) hysterectomy

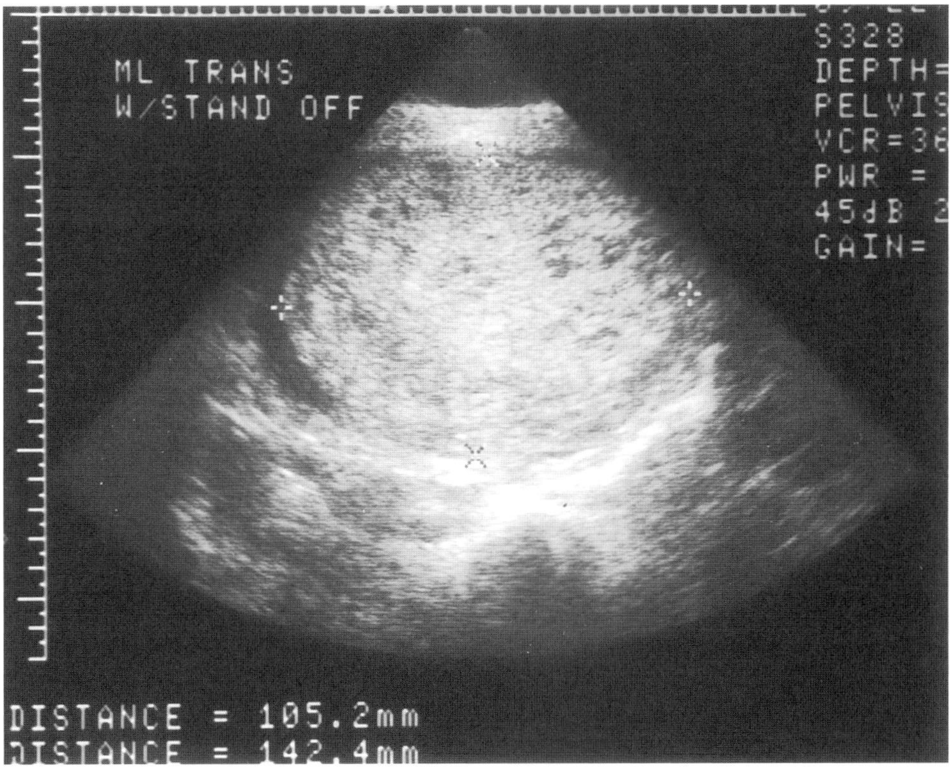

FIG. 39-1. Transverse sonogram showing areas of relative hypoechogenicity and hyperechogenicity (ie, the snowstorm pattern) characteristic of hydatidiform mole.

After the diagnosis of hydatidiform mole is established and the patient is hemodynamically stable, the molar pregnancy should be evacuated. The preferred method of evacuation, independent of uterine size, is suction curettage. After induction of appropriate anesthesia, the cervix should be gently dilated to allow passage of a 12–14-mm suction cannula. The cannula is then introduced into the lower- to miduterine cavity and rotated to evacuate the uterine contents. As the uterus contracts, the evacuation is completed by using gentle suction curettage followed by sharp curettage. An oxytocic agent should be infused intravenously after the start of evacuation and continued for several hours to enhance uterine contractility. If the uterus is larger than 16 weeks of gestational size, at least 2 units of blood should be available, and the patient should be monitored for respiratory distress and blood loss. Prophylactic chemotherapy at the time of molar evacuation is not recommended, since the risk exceeds the benefit.

Hysterectomy is an alternative to suction curettage if childbearing is complete. Hysterectomy not only evacuates the mole and provides for simultaneous sterilization, but also decreases the risk of postmolar gestational trophoblastic tumor from 20% to approximately 3–5%.

Because hysterectomy does not eliminate the potential for persistent disease, follow-up of human chorionic gonadotropin levels is mandatory.

Induction of labor with oxytocin or prostaglandins is less effective therapy than suction curettage. It increases the risk for trophoblastic dissemination and is associated with significantly greater blood loss and incomplete evacuation requiring dilation and curettage. Hysterotomy is also associated with increased blood loss, a classical uterine incision that may lead to the requirement for cesarean delivery in subsequent pregnancies, and a higher frequency of postmolar trophoblastic disease.

Berkowitz RS, Goldstein DP, DuBeshter B, Bernstein MR. Management of complete molar pregnancy. J Reprod Med 1987;32:634–638

Curry SL, Hammond CB, Tyrey L, Creasman WT, Parker RT. Hydatidiform mole: diagnosis, management, and long-term followup of 347 patients. Obstet Gynecol 1975;45:1–8

Schlaerth JB, Morrow CP, Montz FJ, d'Ablaing G. Initial management of hydatidiform mole. Am J Obstet Gynecol 1988;158:1299–1306

40 Evaluation of postmenopausal bleeding

A 61-year-old woman presents with 2 days of light vaginal spotting. She has been menopausal for 9 years, does not take estrogens, and has never had postmenopausal bleeding until now. Physical examination is within normal limits except for atrophic cervicovaginal changes. You perform an office endometrial aspiration biopsy. The uterus sounds to 7 cm, but very little tissue is obtained. The pathologist describes the endometrial sample as mostly blood and mucus with a few fragments of atrophic endometrium.

When the patient returns for follow-up 1 month later, she has had no further bleeding. The most appropriate management at this time is

(A) hysteroscopy
(B) dilation and curettage
(C) transvaginal ultrasound
(D) repeat office endometrial biopsy
* (E) no further evaluation unless bleeding recurs

Abnormal perimenopausal and postmenopausal bleeding should always be investigated. Causes may be nongenital, genital extrauterine, or uterine. Non-genital-tract sites should be considered if the history or examination, including testing for blood in the stool and urine, suggests them. Invasive tumors of the cervix, vagina, and vulva are usually evident on examination, and biopsies should be taken if tumors are discovered. Traumatic bleeding from an atrophic vagina accounts for up to 15% of all cases of postmenopausal bleeding. This diagnosis can be entertained if inspection reveals a thin, friable vaginal wall, but a uterine source of bleeding must first be ruled out. Possible uterine causes of perimenopausal or postmenopausal bleeding include endometrial atrophy, endometrial polyps, estrogen replacement therapy, hyperplasia, and cancer or sarcoma.

Endometrial atrophy is the most common endometrial finding in women with postmenopausal uterine bleeding, accounting for 60–80% of such bleeding. Patients have usually been menopausal for about 10 years, endometrial biopsy often yields insufficient tissue or only blood and mucus, and there is usually no additional bleeding after biopsy.

Endometrial polyps account for 2–12% of postmenopausal bleeding. Polyps are often difficult to detect with office endometrial biopsy or curettage. Hysteroscopy or transvaginal ultrasonography, or both, may be useful adjuncts in identifying endometrial polyps. Unrecognized and untreated polyps may be a source of continued or recurrent bleeding, leading eventually to unnecessary hysterectomy.

Estrogen therapy is an established risk factor for endometrial hyperplasia and cancer. The risk of endometrial cancer is up to eight times greater in postmenopausal women receiving unopposed estrogen replacement therapy, increasing with time and higher estrogen doses. This risk can be decreased by the addition of a progestin to the estrogen either cyclically or continuously. In a patient not taking a progestin, endometrial biopsy should be performed annually and whenever bleeding occurs.

Endometrial hyperplasia is found in 5–10% of patients with postmenopausal uterine bleeding. Sources of excess estrogen that should be considered include obesity, exogenous estrogen, or an estrogen-secreting ovarian tumor. Patients with simple or complex hyperplasia without significant cytologic atypia can be treated with progestins, whereas patients with severe atypical hyperplasia should have a hysterectomy because of the 15–30% incidence of underlying carcinoma. Only 10% of patients with postmenopausal bleeding have endometrial cancer.

Office endometrial aspiration biopsy is currently the accepted first step in evaluating abnormal uterine bleeding. For this patient—whose findings include scant bleeding, a small uterus, and biopsy results compatible with atrophic endometrium, including blood and mucus—no further evaluation is indicated unless bleeding recurs. Hysteroscopy or dilation and curettage, or both, are indicated after a "negative" office endometrial biopsy if the uterus is enlarged and irregular (suggesting that sampling may have been inadequate), if the operator is not confident that the endometrial cavity was entered, or if bleeding is heavy or persistent.

Transvaginal ultrasonography, with or without endometrial fluid instillation (ultrasonohysterography), may be helpful in distinguishing between patients with minimal endometrial tissue whose bleeding is due to perimenopausal anovulation or postmenopausal atrophy and those patients with significant amounts of endometrial tissue or polyps who need further evaluation beyond a negative endometrial biopsy. Repeat endometrial biopsy would not provide any useful information.

Chambers JT, Chambers SK. Endometrial sampling: When? Where? Why? With what? Clin Obstet Gynecol 1992;35:28–39

Choo YC, Mak KC, Hsu C, Wong TS, Ma HK. Postmenopausal uterine bleeding of nonorganic cause. Obstet Gynecol 1985;66:225–228

Fortier KJ. Postmenopausal bleeding and the endometrium. Clin Obstet Gynecol 1986;29:440–445

Lidor A, Ismajovich B, Confino E, David MP. Histopathological findings in 226 women with post-menopausal uterine bleeding. Acta Obstet Gynecol Scand 1986;65:41–43

41

Management of stage IC endometrial carcinoma

An endometrial biopsy reveals grade 2 endometrial adenocarcinoma in a 53-year-old nulligravid woman who has had postmenopausal bleeding. The patient undergoes total abdominal hysterectomy, bilateral salpingo-oophorectomy, and pelvic and paraaortic lymph node sampling. The only pertinent finding at surgery is myometrial invasion of 1.8 cm, with uterine wall thickness of 2.5 cm. Final pathologic analysis confirms the intraoperative assessment of depth of invasion. Pelvic and paraaortic lymph nodes are negative. The most appropriate postoperative therapy for this patient is

* (A) pelvic irradiation
(B) pelvic and paraaortic irradiation
(C) vaginal irradiation
(D) chemotherapy
(E) megestrol acetate

Degree of histologic differentiation is a sensitive indicator of tumor spread. As the tumor grade increases from 1 to 3, the likelihood of deeper myometrial invasion (Table 41-1) and rates of positive pelvic and paraaortic lymph node involvement (Table 41-2) increase. Vascular space involvement also indicates a poorer prognosis. The histologic cell type is related to prognosis: serous, clear cell, and undifferentiated tumors are the most aggressive, with an overall survival of less than 33%, regardless of stage.

Although tumor grade and cell type are important, the single most important identifiable factor correlated with initial treatment failures is depth of myometrial invasion, excluding extension into adenomyosis. One percent of patients with endometrial involvement have metastases to lymph nodes, compared with over 25% of women with involvement of the outer third of the myometrium (Table 41-2). As depth of invasion is related to the grade, prognosis is related to depth of invasion. The accuracy of determining the depth of

TABLE 41-1. Histologic Tumor Grade and Depth of Invasion

	No. (%) with Tumor Grade			
Depth	**G1**	**G2**	**G3**	**Total No. (%)**
Endometrium only	44 (24)	31 (11)	11 (7)	86 (14)
Superficial	96 (53)	131 (45)	54 (35)	281 (45)
Middle	22 (12)	69 (24)	24 (16)	115 (19)
Deep	18 (10)	57 (20)	64 (42)	139 (22)

Adapted from Creasman WT, Morrow CP, Bundy BN, Homesley HD, Graham JE, Heller PB. Surgical pathologic spread patterns of endometrial cancer: a Gynecologic Oncology Group study. Cancer 1987; 60:2037

TABLE 41-2. Frequency of Nodal Metastasis Among Risk Factors

Risk Factor	No. of Patients	No. (%) of Metastases: Pelvic	Paraaortic
Histology			
Adenocarcinoma	459	40 (9)	21 (5)
Others	99	2 (9)	4 (18)
Grade			
1 Well	180	5 (3)	3 (2)
2 Moderate	288	25 (9)	14 (5)
3 Poor	153	28 (18)	17 (11)
Myometrial invasion			
Endometrium only	87	1 (1)	1 (1)
Superficial	279	15 (5)	8 (3)
Middle	116	7 (6)	1 (1)
Deep	139	35 (25)	24 (17)
Site of tumor location			
Fundus	524	42 (8)	20 (4)
Isthmus–cervix	97	16 (16)	14 (14)
Capillary-like space involvement			
Negative	528	37 (7)	19 (9)
Positive	93	21 (27)	15 (19)
Adnexal involvement			
Negative	587	47 (8)	27 (5)
Positive	34	11 (32)	7 (20)
Other extrauterine metastasis			
Negative	586	40 (7)	26 (4)
Positive	35	18 (51)	8 (23)
Peritoneal cytology*			
Negative	537	38 (7)	20 (4)
Positive	75	19 (25)	14 (19)

* Nine patients did not have cytology reported.

Adapted from Creasman WT, Morrow CP, Bundy BN, Homesley HD, Graham JE, Heller PB. Surgical pathologic spread patterns of endometrial cancer: a Gynecologic Oncology Group study. Cancer 1987;60:2038

myometrial invasion by gross visual examination of the cut surface of the uterus in the operating room is 90%.

Staging for endometrial cancer is surgical. Total abdominal hysterectomy, bilateral salpingo-oophorectomy, and pelvic and paraaortic lymph node sampling are required for postoperative staging and form the foundation of therapy; complete lymphadenectomy is not necessary. Because depth of invasion in this patient is greater than one half of the myometrial thickness, her tumor is stage IC.

Optimal treatment for this woman is controversial. Survival data are inconclusive as to the benefit of postoperative pelvic irradiation in cases of stage IC disease, possibly reflecting inadequate power to detect a statistically significant difference because of small sample sizes. Because this patient has an intermediate risk of recurrence due to the tumor grade and depth of invasion, it is likely that adjuvant pelvic radiotherapy will result in improved local and regional control. There is no indication for paraaortic irradiation because the paraaortic lymph nodes are negative. Paraaortic irradiation has been shown to result in 5-year survival for 25–40% of patients with microscopic metastases to paraaortic lymph nodes. Postoperative vaginal irradiation alone would not provide therapy for tumor in pelvic lymph nodes and for that reason would be inadequate. Adjuvant chemotherapy has not been shown to increase survival for patients with stage IC lesions. Adjuvant postoperative therapy with megestrol acetate has not been shown to benefit patients at intermediate or high risk of recurrence.

Creasman WT, Morrow CP, Bundy BN, Homesley HD, Graham JE, Heller PB. Surgical pathologic spread patterns of endometrial cancer: a Gynecologic Oncology Group study. Cancer 1987;60:2035–2041

Doering DL, Barnhill DR, Weiser EB, Burke TW, Woodward JE, Park RC. Intraoperative evaluation of depth of myometrial invasion in stage I endometrial adenocarcinoma. Obstet Gynecol 1989;74:930–933

Morrow CP, Bundy BN, Kurman RJ, Creasman WT, Heller P, Homesley HD, et al. Relationship between surgical-pathological risk factors and outcome in clinical stage I and II carcinoma of the endometrium: a Gynecologic Oncology Group study. Gynecol Oncol 1991;40:55–65

Wilson TO, Podratz KC, Gaffey TA, Malkasian GD Jr, O'Brien PC, Naessens JM, et al. Evaluation of unfavorable histologic subtypes in endometrial adenocarcinoma. Am J Obstet Gynecol 1990;162:418–426

42

Diagnosis of mild atypia in postmenopausal women

You receive a Pap test report of atypical squamous cells of undetermined significance associated with atrophy from a 65-year-old woman. The most appropriate next step in the management of this patient is

(A) colposcopy and directed biopsy
(B) cervical cone biopsy
(C) endocervical curettage
* (D) repeat Pap test after estrogen therapy

A spectrum of benign, reactive morphologic changes may be seen in the Pap test of a postmenopausal patient with vaginal atrophy. Occasionally these changes become so marked that a high-grade squamous intraepithelial lesion or squamous cell carcinoma cannot be excluded.

A diagnosis of atypical squamous cells of undetermined significance associated with atrophy should be interpreted cautiously. Unless the cervix appears to be grossly abnormal, it is likely that the atypical squamous cells are secondary to atrophic changes, with superimposed inflammation resulting from atrophic vaginitis. The cells in such a Pap test show nuclear enlargement and hyperchromasia. In addition, irregularities in nuclear contour and chromatin, as well as pleomorphism, may be observed.

An immediate repeat Pap test would probably show the same changes and therefore is not indicated. The inflammatory changes might also make colposcopy difficult to interpret and result in unnecessary biopsies. Because many such Pap tests are associated with inflammation and repair rather than neoplasia, neither a cervical cone biopsy nor endocervical curettage is indicated at this point in the patient's evaluation. In contrast, a short course of estrogen vaginal cream, followed by a repeat Pap test, will often resolve the problem. Cytologic changes caused by atrophy will resolve after estrogen stimulation, whereas atypical changes resulting from a significant precancerous lesion or carcinoma will persist and be detected more easily in a background of mature cells.

Kurman RJ, Solomon D. The Bethesda System for reporting cervical/vaginal cytologic diagnoses: definitions, criteria, and explanatory notes for terminology and specimen adequacy. New York: Springer-Verlag, 1994:28–29

Sherman ME. Cytopathology. In: Kurman RJ, ed. Blaustein's pathology of the female genital tract. 4th ed. New York: Springer-Verlag, 1994:1097–1130

43

Management of ovarian tumor of low malignant potential

While performing an exploratory laparotomy on a 31-year-old woman for an enlarging complex right adnexal mass, you find an 8-cm cystic and solid mass replacing the right ovary. The remainder of the pelvis and peritoneum are unremarkable. After obtaining cytologic washings and diaphragmatic scrapings, you perform a right salpingo-oophorectomy and send the mass for a frozen-section pathologic analysis. No enlarged lymph nodes are noted on palpation of the pelvic and paraaortic retroperitoneal spaces. The frozen section reveals a serous tumor of low malignant potential (borderline tumor). From preoperative conversation with the patient, you are aware that she would like additional children. The best procedure for this patient is

* (A) omentectomy, peritoneal biopsies, and selected pelvic and paraaortic lymph node biopsies
(B) omentectomy and peritoneal biopsies
(C) termination of the procedure; await permanent paraffin sections
(D) biopsy or bivalving of the other ovary
(E) total abdominal hysterectomy and left salpingo-oophorectomy

Approximately 15% of all ovarian cancers are of the borderline or low malignant potential type. These tumors occur at an earlier age than their invasive counterparts. The average age of patients at diagnosis is about 40 years.

Serous borderline tumors are defined by the World Health Organization as serous neoplasms that show epithelial proliferation greater than that shown in serous cystadenomas (as evidenced by cellular stratification, cytologic atypism, and epithelial tufting) but that exhibit no evidence of stromal invasion. Despite the absence of demonstrable stromal invasion in the primary tumors, extraovarian peritoneal implants are present in 30% of patients. Such implants have a varied histologic appearance. According to the World Health Organization classification of ovarian tumors, the diagnosis of a serous borderline tumor is based on the histologic findings in the primary tumor without consideration of the histologic appearance of the metastases. Recurrence and survival in patients with tumor of low malignant potential are stage dependent.

After a complete surgical staging, about one third of patients with apparent stage I or II ovarian cancer will be found to have more advanced disease. If the pathologist confirms a tumor of low malignant potential on frozen-section analysis, a complete surgical staging procedure is necessary. Palpation of the lymph nodes is insufficient for detecting microscopic disease, because fewer than 10% of patients with lymphatic metastasis have grossly enlarged nodes. The surgical stage of disease is determined by cytologic washings, diaphragmatic scrapings, omentectomy, peritoneal biopsies, and selected pelvic and paraaortic lymph node sampling.

More than 60% of patients have tumor confined to the ovary at diagnosis (ie, stage IA). For patients with surgically documented stage IA disease, there is a role for ovarian tissue conservation. For young patients who have unilateral tumors and have been properly surgically staged, unilateral adnexectomy is the definitive treatment. Twenty to thirty percent of patients with stage I serous tumors of low malignant potential have bilateral tumors. A higher relapse rate is observed in patients treated conservatively with ovarian cystectomy. However, this higher relapse rate does not appear to translate into decreased survival rates.

Because the likelihood of finding microscopic cancer is very low, the contralateral ovary does not require biopsy or bivalving if it appears normal on gross examination. There is a potential risk of postoperative infertility from biopsy or bivalving of the ovary. If a patient with early-stage disease desires future childbearing, a hysterectomy may be deferred.

Bell DA, Weinstock MA, Scully RE. Peritoneal implants of ovarian serous borderline tumors: histologic features and prognosis. Cancer 1988;62:2212–2222

Casey AC, Bell DA, Lage JM, Fuller AF, Nikrui N, Rice LW. Epithelial ovarian tumors of borderline malignancy: long-term follow-up. Gynecol Oncol 1993;50:316–322

Leake JF, Currie JL, Rosenshein NB, Woodruff JD. Long-term followup of serous ovarian tumors of low malignant potential. Gynecol Oncol 1992;47:150–158

44

Estrogen and progesterone receptors and breast cancer

A 76-year-old postmenopausal woman underwent a right modified radical mastectomy for a 2-cm, infiltrating ductal adenocarcinoma of the breast. The tumor was positive for both estrogen and progesterone receptors. The patient was subsequently placed on tamoxifen citrate (Nolvadex) therapy. Which of the following statements is correct?

(A) Hormone-binding assays and sedimentation profiles are the most precise methods for determining estrogen and progesterone receptors.
* (B) Prognosis is directly correlated with the presence of the estrogen receptor.
(C) Prognosis is *not* correlated with the presence of the progesterone receptor.
(D) Use of tamoxifen citrate therapy is based on the presence of progesterone receptors.

The growth and proliferation of breast tissue depend on the effect of a variety of modulatory substances including estrogen, progesterone, and an increasingly long list of identified growth factors. The metastatic potential of breast cancer cells is influenced by the same substances. Estrogen and progesterone exert their effects primarily through interaction with nuclear receptor proteins. Our knowledge of these steroid receptors has been refined over the past 10 years. The human estrogen receptor is a 595-amino-acid protein containing zinc, which interacts with DNA to modulate transcription of specific genes. Similar receptors have been characterized for progesterone, glucocorticoids, thyroid hormones, and other hormones. The receptors have in common a DNA-binding domain and a hormone-binding receptor near the carboxy terminus.

Previously, steroid receptors were crudely quantitated with hormone-binding assays and sedimentation profiles. In the past 10 years monoclonal antibodies and cDNA clones for these receptors have been developed, permitting more precise identification by immunohistochemical methods.

Endocrine therapy for breast cancer includes the use of sex steroid hormone analogs such as tamoxifen. Antiestrogens have both cytostatic and cytotoxic effects on breast cell growth. They probably exert their effect through interaction with the nuclear receptor proteins. Approximately two thirds of patients with breast cancer are positive for the estrogen receptor, and two thirds of these patients will respond to tamoxifen. Patients with progesterone receptor–positive cancers also have a more favorable prognosis. Response rates to tamoxifen increase with higher estrogen receptor levels in the tumor. Although hormone therapy for breast cancer was once selected on the basis of a patient's estrogen receptor status (not her progesterone receptor status), use of tamoxifen as an adjunct to treat metastatic disease is no longer determined entirely on this basis.

Osborne CK, Yochmowitz MG, Knight WA III, McGuire WL. The value of estrogen and progesterone receptors in the treatment of breast cancer. Cancer 1980;46:2884–2888

Read LD, Katzenellenbogen BS. Characterization and regulation of estrogen and progesterone receptors in breast cancer. In: Dickson RB, Lippman ME, eds. Genes, oncogenes, and hormones: advances in cellular and molecular biology of breast cancer. Boston: Kluwer Academic Publishers, 1991:277–299

Wiebe VJ, Osborne CK, Fuqua SAW, DeGregorio MW. Tamoxifen resistance in breast cancer. Crit Rev Oncol Hematol 1993;14:173–188

45

Treatment for early stage cervical carcinoma

A 37-year-old woman with intermenstrual and postcoital bleeding has a 2.6 × 2.0 cm lesion of the anterior cervix. Biopsy shows an invasive squamous cell carcinoma. Invasion is through the entire depth of the biopsy (4 mm). There is no vaginal or parametrial extension. Physical examination is otherwise unremarkable. Chest X-ray and computed tomography (CT) scan of the abdomen and pelvis are normal. Of the following options, the best next step in management is

(A) cone biopsy
(B) simple hysterectomy and bilateral pelvic lymphadenectomy
(C) radical hysterectomy
* (D) radical hysterectomy and bilateral pelvic lymphadenectomy

Carcinoma of the cervix is diagnosed in approximately 15,000 women in the United States annually and causes an estimated 4,600 deaths. The International Federation of Gynecology and Obstetrics staging classification for cervical cancer is shown in Table 3 of the Appendix.

Of all the cervical cancers diagnosed, 42% are confined to the cervix (stage IB). This patient has a stage IB cervical cancer because the lesion is visible, disease has been documented to invade the cervical stroma to a depth of 4 mm, there is no evidence of disease spread beyond the cervix on physical examination, and metastasis is not evident on chest X-ray. A cone biopsy would be unnecessary and is contraindicated, because sufficient information is already available to stage the disease. The cure rate for women with stage IB carcinoma of the cervix is 84–88%. This cure rate will be achieved with either radical hysterectomy and bilateral pelvic lymphadenectomy or radical radiotherapy. There is no significant difference in either the cure rate or the frequency of serious complications between these two therapies. Advantages for surgical therapy include a shorter treatment interval, lower cost, ability to preserve ovarian function, better vaginal function, avoidance of short-term and long-term radiation complications, and better definition of prognostic factors.

Advantages of radiation therapy include avoidance of a major surgical procedure (often an important concern in patients who are very obese or have significant medical problems) and avoidance of short-term and long-term surgical complications. Although some authorities have used age as a criterion for selecting patients for radiation therapy, the preponderance of medical literature indicates that older patients with good performance status tolerate radical surgery as well as younger patients.

There is no evidence that cervical cancers respond differently to either surgical therapy or irradiation based on histologic cell type. Although adenocarcinoma and adenosquamous carcinoma have been shown to have a worse prognosis in some studies, choice of therapy does not affect prognosis.

The risk of lymph node metastases is 14–18% in patients with stage IB cervical cancer. Therapy for stage IB disease should therefore include either removal (surgical therapy) or treatment (irradiation) of the regional lymphatics and lymph nodes.

Simple hysterectomy is adequate therapy for stage IA1 cervical cancers with invasion of less than 3 mm and no lymph-vascular space invasion because the risk of lymphatic involvement is low. For lesions that invade to a depth greater than 3 mm, radical hysterectomy and bilateral pelvic lymphadenectomy are necessary to remove the parametria and pelvic lymph nodes. Addition of pelvic lymphadenectomy to simple hysterectomy would fail to adequately treat the parametrial tissues and lymphatics.

Fuller AF Jr, Elliott N, Kosloff C, Hoskins WJ, Lewis JL Jr. Determinants of increased risk for recurrence in patients undergoing radical hysterectomy for stage IB and IIA carcinoma of the cervix. Gynecol Oncol 1989;33:34–39

Hoskins WJ, Ford JH Jr, Lutz MH, Averette HE. Radical hysterectomy and pelvic lymphadenectomy for the management of early invasive cancer of the cervix. Gynecol Oncol 1976;4:278–290

Perez CA, Kurman RJ, Stehman FB, Thigpen JT. Uterine cervix. In: Hoskins WJ, Perez CA, Young RC, eds. Principles and practice of gynecologic oncology. Philadelphia: JB Lippincott, 1992:591–662

46

Treatment of germ cell tumor in a teenager

A 16-year-old woman was diagnosed with an endodermal sinus tumor (yolk sac tumor), stage IV. A unilateral salpingo-oophorectomy was performed, along with excision of the involved supraclavicular node. A preoperative alpha-fetoprotein (AFP) level was greater than 4,000 ng/ml. After surgery, she had three cycles of chemotherapy with bleomycin sulfate (Blenoxane), etoposide (VePesid), and cisplatin (Platinol). Her AFP level has been normal since she completed her first cycle of therapy. By noninvasive testing and physical examination, she is in complete clinical remission. Subsequent management requires

* (A) no further therapy
(B) laparoscopic oophorectomy of the contralateral ovary
(C) three additional cycles of chemotherapy
(D) consolidation therapy with ^{32}P
(E) second-look laparotomy

Malignant ovarian tumors in young women are rare. The most common presenting symptoms and signs are abdominal pain, abdominal swelling, and pelvic mass. Ovarian masses in premenarchal girls are more often malignant, whereas in postmenarchal girls and in menstruating women ovarian masses are often functional cysts. The incidence of neoplastic lesions is estimated to be 2.6 cases per 100,000 women under age 18 per year.

Most malignant germ cell tumors are unilateral. Bilateral ovarian involvement with germ cell tumors is rare, except in the case of dysgerminoma, in which 10–15% are bilateral. Therefore, unilateral salpingo-oophorectomy with preservation of the contralateral ovary and the uterus is appropriate surgical management for most patients with malignant germ cell tumors. In 5–10% of patients with malignant germ cell tumors, a benign cystic teratoma may coexist. An ovarian cystectomy for the benign cystic tumor with preservation of the normal ovarian tissue is recommended.

Eighty-five percent of patients with endodermal sinus (yolk sac) tumors will die if no postoperative therapy is given, even if the disease is discovered at stage I. Three cycles of bleomycin, etoposide, and cisplatin are curative in more than 95% of patients with all stages of these germ cell tumors if visible disease was completely resected. Additional cycles of chemotherapy have not improved survival rates for patients in complete clinical remission. Likewise, consolidation therapy with ^{32}P is not indicated for this patient. Treatment after achieving a complete clinical response or a pathologic complete response is termed consolidation therapy, because it is administered to consolidate the response. No further therapy is needed for a patient with germ cell tumor who is in complete clinical remission.

Second-look laparotomy is not warranted in the management of patients with malignant germ cell tumors, except for those with grade 2 or 3 immature teratomas who had residual disease at the onset of chemotherapy.

Although ovarian dysfunction or failure is a risk of chemotherapy, most survivors who are younger than 35 years of age at the time of treatment can anticipate normal menstrual and reproductive function. According to published data, treatment with chemotherapy does not increase the frequency of congenital anomalies in the offspring of these patients. Successful pregnancies without evidence of genetic damage have been documented after treatment with combination chemotherapy in patients with malignant ovarian germ cell tumors.

Although no reports of other late effects of chemotherapy on patients treated for ovarian germ cell tumors are available, several articles regarding men with testicular cancer have reported late toxicities including high-tone hearing loss, neurotoxicity, renal dysfunction, pulmonary toxicity, skin changes, leukemia, ischemic heart disease, and Raynaud phenomenon (see box).

Toxicities Associated with Chemotherapy

Bleomycin
Pulmonary fibrosis
Skin hyperpigmentation

Cisplatin
Ototoxicity
Neurotoxicity
Nephrotoxicity
Raynaud phenomenon
Ischemic heart disease

Gershenson DM. Update on malignant ovarian germ cell tumors. Cancer 1993;71:1581–1590

Gribbon M, Ein SH, Mancer K. Pediatric malignant ovarian tumors: a 43-year review. J Pediatr Surg 1992;27:480–484

Skinner MA, Schlatter MG, Heifetz SA, Grosfeld JL. Ovarian neoplasms in children. Arch Surg 1993;128:849–854

Williams SD, Loehrer PJ, Nichols CR, Einhorn LN. Chemotherapy of male and female germ cell tumors. Semin Oncol 1992;19:19–24

47

Treatment for cervical intraepithelial neoplasia

A 32-year-old woman, gravida 3, para 3, has seen you for annual visits for the past 6 years. A high-grade squamous intraepithelial lesion is detected on Pap test. She has completed her family, and her gynecologic history is unremarkable.

An area of acetowhite epithelium with focal mosaicism at the 4-o'clock position is noted on colposcopic examination. The lesion extends into the endocervical canal, and the upper margin is not visualized. Biopsy of the lesion reveals cervical intraepithelial neoplasia grade II (CIN II). An endocervical curettage reveals CIN III.

The recommendation for optimal management is

(A) cryotherapy of the cervix
(B) laser vaporization of the cervix
* (C) excision by conization
(D) hysterectomy

The treatment of cervical dysplasia is predicated primarily on the location of the lesion and secondarily on the surface contour of the cervix. Except for CIN I, the severity or grade of dysplasia should not influence the recommendation for treatment.

Treatment methods based on tissue destruction require that invasive disease be excluded and that the entire lesion be accessible. Both cryotherapy and laser vaporization are appropriate for lesions confined to the ectocervix. Comparable success rates are reported for the two methods. With cryotherapy, treatment of cervical dysplasia is associated with a failure rate of 5.7%. When the grade of dysplasia alone is considered, the failure rates are 4.9% for CIN I and 6.5% for CIN III. With laser vaporization, the average failure rate is 6.2%. When the grade of dysplasia is considered, the failure rates are 8.9% for CIN I and 4.1% for CIN III. The size of the lesion is also an important predictor of success in that recurrent dysplasia is more likely in larger lesions regardless of treatment modality.

In general, laser therapy is more expensive than cryotherapy and is not as readily available in the office setting. Laser therapy causes more pain and is associated with more complications than cryotherapy. However, cryotherapy may be associated with prolonged and profuse vaginal discharge. In addition, cryotherapy may not be suitable for a patient with a distorted surface contour of the cervix, which may result from vaginal delivery. In this situation, it is difficult to achieve an extensive application of the cryoprobe to the cervix.

Endocervical involvement, evidenced by a positive endocervical curettage or an inability to visualize the upper extent of an ectocervical lesion, mandates surgical excision of the transformation zone and the distal portion of the endocervical canal. This may be accomplished by cervical conization or the loop electrode excision procedure.

Hysterectomy is not the treatment of choice for this patient with CIN III on endocervical curettage, because the diagnosis of invasive carcinoma has not been confidently excluded. Even when invasive carcinoma has been excluded, hysterectomy is not recommended as the treatment of choice in the absence of gynecologic indications such as symptomatic fibroids or menometrorrhagia unresponsive to medical management.

American College of Obstetricians and Gynecologists. Ethical considerations in sterilization. ACOG Committee Opinion 73. Washington, DC: ACOG, 1989

Baggish MS, Dorsey JH, Adelson M. A ten-year experience treating cervical intraepithelial neoplasia with the CO_2 laser. Am J Obstet Gynecol 1989;161:60–68

Benedet JL, Miller DM, Nickerson KG, Anderson GH. The results of cryosurgical treatment of cervical intraepithelial neoplasia at one, five, and ten years. Am J Obstet Gynecol 1987;157:268–273

Ferenczy A. Comparison of cryo- and carbon dioxide laser therapy for cervical intraepithelial neoplasia. Obstet Gynecol 1985;66:793–798

Roman LD, Morris M, Eifel P, Burke TW, Gershenson DM, Wharton JT. Reasons for inappropriate simple hysterectomy in the presence of invasive cancer of the cervix. Obstet Gynecol 1992;79:485–489

48 Management of vaginal vault prolapse

An 87-year-old woman presents with symptomatic vaginal vault prolapse, 45 years after an abdominal hysterectomy. She has tried a number of pessaries without success. She requests surgical correction of the vault prolapse. She does not desire future sexual activity.

A review of the patient's medical history is pertinent for chronic congestive heart failure, hypertension, and diabetes mellitus. The optimal procedure for her is

* (A) complete colpocleisis
(B) LeFort partial colpocleisis
(C) abdominal sacrocolpopexy
(D) sacrospinous ligament suspension

Vaginal vault prolapse may be corrected by using any of the procedures listed above. The procedure that is recommended is based on pelvic anatomy, assessment of surgical risk, and the patient's wishes concerning vaginal intercourse. Chronic congestive heart failure, hypertension, and diabetes mellitus increase this patient's risk of perioperative complications, and the least stressful operative procedure should be chosen.

Complete colpocleisis (Fig. 48-1) is the procedure of choice for this patient, who is not interested in vaginal intercourse. This procedure is less extensive than abdominal sacrocolpopexy, sacrospinous ligament suspension, or posterior shelf colpopexy, and it would pose less surgical stress to the patient. The mucosa of the vaginal walls is dissected free, and the vagina is closed with successive purse-string sutures. Vaginal vault colpocleisis has a success rate greater than 85%. Complications of the procedure include urinary incontinence, rectal prolapse, labial herniation, and recurrent intestinal herniation.

The LeFort partial colpocleisis (Fig. 48-2) is performed in the presence of total uterine procidentia without resorting to hysterectomy and its associated complications. Only anterior and posterior segments of the vaginal epithelium are excised, leaving lateral vaginal tissues intact to allow uterine drainage if necessary. Suturing of the anterior vaginal tissues to the posterior tissues in front of the cervix in multiple layers replaces the uterus into the pelvis.

With the abdominal sacrocolpopexy procedure (Fig. 48-3), the apex of the vagina is suspended to the anterior surface of the sacrum at the level of the promontory by using a sling made of a synthetic material or fascia lata. This procedure is used when the vagina is too short to reach the ischial spine, when abdominal exploration is indicated for another reason, or when there is simultaneous prolapse of the rectum and vagina. However, the complications of general anesthesia and the risk of fluid overload are of concern in this patient.

Sacrospinous ligament suspension (Fig. 48-4) would avoid the potential pulmonary complications associated with abdominal surgery. With this vaginal procedure, the apex of the vagina is suspended from the sacrospinous ligament. Potential complications of this procedure include laceration of the pudendal vessels, sciatic nerve entrapment, and buttock pain.

Morley GW, DeLancey JOL. Sacrospinous ligament fixation for eversion of the vagina. Am J Obstet Gynecol 1988;158:872–881

Ridley JH. Evaluation of the colpocleisis operation: a report of fifty-eight cases. Am J Obstet Gynecol 1972;113:1114–1119

Seigworth GR. Vaginal vault prolapse with eversion. Obstet Gynecol 1979;54:255–260

Valaitis SR, Stanton SL. Sacrocolpopexy: a retrospective study of a clinician's experience. Br J Obstet Gynaecol 1994;101:518–522

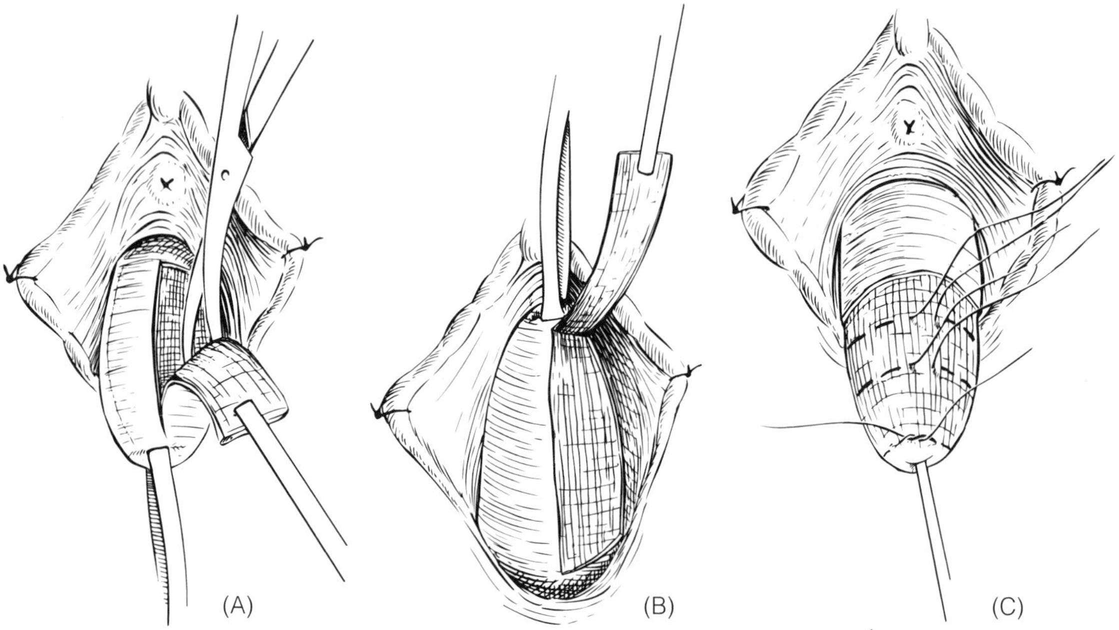

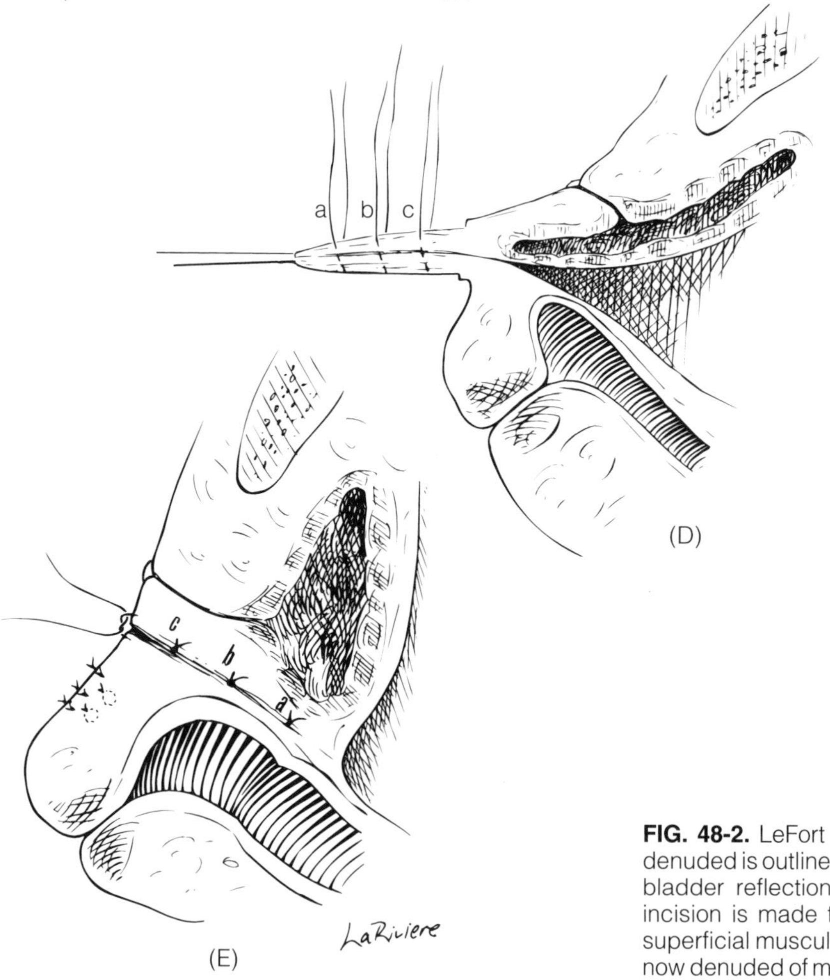

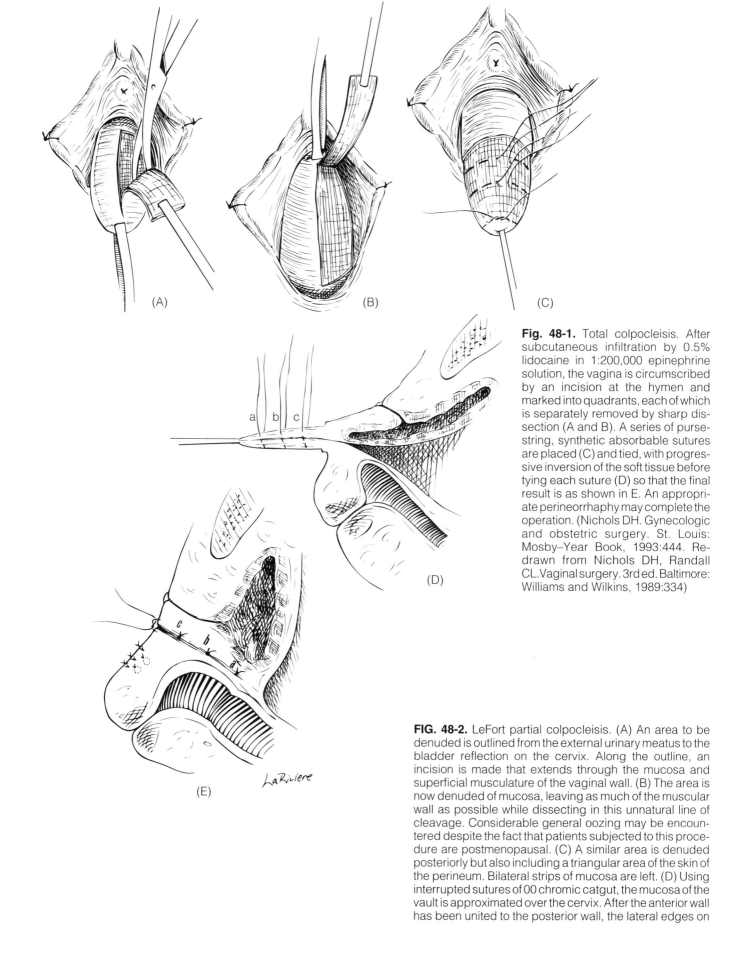

Fig. 48-1. Total colpocleisis. After subcutaneous infiltration by 0.5% lidocaine in 1:200,000 epinephrine solution, the vagina is circumscribed by an incision at the hymen and marked into quadrants, each of which is separately removed by sharp dissection (A and B). A series of purse-string, synthetic absorbable sutures are placed (C) and tied, with progressive inversion of the soft tissue before tying each suture (D) so that the final result is as shown in E. An appropriate perineorrhaphy may complete the operation. (Nichols DH. Gynecologic and obstetric surgery. St. Louis: Mosby–Year Book, 1993:444. Redrawn from Nichols DH, Randall CL. Vaginal surgery. 3rd ed. Baltimore: Williams and Wilkins, 1989:334)

FIG. 48-2. LeFort partial colpocleisis. (A) An area to be denuded is outlined from the external urinary meatus to the bladder reflection on the cervix. Along the outline, an incision is made that extends through the mucosa and superficial musculature of the vaginal wall. (B) The area is now denuded of mucosa, leaving as much of the muscular wall as possible while dissecting in this unnatural line of cleavage. Considerable general oozing may be encountered despite the fact that patients subjected to this procedure are postmenopausal. (C) A similar area is denuded posteriorly but also including a triangular area of the skin of the perineum. Bilateral strips of mucosa are left. (D) Using interrupted sutures of 00 chromic catgut, the mucosa of the vault is approximated over the cervix. After the anterior wall has been united to the posterior wall, the lateral edges on

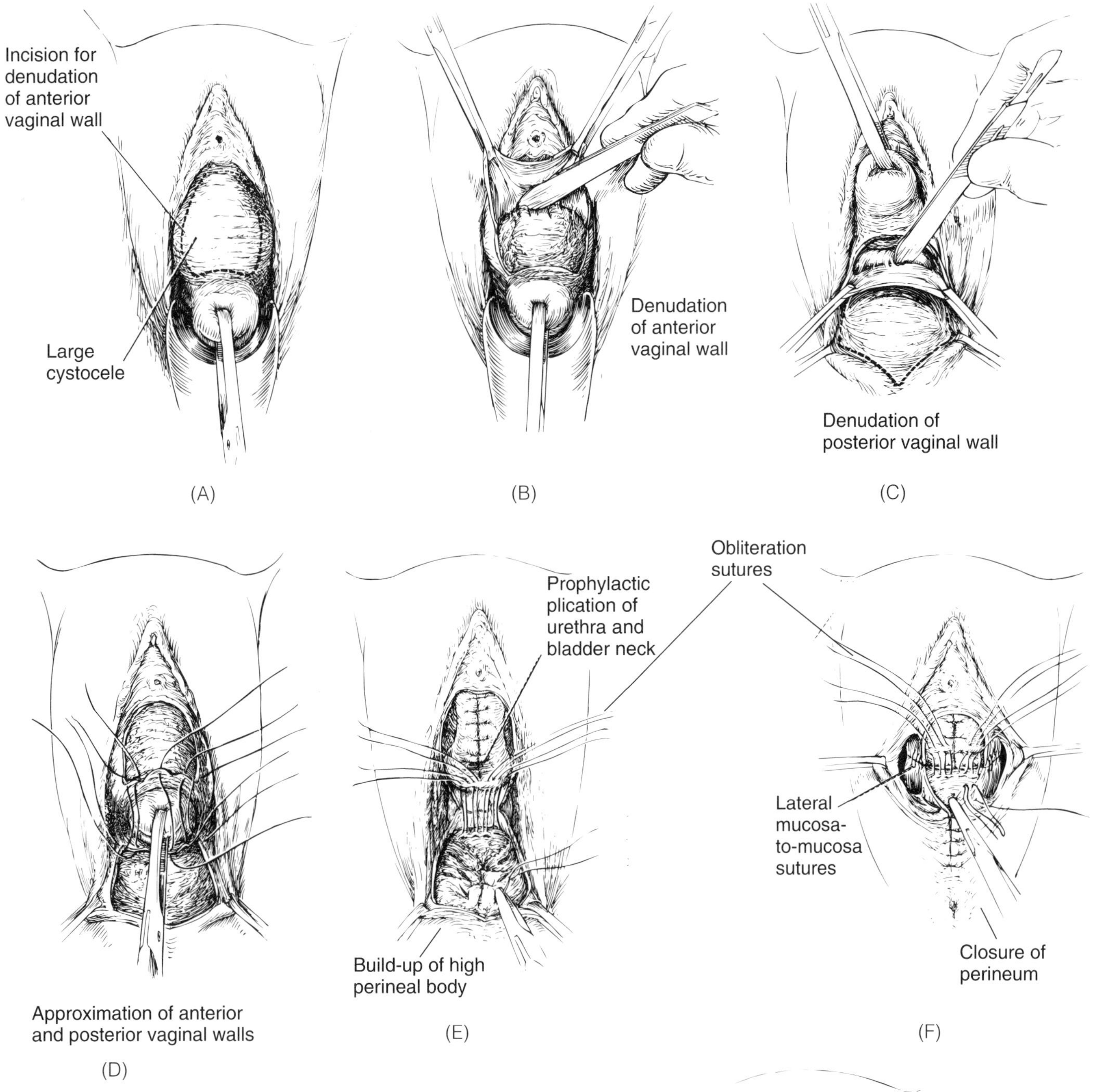

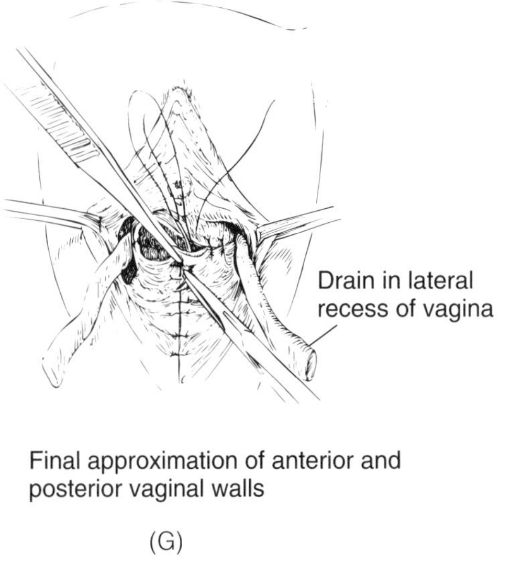

each side are approximated. (E) The denuded vaginal wall is approximated anteroposteriorly by a series of mattress sutures in conjunction with the mucosal closure. When the area of the bladder neck is reached, this is plicated not only in the event of stress incontinence, but also for prophylactic purposes. (F) The musculature of the perineal body is built up with interrupted sutures to aid in the obliteration of the genital aperture. Successive rows of mattress sutures continue the obliteration of the vaginal canal. The skin of the perineum is approximated in the midline by interrupted sutures. (G) The remainder of the anteroposterior approximation is done, and drains are placed in both of the lateral tunnels of the vagina that result. (Reprinted with permission from Ball TL. Gynecologic surgery and urology. St Louis: Mosby Year Book, 1963; Daisy Stillwell, medical illustrator)

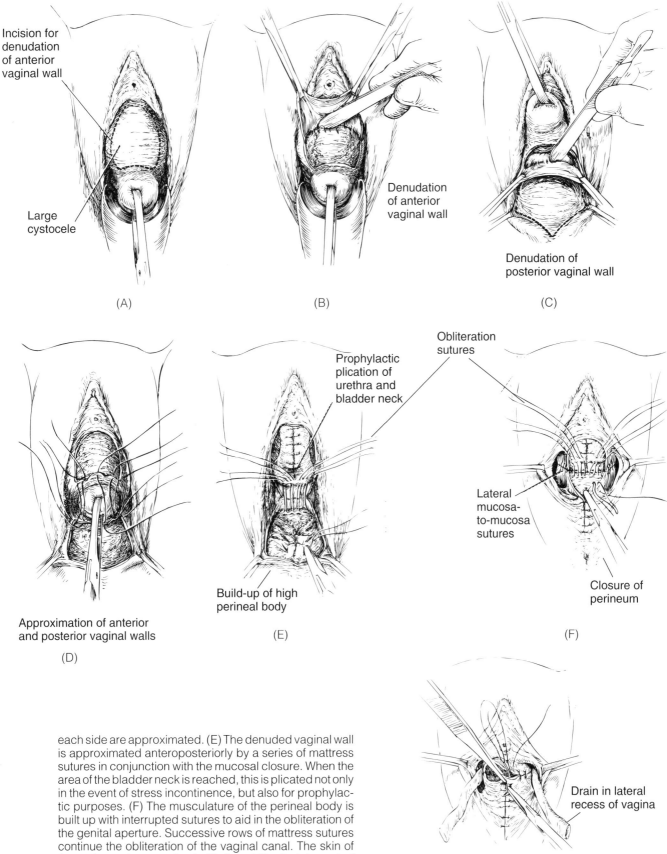

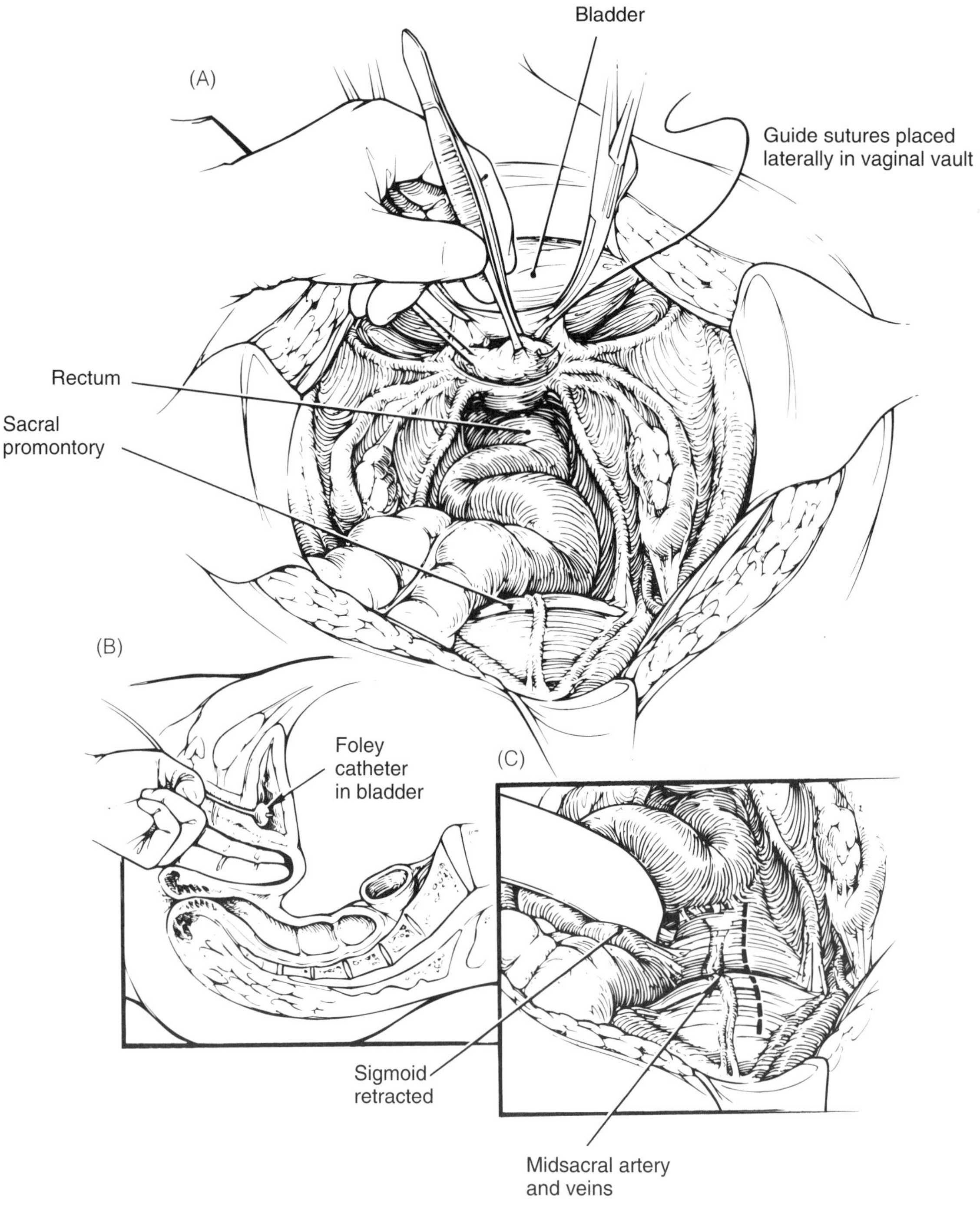

FIG. 48-3. Abdominal sacrocolpopexy. (A) The abdomen has been opened by a midline incision. The vaginal vault is manually elevated, as shown in (B), and the peritoneum covering it is incised transversely. Bowel is packed out of the way, and the promontory of the sacrum is exposed. The peritoneum overlying the promontory is incised as shown by the broken line (C). The tissues are carefully separated (D), exposing the presacral fascia (E). The fascia lata is sewn to the vaginal vault (F). (Nichols DH. Gynecologic and obstetric surgery. St Louis: CV Mosby, 1993:458–459)

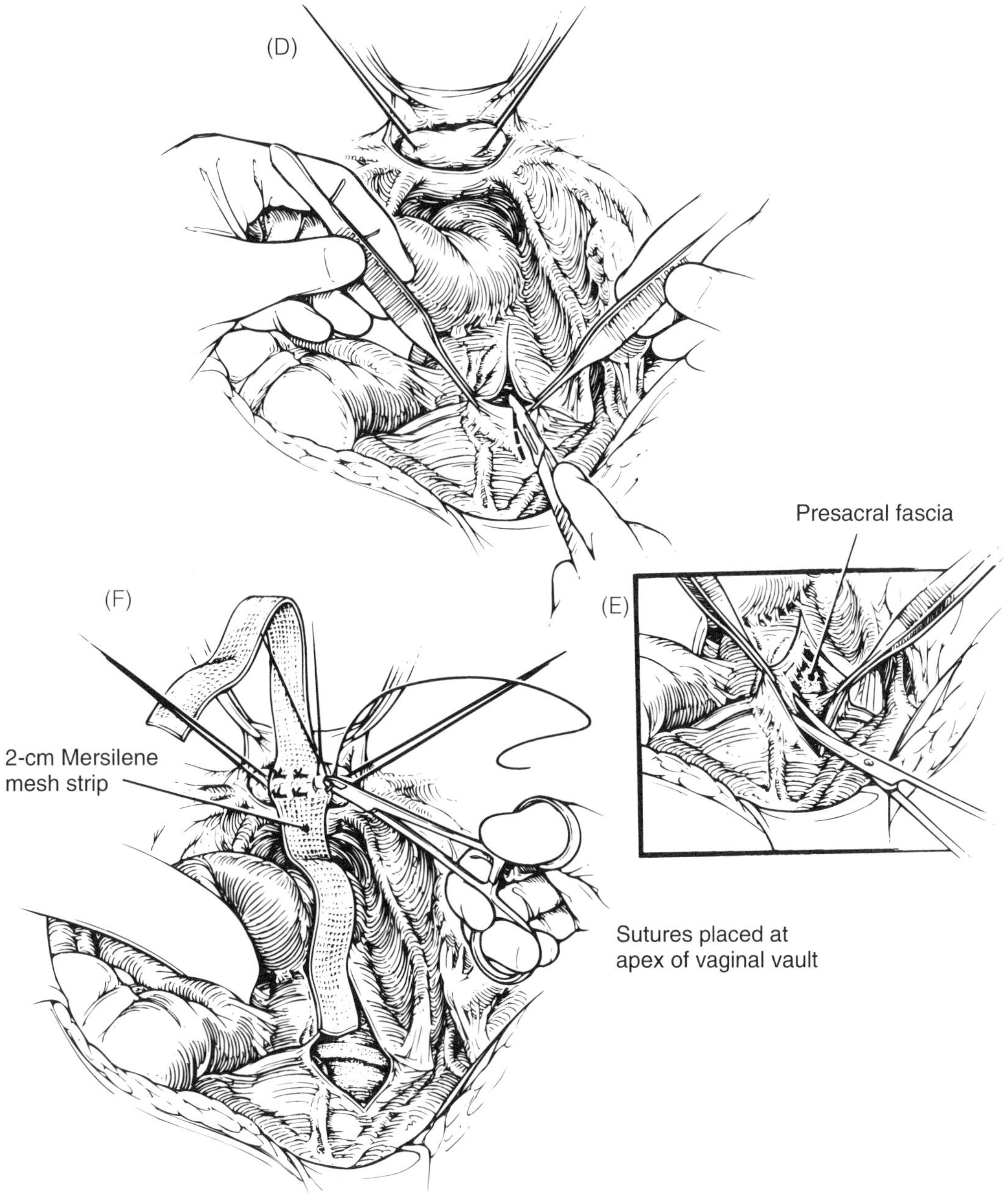
(D)
Presacral fascia
(F)
(E)
2-cm Mersilene
mesh strip
Sutures placed at
apex of vaginal vault

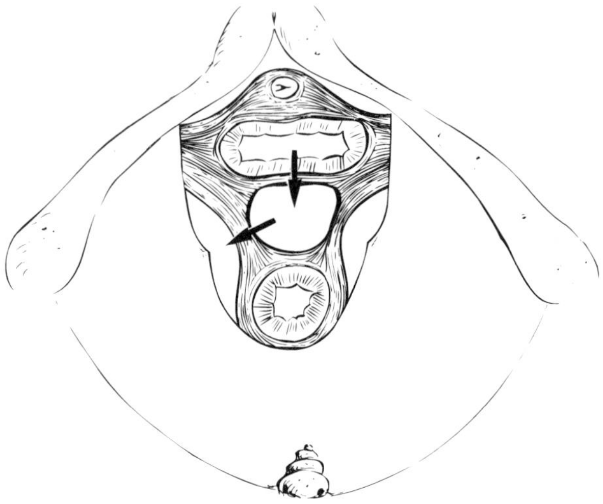

(A)

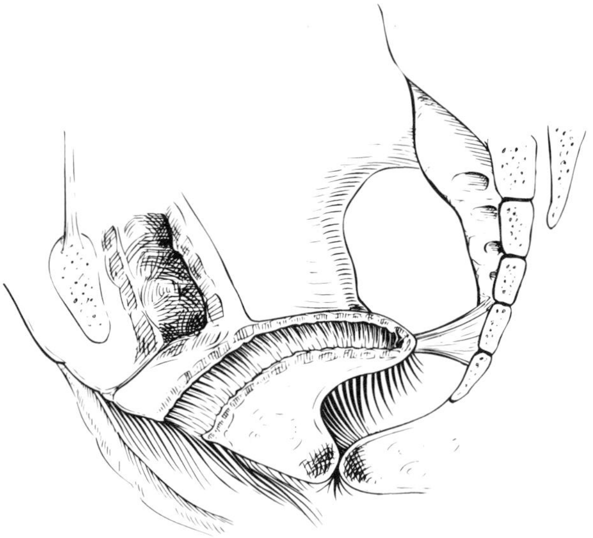

(B)

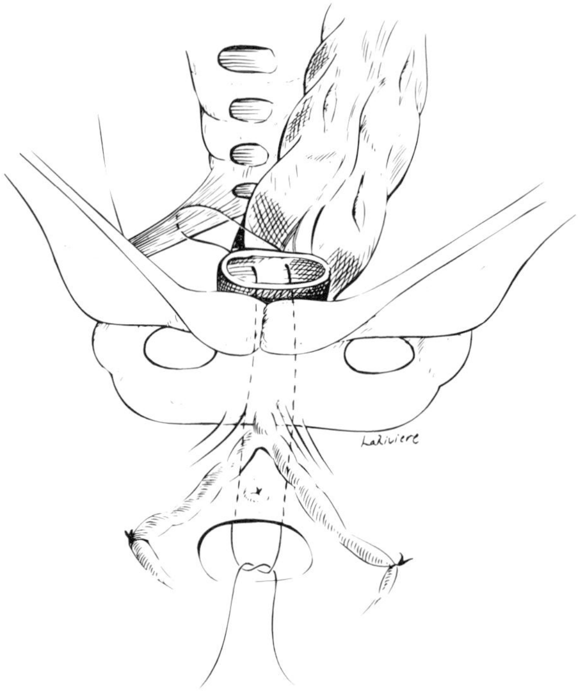

(C)

FIG. 48-4. Sacrospinous ligament fixation. (A) A path of dissection through the posterior vaginal wall into the rectovaginal space and then through a window in the descending rectal septum into the right pararectal space. The dissection always proceeds toward the ischial spine in the lateral wall of the pararectal space. The vagina is sewn to the right sacrospinous ligament–coccygeal muscle complex at a point one and one-half fingerbreadths medial to the right ischial spine (B). After the fixation stitches have been tied, the vagina is attached to the right sacrospinous ligament (C), indicating after appropriate colporrhaphy, a fairly normal vaginal depth and axis. (Nichols DH. Gynecologic and obstetric surgery. St Louis: CV Mosby, 1993:446–447)

49

Diagnosis of fibrocystic change

A 38-year-old woman seeks advice about her progressive unilateral breast pain, which is premenstrual, bilateral, and diffuse. The single most useful procedure in reassuring this patient is

* (A) clinical breast examination
(B) fine-needle aspiration
(C) breast ultrasonography
(D) thermography
(E) open surgical biopsy

Premenstrual progressive cyclic mastalgia is associated with fibrocystic changes of the breast, a condition that is not considered a disease but rather is associated with nonspecific histologic changes in normal breast tissue. Fibrocystic changes are focally present in the breasts of 90% of women. A clinical impression of fibrocystic changes of the breast without a dominant mass is not an indication for biopsy.

Clinical breast examination is the single most useful procedure for obtaining a clinical impression consistent with the histopathologic description of fibrocystic changes. Mammography can give an impression suggestive of histopathologic fibrocystic changes, which can be confirmed by breast examination. An adequate cellular sample obtained by fine-needle aspiration can show cytologic findings suggestive of histopathologic fibrocystic changes, but it is not diagnostic. Breast ultrasonography can identify breast cysts and present a sonographic picture suggestive of the histopathologic description of fibrocystic changes, but it is not specific enough to be diagnostic.

Thermography demonstrates differences in temperature of the breast tissue, which correlate with increased vascularity. These changes are nonspecific and not diagnostic. Multiple studies with thermography reported numerous false-positive and false-negative diagnoses, especially when compared with histopathologic diagnoses of malignancy by open surgical biopsy.

Only surgery provides tissue for the definitive histopathologic description of fibrocystic changes. However, in the absence of a dominant mass or other suspicion of malignancy, a biopsy to establish this diagnosis is not indicated.

Cyclic breast pain is common in menstruating women, particularly during the early reproductive years. The underlying fear of breast cancer motivates many women with cyclic breast pain to seek medical evaluation. After thorough evaluation, as many as 80% of women who present with the primary symptom of cyclic breast pain (mastalgia without an associated mass) require no further treatment other than appropriate reassurance that there is no evidence of cancer.

Ayers JWT, Gidwani GP. The "luteal breast": hormonal and sonographic investigation of benign breast disease in patients with cyclic mastalgia. Fertil Steril 1983;40:779–784

Dowle CS. Breast pain: classification, aetiology and management. Aust N Z J Surg 1987;57:423–428

Goodwin PJ, Neelam M, Boyd NF. Cyclical mastopathy: a critical review of therapy. Br J Surg 1988;75:837–844

Hughes LE, Mansel RE, Webster DJT. Benign disorders and diseases of the breast. London: Baillière Tindall, 1989:75–92

Is "fibrocystic disease" of the breast precancerous? Arch Pathol Lab Med 1986;110:171–173

Page DL, Simpson JF. Benign, high-risk, and premalignant lesions of the mamma. In: Bland KI, Copeland EM III, eds. The breast: comprehensive management of benign and malignant diseases. Philadelphia: WB Saunders, 1991:113–134

50

Combination chemotherapy for epithelial ovarian cancer

A 58-year-old woman is diagnosed with stage IIIC serous cystadenocarcinoma of the ovary after total abdominal hysterectomy, bilateral salpingo-oophorectomy, and surgical staging. She is morbidly obese and has well-controlled hypertension and moderate renal insufficiency secondary to diabetic nephropathy. The optimal chemotherapy for this patient is

* (A) paclitaxel (Taxol) and a platinum compound
(B) cyclophosphamide (Cytoxan) and a platinum compound
(C) melphalan (Alkeran)
(D) altretamine (Hexalen)
(E) doxorubicin hydrochloride–cyclophosphamide

The decision regarding chemotherapy for a patient with ovarian cancer is based on the anticipated response to a particular regimen, the stage of disease, the histologic type of cancer, and consideration of toxicities that would be exacerbated by comorbid illnesses.

Currently, combination chemotherapy with paclitaxel and either cisplatin or carboplatin is the treatment of choice for epithelial ovarian cancer after surgical debulking. Published data have shown that the combination of paclitaxel and cisplatin is superior to cisplatin and cyclophosphamide. The major toxicities of cisplatin are nephrotoxicity and neurotoxicity. In this patient with diabetes and renal insufficiency, carboplatin in addition to paclitaxel may be preferable to avoid exacerbation of her existing renal insufficiency. Although the regimen of paclitaxel and carboplatin has not completed phase III trials, it is known that cisplatin and carboplatin have comparable efficacy. Carboplatin is associated with myelosuppression.

Melphalan, an alkylating agent, was previously used in the treatment of patients with advanced-stage ovarian cancer. The response rate was 35–65%, and the median survival was 8–19 months. With the introduction of platinum-based regimens, melphalan is rarely used for the treatment of advanced-stage disease. Melphalan has also been used to treat patients with stage I ovarian cancer. However, the risk of leukemia after long-term alkylating therapy has resulted in the use of other chemotherapeutic agents.

Altretamine, a synthetic compound, is occasionally used as second-line therapy after treatment with platinum-based combination chemotherapy. It is not used as first-line therapy in the treatment of epithelial ovarian cancer.

Doxorubicin hydrochloride–cyclophosphamide is not as effective as platinum-based combination therapy and is not used as first-line treatment for epithelial ovarian cancer.

Fanning J, Bennett TZ, Hilgers RD. Meta-analysis of cisplatin, doxorubicin, and cyclophosphamide versus cisplatin and cyclophosphamide chemotherapy of ovarian carcinoma. Obstet Gynecol 1992;80:954–960

McGuire WP, Hoskins WJ, Brady MF, Kucera PR, Partridge EE, Look KY, et al. Cyclophosphamide and cisplatin compared with paclitaxel and cisplatin in patients with stage III and stage IV ovarian cancer. N Engl J Med, 1996;334:1–6

Moore DH, Fowler WC Jr, Jones CP, Crumpler LS. Hexamethylmelamine chemotherapy for persistent or recurrent epithelial ovarian cancer. Am J Obstet Gynecol 1991;165:573–576

Rubin SC, Wong GYC, Curtin JP, Barakat RR, Hakes TB, Hoskins WJ. Platinum-based chemotherapy of high-risk stage I epithelial ovarian cancer following comprehensive surgical staging. Obstet Gynecol 1993;82:143–147

Thigpen JT, Vance, RB, Khansur T. Second-line chemotherapy for recurrent carcinoma of the ovary. Cancer 1993;71(4 suppl):1559–1564

51

Repair of rectovaginal fistula

A patient with documented Crohn disease is seen because of a history of foul-smelling discharge and passage of flatus per vagina. She has not required medical therapy for 1 year. Examination shows a 2.5-cm fistula between the lower vagina and rectum. The therapy most likely to correct the fistula and lead to normal bowel function is

(A) simple fistulectomy with metronidazole coverage
(B) fecal diversion and healing of the perineum by granulation
(C) systemic corticosteroid therapy and transanal repair with an anterior rectal advancement flap
* (D) fistula repair and bulbocavernosus fat flap (Martius graft)

Surgical and obstetric injuries are the most frequent causes of rectovaginal fistulae. The obstetric trauma is often a third- or fourth-degree perineal laceration or unrecognized rectal injury at the time of forceps or precipitate vaginal delivery. Necrosis of the vaginal septum from prolonged compression by the presenting fetal part is still a predisposing factor in the Third World. Surgical procedures that involve the posterior vaginal wall, anus, and rectum as well as difficult hysterectomy also predispose a patient to fistula formation.

The incidence of rectovaginal fistula formation in Crohn disease is reported to be 0.91% to 18%. Hallmarks of underlying Crohn disease include perianal disorders such as fistulae, abscesses, fissures, and edematous cyanotic anal skin tags. In particular, colonic involvement in Crohn disease, as opposed to regional ileitis, appears to predispose a patient to rectovaginal fistulae.

In the management of a rectovaginal fistula, distinction is drawn between a situation in which the tissues are essentially healthy, such as after obstetric trauma, and one in which the tissues are unhealthy, such as after irradiation or in cases of Crohn disease. In patients with Crohn disease, the poor healing qualities of the rectum are compounded by the effect of systemic corticosteroid therapy as well as the tendency to diarrhea. Local vaginal repair of rectovaginal fistulae in these patients has been associated historically with unacceptable recurrence rates that have led some to either advocate abdominoperineal resection or fecal diversion and healing of the perineum by granulation.

In the last decade, however surgical procedures that preserve rectal function have evolved. Medical therapy may control symptoms of the disease at the time of surgical repair. Immunosuppressive therapy reduces the need for corticosteroid therapy. Hyperalimentation, low-residue diets, sulfasalazine, 5-acetylsalicylic acid enemas, and metronidazole therapy contribute to the success of the repair.

The fistula repair is performed when tissues are as healthy as feasible, preferably without evidence of infection or induration. Preoperative bowel cleansing is a prerequisite. The critical surgical principles for fistula repair are as follows:

1. Wide mobilization of the tissues around the vaginal and rectal orifices of the fistula
2. Excision of the entire fistulous tract
3. Meticulous closure of the rectal orifice of the fistula
4. Reapproximation of broad tissue surface to broad tissue surface without tension

The choices of fistula repair are:

- Use of the Martius graft
- Transverse transperitoneal repair
- Development and advancement of a rectal flap
- Development and advancement of a vaginal flap
- Interposition of the levator muscle and fascia of Colles between the vaginal and rectal tissues

The Martius graft may be used in conjunction with the other procedures listed and provides additional benefits. It obliterates the dead space in the dissected area and also brings a new blood supply to the devascularized area. It is, therefore, the optimal treatment for this patient. The rich blood supply of the labial area is shown in Fig. 51-1, and the steps in the mobilization and

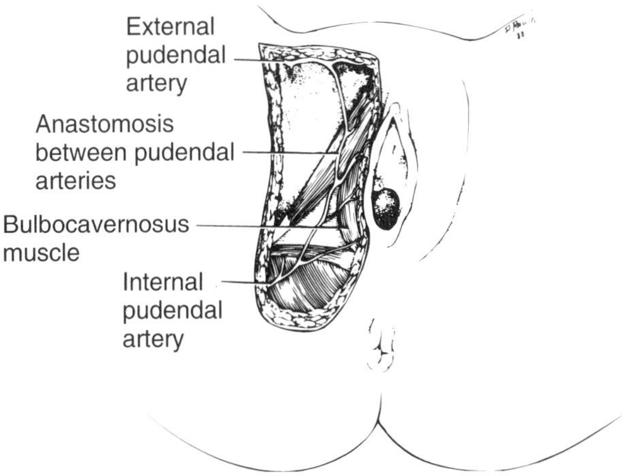

FIG. 51-1. Blood supply to the labial area. (Given FT Jr, Acosta AA. The Martius procedure—bulbocavernosus fat flap: a review. Obstet Gynecol Surv 1990;45:34)

transposition of the graft are shown in Fig. 51-2. Besides the use of the simple bulbocavernosus flap, skin may be included with the graft in the form of a myocutaneous labial flap or as an island skin patch.

Bauer JJ, Sher ME, Jaffin H, Present D, Gelerent I. Transvaginal approach for repair of rectovaginal fistulae complicating Crohn's disease. Ann Surg 1991;213:151–158

Given FT Jr, Acosta AA. The Martius procedure—bulbocavernosus fat flap: a review. Obstet Gynecol Surv 1990;45:34–40

Scott NA, Nair A, Hughes LE. Anovaginal and rectovaginal fistula in patients with Crohn's disease. Br J Surg 1992;79:1379–1380

Tancer ML, Lasser D, Rosenblum N. Rectovaginal fistula or perineal and anal sphincter disruption, or both, after vaginal delivery. Surg Gynecol Obstet 1990;171:43–46

Wiskind AK, Thompson JD. Transverse transperineal repair of rectovaginal fistulas in the lower vagina. Am J Obstet Gynecol 1992;167:694–699

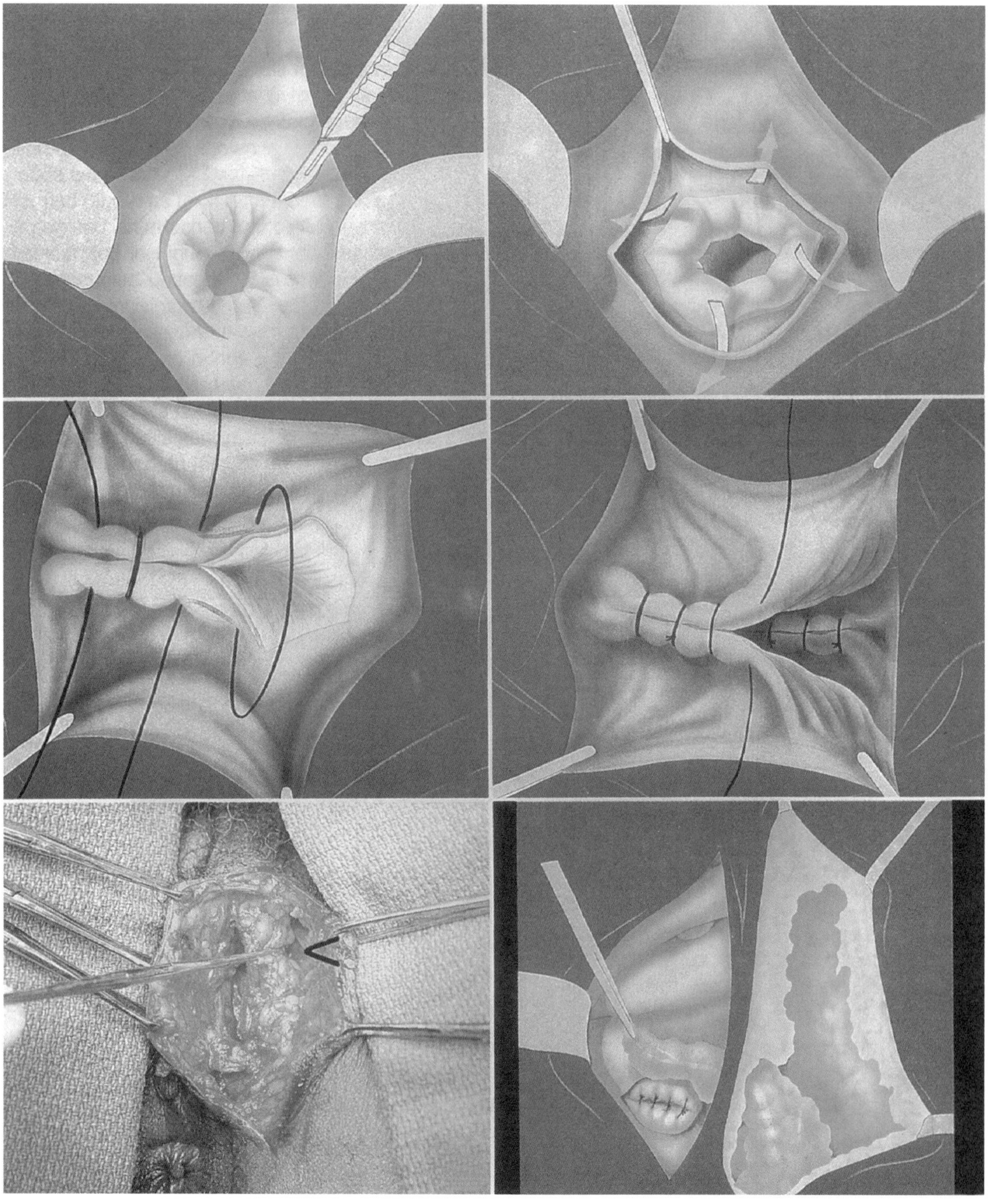

(A) (B) (C) (D) (E) (F)

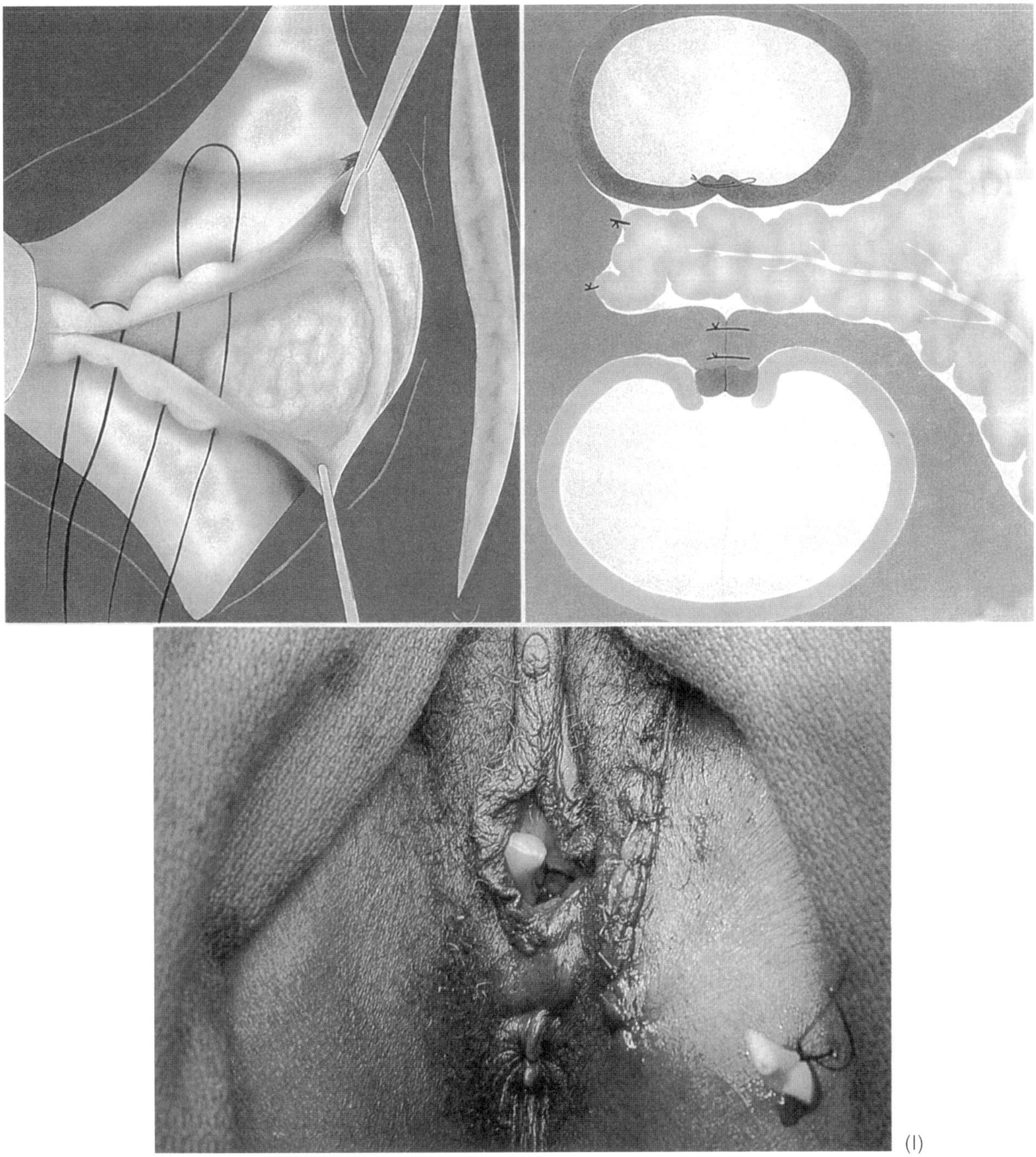

(G) (H)

(I)

FIG. 51-2. Steps in the bulbocavernosus flap procedure. (A) Initial incision around fistula. (B) Wide mobilization of tissues. (C) First-layer closure using inverting stitches. (D) Second-layer closure using inverting suture. (E) Dissection of bulbocavernosus fat flap. (F) Bulbocavernosus fat flap tunneled in the site of the repair. (G) Closure of the vaginal mucosa. (H) Diagrammatic cross-section of the repair. (I) Labial closure. (Given FT Jr, Acosta AA. The Martius procedure—bulbocavernosus fat flap: a review. Obstet Gynecol Surv 1990;45:35–36)

52

Surgical creation of a neovagina

A 48-year-old woman with invasive cervical cancer received radiation therapy as initial treatment. She presents with recurrence involving the bladder and bowel 1 year later. A total supralevator exenteration with removal of the bladder, uterus, cervix, rectum, and all of the vagina is planned with a colostomy and ileal pouch. She requests that a neovagina be created at the time of surgery. The surgical technique for creating a neovagina that is the most feasible technically for this patient and is likely to have the fewest complications is

(A) split-thickness skin graft
(B) gracilis myocutaneous graft
(C) vulvobulbocavernosus cutaneous graft
* (D) rectus abdominis myocutaneous graft

Formation of a neovagina after exenterative surgery may be an essential step in helping a patient restore a normal self-image. Several techniques have been described to form a neovagina after vaginectomy.

The split-thickness skin graft (Fig. 52-1) has been used for many years for neovaginoplasty for women with congenital absence of the vagina. It has also been offered to women after vaginectomy, simple or radical, and to women with vaginal stenosis after radiation therapy. The split-thickness skin graft is the simplest operation of those listed and is the easiest to perform. There is a tendency for the neovagina to shrink in the postoperative period, and it may be necessary for the patient to wear a mold for a protracted period of time. Patients with prior radiation therapy may be more prone to stricture formation, and the attachment of the skin graft may be less complete.

An essential requirement for a split-thickness skin graft is a well-vascularized recipient site. The rectum may serve as the recipient site in patients undergoing anterior exenteration, and the omentum can be brought down as a recipient site for the lateral and anterior vaginal surfaces. After total exenteration there usually is not a suitable, well-vascularized recipient site for the split-thickness skin graft; therefore, it should not be used in this patient. A technique that uses a modification of the omental J flap as the recipient site has been described. Normally, the omental J flap is used to close off the pelvic inlet after total pelvic exenteration, but it may be modified into a cylinder suitable for a split-thickness skin graft neovaginoplasty. This option requires a sufficient amount of well-mobilized omentum.

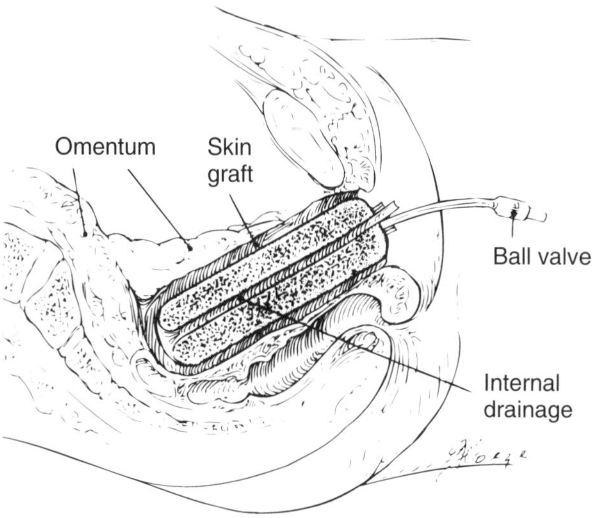

FIG. 52-1. Split-thickness skin graft. The omentum is used to create a "pocket" for the placement of the graft. (Berek JS, Hacker NF, Lagasse LD. Vaginal reconstruction performed simultaneously with pelvic exenteration. Reprinted with permission from The American College of Obstetricians and Gynecologists [Obstetrics and Gynecology 1984, 63, 318])

The myocutaneous grafts have often been used for neovaginal construction after pelvic exenteration. The bilateral gracilis myocutaneous graft (Fig. 52-2) is a good option for neovaginoplasty after total pelvic exenteration when the perineal body and anus are removed. It sufficiently fills the pelvic space and offers a new blood supply, which decreases postoperative morbidity associated with exenteration itself. The neovagina includes subcutaneous fat and muscle, which offer additional reenforcement and pliability to the graft. The gracilis muscle, the most superficial adductor muscle, has a stable neurovascular blood supply and overlying skin.

Gracilis flaps are usually successful, but occasionally there may be loss of skin necessitating a split-thickness skin graft. The principal disadvantage of the gracilis myocutaneous graft is a 10–20% incidence of flap loss because of vascular compromise. There is a greater potential for prolapse of the neovagina. This procedure also has a higher incidence of partial pedicle loss and requires bilateral flaps to provide a complete vaginal pouch. The sensitivity of the transposed skin is different from that of a normal vagina. Pressure sensitivity is excellent, but tactile sensitivity is diminished.

The gracilis myocutaneous flap does not yield a satisfactory result in patients undergoing anterior exenteration or total exenteration when the perineal body and anus are preserved. The graft is too large to position in the vagina without compromising the vascular pedicle.

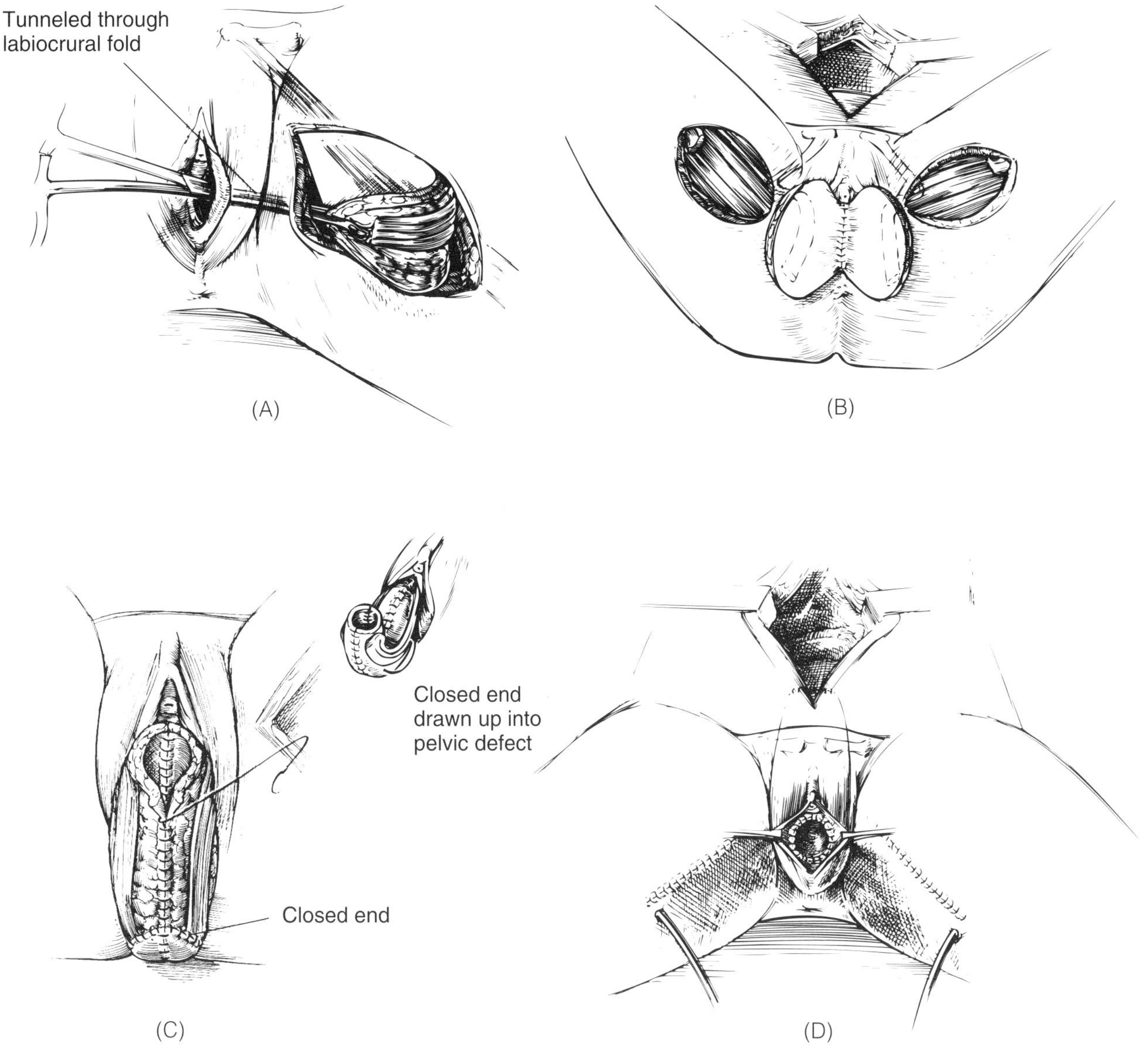

FIG. 52-2. Gracilis myocutaneous graft. (A) The distal end of the graft is grasped with a Babcock instrument and guided through the subcutaneous labiocrural tunnel. The procedure is performed on both legs, producing bilateral grafts, which are then opposed and the skin edges sutured, except the proximal (upper) portions of the grafts as they lie in front of the perineum. (B) The two grafts are sutured into a tubal structure. (C) The inferior (closed) end is drawn up into the pelvic defect. (D) The graft is anchored laterally to the pelvic fascia and the retropubic fascia. The open end of the tube is circumferentially sutured to the skin surrounding the introitus. The thigh wounds are closed in layers over subfascial suction drains. (Gershenson DM, DeCherney AH, Curry SL. Operative gynecology. Philadelphia: WB Saunders, 1993:617)

The vulvobulbocavernosus cutaneous graft or the rectus abdominis graft is preferable in this circumstance.

The vulvobulbocavernosus cutaneous graft includes the skin, fat, and underlying bulbocavernosus muscle and tissue. The pudendal artery provides the vascular supply. The graft is not large enough to form an entire vagina in most patients. An additional disadvantage is that the inclusion of vulvar hair may result in vaginal discharge of desquamated keratinized cells and sebaceous material, which has led some patients to request vaginectomy and split-thickness skin graft within a year of the initial procedure. Tactile sensation may be more physiologic than that with the other procedures, because the neovaginal tissue is enervated by the pudendal nerve.

The rectus abdominis myocutaneous flap (Fig. 52-3) has as its vascular supply the deep inferior epigastric vessels and periumbilical perforating vessels. The rectus muscle is freed from its attachment to the pubic symphysis and is mobilized so that the overlying skin

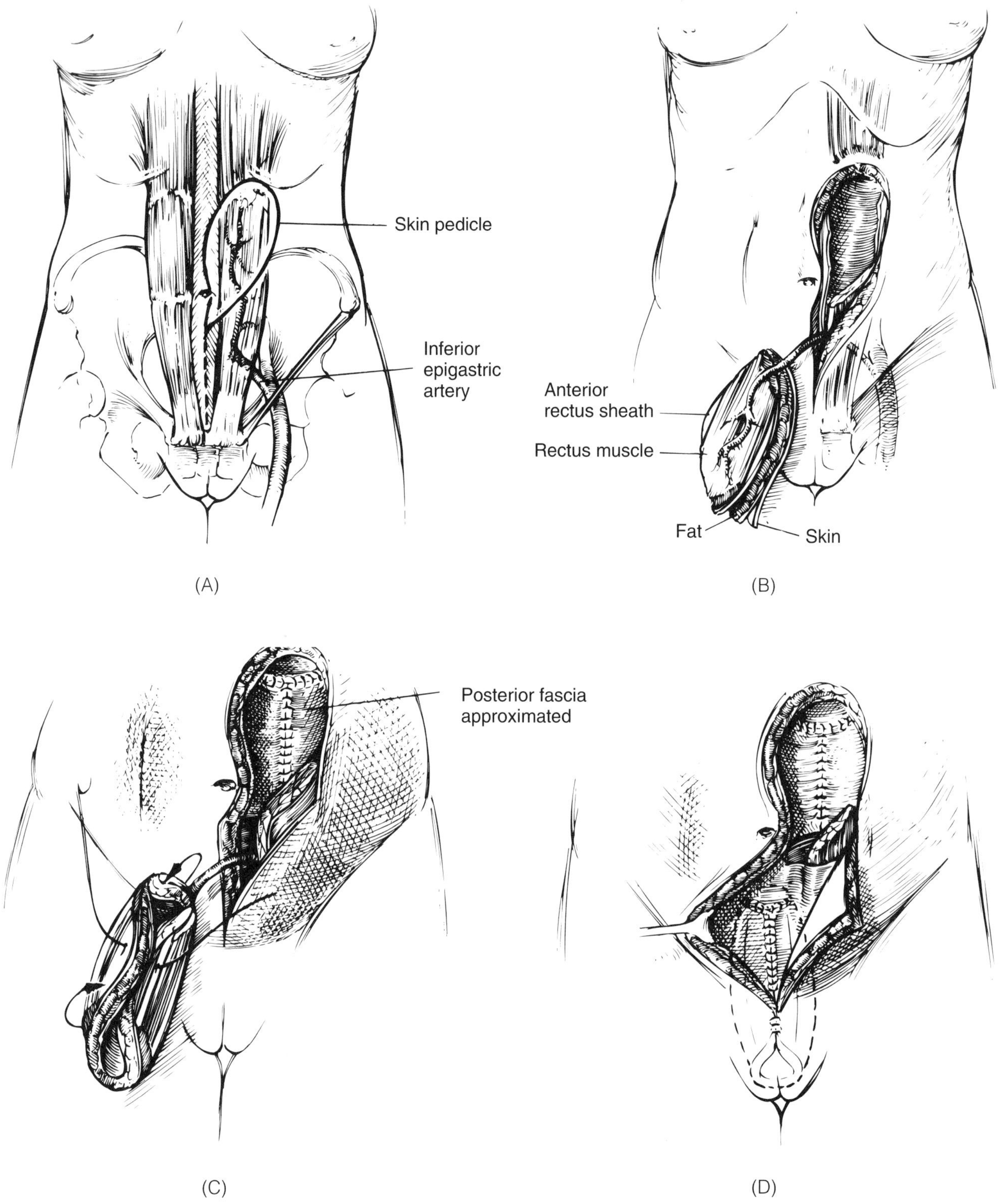

FIG. 52-3. Rectus abdominis myocutaneous graft. (A) The rectus abdominis is based on an inferior pedicle with the vascular supply from the inferior epigastric vessels off the external iliacs. (B) The pedicle is usually 10–14 cm in horizontal width and 14–20 cm in vertical length, and the upper border is adjacent to the inferior costal margin. The rectus abdominis muscle is transected superiorly and dissected free from its fascial bed (although the anterior rectus fascia adjacent to the pedicle is mobilized with the pedicle). (C) The vaginal tube is developed by inverting the lateral and inner margins. (D) The neovagina is sutured into place, and the abdomen is closed. (Gershenson DM, DeCherney AH, Curry SL. Operative gynecology. Philadelphia: WB Saunders, 1993:619)

may be attached to the vaginal introitus. Like the myocutaneous graft, it fills the pelvic space, provides suppleness to the neovagina, and helps reduce postoperative morbidity. It usually provides approximately 10 × 20 cm of skin, which is adequate for creating a neovagina. The overall results with the rectus abdominis myocutaneous flap have been excellent, and it appears to have the lowest incidence of vascular compromise. This procedure is the preferred surgical technique for the patient described.

Benson C, Soisson AP, Carlson J, Culbertson G, Hawley-Bowland C, Richards F. Neovaginal reconstruction with a rectus abdominis myocutaneous flap. Obstet Gynecol 1993;81:871–875

Cain JM, Diamond A, Tamimi HK, Greer BE, Figge DC. The morbidity and benefits of concurrent gracilis myocutaneous graft with pelvic exenteration. Obstet Gynecol 1989;74:185–189

Carlson JW, Soisson AP, Fowler JM, Carter JR, Twiggs LB, Carson LF. Rectus abdominis myocutaneous flap for primary vaginal reconstruction. Gynecol Oncol 1993;51:323–329

Hatch KD. Neovaginal reconstruction. Cancer 1993;71:1660–1663

Tobin GR, Pursell SH, Day TG Jr. Refinements in vaginal reconstruction using rectus abdominis flaps. Clin Plast Surg 1990;17:705–712

Wheeless CR Jr. Neovagina constructed from an omental J flap and a split thickness skin graft. Gynecol Oncol 1989;35:224–226

53

Universal precautions in the operating room

When initially instructing first-year medical students regarding universal precautions, you teach them that universal precautions include

(A) double gloving in the operating room
(B) double gowning in the operating room
(C) careful recapping of all used needles
* (D) hand-washing after glove removal

The increasing prevalence of human immunodeficiency virus (HIV) increases the risk that health care workers will be exposed to blood or other body fluids from infected patients. Exposure to hepatitis B virus continues to be of concern. Health care workers should consider all patients as potentially infected with HIV and hepatitis B virus and adhere rigorously to infection control precautions recommended by the Occupational Safety and Health Administration and the Centers for Disease Control and Prevention. These new regulations require that universal precautions be implemented in all clinical settings in which the potential for exposure to blood and body fluids exists (Title 29 of the Code of Federal Regulations, Section 1910.1030).

Universal precautions require hand-washing after glove removal. Double gloving and double gowning are not specifically addressed by the Occupational Safety and Health Administration, although double gloving in the operating room has been shown to decrease the risk of exposure to body fluids. The recapping of used needles is specifically discouraged because of the risk of needlestick injury.

Universal precautions include the following:

- Routinely use appropriate barrier precautions to prevent skin and mucous membrane exposure when contact with blood or other body fluids of any patient is anticipated.

  Wear gloves when touching blood, body fluids, mucous membranes, nonintact skin, and items soiled with any body fluids. Change gloves after contact with each patient and wash hands immediately after gloves are removed.

  Wear a gown, mask, and protective eyewear when performing procedures that are likely to generate droplets of blood or other body fluids.
- Wash hands and other skin surfaces immediately and thoroughly with soap and water if contaminated with blood or other body fluids.
- To prevent needlestick injuries, do not recap, purposely bend or break needles by hand, remove them from disposable syringes, or otherwise manipulate them by hand.
- Dispose of syringes, needles, and scalpel blades in a puncture-resistant container.
- Have mouthpieces, resuscitation bags, or other devices available for use in areas in which the need for resuscitation is predictable.
- Health care workers who have skin breaks such as open sores or weeping dermatitis should refrain from all direct patient care.

Centers for Disease Control. Guidelines for prevention of transmission of human immunodeficiency virus and hepatitis B virus to health-care and public-safety workers. MMWR 1989;38(Suppl 6):1–37

Occupational Safety and Health Administration, Department of Labor. Occupational exposure to bloodborne pathogens; final rule. Part II. Federal Register. December 6, 1991;56:64004–64182

54

Mammogram findings of breast cancer

Your patient, a 50-year-old woman, has been told by the radiologist that the mammography performed today showed abnormal results. Her sister was diagnosed and treated for ductal carcinoma in situ (DCIS) at age 58. Which of the following mammographic findings would suggest that your patient also has DCIS?

(A) Irregular mass with spiculated margins
(B) Circumscribed mass with indistinct margins
(C) Architectural distortion
* (D) Grouped fine linear calcifications
(E) Skin thickening

Clustered (grouped), irregular, dense, fine, linear, or branching calcifications are mammographically typical of DCIS (Fig. 54-1). In contrast, a distinct mass is usually seen with invasive ductal carcinoma (Fig. 54-2).

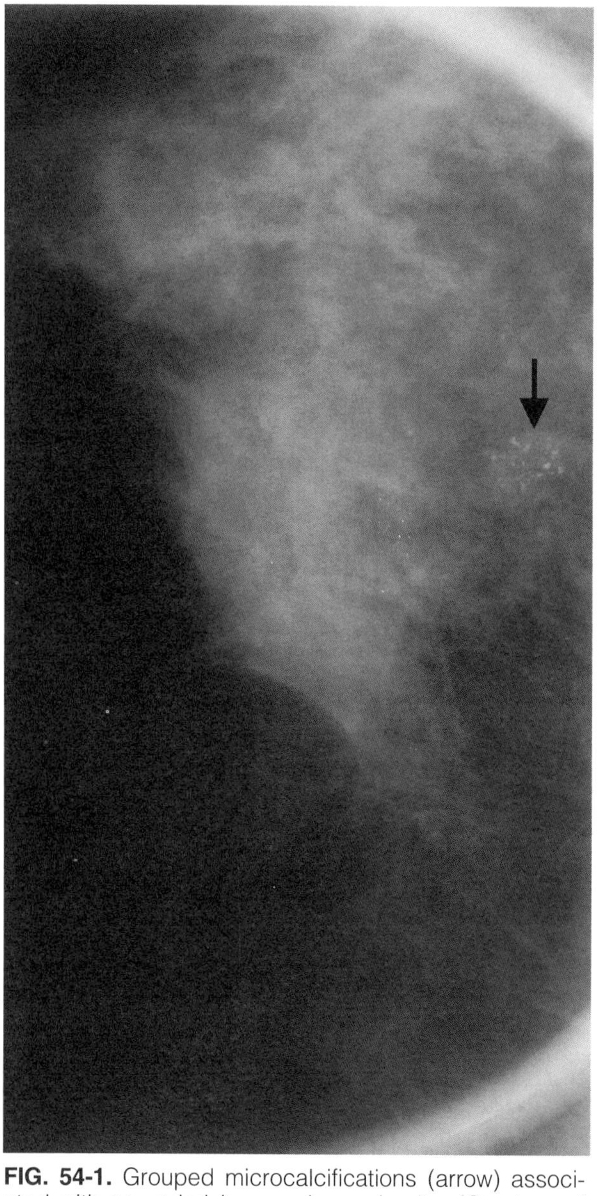

FIG. 54-1. Grouped microcalcifications (arrow) associated with an underlying carcinoma in situ. (Courtesy of Richard W. Cross, MD)

Typically, an invasive ductal carcinoma mass has an irregular shape with spiculated margins. Less commonly, such a mass is circumscribed with indistinct margins. Architectural distortion without a mass can also be a sign of invasive ductal carcinoma. Skin thickening on mammography is a finding that is associated with a malignant mass or inflammatory breast cancer.

When no palpable mass is noted on physical examination, needle localization biopsy (with specimen radio-

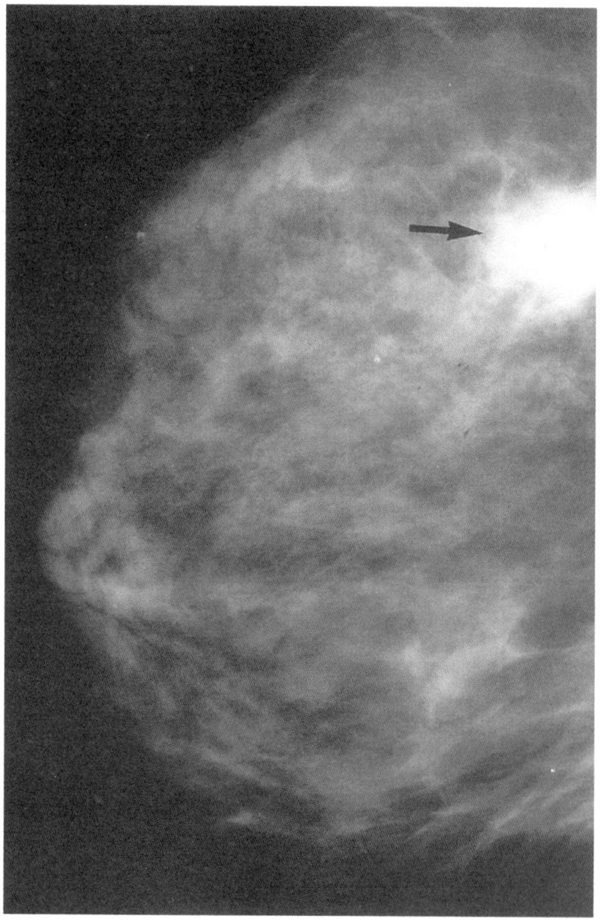

FIG. 54-2. Mammogram demonstrating an irregular stellate lesion (arrow) characteristic of malignancy.

graph confirmation that the lesion seen on the mammogram is in the excised breast tissue) is required for definitive histopathologic diagnosis.

American College of Radiology. BIRADS: Breast Imaging Reporting and Data System. Reston, Virginia: American College of Radiology, 1993

Andersson I. Mammography in clinical practice. Med Radiogr Photogr 1986;62(2):2–40

D'Orsi CJ, Kopans DB. Mammographic feature analysis. Semin Roentgenol 1993;28:204–230

Tabár L, Dean PB. Teaching atlas of mammography. 2nd ed, revised. New York: Thieme, 1985

55

Therapy for uterine leiomyosarcoma

A 52-year-old woman undergoes total abdominal hysterectomy and bilateral salpingo-oophorectomy for an enlarging myomatous uterus associated with irregular perimenopausal bleeding. Preoperative evaluation, including endometrial biopsy and chest X-ray, is negative. There appears to be a single large uterine tumor, with no obvious clinical evidence of disease elsewhere in the pelvis or abdomen at surgery.

Routine pathologic examination of the uterus reveals a 7-cm malignant smooth muscle tumor with 10 mitoses per 10 high-power fields (hpf), pushing margins, and areas of necrosis. The most appropriate postoperative management for this patient is

(A) reoperation with omentectomy, pelvic and paraaortic lymph node biopsies, and peritoneal cytology
(B) pelvic irradiation
(C) chemotherapy with doxorubicin hydrochloride
* (D) follow-up at 3-month intervals

Leiomyosarcoma comprises about 40% of uterine sarcomas, or about 1–2% of all uterine malignancies. The average age at diagnosis is 53 years, with premenopausal patients tending to have a better prognosis. The most common presenting symptoms in order of frequency are abnormal uterine bleeding, pelvic pain or pressure, and awareness of an abdominal–pelvic mass. The principal physical finding is the presence of a pelvic mass. The diagnosis should be considered if rapid uterine enlargement occurs in a perimenopausal or postmenopausal woman. Although diagnosis is made by endometrial curettage in 15–33% of patients with leiomyosarcoma, most of these patients are diagnosed incidentally at the time of surgery for presumed uterine leiomyomata. Fewer than 1% of women over age 40 undergoing surgery for uterine leiomyoma are found to have leiomyosarcoma. Obvious clinical extension beyond the uterus at the time of presentation is unusual.

Uterine smooth muscle tumors with more than 10 mitoses per 10 hpf or 5–10 mitoses per 10 hpf with moderate to severe cellular atypia are considered to be malignant, whereas tumors with fewer than 5 mitoses per 10 hpf usually behave in a benign fashion. In addition to low mitotic count, other pathologic features that are associated with a more favorable prognosis are pushing versus infiltrating tumor margins, hyalinization, absence of necrosis, origin within a leiomyoma, and size less than 5 cm. Tumor spread beyond the uterus at the time of diagnosis is the worst prognostic indicator, followed by high mitotic count. With leiomyosarcoma apparently confined to the uterus, recurrences develop in 50–75% of patients with 10 or more mitoses per 10 hpf and in one third of those with 5–9 mitoses per 10 hpf. Isolated pelvic recurrences are uncommon; 40% of treatment failures occur both in the pelvis and at distant sites, whereas distant metastases to the upper abdomen and lung account for about 50% of recurrences.

Uterine leiomyosarcoma is best treated by initial exploratory laparotomy, total abdominal hysterectomy, and bilateral salpingo-oophorectomy. Based on spread and recurrence patterns, lymph node sampling, partial omentectomy, and peritoneal cytology are also recommended if the diagnosis is known at the time of surgery, but their impact on planning treatment and survival is uncertain. Irradiation has no apparent value in the treatment of uterine leiomyosarcoma.

Because of the relatively high rate of recurrence in cases of presumed localized disease and the predominance of distant metastases, patients with uterine leiomyosarcoma would theoretically be excellent candidates for adjuvant chemotherapy. Unfortunately, most studies have been unable to demonstrate a clear improvement in survival when postoperative adjuvant chemotherapy was used in patients with early uterine sarcoma. Although the randomized adjuvant doxorubicin hydrochloride (Adriamycin) study by the Gynecologic Oncology Group did not show a statistically significant difference in survival for stage I and II patients, the patients receiving doxorubicin had fewer distant metastases. When there is extrauterine or metastatic uterine leiomyosarcoma, doxorubicin-based chemotherapy is indicated.

Most recently, a combination of doxorubicin hydrochloride, ifosfamide (IFEX) with the uroprotector mesna, and dacarbazine (DTIC-Dome) has been used. At present, in the absence of an appropriate investigational study, the recommended management for uterine leiomyosarcoma, stage I or II disease, is follow-up examinations and testing after surgery, with subsequent therapy if metastatic or recurrent tumor develops.

Berchuck A, Rubin SC, Hoskins WJ, Saigo PE, Pierce VK, Lewis JL Jr. Treatment of uterine leiomyosarcoma. Obstet Gynecol 1988;71:845–850

Evans HL, Chawla SP, Simpson C, Finn KP. Smooth muscle neoplasms of the uterus other than ordinary leiomyoma: a study of 46 cases, with emphasis on diagnostic criteria and prognostic factors. Cancer 1988;62:2239–2247

Leibsohn S, d'Ablaing G, Mishell DR Jr, Schlaerth JB. Leiomyosarcoma in a series of hysterectomies performed for presumed uterine leiomyomas. Am J Obstet Gynecol 1990;162:968–976

Omura GA, Blessing JA, Major F, Lifshitz S, Ehrlich CE, Mangan C, et al. A randomized clinical trial of adjuvant Adriamycin in uterine sarcomas: a Gynecologic Oncology Group study. J Clin Oncol 1985;3:1240–1245

56

Treatment of vaginal intraepithelial neoplasia

A 48-year-old sexually active woman is referred to you for evaluation and treatment of an abnormal vaginal vault Pap test. She had a hysterectomy several years ago for grade 3 cervical intraepithelial neoplasia. Colposcopic examination and biopsies reveal multifocal grade 3 vaginal intraepithelial neoplasia (VAIN) at the apex of the vaginal vault (Fig. 56-1; see color plates). Of the following options, the best treatment is

(A) estrogen cream and repeat colposcopy
(B) intravaginal radiotherapy
* (C) laser vaporization
(D) cryotherapy
(E) upper vaginectomy

Vaginal intraepithelial neoplasia is diagnosed much less frequently than intraepithelial lesions of the cervix and vulva, accounting for 0.4% of lower genital tract intraepithelial neoplasia. The process most commonly occurs in the upper third of the vagina and is frequently multifocal (Fig. 56-1). Vaginal intraepithelial neoplasia grade 3 is also considered to be carcinoma in situ, or stage 0 (Appendix, Table 4). If a patient has had a hysterectomy for cervical intraepithelial neoplasia, she is at higher risk for developing vaginal or vulvar intraepithelial neoplasia (field effect).

Colposcopic evaluation and biopsy of vaginal lesions determine the appropriate therapy. In a patient who has had a hysterectomy, colposcopic evaluation may be difficult, especially if the vault suspension has produced deep vaginal angles at the apex. Before colposcopic assessment of either a postmenopausal woman or a woman who has undergone previous pelvic radiotherapy, a 3-week course of estrogen therapy will thicken the vaginal epithelium and facilitate the examination. In this patient the colposcopy was adequate (Fig. 56-1); therefore, there is no need to use vaginal estrogen.

Radiotherapy has largely been abandoned in the treatment of VAIN because of the frequent problems of posttreatment vaginal stenosis, dyspareunia, and difficulty in follow-up of patients so treated. Cryotherapy is often technically difficult to deliver, because surgical scarring and changes prevent precise application of the cryoprobe to the distorted vaginal apex. Currently, laser ablation, topical 5-fluorouracil (5-FU), and local surgical excision are the most commonly used treatment modalities. Overall, these techniques are remarkably similar in efficacy.

The prerequisites for the ablative techniques include expert colposcopy with complete visualization of the lesion and the epithelium at risk, as well as the procurement of adequate biopsy specimens to rule out invasive disease. Laser vaporization to a depth of 2–3 mm will destroy the vaginal epithelium. Laser vaporization should not be performed unless the full extent of the abnormal vaginal epithelium can be visualized and there is no suspicion of an invasive lesion. If there is gross scarring or distortion of the vagina after hysterectomy, laser vaporization may not be technically feasible. However, laser vaporization is feasible in most patients, and results are good.

Topical 5-FU treatment has the theoretical advantage of permitting more comprehensive treatment of the entire vaginal mucosa. Published studies indicate that patients with extensive or multifocal lesions obtain better therapeutic effects from topical 5-FU than from laser vaporization. A major problem with topical 5-FU therapy is the intense acute chemical vulvovaginitis that occurs in many patients treated with continuous daily regimens. Topical 5-FU causes fewer acute ulcerations when it is used as a single weekly dose for 10 weeks. Chronic mucosal ulcerations following prolonged therapy with 5-FU have been described. Vaginal adenosis has been reported after combined therapy with 5-FU and laser vaporization. Systemic toxicity through vaginal absorption has not been noted.

Removal of the abnormal tissue by partial or total vaginectomy provides a specimen for complete histologic view. One of the complications of vaginectomy is vaginal shortening and stenosis. For this reason, the procedure is not often used to treat VAIN. Preventive measures include not closing the mucosa and using a dilator with estrogen vaginal cream in the early postoperative period. With large defects, a skin graft can be used to cover the excised area.

Benedet JL. Vaginal malignancy. Curr Opin Obstet Gynecol 1991;3:7377

Hoffman MS, DeCesare SL, Roberts WS, Fiorica JV, Finan MA, Cavanagh D. Upper vaginectomy for in situ and occult, superficially invasive carcinoma of the vagina. Am J Obstet Gynecol 1992;166:30–33

Hoffman MS, Roberts WS, LaPolla JP, Fiorica JV, Cavanagh D. Laser vaporization of grade 3 vaginal intraepithelial neoplasia. Am J Obstet Gynecol 1991;165:1342–1344

Krebs HB. Treatment of vaginal intraepithelial neoplasia with laser and topical 5-fluorouracil. Obstet Gynecol 1989;73:657–660

57

Basal cell carcinoma of the vulva

A 69-year-old woman has a 2-cm ulcerative lesion of the right anterior labium majus. A punch biopsy of the lesion reveals basal cell carcinoma. The best recommendation for therapy is

(A) simple vulvectomy
(B) radical vulvectomy
* (C) wide local excision
(D) wide local excision with ipsilateral lymphadenectomy
(E) topical therapy with 5-fluorouracil cream

Although basal cell carcinomas are the most common malignancy of the skin, basal cell carcinomas of the vulva are rare, accounting for about 2% of all vulvar cancers. They occur predominantly in postmenopausal Caucasian women. These lesions, which occur most frequently on the labia majora, usually present as "rodent ulcers" with central ulceration and peripheral rolled edges (Fig. 57-1A; see color plate). Red macules and hypertrophic polypoid lesions have also been described. The histologic appearance of basal cell carcinomas is characteristic, with peripheral palisading of tumor cells. The cells are typically small, with hyperchromatic nuclei (Fig. 57-1B; see color plate). Although giant basal cell carcinomas up to 10 cm have been reported, most lesions are less than 2 cm in diameter.

Common symptomatology is the presence of a mass and pruritus. These cancers rarely cause pain. Metastases to regional lymph nodes have been documented but are rare. The chance of developing basal cell carcinoma relates directly to the number of previous basal cell carcinomas. For example, a person who has had 10 basal cell carcinomas is at risk for developing one new tumor each year thereafter. Other conditions that may predispose to the development of basal cell carcinoma include other primary malignancies, especially lymphoreticular types; immunodeficiency states; and trauma.

The treatment of vulvar basal cell carcinoma consists of local excision with clear margins. If a surgical margin is found to be involved, the patient should undergo a wider excision. Like vulvar intraepithelial neoplasia and Paget disease, these lesions are prone to recur. Recurrences are treated by wide local excision. There is no indication for vulvectomy, either simple or radical. Lymphadenectomy is not indicated in a patient with no palpable inguinal lymph nodes. If lymph nodes are palpable, a biopsy rather than lymphadenectomy should be performed because of the infrequency of nodal metastases in basal cell carcinomas.

Treatment with topical chemotherapy is ineffective, and the lesion should not be treated with electrocautery or laser vaporization.

Friedrich EG Jr. Vulvar disease. Philadelphia: WB Saunders, 1983:98

Hacker NF, Eifel P, McGuire W, Wilkinson EJ. Vulva. In: Hoskins WJ, Perez CA, Young RC, eds. Principles and practice of gynecologic oncology. Philadelphia: JB Lippincott, 1992:537–566

Hoffman MS, Roberts WS, Ruffolo EH. Basal cell carcinoma of the vulva with inguinal lymph node metastases. Gynecol Oncol 1988;29:113–119

58

Receptors in corpus adenocarcinoma

A 64-year-old woman was diagnosed with moderately well-differentiated adenocarcinoma of the endometrium and underwent an abdominal hysterectomy and bilateral salpingo-oophorectomy. Presence of the estrogen receptor was documented by an immunohistochemical method.

Compared with the classical biochemical assay of steroid binding, the immunohistochemical method

* (A) can be performed on either frozen-section material or tissue fixed in formaldehyde solution and embedded in paraffin
(B) allows quantitation of the estrogen receptor, expressed as femtomoles per milligram of cytosol protein
(C) provides results that are in agreement with the biochemical assay in over 90% of cases
(D) requires special expertise and laboratory equipment

The presence of the estrogen receptor is correlated with several clinical prognostic factors in adenocarcinoma of the endometrium (Fig. 58-1; see color plate), including stage of disease, histologic grade, and 5-year survival. Presence of the estrogen receptor is considered a favorable prognostic indicator. The progesterone receptor is more prognostic, and its presence is associated with an even more favorable outcome.

The estrogen receptor has conventionally been detected with a biochemical assay of steroid binding. More recently, techniques have been developed that permit the detection of this receptor with immunohistochemical methods. Comparison of the two methods reveals some important differences.

Biochemical assays to detect the estrogen receptor cannot be performed on tissue fixed in formaldehyde solution. These assays must be performed on fresh tissue or tissue that has been stored at –70°C before analysis. Delay in freezing of the tissue or storage at warmer temperatures permits enzymatic degradation of the receptor and results in test values that are falsely lowered. Biochemical assays permit quantitation of the amount of receptor, expressed as femtomoles per milligram of cytosol protein. However, the results are influenced by the proportion of contaminating benign glandular and stromal cells that are present. When the proportion of benign estrogen receptor–negative cells is high, the amount of the estrogen receptor is falsely lowered. Myometrial cells express the estrogen receptor, and contamination of an adenocarcinoma with these cells would yield a falsely elevated value.

In contradistinction to biochemical assays of the estrogen receptor, immunohistochemical methods of detection can be performed on frozen-section material as well as tissue fixed in formaldehyde solution and embedded in paraffin. As is the case with all immunohistochemical methods of antigen detection, quantitation of the results is difficult. Most laboratories use a semiquantitative scoring system that incorporates the number of positive neoplastic cells and the intensity of staining per cell.

The biochemical and immunohistochemical methods of detecting the estrogen receptor have been compared in endometrial neoplasms. With the biochemical method as reference, the sensitivity of the immunohistochemical method of detecting the estrogen receptor ranges from 63% to 91.5%, and the specificity ranges from 58.2% to 93.1%. The overall agreement between the two methods is approximately 70.3%. Some explanations that have been offered for discrepancies between the two methods include alterations of the hormone receptor antigen during formalin fixation, delays in tissue processing that result in receptor degradation, molecular heterogeneity of the receptor, and insufficient numbers of neoplastic cells that express the hormone receptor.

Immunohistochemical methods of detecting the estrogen receptor are versatile and can be performed by virtually any surgical pathology laboratory. Special expertise and equipment are not required. The ability to visualize the distribution of the receptor and qualitatively assess receptor density in the neoplastic cell population is an advantage that is not provided by biochemical methods. The ability to study archival material that has been fixed in formalin and embedded in paraffin is an advantage for the performance of retrospective studies.

Beck T, Weikel W, Brumm C, Wilkens C, Pollow K, Knapstein P-G. Immunohistochemical detection of hormone receptors in breast carcinomas (ER-ICA, PgR-ICA): prognostic usefulness and comparison with the biochemical radioactive-ligand-binding assay (DCC). Gynecol Oncol 1994;53:220–227

Chambers JT, Carcangiu ML, Voynick IM, Schwartz PE. Immunohistochemical evaluation of estrogen and progesterone receptor content in 183 patients with endometrial carcinoma. Am J Clin Pathol 1990;94:255–260

Mutch DG, Soper JT, Budwit-Novotny DA, Cox EB, Creasman WT, McCarty KS, et al. Endometrial adenocarcinoma estrogen receptor content: association of clinicopathologic features with immunohistochemical analysis compared with standard biochemical methods. Am J Obstet Gynecol 1987;157:924–931

59

Therapy for vulvar melanoma

A 76-year-old white woman presents for an annual examination after no visits to a doctor for 23 years. Pelvic examination reveals a 2.3×2.0-cm irregular black nodular induration superior to the edematous clitoris (Fig. 59-1; see color plate). Several other areas of hyperpigmentation are observed. The remainder of the pelvic examination and the general physical examination are normal. A biopsy is taken. Given the most likely diagnosis, the appropriate management of this lesion is

(A) local excision
(B) local excision with unilateral groin lymph node dissection
* (C) radical wide excision
(D) radical vulvectomy with bilateral groin and pelvic lymph node dissection

This patient has malignant melanoma of the vulva. Although this condition is rare, it is the second most common vulvar malignancy. It occurs mainly on the labia minora and clitoris and most frequently in white women between the ages of 50 and 80 years. It may arise from a preexisting junctional nevus, the junctional component of a compound nevus, or de novo. Although these lesions are often asymptomatic, patients may present complaining of a lump, itching, enlargement of a mole, discharge or bleeding from a lesion, or rarely a groin mass.

Women who have either a family history of melanoma or dysplastic nevi elsewhere on the body are at increased risk for the development of melanoma. Between 2% and 5% of Caucasian adults have dysplastic melanocytic nevi; this incidence is increased to 33% in patients with cutaneous melanoma.

Nodular melanoma is the most aggressive of the melanomas and has the worst prognosis. It has a relatively uniform blue-black color, penetrates deeply, and may metastasize early. It may appear as a uniform nodule beneath the epidermal surface or as an elevated blue-black plaque with an irregular outline, or it may be exophytic and ulcerated.

Involvement of clitoral lymphatics in melanoma is evident in this patient's tumor because of clitoral edema (Fig. 59-1). Radical wide excision, with 2-cm lateral margins to the level of the deep perineal fascia, is required for this lesion. It is particularly important that the inner vaginourethral margin is adequate, because this is a common site of recurrence because of failure to perform a complete resection. Local excision only would be predictably incomplete at the lateral and deep margins. Investigational protocols have shown that lymphadenectomy does not affect survival. For patients with small, superficially invasive lesions, lymph node biopsies should be performed to further establish the prognosis.

Radical wide local excision results in a prognosis comparable to that of radical vulvectomy but without the postsurgical and psychologic morbidity observed after the latter procedure. Immunotherapy and chemotherapy have not been successful for melanoma, although estrogen receptors have been demonstrated in some tumors that have responded to tamoxifen citrate (Nolvadex) therapy. Surgery is the principal mode of therapy.

Look KY, Roth LM, Sutton GP. Vulvar melanoma reconsidered. Cancer 1993;72:143–146

Masiel A, Buttrick P, Bitran J. Tamoxifen in the treatment of malignant melanoma. Cancer Treat Rep 1981;65:531–532

Phillips GL, Twiggs LB, Okagaki T. Vulvar melanoma: a microstaging study. Gynecol Oncol 1982;14:80–88

Rose PG, Piver MS, Tsukada Y, Lau T. Conservative therapy for melanoma of the vulva. Am J Obstet Gynecol 1988;159:52–55

60

Histopathology of intraductal carcinoma

A 35-year-old woman whose mother had breast carcinoma has an abnormal mammogram. An excisional biopsy is performed to remove the suspicious area. Histologically there is a small focal lesion (Fig. 60-1; see color plates) containing a proliferation of cells that bridge the lumen and are arranged around sharply defined spaces in a cribriform pattern. This lesion is characteristic of

* (A) intraductal carcinoma
(B) atypical intraductal hyperplasia
(C) lobular carcinoma in situ
(D) infiltrating ductal carcinoma
(E) infiltrating lobular carcinoma

Intraductal carcinoma has been identified more frequently in recent years because of the widespread use of mammography. Most intraductal carcinomas are detected by mammography or as incidental findings during microscopic examination of adjacent breast tissue from benign palpable lesions. Microscopically, intraductal carcinoma may display a variety of patterns including the comedo, cribriform, solid, and micropapillary patterns. In Fig. 60-1A, a low magnification, ducts containing a proliferation of cells are arranged around rounded spaces in a cribriform pattern. Figure 60-1B, a high magnification of one of these ducts, shows a uniform population of small cells characteristic of intraductal carcinoma.

It may be difficult to distinguish atypical intraductal hyperplasia from intraductal carcinoma. Atypical intraductal hyperplasia shows features that are suggestive of, but fall short of, the changes seen in intraductal carcinoma. In intraductal carcinoma, the cells tend to be more evenly distributed, and the luminal spaces have a more rigid appearance.

Lobular carcinoma in situ is characterized by clusters of lobules and associated terminal ducts that are distended by a uniform population of cells. The latter are relatively small and uniform, completely filling and expanding the lobules. The cells have a relatively high nuclear to cytoplasmic ratio.

Infiltrating ductal and lobular carcinomas are composed of nests and columns of cells that diffusely infiltrate the stroma in a haphazard pattern. In the case of infiltrating lobular carcinoma, the neoplastic cells tend to be small and infiltrate the breast tissue in rows, aligned in a single-file pattern.

Data on the follow-up of patients with intraductal carcinoma treated by local removal or excisional biopsy alone are still relatively limited and therefore somewhat controversial. With untreated lesions, the frequency of development of invasive carcinoma has been estimated to range from 27% to 75%. However, recent studies strongly suggest that the multifocality, size, and pattern of intraductal carcinoma may be important prognostic factors. Specifically, small, inconspicuous intraductal carcinomas displaying a cribriform pattern with an absence of necrosis are associated with a low risk of subsequent carcinoma in the same breast. Although mastectomy guarantees a cure, in recent years more conservative surgical procedures such as lumpectomy with or without radiation therapy have been advocated.

Fechner RE, Mills SE. Breast pathology: benign proliferations, atypias and in situ carcinomas. Chicago: ASCP Press, 1990:119

Lagios MD. Duct carcinoma in situ: pathology and treatment. Surg Clin North Am 1990;70:853–871

Lagios MD, Margolin FR, Westdahl PR, Rose MR. Mammographically detected duct carcinoma in situ. Frequency of local recurrence following tylectomy and prognostic effect of nuclear grade on local recurrence. Cancer 1989;63:618–624

Page DL, Dupont WD, Rogers LW, Landenberger M. Intraductal carcinoma of the breast: follow-up after biopsy only. Cancer 1982;49:751–758

61

Bladder injury at vaginal hysterectomy

You are called to the operating room to assist a colleague, who has entered the bladder and encountered excessive bleeding while attempting to perform a laparoscopically assisted vaginal hysterectomy on a patient. In reviewing the chart before scrubbing, you note that the patient is a 36-year-old woman with a history of endometriosis and two previous cesarean deliveries. The appropriate surgery in this situation is

(A) continue the hysterectomy vaginally and repair the bladder injury vaginally
(B) complete the hysterectomy vaginally and repair the injured bladder at laparoscopy
(C) repair the bladder injury at laparoscopy and plan an abdominal hysterectomy in 2 weeks' time
* (D) perform an abdominal hysterectomy immediately and repair the bladder

The selection of the correct operative procedure is key to avoiding complications. Selection is based on the extent of surgical intervention required to cure the disease as well as the ability of the surgeon to perform the procedure. In this instance, it was likely that the patient's history of endometriosis and two previous cesarean deliveries would make bladder dissection difficult. Because of the extent of adhesive disease, the optimal management is to perform an abdominal hysterectomy and repair the bladder concomitantly.

Bladder injury may occur if the bladder has not been decompressed intraoperatively and if there is distorted anatomy, especially of the bladder base. Bladder injury is common in patients who have had a previous low flap cesarean delivery. Most bladder injuries are sustained during abdominal procedures, in keeping with the fact that more difficult cases are performed abdominally. The advent of laparoscopically assisted vaginal hysterectomy appears to have increased the incidence of bladder injuries. This increase probably reflects variously the inappropriate selection of patients, inexperience of the surgeon, and limitations of the laparoscopic procedure.

Intraoperative recognition of the injury is crucial. A sudden increase in bleeding is suggestive of injury; the appearance of a urethral catheter in the operative field is conclusive. Retrograde instillation of dye solution or sterile milk can further identify the site of injury. Sudden distension of the bladder drainage bag with gas is peculiar to laparoscopy-associated bladder injury. Once an injury is suspected, the ureters as well as the bladder should be inspected. For this inspection, a laparotomy is necessary.

If an injury to the bladder has occurred, either a one- or two-layer closure of the bladder is performed. Bladder drainage is then continued for at least a week. At vaginal hysterectomy, the bladder may be repaired through the vagina. In this patient, the bleeding and scarring preclude a vaginal approach.

In some instances in which extensive pathology has not contributed to the injury, repair of the bladder might be feasible at laparoscopy. The safety and effectiveness of such a repair have not, however, been confirmed in any large studies.

Brubaker LT, Wilbanks GD. Urinary tract injuries in pelvic surgery. Surg Clin North Am 1991;71:963–976

Font GE, Brill AI, Stuhldreher PV, Rosenzweig BA. Endoscopic management of incidental cystotomy during operative laparoscopy. J Urol 1993;149:1130–1131

Kovac SR, Cruikshank SH, Retto HF. Laparoscopy-assisted vaginal hysterectomy. J Gynecol Surg 1990;6:185–193

Lee C-L, Soong Y-K. Laparoscopic hysterectomy with the Endo GIA 30 stapler. J Reprod Med 1993;38:582–586

Moriel EZ, Meirow D, Zilberman M, Farkas A. Experience with the immediate treatment of iatrogenic bladder injuries and the repair of complex vesico-vaginal fistulae by the transvesical approach. Arch Gynecol Obstet 1993;253:127–130

Nezhat C, Nezhat F, Silfen SL. Laparoscopic hysterectomy and bilateral salpingo-oophorectomy using Multifire GIA surgical stapler. J Gynecol Surg 1990;6:287–288

Nezhat CH, Nezhat F, Nezhat C, Rottenberg H. Laparoscopic repair of a vesicovaginal fistula: a case report. Obstet Gynecol 1994;83:899–901

Ostrzenski A. Endoscopic bladder repair during total modified laparoscopic hysterectomy: a case report. J Reprod Med 1993;38:558–560

Reich H, McGlynn F. Laparoscopic repair of bladder injury. Obstet Gynecol 1990;76:909–910

62

Protection from ovarian cancer by oral contraceptives

A 23-year-old woman consults you for contraceptive advice. Her mother was recently diagnosed with ovarian cancer. She inquires about the association between oral contraceptives and ovarian cancer. You explain that the use of oral contraceptives

(A) increases ovarian cancer risk both in the general population and in women with a family history of the disease
(B) reduces ovarian cancer risk in the general population but not in women with a family history of the disease
* (C) reduces ovarian cancer risk both in the general population and in women with a family history of the disease
(D) reduces the risk of ovarian, endometrial, breast, and cervical cancer
(E) does not alter the risk of any gynecologic cancer

Although the etiology of ovarian cancer is not known, some women can be identified to be at increased risk of developing the disease. Factors that increase the risk of ovarian cancer include advancing age, postmenopausal status, nulliparity, prolonged ovulation (early menarche or late menopause), and a family history of ovarian cancer. Conversely, multiparity, premenopausal status, no family history of ovarian cancer, and a shortened period of menstruation are associated with a decreased risk of developing ovarian cancer.

The use of oral contraceptives has been shown to reduce the risk of developing ovarian cancer. The Cancer and Steroid Hormone (CASH) Study of the Centers for Disease Control and Prevention and the National Institute of Child Health and Human Development reported that oral contraceptive use was associated with a decreased relative risk of ovarian cancer and that the decrease in risk was greatest in women who took oral contraceptives for longer periods of time. Although the relative risk decreased with prolonged use, even very short periods of oral contraceptive use were associated with a significant decrease in the risk of ovarian cancer (Table 62-1). All combination estrogen–progesterone contraceptive formulations were associated with a decrease in the relative risk of developing the disease.

Until recently, studies of the decrease in relative risk of ovarian cancer in oral contraceptive users focused on the general population and did not evaluate individuals with a family history of ovarian cancer. Recently, investigators evaluated oral contraceptive use in women with a family history, and a similar decrease in ovarian cancer was shown in these women (Table 62-2).

The use of oral contraceptives decreases the risk of endometrial cancer but is associated with a slight increase in the risk of cervical cancer and breast cancer (in certain subsets of populations). Noncontraceptive estrogen use (estrogen replacement therapy), on the other hand, increases the risk of developing endometrial can-

TABLE 62-1. Cumulative Duration of Oral Contraceptive Use by Women with Epithelial Ovarian Cancer and Control Subjects*

Duration of Use	Case Subjects	Control Subjects	Relative Risk†	95% Confidence Interval
Never	242	1,532	1	(Referent)
3–6 mo	26	280	0.6	0.4–0.9
7–11 mo	14	134	0.7	0.4–1.3
1–2 y	65	602	0.7	0.5–0.9
3–4 y	40	397	0.6	0.4–0.9
5–9 y	39	594	0.4	0.3–0.6
≥10 y	13	328	0.2	0.1–0.4

* Excluded from the study were 8 case and 88 control subjects whose durations of use were unknown, 44 case and 253 control subjects without 3 or more months of consecutive use, and 1 case and 20 control subjects whose parity was unknown.

† Relative risk is adjusted for age and parity.

Reprinted by permission of The New England Journal of Medicine from The Cancer and Steroid Hormone Study of the Centers for Disease Control and the National Institute of Child Health and Human Development. The reduction in risk of ovarian cancer associated with oral-contraceptive use. N Engl J Med 1987;316:653; copyright 1987, Massachusetts Medical Society

TABLE 62-2. Cumulative Number of Cases of Epithelial Ovarian Cancer per 100,000 Women*

Group	Years of Oral Contraceptive Use			
	Never	1	5	10
Positive family history				
Age 40	218	165	111	95
Age 50	644	475	307	248
Age 55	1,007	736	471	377
Negative family history				
Age 40	100	76	51	44
Age 50	298	219	142	115
Age 55	466	340	218	174
Parous				
Age 40	82	62	41	35
Age 50	270	199	128	102
Age 55	429	313	199	158
Nulliparous				
Age 40	165	125	83	70
Age 50	543	399	256	206
Age 55	862	628	401	319

* Data are presented as total number of cases arising from age 20 years to ages 40, 50, and 55 years. Oral contraceptive use is assumed to begin at age 20 years and to be continuous.

Gross TP, Schlesselman JJ. The estimated effect of oral contraceptive use on the cumulative risk of epithelial ovarian cancer. Reprinted with permission from The American College of Obstetricians and Gynecologists (Obstetrics and Gynecology 1994, 83, 421)

cer and may increase the risk of breast cancer but has no effect on the risk of developing cervical or ovarian cancer.

Booth M, Beral V, Smith P. Risk factors for ovarian cancer: a case-control study. Br J Cancer 1989;60:592–598

The Cancer and Steroid Hormone Study of the Centers for Disease Control and the National Institute of Child Health and Human Development. The reduction in risk of ovarian cancer associated with oral-contraceptive use. N Engl J Med 1987;316:650–655

Gross TP, Schlesselman JJ. The estimated effect of oral contraceptive use on the cumulative risk of epithelial ovarian cancer. Obstet Gynecol 1994;83:419–424

The WHO Collaborative Study of Neoplasia and Steroid Contraceptives. Epithelial ovarian cancer and combined oral contraceptives. Int J Epidemiol 1989;18:538–545

63

Diagnosis of rectal prolapse

A healthy 60-year-old woman had surgery for pelvic organ prolapse 1 year ago. On physical examination, rectal mucosa is noted to protrude approximately 5 cm from the rectal opening. The patient has difficulty with fecal evacuation and has periods of fecal incontinence. When counseling her, you explain that the diagnosis of rectal prolapse is made by

* (A) clinical examination
(B) defecating proctography
(C) anorectal manometry
(D) colon transit studies

Rectal prolapse occurs in women 3–10 times more often than in men. The incidence increases with age, peaking in the sixth or seventh decade.

Complete rectal prolapse is diagnosed as the patient strains and the rectum protrudes. Rectal prolapse can be differentiated from prolapsed internal hemorrhoids and mucosal prolapse. Prolapsed hemorrhoids (with edema and thrombosis) resemble rectal prolapse, the difference being that radial grooves are apparent between the hemorrhoidal tissue. In rectal prolapse, concentric rings of mucosa are seen at the circumference of the protruding mass. With mucosal prolapse, the exposed mucosal folds are arranged in a radial fashion. Mucosal prolapse protrudes no more than 1–2 cm from the anal sphincter, whereas rectal prolapse protrudes at least 4 cm beyond the anal sphincter. The mass of mucosal prolapse is thin compared with the thick, concentric layers in rectal prolapse.

The diagnosis of rectal prolapse is clinical. Further studies may identify other associated conditions. Flexible sigmoidoscopy can rule out neoplasm, inflammatory bowel disease, and diverticular disease. Defecating proctography would add little to the clinical diagnosis.

Anorectal manometry will quantify internal and external anal sphincter function. Lower resting and squeeze pressures are the norm in patients with complete rectal prolapse and fecal incontinence. Patients who have rectal prolapse without fecal incontinence have normal pressures.

In patients with a history of severe chronic constipation, transit studies of the colon are performed to identify those with slow transit time. Patients with delay in transit time may be candidates for selective colonic resection in addition to rectal prolapse repair.

Medical management is not effective for repeated rectal prolapse. Surgery is indicated.

Levin KE, Pemberton JH. Rectal prolapse: pathogenesis and management. In: Benson JT, ed. Female pelvic floor disorders: investigation and management. New York: Norton Medical Books, 1992:363–379

Neill ME, Parks AG, Swash M. Physiological studies of the anal sphincter musculature in faecal incontinence and rectal prolapse. Br J Surg 1981;68:531–536

64

Follow-up of diethylstilbestrol-exposed patients

A 33-year-old nulligravid woman tells you that her mother took diethylstilbestrol (DES) during the first month of pregnancy because of vaginal bleeding. The patient has had normal pelvic examinations and Pap tests every 6 months since her premarital examination 14 years ago. She has vaginal adenosis and has been told that it is improving. Appropriate management for this patient includes

(A) annual biopsies of vaginal adenosis
(B) annual colposcopy
* (C) annual palpation and cytologic smear of the vagina
(D) Pap test every 6 months

In most cases, vaginal adenosis and clear cell vaginal adenocarcinoma have a common origin: a synthetic estrogen, DES, which was first made commercially available in 1938. In the late 1940s and the 1950s, DES was given to pregnant women who had recurrent or threatened abortion. As many as 2 million women may have received DES or the comparable synthetic estrogens dienestrol or hexestrol by 1971, when an association between in utero exposure to DES and the development of clear cell adenocarcinoma of the vagina was first noted. That year, the U.S. Food and Drug Administration banned these drugs from use during pregnancy. Adverse effects are shown in the box.

Adenosis of the vagina and cervix, which is much more common than adenocarcinoma in these patients, is associated with almost all vaginal and half of cervical clear cell adenocarcinomas. The frequency of vaginal adenosis after in utero DES exposure is related to gestational age at initiation of treatment. The frequency is 90% if maternal ingestion occurred before 8 weeks of gestation, but less than 10% if exposure occurred after 16 weeks. Vaginal adenosis is more likely to develop if a larger total dose of DES was taken by the mother before 22 weeks of gestation and if DES was taken over a longer period of time.

Adenosis is more commonly observed on the proximal third of the anterior vaginal wall, but it also can be lateral or posterior and may even extend to the introitus. As females with adenosis mature, glands are replaced by squamous epithelium through squamous metaplasia, and the adenosis disappears. Metaplastic changes associated with adenosis require careful assessment, because dysplasia may be reported on Pap tests and biopsies when, in fact, it is not present.

Adverse Effects on Female Progeny of In Utero Exposure to Diethylstilbestrol

Anatomic Abnormalities

- Lower genital tract
  - Adenosis and clear cell adenocarcinoma of the vagina or cervix
  - Cervicovaginal structural abnormalities
    - Collars, hoods, septa, and cockscombs
    - Cervical mucus effects
    - Cervical incompetence
- Upper genital tract
  - Uterine structural abnormalities
  - Fallopian tube structural abnormalities

Reproductive Abnormalities

- Menstrual dysfunction
- Reproductive dysfunction
  - Infertility
  - Adverse pregnancy outcome
    - Spontaneous abortion
    - Ectopic pregnancy
    - Premature delivery
    - Perinatal death

Reprinted with permission from Stillman RJ. In utero exposure to diethylstilbestrol: adverse effects on the reproductive tract and reproductive performance in male and female offspring. Am J Obstet Gynecol 1982;142:906

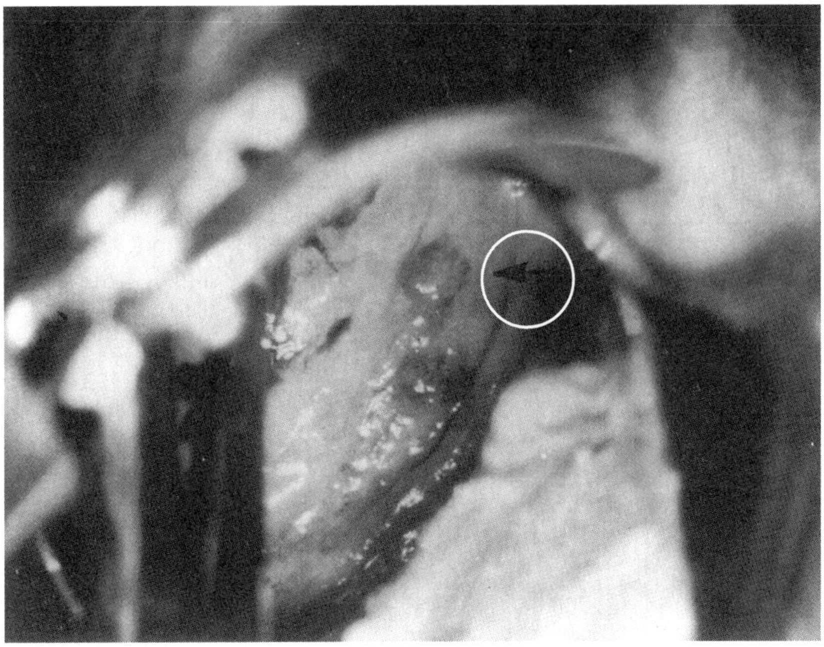

FIG. 64-1. Palpable raised nodule in left fornix (circled arrow). Although similar in appearance to adenosis, this lesion was found to be a clear cell adenocarcinoma at biopsy. (Kaufman RH, Korhonen MO, Strama T, Adam E, Kaplan A. Development of clear cell adenocarcinoma in DES-exposed offspring under observation. Reprinted with permission from The American College of Obstetricians and Gynecologists [Obstetrics and Gynecology 1982, 59, 69S])

New cases of DES-associated clear cell adenocarcinoma are still being reported. The age range of DES-exposed women who have developed clear cell adenocarcinoma extends from 7 to 42 years, with 91% of patients being diagnosed between ages 15 and 27 years and diagnosis occurring at a median age of 19.5 years. For DES-exposed women, the incidence of this cancer ranges from 0.14 to 1.4 per thousand.

Clear cell adenocarcinoma (Fig. 64-1) usually develops anteriorly in the upper third of the vagina or on the posterior ectocervix. Although the tumors are most often reddish in color, some tumors are not visible and are discovered only as an induration palpable through normal mucosa. Vaginal bleeding or discharge usually precedes tumor detection.

Observation is usually adequate to make a tentative diagnosis of surface adenosis. All abnormalities should be described in writing and in a drawing before biopsies are taken. Biopsy is required for confirmation and should be performed if a palpable nodule develops. Approximately 17% of patients with in utero DES exposure require biopsy to rule out premalignant or malignant lesions. Although colposcopy was routinely recommended for these patients in the past, it should be reserved for evaluation of abnormal-appearing areas or as follow-up of an abnormal Pap test.

Palpation is an important part of the initial and follow-up evaluation of DES-exposed women. A careful single-digit examination of the vaginal surfaces and cervix is particularly important for the detection of cancers that are palpable but not visible. Palpation is followed by a thorough inspection of the cervix and all vaginal surfaces. A Pap test should be performed annually, covering the entire cervix and proximal vaginal surfaces.

The optimal interval between screening examinations for clear cell carcinoma is unknown; a 6-month interval was initially recommended, but annual examination appears to be adequate if cytology and any biopsy results are normal. Neither special instruments nor special methods are required.

Herbst AL, Ulfelder H, Poskanzer DC. Adenocarcinoma of the vagina. Association of maternal stilbestrol therapy with tumor appearance in young women. N Engl J Med 1971;284:878–881

Jefferies JA, Robboy SJ, O'Brien PC, Bergstralh EJ, Labarthe DR, Barnes AB, et al. Structural anomalies of the cervix and vagina in women enrolled in the Diethylstilbestrol Adenosis (DESAD) Project. Am J Obstet Gynecol 1984; 148:59–66

Noller KL. Role of colposcopy in the examination of diethylstilbestrol-exposed women. Obstet Gynecol Clin NorthAm 1993;20:165–176

Robboy SJ, Szyfelbein WM, Goellner JR, Kaufman RH, Taft PD, Richard RM, et al. Dysplasia and cytologic findings in 4,589 young women enrolled in Diethylstilbestrol–Adenosis (DESAD) Project. Am J Obstet Gynecol 1981; 140:579–586

65

Management of koilocytosis

A 25-year-old woman has had a recent Pap test interpreted as koilocytotic atypia. Of the following options, the best next step in management is

(A) repeat Pap test immediately
* (B) repeat Pap test in 4–6 months
(C) electroexcisional biopsy of the transformation zone
(D) intravaginal 5-fluorouracil
(E) cryosurgery of the transformation zone

Koilocytosis (koilocytotic atypia) in the lower female genital tract is defined as cytoplasmic vacuolization and nuclear enlargement and/or atypia in squamous cells. It is a marker of epithelium altered by human papillomavirus infection. Because it is not currently possible to reliably distinguish koilocytosis from mild dysplasia or cervical intraepithelial neoplasia (CIN 1), the Bethesda System recommendation is to classify Pap tests showing koilocytosis either alone or with mild dysplasia as low-grade squamous intraepithelial lesions (SIL). Moderate dysplasia (CIN 2) and severe dysplasia (carcinoma in situ or CIN 3) are classified as high-grade SIL.

When colposcopically directed biopsies are performed on patients with Pap tests showing koilocytosis only, 15–20% show high-grade SIL. Also, in prospective follow-up studies comparing patients with Pap tests showing koilocytosis alone to patients with CIN 1, the progression rate to high-grade SIL, specifically CIN 3, is essentially the same in both groups (approximately 15%). On the other hand, spontaneous regression of low-grade SIL occurs in approximately 60% of patients.

Management of low-grade SIL (CIN 1) is controversial. Although many gynecologists perform colposcopic biopsies and treat a histologically confirmed low-grade SIL by CO_2 laser vaporization, electroexcisional biopsy, or cryosurgery of the transformation zone, there are no data indicating that any of these procedures is more efficacious than observation alone in view of the high spontaneous regression rate of these lesions. Follow-up with Pap tests every 4–6 months for 2 years is used by many clinicians and is an established method of management of women with low-grade SIL in other countries. For example, in the Netherlands and in parts of Canada where follow-up is reliable, this method is the standard of practice. In contrast, there is general agreement that high-grade SIL (CIN 2 and 3) should be treated.

Colposcopy, endocervical curettage, and directed biopsy of any abnormal area on the ectocervix are other appropriate management options, because high-grade SIL is present in 15% of women with a cytologic diagnosis of low-grade SIL. If a biopsy is performed, tissue should be obtained by using the least traumatic method in an effort to confirm the presence of a lesion histologically. The term *directed biopsy* may mean individual biopsies of atypical areas or colposcopically directed loop electrode excision procedure with a small loop.

Routine electroexcision of the transformation zone as a method of evaluating a Pap test diagnosis of low-grade SIL is not appropriate. Similarly, in the absence of a histologic diagnosis of SIL, ablative treatment such as intravaginal 5-fluorouracil, CO_2 laser vaporization, or cryosurgery of the transformation zone is overtreatment. A repeat Pap test performed immediately would be of no value. A negative test would probably represent a false-negative result, whereas a positive test would merely confirm what is already known.

Campion MJ, Cuzick J, McCance DJ, Singer A. Progressive potential of mild cervical atypia: prospective cytological, colposcopical and virological study. Lancet 1986;2:237–240

Kaufman R, Kurman RJ, Meisels A, Okagaki T, Patten SF, Koss LG, et al. Caution in interpreting papillomavirus-associated lesions. Obstet Gynecol 1983;62:269–270

The 1988 Bethesda System for reporting cervical/vaginal cytologic diagnoses. National Cancer Institute Workshop. JAMA 1989;262:931–934

Syrjanen K, Vayrynen M, Saarikoski S, Mantyjarvi R, Parkkinen S, Hippelainen M, et al. Natural history of cervical human papillomavirus (HPV) infections based upon prospective follow-up. Br J Obstet Gynaecol 1986;92:1086–1092

66

Appropriateness of screening tests for ovarian cancer

A 45-year-old nulligravid woman is seen for an initial office visit. Her family history reveals that a maternal aunt died of ovarian cancer at age 60 (cause of death was documented by pathology records). A complete family pedigree is obtained and does not reveal any other cancers. The patient is very fearful of developing cancer and requests a complete workup and any available tests that might detect ovarian cancer. In counseling her about the appropriateness of screening for ovarian cancer, you advise her to have an annual pelvic examination and

* (A) no further testing
(B) CA 125 evaluation
(C) endovaginal sonography
(D) CA 125 evaluation and endovaginal sonography
(E) color-flow Doppler examination

Early detection and treatment of precursor lesions and asymptomatic neoplasms can reduce cancer morbidity and mortality. Recent media attention has generated considerable publicity, causing anxiety about the familial nature of ovarian cancer and poor survival associated with the disease. This high level of public awareness sometimes leads to inappropriate requests and inappropriate management.

Although patients may request testing, a screening test must meet certain criteria before it can be approved for screening in the general population. It should have high specificity and sensitivity, be cost-effective, and result in a decrease in mortality. A recent National Institutes of Health consensus conference on ovarian cancer considered but did not recommend the use of CA 125 and ultrasonography (pelvic or endovaginal, with or without color-flow Doppler) as screening tests for the early detection of ovarian cancer. A large prospective National Cancer Institute trial is evaluating these methods of screening in women age 60 years and older. Until this study establishes the effectiveness of screening a large population with CA 125 and ultrasonography, these tests cannot be routinely recommended, especially for women with no known risk factors. Although pelvic examination lacks sensitivity, it is currently the only recommended procedure to screen for ovarian cancer. Therefore, this patient requires no further testing.

There are more than 43 million women in the United States age 45 years or older. If every woman in this age group had an annual CA 125 evaluation and a pelvic ultrasound examination, it is estimated that health care costs would increase more than $13 billion per year. With false-positive results, additional unnecessary testing and surgery might be performed. A study of more than 5,000 apparently healthy women, monitored by CA 125, reported 247 patients with a CA 125 level above 30 U/ml. Ovarian cancer was detected in only eight of these women. Six other women with normal CA 125 levels were found to have ovarian cancer.

Women with a documented family history, such as this patient, or with a familial ovarian cancer syndrome may be given the opportunity to participate in clinical trials that will prospectively evaluate the efficacy of CA 125, ultrasonography, and other methods of testing as screening tools. This patient, whose second-degree relative had ovarian cancer, has a risk of developing ovarian cancer of 4.5%, only slightly above that of the population in general (1.5%) (Table 66-1). Use of CA 125, endovaginal ultrasonography, or Doppler color flow of the ovaries for screening, except in clinical trials, is not warranted. Patients with a sporadic family history should not be tested.

Based on pedigree analysis, the risk of ovarian cancer for family members can be estimated. Patients whose family history indicates hereditary ovarian cancer syndrome (more than two first-degree relatives with ovarian cancer or related cancers) have a 30–50% chance of developing ovarian cancer. They will need extensive counseling regarding the decision to undergo testing and the options for screening and preventive surgery. They will also need support to cope with the psychologic stress induced by obtaining this information. Clinical screening studies to prospectively evaluate the risks and benefits of screening for ovarian cancer are best administered by a multidisciplinary team with expertise in the following areas: screening and management of ovarian cancer, pattern of inheritance (pedigree), DNA testing (when available), and psychosocial counseling.

The discovery of genetic markers for cancer risk will require new knowledge about how to communicate risk information and how to motivate adherence to cancer prevention and early detection guidelines. Ethical issues need to be addressed. Who is to have access to this new information, and what safeguards are necessary to protect patients? For example, shall insurance companies and employers be allowed to access this information? More effective methods are needed for providing informed consent to those being screened about potential psychologic and social sequelae of participation in screening programs. Although cancer screening has the potential to reduce morbidity and mortality, notification of patients with true-positive and false-positive results

TABLE 66-1. Lifetime Probability of Ovarian Cancer by Age in Women with One Relative with Ovarian Cancer

Age (y)	Lifetime Probability of Ovarian Cancer (%)*	Lifetime Probability of Ovarian Cancer with One Relative with Ovarian Cancer (%)†
30	1.6	5.0
35	1.6	5.0
40	1.6	4.8
45	1.5	4.5
50	1.4	4.4
55	1.3	4.1
60	1.2	3.6

*Probabilities are based on surveillance, epidemiology, and end-results cancer statistics.

† Probabilities are based on surveillance, epidemiology, and end-results cancer statistics and a pooled odds ratio of 3.1 in a woman with one relative with ovarian cancer.

Kerlikowske K, Brown JS, Grady DG. Should women with familial ovarian cancer undergo prophylactic oophorectomy? Reprinted with permission from The American College of Obstetricians and Gynecologists (Obstetrics and Gynecology 1992, 80, 704)

might have significant psychologic sequelae. Common reactions to genetic cancer risk information have included denial, low self-esteem, anxiety, and guilt. Cancer control programs should be designed to maximize adherence to prevention and surveillance regimens and to minimize the adverse psychologic, social, and ethical consequences.

American College of Obstetricians and Gynecologists. Genetic risk and screening techniques for epithelial ovarian cancer. ACOG Committee Opinion 117. Washington, DC: ACOG, 1992

Biesecker BB, Boehnke M, Calzone K, Markel DS, Garber JE, Collins FS, et al. Genetic counseling for families with inherited susceptibility to breast and ovarian cancer. JAMA 1993;269:1970–1974

Creasman WT, DiSaia PJ. Screening in ovarian cancer. Am J Obstet Gynecol 1991;165:7–10

Einhorn N, Sjovall K, Knapp RC, Hall P, Scully RE, Bast RC Jr, et al. Prospective evaluation of serum CA125 levels for early detection of ovarian cancer. Obstet Gynecol 1992;80:14–18

Lerman C, Rimer BK, Engstrom PF. Cancer risk notification: psychosocial and ethical implications. J Clin Oncol 1991;9:1275–1282

National Institutes of Health Consensus Development Conference Statement. Ovarian cancer: screening, treatment, and follow-up. Gynecol Oncol 1994;55:S4–S14

Schwartz PE, Chambers JT, Taylor KJ, Pellerito J, Hammers L, Cole LA, et al. Early detection of ovarian cancer: background, rationale, and structure of the Yale Early Detection Program. Yale J Biol Med 1991;64:557–571

67

Methods of monitoring patients under anesthesia

A 69-year-old woman with grade 2 endometrial carcinoma is scheduled for a staging laparotomy and hysterectomy. She has a history of hypertension and congestive heart failure. She is taking digoxin and a diuretic but still has moderate dyspnea with exertion. In addition to routine monitoring of blood pressure, pulse, and oxygen saturation during anesthesia, the most important parameter to monitor is

* (A) pulmonary capillary wedge pressure
(B) cardiac index
(C) systemic vascular resistance
(D) peripheral pulse pressure in the femoral artery
(E) central venous pressure

In early stages, endometrial cancer is highly curable by hysterectomy. Historically, alternative treatment with irradiation resulted in inferior survival. It is important for the patient described to have surgery, if surgery is medically feasible.

Many patients with mild to moderately impaired cardiac function can safely undergo surgery, provided their cardiac function is monitored properly. This patient will require preoperative placement of a pulmonary artery balloon (Swan–Ganz) catheter to optimize monitoring of her status. In addition to routine anesthetic monitoring, the combination of the Swan–Ganz catheter and the intraarterial pressure catheter provides information on the major hemodynamic variables of arterial blood pressure, cardiac output, and left ventricular filling pressure and can be used before, during, and after surgery. The Swan–Ganz catheter continuously monitors the pulmonary artery pressure and allows periodic measurement of the wedge (left ventricular filling) pressure.

With the thermodilution technique, the Swan–Ganz catheter can also be used to measure cardiac output. This will allow the anesthesiologist to accurately maximize the preload by infusion of fluids, to modify the afterload with drugs that affect vascular resistance, and to monitor cardiac output and left ventricular function. Inotropic agents may be necessary to improve cardiac function before, during, or after surgery. The effect of these agents can be measured by the arterial pressure catheter and the Swan–Ganz catheter.

This patient will require continuous monitoring of intraarterial pressure. An upper-extremity artery is usually cannulated, although any peripheral artery can be used. Catheterization of the radial artery is associated with fewer complications and is more convenient than catheterization of the femoral artery. It is not usually necessary to calculate cardiac index (L/min/m^2) or systemic vascular resistance (dyne/s/cm^{-5}) during surgery. These parameters are more useful postoperatively.

The central venous pressure may provide some indication of hydration status, but it does not provide the detailed information about left ventricular filling pressure and cardiac output needed to optimally manage a patient with cardiac disease.

Glower DD, Spratt JA, Snow ND, Kabas JS, Davis JW, Olsen CO, et al. Linearity of the Frank-Starling relationship in the intact heart: the concept of preload recruitable stroke work. Circulation 1985;71:994–1009

Orr JW Jr, Browne KF Jr. Cardiovascular complications. In: Orr JW Jr, Shingleton HM, eds. Complications in gynecologic surgery: prevention, recognition, and management. Philadelphia: JB Lippincott, 1994:1–51

Shoemaker WC, Kram HB, Appel PL, Fleming AW. The efficacy of central venous and pulmonary artery catheters and therapy based upon them in reducing mortality and morbidity. Arch Surg 1990;125:1332–1338

Wilmore DW, Brennan MF, Harlen AH, Holcroft JW, Meakins JL, eds (American College of Surgeons). Care of the surgical patient. Vol 1: Critical care. A publication of the Committee on Pre and Postoperative Care. New York: Scientific American, 1991

68

Therapy for vulvar Paget disease

A 62-year-old woman is diagnosed with vulvar Paget disease. Palpation reveals no cutaneous or subcutaneous induration of the vulva. The distribution of the disease is depicted in Fig. 68-1 (see color plate). The optimal therapy for this patient is

(A) laser therapy
(B) topical 5-fluorouracil
(C) radical vulvectomy
* (D) wide local excision

Extramammary Paget disease of the vulva is an intraepithelial neoplasm. Although this lesion is rarely locally invasive, there have been isolated reports of inguinal node metastases. Because an underlying invasive adenocarcinoma may be present in as many as 20% of patients with vulvar Paget disease, laser therapy is not appropriate as primary therapy. For the same reason, topical 5-fluorouracil is also not the initial treatment of choice. The hyperkeratosis that often accompanies the disease impedes drug penetration to the Paget cells. Even in the absence of hyperkeratosis, drug penetration may be inadequate when the Paget cells invade the skin appendages to a depth of 5–7 mm below the epithelial surface.

Surgical resection is the optimal treatment for vulvar Paget disease. In the past, radical resection was advocated as treatment for all patients with the disease. Because it is now recognized that this is generally a noninvasive, intraepithelial lesion, less extensive surgery is currently advocated. An adequate deep margin can be achieved by wide local excision, which yields better cosmetic and functional results than does radical resection. If an underlying adenocarcinoma is present on permanent pathology, an additional procedure can be performed. A depth of resection to the level of the deep perineal fascia, such as that performed as part of radical vulvectomy, is not required in the absence of an underlying invasive adenocarcinoma. Similarly, inguinofemoral dissection is not required.

Histologically negative lateral margins may be difficult to achieve at the time of wide local excision because the histologic extent of the disease typically exceeds the assessment of the extent of the disease by visualization. Assessment of the surgical margins by frozen section has been historically used to determine the adequacy of resection. More recently, the intravenous administration of fluorescein as a means to assess surgical margins has been described. Dilated vessels invariably accompany Paget disease. The ultraviolet excitement of fluorescein permits the visualization of areas of tissue with an increased number of dilated vessels. Resection of all fluorescein-positive areas ensures removal of histologically positive tissue. Fluorescein infusions to delineate surgical margins have a positive predictive value of 97.4% and a negative predictive value of 99.9%.

Bergen S, DiSaia PJ, Liao SY, Berman ML. Conservative management of extramammary Paget's disease of the vulva. Gynecol Oncol 1989;33:151–156

Misas JE, Cold CJ, Hall FW. Vulvar Paget disease: fluorescein-aided visualization of margins. Obstet Gynecol 1991;77:156–159

Stacy D, Burrell MO, Franklin EW III. Extramammary Paget's disease of the vulva and anus: use of intraoperative frozen-section margins. Am J Obstet Gynecol 1986;155:519–523

69

Management of leiomyomata and rectocele

A 40-year-old woman who has had four vaginal deliveries desires surgical sterilization. Her history reveals no pelvic inflammatory disease and no pelvic or abdominal surgery. Her history reveals symptoms of menorrhagia, pelvic pressure in the upright position, and difficulty with defecation. Examination reveals grade 2 enterocele, descensus, and a uterus of 10 weeks' gestational size that is nodular, firm, and nontender but mobile. The pubic arch is wide. Rectal examination reveals a free cul-de-sac and no tenderness or nodularity of the uterosacral ligaments. Evaluation of her abnormal bleeding by hysteroscopy reveals a broad-based deep submucous myoma, and a timed endometrial biopsy shows secretory endometrium.

After discussing all of the options with the patient, you recommend

* (A) vaginal hysterectomy, culdoplasty, and posterior repair
(B) abdominal hysterectomy and posterior repair
(C) laparoscopy-assisted vaginal hysterectomy
(D) laparoscopy-assisted vaginal hysterectomy and posterior repair

Hysterectomy is indicated for this patient because of symptomatic uterine leiomyomata. She also has a symptomatic rectocele that requires surgical correction, and she desires surgical sterilization. Vaginal hysterectomy and posterior repair will remove the pelvic pathology and relieve all of her symptoms. Factors favoring vaginal hysterectomy over abdominal hysterectomy are her wide pubic arch and uterine descensus. The vaginal approach is also logical because of the need to repair the posterior vaginal wall. Benefits of vaginal hysterectomy include shorter operating time, less postoperative discomfort, and shorter hospital stay. The vaginal hysterectomy should include culdoplasty to correct the enterocele.

Laparoscopy-assisted vaginal hysterectomy or laparoscopy-assisted vaginal hysterectomy with posterior repair is not indicated because the patient does not have a history of pelvic or abdominal surgery and has no evidence of pelvic inflammatory disease, pelvic adhesions, or endometriosis. Furthermore, salpingo-oophorectomy is not planned. Laparoscopic assistance would add to the operative and anesthesia time and increase the cost.

Masterson BJ. Manual of gynecologic surgery. 2nd ed. New York: Springer-Verlag, 1986:48–52

Poma PA. Tubal sterilization and later hospitalizations. J Reprod Med 1980; 25:272–278

Summitt RL Jr, Stovall TG, Lipscomb GH, Ling FW. Randomized comparison of laparoscopy-assisted vaginal hysterectomy with standard vaginal hysterectomy in an outpatient setting. Obstet Gynecol 1992;80:895–901

Wheeless CR Jr. Tubal sterilization. In: Thompson JD, Rock JA, eds. Te Linde's operative gynecology. 7th ed. Philadelphia: JB Lippincott, 1992:343–359

70

Therapy for low-grade stromal sarcoma

A 41-year-old woman, gravida 1, para 0, has a 9-month history of increasing menometrorrhagia and an enlarging uterus. Endometrial biopsy reveals proliferative endometrium and a few atypical stromal cells. Physical examination is within normal limits except for a 10-week-size, irregular uterus. Her hemoglobin is 9.8 g/dl. Chest X-ray and serum chemistries are normal.

The patient undergoes a vaginal hysterectomy for the presumed diagnosis of uterine leiomyomata. The pathology report reveals an extensive low-grade stromal sarcoma (endolymphatic stromal myosis) with microscopic parametrial invasion. The mitotic rate is 2–4 per 10 high-power fields. Postoperative computed tomographic scans of the chest, abdomen, and pelvis are negative. The preferred plan of management for this patient is

(A) radical removal of the parametria, bilateral salpingo-oophorectomy, and lymph node biopsies
* (B) bilateral salpingo-oophorectomy, pelvic radiotherapy, and progestins
(C) pelvic radiotherapy
(D) progestins
(E) chemotherapy

Low-grade endometrial stromal sarcoma has fewer than 10 and usually fewer than 5 mitoses per 10 high-power fields, a characteristic pattern of myometrial invasion manifested by masses of endometrial stromal cells with minimal cytologic atypia diffusely infiltrating the myometrium, as well as vascular invasion. It typically has a protracted clinical course characterized by late recurrences, which are local rather then distant. Although it often behaves in a clinically aggressive fashion, it lacks the aneuploid DNA content commonly associated with malignancy.

Low-grade stromal sarcoma occurs predominantly in premenopausal women. Patients usually present with abnormal uterine bleeding with or without associated pelvic pain. The diagnosis is seldom made preoperatively. Most patients undergo surgery for uterine leiomyomata or a pelvic mass. The diagnosis may be suspected preoperatively by the finding of fragments of hypercellular endometrial stromal tissue with few glands on endometrial biopsy or intraoperatively by the discovery of rubbery, worm-like, yellow-gray cords of tumor extending through the myometrium into blood vessels within the adnexa, broad ligaments, and parametria.

Low-grade stromal sarcoma has extended beyond the uterus in 40% of patients at the time of diagnosis, but two thirds of the extrauterine spread is confined to the pelvis. Almost 50% of patients experience recurrence after initial surgical therapy. The interval between initial treatment and the diagnosis of recurrent or metastatic tumor averages about 5 years, but recurrences as late as 25 years after initial treatment have been reported. Prolonged survival and cure are possible even in the presence of extrauterine spread or after the development of recurrent or metastatic disease.

Initial therapy for patients with low-grade stromal sarcoma consists of surgical excision of all grossly detectable tumor. Total hysterectomy and bilateral salpingo-oophorectomy should be performed. Radical hysterectomy may improve local control, but there are no clinical data to support this approach, and its applicability is limited because the diagnosis is usually made during or after surgery. For this patient, reoperation with radical removal of the parametria would be difficult, and there are no data to support use of the procedure in this setting. Because lymph node involvement is unusual, lymphadenectomy is of questionable value. The adnexa should be removed because of the propensity for tumor extension into the broad ligament and adnexal structures, as well as the possible stimulating effect of estrogen from retained ovaries on the tumor.

Postoperative therapy is warranted in patients with parametrial extension, as well as in patients with extrapelvic disease. The concurrent use of high-dose progestin and pelvic irradiation seems to be effective therapy. Pelvic irradiation is recommended for recurrent or inadequately excised pelvic disease. Estrogen and progesterone receptors have been identified in high concentrations in some of these tumors, explaining the tumors' responsiveness to progestin therapy. Megestrol acetate, 160 mg/day orally, should be given. Estrogen replacement therapy is contraindicated.

Recurrent or metastatic lesions, especially in the pelvis and lungs, may be amenable to surgical excision. Chemotherapy should be recommended only if disease progresses or is beyond the scope of standard therapy.

Krieger PD, Gusberg, SB. Endolymphatic stromal myosis—a grade 1 endometrial sarcoma. Gynecol Oncol 1973;1:299–313

Lurain JR, Piver MS. Uterine sarcomas: clinical features and management. In: Coppleson M, ed. Gynecologic oncology: fundamental principles and clinical practice. 2nd ed. Edinburgh: Churchill Livingstone, 1992:827–840

Piver MS, Rutledge FN, Copeland L, Webster K, Blumenson L, Suh O. Uterine endolymphatic stromal myosis: a collaborative study. Obstet Gynecol 1984;64:173–178

71

Terminal care for patients with gynecologic cancer

A 56-year-old woman has recurrent cervical cancer. Evaluation reveals involvement of the left pelvic sidewall with ureteral obstruction and bilateral, multiple lung metastases. Chemotherapy is offered. The patient is told that the chance of response is 30–40% and that the average duration of response is 6 months. She declines chemotherapy and requests information about pain control and arrangements for dying at home. Which of the following statements best reflects your obligation to this patient?

(A) You should insist on psychiatric consultation.
(B) You should try to convince her to undergo therapy.
(C) You should support her decision, but warn her of the danger of addiction to narcotics.
* (D) You should inform her that pain can be controlled with narcotics and home hospice care.
(E) You should explain that symptoms can only be controlled in the hospital and encourage her to plan admission.

As physicians, we have devoted most of our working lives to the treatment of disease, and failure to obtain a cure is a difficult situation that threatens our sense of professional competence. We often are not well suited to the emotional difficulties of helping a patient die. Despite our efforts, in some patients therapy will fail and death will result.

For the patient described, death from disease is almost a certainty. Although response rates from combination chemotherapy are in the 30–40% range for patients with recurrent cervical cancer, these responses rarely last more than 6 months. Such patients spend the last months of their lives receiving therapy that has side effects that interfere with quality of life. In view of these considerations, some patients decline therapy. The obligation of the physician is to ensure that the patient understands all of the options and that she has the support needed to carry out her decision. It is preferable for the patient to have at least two opinions as to therapy and to have the option of psychologic support for herself and her family. Although it is not appropriate to force psychiatric consultation, patients usually respond favorably to the explanation that such support is of benefit.

With rare exceptions, the control of pain and other symptoms of terminal cancer is possible with narcotic medications or combinations of narcotic and nonnarcotic preparations. Hospital admission is not required for pain control. Although increasing doses are required and total doses may be large, addiction is not an issue. Patients should be assured that the goal of therapy is control of symptoms with a minimum of side effects.

Early contact should be made with a hospice facility, and the patient and her family should evaluate both home hospice and residence hospice facilities. Advantages of home hospice care include lower cost and the comfort of one's own surroundings. Disadvantages include the need for substantial family involvement in rendering care, which may be troubling to both the patient and the family. Advantages of a residence hospice center are the physical comforts these facilities provide, but a disadvantage is separation of the dying patient from family members. The cost of residence hospice care may be little different from that of a regular hospital facility.

The issue of advance directive and power of attorney should be discussed, and the patient should clearly express in writing her wishes regarding resuscitation and terminal care to the physician and the family. The physician will need to guide the patient with a description of her options and the decision-making process.

Brown JH, Henteleff P, Barakat S, Rowe CJ. Is it normal for terminally ill patients to desire death? Am J Psychiatry 1986;143:208–211

Coyle N, Adelhardt J, Foley KM, Portenoy RK. Character of terminal illness in the advanced cancer patient: pain and other symptoms during the last four weeks of life. Journal of Pain and Symptom Management 1990;5:83–93

Greer DS, Mor V, Morris JN, Sherwood S, Kidder D, Birnbaum H. An alternate in terminal care: results of the National Hospice Study. J Chronic Dis 1986;39:9–26

Havlir D, Brown L, Rousseau GK. Do not resuscitate discussions in a hospital based home care program. J Am Geriatr Soc 1989;37:52–54

Wallston KA, Burger C, Smith RA, Baugher RJ. Comparing the quality of death for hospice and non-hospice cancer patients. Med Care 1988;26:177–182

Youngner SJ, Lewandowski W, McClish DK, Juknialis BW, Coulton C, Bartlett ET. "Do not resuscitate" orders. Incidence and implications in a medical-intensive care unit. JAMA 1985;253:54–57

72

Therapy for vulvar intraepithelial neoplasia

A 63-year-old woman presents with a 2-cm erythematous lesion on the left labium majus. Biopsies of the lesion reveal grade 3 vulvar intraepithelial neoplasia (VIN). The optimal treatment for this patient is

(A) simple vulvectomy
* (B) wide local excision
(C) laser vaporization
(D) topical 5-fluorouracil

The treatment of choice for VIN, grade 3, is surgical excision. Vulvectomy was the recommended treatment in the 1960s but was subsequently abandoned in favor of wide local excision. For this patient, wide local excision is the treatment of choice for several reasons:

- The risk of progression to cancer is low; because progression occurs over a prolonged period of time, radical resections are not required.
- Because the disease tends to be unifocal in older patients, a vulvectomy is unnecessary.
- Wide local excision has better cosmetic results than the more extensive procedure without compromising cure.
- Excision verifies the punch biopsy diagnosis and excludes an early invasive carcinoma.
- Sexual function is not impaired.

Although laser vaporization can be used for the treatment of premalignant lesions of the vulva, it is not the preferred treatment in older women because of the risk of a concomitant early invasive carcinoma.

In patients with VIN, topical 5-fluorouracil has a failure rate exceeding 50%. Variables that influence the likelihood of success include size and accessibility of the lesion, the way in which the medication is prescribed (ie, frequency of application and duration of use), and patient compliance. Local toxicity consisting of an intense chemical vulvovaginitis is the major side effect.

Chafe W, Richards A, Morgan L, Wilkinson E. Unrecognized invasive carcinoma in vulvar intraepithelial neoplasia (VIN). Gynecol Oncol 1988;31:154–162

Roman LD, Mitchell MF, Burke TW, Silva EG. Unsuspected invasive squamous cell carcinoma of the vulva in young women. Gynecol Oncol 1991;41:182–185

Sillman FH, Sedlis A, Boyce JG. A review of lower genital intraepithelial neoplasia and the use of topical 5-fluorouracil. Obstet Gynecol Surv 1985;40:190–220

73

Sacrospinous ligament fixation

A 65-year-old woman, gravida 3, para 3, has third-degree uterine prolapse including prolapse of the uterine cervix to the introitus, a cystocele that protrudes from the introitus with the Valsalva maneuver, and a symptomatic rectocele. Her uterosacral–cardinal ligaments are attenuated and lax. A stress test, with the uterine prolapse reduced by the placement of a pessary, reveals no genuine stress incontinence. After a full discussion of therapeutic options with the patient, you recommend a vaginal hysterectomy with bilateral salpingo-oophorectomy, anterior and posterior colporrhaphy, culdoplasty, and possibly vaginal sacrospinous ligament fixation.

The patient understands the need for each of these procedures except vaginal sacrospinous ligament fixation. To assist her understanding of this procedure, you explain that the sacrospinous ligament fixation

(A) is routinely performed with vaginal hysterectomy for uterine prolapse
(B) is part of the usual culdoplasty procedures when an enterocele is present
* (C) is used when the uterosacral–cardinal support is attenuated
(D) is performed when there is concern about vaginal depth

Numerous techniques to prevent vaginal vault prolapse are described in the literature. In the United States there is renewed interest in the use of sacrospinous ligament fixation to prevent this condition.

Although sacrospinous ligament fixation (Fig. 73-1) has traditionally been regarded as a therapeutic tool used for repair of posthysterectomy vaginal vault prolapse, it may be used as an adjunct to vaginal hysterectomy to

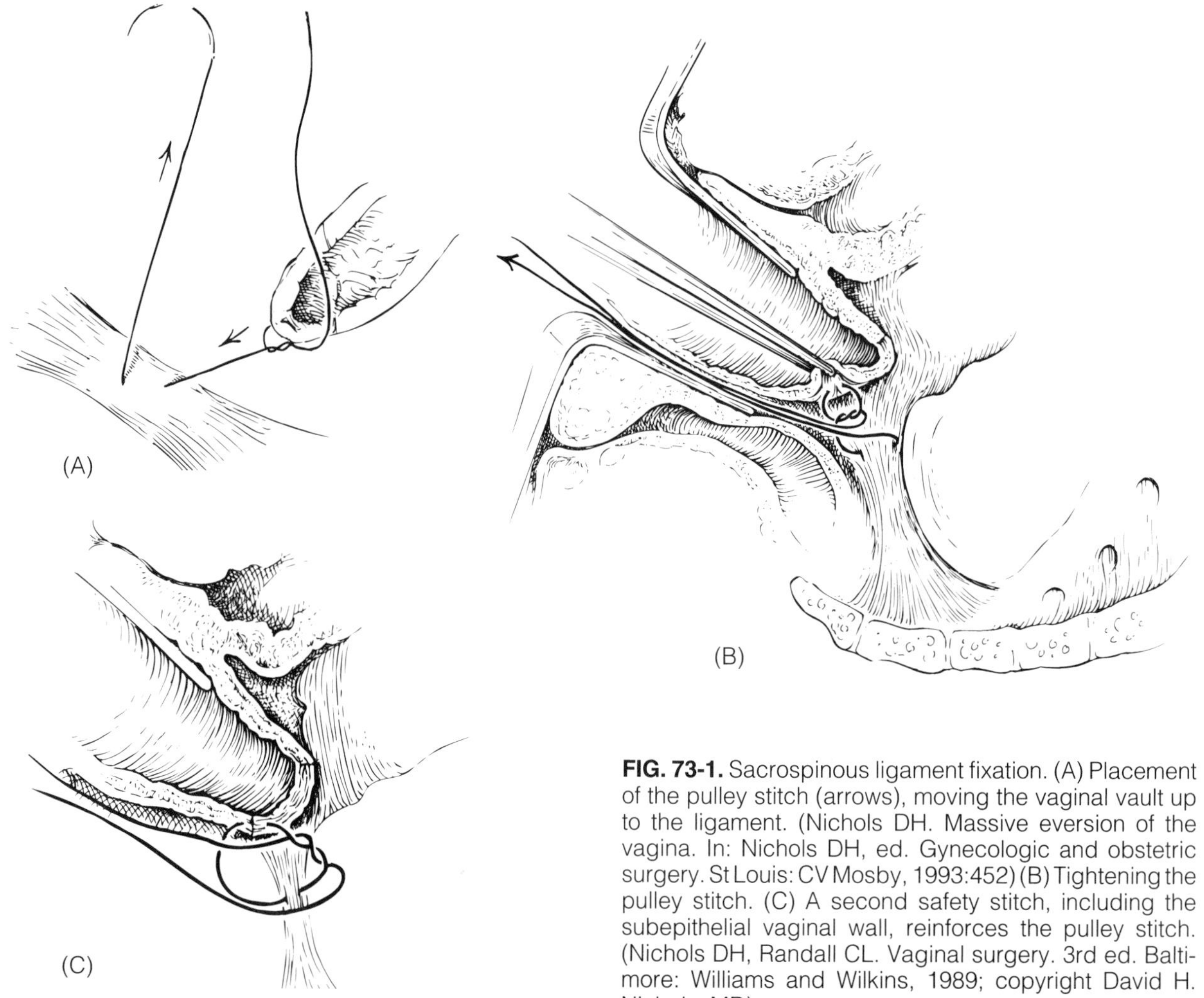

FIG. 73-1. Sacrospinous ligament fixation. (A) Placement of the pulley stitch (arrows), moving the vaginal vault up to the ligament. (Nichols DH. Massive eversion of the vagina. In: Nichols DH, ed. Gynecologic and obstetric surgery. St Louis: CV Mosby, 1993:452) (B) Tightening the pulley stitch. (C) A second safety stitch, including the subepithelial vaginal wall, reinforces the pulley stitch. (Nichols DH, Randall CL. Vaginal surgery. 3rd ed. Baltimore: Williams and Wilkins, 1989; copyright David H. Nichols, MD)

prevent future vaginal vault prolapse. A patient with extensive prolapse who is undergoing a vaginal hysterectomy is a potential candidate for this procedure if deficient pelvic supportive structures (uterosacral–cardinal ligament complex) are present.

Although sacrospinous ligament fixation is not commonly required, the operation is straightforward if there are no adhesions from previous surgery to alter the tissue planes and spaces. A successful procedure results in a well-supported vagina of adequate length with preservation of normal coital ability. Although long-acting polydioxanone or polyglactin 910 (Vicryl) sutures may be used, these sutures are absorbable, and their use may result in recurrence of the vaginal vault prolapse. Nonabsorbable monofilament sutures such as polypropylene (Prolene) are more likely to give permanent tissue support.

During the surgical procedure, any potential space that could later result in enterocele formation should be obliterated. Whether repairing or attempting to prevent an enterocele, the surgical objective is to restore normal anatomy and function. Failure to close a deep cul-de-sac at the time of hysterectomy can lead to the development of such a hernia.

Multiple surgical techniques have been described to obliterate potential and apparent enterocele sacs. Culdoplasty (Fig. 73-2) is an important aspect of a vaginal hysterectomy. A culdoplasty aids in the prevention of a potential or apparent enterocele. Securing the supportive uterosacral–cardinal ligaments to the vaginal angles at the time of hysterectomy assists in maintaining functional vaginal depth.

Sacrospinous ligament fixation is not routine when a culdoplasty is performed. The indications for sacrospinous ligament fixation are distinct and separate.

Preserving functional vaginal depth is an integral part of any pelvic operation. A sacrospinous ligament fixation secures the vaginal apex in its normal anatomic position, but it is not performed to maintain vaginal depth.

Cruikshank SH, Cox DW. Sacrospinous ligament fixation at the time of transvaginal hysterectomy. Am J Obstet Gynecol 1990;162:1611–1619

Cruikshank SH, Pixley RL. Methods of vaginal cuff closure and preservation of vaginal depth during transvaginal hysterectomy. Obstet Gynecol 1987;70:61–63

Nichols DH. Massive eversion of the vagina. In: Nichols DH, ed. Gynecologic and obstetric surgery. St Louis: CV Mosby, 1993:431–464

Porges RF, Smilen SW. Long-term analysis of the surgical management of pelvic support defects. Am J Obstet Gynecol 1994;171:1518–1528

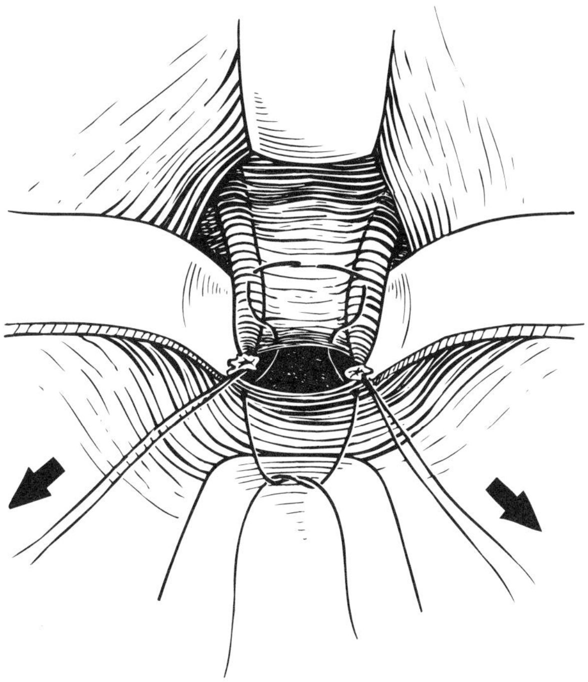

FIG. 73-2. Modified culdoplasty stitch. The enterocele sac has been resected, and a bite of absorbable long-lasting polyglycolic acid–type suture has been placed through the full thickness of the posterior vaginal wall at a spot selected to become the highest point of the reconstructed vaginal vault. Traction is made on the uterosacral ligament pedicles, and suture picks up the cut edge of peritoneum and the peritoneal site of each uterosacral ligament at the level to which the vaginal vault will be fixed. Suture is returned through the peritoneum between the uterosacral ligaments and then through the uterosacral ligament, peritoneum, and vaginal vault of the opposite side. (Nichols DH. Massive eversion of the vagina. In: Nichols DH, ed. Gynecologic and obstetric surgery. St Louis: CV Mosby, 1993:320. Modified from Nichols DH, Randall CL. Vaginal surgery. 3rd ed. Baltimore: Williams and Wilkins, 1989; copyright David H. Nichols, MD)

74

Abnormal wound healing

A 22-year-old woman has undergone an ovarian cystectomy by laparoscopy for removal of a unilateral 6-cm endometrioma. Under which of the following circumstances are adhesions most likely to occur postoperatively?

* (A) The cystic ovary is surgically dissected from the pelvic sidewall, to which it was fixed by scarring.
(B) Both ovaries are incised to locate the endometrioma.
(C) The small bowel is dissected from the medial aspect of the ovary.
(D) The adherent ovary is mobilized, and the ovarian ligament is plicated to distance the ovary from the pelvic sidewall.

The principles of formation of postoperative adhesions are now better defined. Three factors predispose to scar formation:

- The presence of two or more injured surfaces, as opposed to a single injured surface
- Contact of two injured surfaces
- Lack of hemostasis

Medical therapies to prevent scarring have not been consistently effective. The coating of the raw surfaces with expanded polytetrafluoroethylene (Gore-Tex Surgical Membrane) or oxidized regenerated cellulose (Interceed) has been demonstrated to retard adhesion formation in some large clinical studies. However, animal models have failed to confirm such an effect. The role of these therapies has not been defined.

In the laboratory setting, adhesion formation is greatest when two injured surfaces are placed in immobile juxtaposition (Fig. 74-1), with a 59% frequency of adhesions compared with a 13% frequency of adhesions when there is a single injury site (Fig. 74-2). Where there is mobility of the injured organs, and thus distance

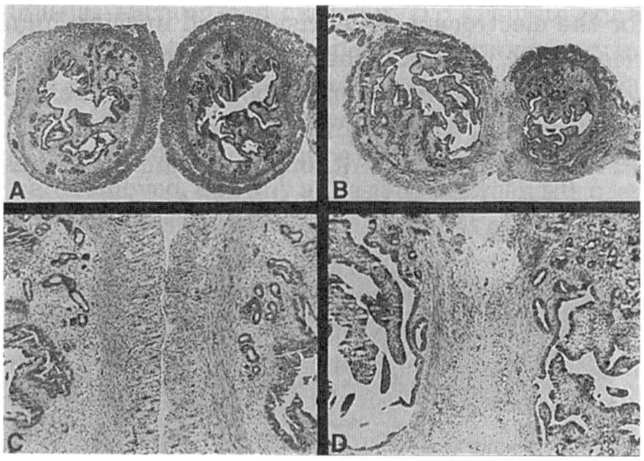

FIG. 74-1. Cross section of uterine horns showing adhesion formation with double-surface injury. Views of the sham-operated control (A) and electrocoagulation-injured (B) uterine horns are shown 7 days postoperatively (magnification ×23). Higher-power photomicrographs of the same horns are shown in panels C and D, respectively (magnification ×68). In the control (A and C), the intact uterine serosa overlying the outer longitudinal and inner circular uterine muscle layers are obvious. When adhesions are present (B and D), the horns are fused by a connective tissue matrix composed of tissue repair cells. The deposition of collagen indicates the permanence of the adhesion. (From Haney AF, Doty E. The formation of coalescing peritoneal adhesions requires injury to both contacting peritoneal surfaces. Fertil Steril 1994;61:772. Reproduced with permission of the publisher, the American Society for Reproductive Medicine [The American Fertility Society])

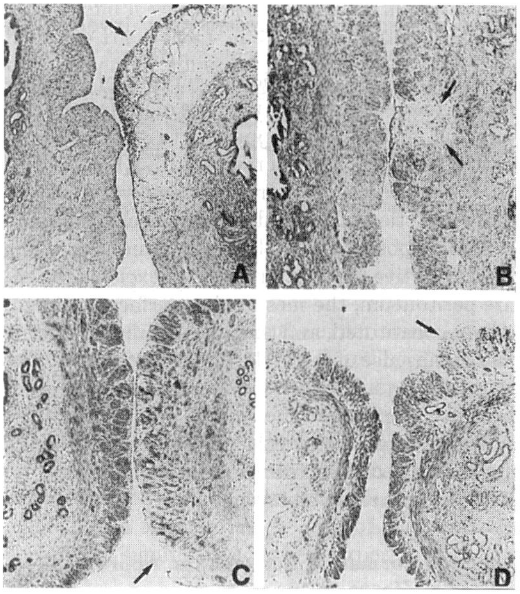

FIG. 74-2. Cross section of uterine horns showing lack of adhesions with single surface injury. Arrows point to the injury on each uterine horn 3 days after injury (magnification ×68). For comparative purposes, the opposing non-injured control uterine horn site is shown on the left in each photomicrograph. The electrocautery injury is shown in panel A; notably, the injury extends throughout the entire muscular wall. In the excision injury (B), the defect is replaced with tissue repair cells and a connective tissue matrix without any intervening muscular wall. In the incision (C) and scrape (D) injuries, the histologic disruption is confined to the surface except for edema in the area under the injury site. (From Haney AF, Doty E. The formation of coalescing peritoneal adhesions requires injury to both contacting peritoneal surfaces. Fertil Steril 1994;61:772. Reproduced with permission of the publisher, the American Society for Reproductive Medicine [The American Fertility Society])

between the structures, the incidence of adhesions is decreased to 3%. The role of hemostasis in protecting against adhesion formation is less clear. It is prudent, therefore, to ensure that hemostasis is absolute at the conclusion of the surgery.

Based on these principles, the first setting described is the most likely to result in scar formation. Here the endometrioma is adherent to the pelvic sidewall, and the ovary is surgically dissected from that location with the creation of two raw surfaces. The ovary will return to its original position, to oppose the two injured surfaces.

In the second situation described, both ovaries are incised, there is distance between the incisions, and the raw surfaces are mobile. In the third setting, the enterolysis confers mobility on the small bowel and separates the denuded surfaces. In the final setting, plication of the ovarian ligament elevates the ovary from the pelvic sidewall to distance the raw surfaces. In each of these three instances, the risk of postoperative adhesion formation is reduced by the distance between the incisions and the mobility of the organs. If adhesion reformation is likely, adhesion-reducing strategies should be considered.

Haney AF, Doty E. Comparison of the peritoneal cells elicited by oxidized regenerated cellulose (Interceed) and expanded polytetrafluoroethylene (Gore-Tex Surgical Membrane) in a murine model. Am J Obstet Gynecol 1992;166:1137–1149

Haney AF, Doty E. The formation of coalescing peritoneal adhesions requires injury to both contacting peritoneal surfaces. Fertil Steril 1994;61:767–775

Ryan GB, Grobéty J, Majno G. Mesothelial injury and recovery. Am J Pathol 1973;71:93–112

75

Reducing the risk of ovarian cancer

A 36-year-old woman, para 2, is concerned about her risk of ovarian cancer. She does not desire any more children. Her mother and maternal aunt died of the disease in their sixties. She has two older sisters who are alive and well. She is a nonsmoker. You advise her that the best management is

(A) prophylactic bilateral salpingo-oophorectomy
(B) prophylactic hysterectomy and bilateral salpingo-oophorectomy
* (C) oral contraceptives
(D) periodic serial tumor markers
(E) periodic endovaginal sonography

One in 70 women (1.4%) will develop ovarian cancer in her lifetime. Annual incidence rates increase with age. Several factors may increase the risk of ovarian cancer, including nulliparity, low parity, infertility, early menarche, late menopause, late first pregnancy, and a family history of ovarian cancer.

Familial ovarian cancer usually refers to the hereditary ovarian cancer syndromes as well as the sporadic occurrence of ovarian cancer in families. The hereditary ovarian cancer syndrome includes 1) site-specific ovarian cancer syndrome, 2) hereditary breast–ovarian cancer syndrome, and 3) hereditary nonpolyposis colorectal cancer (Lynch syndrome II). The average age at diagnosis of ovarian cancer in the general population is 59 years. Women with ovarian cancer from families with one of these syndromes tend to be 7–14 years younger at diagnosis. Hereditary ovarian cancer syndrome may involve an autosomal dominant inheritance pattern. Thus, a woman from a family with an ovarian cancer syndrome may have a lifetime probability of developing ovarian cancer as high as 50%. Such hereditary ovarian cancer syndromes are rare. Because this patient has only one first-degree relative and one second-degree relative with ovarian cancer, she does not meet the criteria for a hereditary ovarian cancer syndrome.

About 5–7% of women with ovarian cancer report a family history of ovarian cancer, and of these women, over 90% have only one relative with the disease. For women at age 35 who have two or three relatives with ovarian cancer (one first-degree relative and/or one or more second-degree relatives), the lifetime probability is 7.2%, compared with a lifetime probability of 1.6% in a 35-year-old woman without a family history of ovarian cancer (Table 75-1).

A 7% lifetime probability of ovarian cancer may motivate some women to request prophylactic oophorectomy. However, the potential morbidity and mortality of surgery, the risks associated with early menopause, and the need for long-term hormone replacement therapy will outweigh the risk of ovarian cancer for most women. Thus, a recommendation for bilateral salpingo-oophorectomy with or without a hys-

TABLE 75-1. Lifetime Probability of Ovarian Cancer and Life Expectancy in Women With Familial Ovarian Cancer

Family History of Ovarian Cancer	Estimated Odds Ratio (95% Confidence Interval)	Lifetime Probability of Ovarian Cancer in a 35-Year-Old Woman (%)*	Life Expectancy of a 35-Year-Old Woman (y)†
No family history of ovarian cancer	1.0 (comparison group)	1.6	82.4
One relative with ovarian cancer	3.1 (2.2–4.4)‡	5.0	82.1
One first-degree relative with ovarian cancer	3.1 (2.1–4.5)§	5.0	82.1
Two or three relatives with ovarian cancer	4.6 (1.1–18.4)¶	7.2	81.8
Hereditary ovarian cancer syndrome	Not available	50	74.7

* Probabilities are based on surveillance, epidemiology, and end-results cancer statistics and estimated odds ratios.

† Probabilities are based on surveillance, epidemiology, and end-results cancer statistics, United States Department of Health and Human Services vital statistics, and estimated odds ratios.

‡ Probabilities are based on pooled odds ratios from seven case–control studies with a family history of one first- or one second-degree relative.

§ Probabilities are based on pooled odds ratios from five case–control studies with a family history of one first-degree relative with ovarian cancer.

¶ Probabilities are calculated from cancer and steroid hormone study data by Schildkraut and Thompson; two or three relatives refers to one first-degree relative and/or one or more second-degree relatives.

Kerlikowske K, Brown JS, Grady DG. Should women with familial ovarian cancer undergo prophylactic oophorectomy? Reprinted with permission from The American College of Obstetricians and Gynecologists (Obstetrics and Gynecology 1992, 80, 703)

terectomy may result in substituting one disease for another (ie, ovarian cancer for osteoporosis or heart disease, or both).

A recent large prospective cohort study confirmed the protective effect of tubal sterilization against ovarian cancer. The mechanism of protection is unknown. A weaker association was noted for hysterectomy.

Administration of high-dose (>50 μg) oral contraceptives has been demonstrated to decrease the ovarian cancer risk by 40–50%. Lower-dose oral contraceptives appear to have a similar protective effect, although fewer studies have evaluated these pills. Oral contraceptives decrease gonadotropins and inhibit ovulation. Nulliparous women appear to receive more protection than do multiparous women. The protective effect appears to increase with duration of use and to persist for 10–15 years after oral contraceptives have been discontinued.

Some experts have recommended yearly or twice yearly screening of patients with serum CA 125 determination, vaginal ultrasonography, and color-flow Doppler imaging of the ovarian vascular tree. These screening strategies are expensive, and their efficacy is unproven.

American College of Obstetricians and Gynecologists. Prophylactic bilateral oophorectomy to prevent epithelial carcinoma. ACOG Criteria Set 2. Washington, DC: ACOG, 1994

The Cancer and Steroid Hormone Study of the Centers for Disease Control and the National Institute of Child Health and Human Development. The reduction in risk of ovarian cancer associated with oral-contraceptive use. N Engl J Med 1987;316:650–655

Hankinson SE, Hunter DJ, Colditz GA, Willett WC, Stampfer MJ, Rosner B, et al. Tubal ligation, hysterectomy, and risk of ovarian cancer: a prospective study. JAMA 1993;270:2813–2818

Kerlikowske K, Brown JS, Grady DG. Should women with familial ovarian cancer undergo prophylactic oophorectomy? Obstet Gynecol 1992;80:700–707

Runowicz CD. Advances in the screening and treatment of ovarian cancer. CA Cancer J Clin 1992;42:327–349

76

Needlestick injury

A 23-year-old woman who is antibody positive for human immunodeficiency virus type I (HIV-I) is undergoing an emergency laparotomy for a ruptured ectopic pregnancy. During the surgical procedure, the surgeon sustains a suture needle puncture injury. Which of the following statements is true regarding this injury during gynecologic surgery?

(A) Reported percutaneous injury rates range from 5–25%.
(B) The risk of HIV-I acquisition as a result is 0.3–0.4%.
(C) Prompt administration of zidovudine (Retrovir) will kill the HIV-I virus.
* (D) Routine surveillance for HIV-I should be performed at baseline, 6 weeks, 3 months, and 6 months after the exposure.

Most women who acquire HIV infection do so through heterosexual transmission between the ages of 20 and 54 years, the time span during which most elective and emergency pelvic surgical procedures are performed. Reported percutaneous injury rates during gynecologic surgical procedures range from 2–10%. The gynecologic surgeon's risk of acquiring infection by exposure to blood or other body fluids in the operating room is low. Nevertheless, universal precautions must be practiced. Up to 85% of operating room blood contacts are avoidable by the use of additional barriers. For example, double gloving reduces the risk of exposure to the patient's blood.

There is a definite risk of acquisition of HIV-I as a result of exposure to patient blood by needlestick injury. The highest likelihood of antibody conversion is 0.3–0.4% and occurs after hollow, not solid, needle injury. Surgical injuries occur primarily in the distal forefinger or thumb of the nondominant hand of the surgeon or first assistant. These injuries are usually from sticks with a solid needle and result when the fingers are used to guide needle placement. Risk factors for skin injury include prolonged operating time, use of large numbers of sutures during the case, emergency surgery, and a large amount of blood loss.

Management of a health care worker with percutaneous occupational exposure to HIV-I is controversial. The Clinical Center of the National Institutes of Health suggests offering and providing zidovudine to health care workers within 4 hours of parenteral exposure as an option. Although zidovudine inhibits HIV-I replication, it is not virucidal. In one report, there were no seroconversions in over 160 health care workers who took zidovudine after a parenteral exposure.

Animal data do not indicate that zidovudine will prevent seroconversion. In animal studies, large inocula were generally used and were given intravenously; these data may not be applicable to a small, nonintravenous inoculum. Failure to demonstrate efficacy of zidovudine in a primate model is, however, consistent with the hypothesis that the drug is not an effective chemoprophylactic agent for HIV-I in humans. Zidovudine chemoprophylaxis failures in humans have been documented in at least 16 anecdotal case reports. Recognizing the controversy, a health care worker who has sustained a percutaneous injury could elect to take zidovudine until it is known whether the patient is HIV positive.

Many health care workers who begin taking prophylactic zidovudine choose to discontinue it because of side effects, the most common of which are headache, fatigue, sleep disturbance, and gastrointestinal complaints. Some of these symptoms may be associated with the stress that accompanies parenteral exposure in a health care worker, who is knowledgeable about the potential sequelae.

Zidovudine is metabolized by glucuronidation in the liver and is eliminated primarily by renal excretion. Anemia and granulocytopenia may occur. For these reasons, if zidovudine is taken, complete blood count and liver function tests are recommended biweekly to detect toxicity or an indication for reducing the dose or discontinuing treatment. Arguments against the routine use of an expensive agent without proven efficacy and with uncertain long-term toxicity in otherwise healthy adults have been posed.

After exposure, routine surveillance of health care workers with HIV-I testing should be performed at baseline, 6 weeks, 3 months, and 6 months. In addition, health care workers taking zidovudine should undergo testing again at 12 months. Theoretically, delayed seroconversion may result from zidovudine prophylaxis.

Gerberding JL, Henderson DK. Management of occupational exposures to bloodborne pathogens: hepatitis B virus, hepatitis C virus, and human immunodeficiency virus. Clin Infect Dis 1992;14:1179–1185

Gerberding JL, Littell C, Tarkington A, Brown A, Schecter WP. Risk of exposure of surgical personnel to patients' blood during surgery at San Francisco General Hospital. N Engl J Med 1990;322:1788–1793

Panlilio AL, Foy DR, Edwards JR, Bell DM, Welch BA, Parrish CM, et al. Blood contacts during surgical procedures. JAMA 1991;265:1533–1537

Tokars JI, Bell DM, Culver DH, Marcus R, Mendelson MH, Sloan EP, et al. Percutaneous injuries during surgical procedures. JAMA 1992;267:2899–2904

77

Complications of molar pregnancy

A 16-year-old primigravid woman presents 14 weeks from her last menstrual period with nausea and vomiting of 2 weeks' duration and the recent onset of heavy uterine bleeding. Physical examination reveals a 20-week-size uterus, no fetal heart sounds, and a blood pressure of 170/100 mm Hg. A pelvic ultrasound examination is consistent with the diagnosis of complete hydatidiform mole and bilateral 8-cm ovarian cysts. A complete blood count and serum chemistries are within normal limits except for hemoglobin of 8.2 g/dl and hematocrit of 25%. The serum human chorionic gonadotropin level is 160,000 mIU/ml. Thyroid function tests are normal. A preoperative chest X-ray is normal.

At the time of suction evacuation of the uterus, blood loss is estimated to be 400 ml. Two units of packed red blood cells and 2,000 ml of crystalloid are administered during and shortly after the procedure. Thirty minutes later in the recovery room the patient is found to be extremely dyspneic with cough. Her blood pressure is 180/100 mm Hg. Examination reveals tachycardia, tachypnea, distended jugular veins, and extensive rales throughout both lung fields. A chest X-ray and arterial blood gases are ordered. Your initial step in managing this patient is

(A) Swan–Ganz catheter placement
(B) digoxin therapy
(C) magnesium sulfate therapy
* (D) oxygen and diuretic therapy
(E) administration of heparin

Many potential causes of respiratory distress are associated with evacuation of a hydatidiform mole, including trophoblastic deportation, high-output congestive heart failure caused by anemia or hyperthyroidism, preeclampsia, or iatrogenic fluid overload. This syndrome of acute respiratory compromise after evacuation of a molar pregnancy usually has multiple contributing factors and occurs in patients with already established hemodynamic instability or recognizable risk factors.

These patients have an increased plasma volume and decreased erythrocyte volume that, when combined with the vaginal bleeding most often associated with molar pregnancy, can lead to marked anemia. In a patient with a molar pregnancy who presents with tachycardia, bleeding, and a decreased hematocrit, administration of blood or plasma expanders may overload an already expanded vascular space and precipitate acute pulmonary edema. The need for blood replacement may also be overestimated because of the large volume of sanguinous molar tissue obtained during evacuation.

Other factors that may contribute to the hemodynamic complexities of molar pregnancy are hyperthyroidism and preeclampsia. Thyrotoxicosis, which is present in up to 10% of patients with hydatidiform mole, produces an additional metabolic demand with a rise in heart rate and can be associated with high-output cardiac failure. In preeclampsia, which complicates molar pregnancy in 25% of patients, there is increased peripheral resistance, decreased blood volume, decreased glomerular filtration rate, and retention of sodium and water; all of these factors contribute to the cumulative cardiovascular stress.

Massive trophoblastic embolization can presumably lead to acute cardiorespiratory embarrassment. Some degree of trophoblastic embolization probably follows evacuation of most hydatidiform moles, but it rarely causes severe pulmonary compromise. Only scanty amounts of trophoblastic cells have been recovered from the pulmonary arteries of patients undergoing molar evacuation. Volume overload is important in the etiology of pulmonary edema in these patients.

Factors that are most likely to predict acute pulmonary complications of molar pregnancy—besides anemia, preeclampsia, and hyperthyroidism—are a large uterus and theca–lutein cysts. Pulmonary complications are observed in one fourth of patients with a uterus greater than 16 weeks of gestational size. Preevacuation identification of this high-risk group will allow for appropriate planning and management, including arterial blood gas determination, central venous pressure monitoring, and judicious administration of fluids and oxytocin.

The mainstays of therapy in patients with respiratory distress and evidence of fluid overload in the immediate postevacuation period are oxygen, usually administrated by nasal cannula, and intravenous diuretics, with or without morphine. Intake and output should be carefully monitored. Chest X-ray and arterial blood gases should be obtained to document pulmonary edema and the level of hypoxemia. Ventilatory assistance and invasive cardiac monitoring are rarely required. Digoxin therapy for cardiac failure or treatment of preeclampsia with magnesium sulfate is not indicated for this patient. Although the diagnosis of acute pulmonary embolus from a deep vein thrombosis may be considered, the most likely diagnosis in this clinical situation is trophoblastic embolization or fluid overload, or both. Heparin should not be administered without further documentation of a deep vein thrombosis as a probable cause.

Most patients respond rapidly to administration of oxygen and diuretics, with rapid clearing of their chest X-ray and resolution of hypoxemia. Patients with pulmonary complications of molar pregnancy are up to five times more likely to develop postmolar gestational trophoblastic tumor requiring chemotherapy. Prophylactic chemotherapy may, therefore, be considered for this group of patients in the immediate postevacuation period.

Cotton DB, Bernstein SG, Read JA, Benedetti TJ, D'Ablaing G, Miller FC, et al. Hemodynamic observations in evacuation of molar pregnancy. Am J Obstet Gynecol 1980:138:6–10

Hankins GDV, Wendel GD, Snyder RR, Cunningham FG. Trophoblastic embolization during molar evacuation: central hemodynamic observations. Obstet Gynecol 1987;69:368–372

Kohorn EI. Clinical management and the neoplastic sequelae of trophoblastic embolization associated with hydatidiform mole. Obstet Gynecol Surv 1987; 42:484–488

Twiggs LB, Morrow CP, Schlaerth JB. Acute pulmonary complications of molar pregnancy. Am J Obstet Gynecol 1979;135:189–194

78

Patient selection for vaginal hysterectomy

A 47-year-old nulliparous woman who is 50% above ideal body weight presents with increasing menometrorrhagia unresponsive to medical management. Pelvic examination indicates a 12-week-size, irregular uterus; adnexal structures cannot be adequately assessed. Pelvic ultrasonography reveals multiple uterine leiomyomata, including several in the submucosa, and a 5-cm cystic and solid left adnexal mass persistent through two menstrual cycles. Endometrial sampling reveals proliferative endometrium. A hysterectomy is planned. The most compelling reason to choose abdominal over vaginal hysterectomy for this patient is

(A) nulliparity
(B) obesity
(C) uterine leiomyomata
* (D) adnexal mass
(E) abnormal uterine bleeding

Vaginal hysterectomy offers several advantages over abdominal hysterectomy:

- The opportunity to perform hysterectomy with less bowel manipulation
- The opportunity to correct vaginal wall relaxation
- Less compromise of pulmonary function
- Avoidance of complications of abdominal incision including infection, incisional hernia, and dehiscence
- Decreased postoperative pain and discomfort
- Earlier ambulation and return of bowel function
- Less intraabdominal postoperative adhesion formation

If the therapeutic aim can be safely and effectively accomplished with a vaginal approach, it is preferred over an abdominal hysterectomy. However, abdominal hysterectomy should be performed if any of the following are present:

- Suspected adnexal pathology, either benign or malignant
- Tuboovarian abscesses
- Extensive endometriosis involving the ovaries or with cul-de-sac obliteration
- Need for exploration of the abdomen

Nulliparity and absence of uterine descensus may make vaginal hysterectomy technically more difficult but are not contraindications to vaginal hysterectomy per se. Obesity complicates both vaginal hysterectomy and abdominal hysterectomy, but in an obese patient, vaginal hysterectomy may be easier to perform than abdominal hysterectomy. Removing a large leiomyomatous uterus vaginally may also be more challenging surgically, and some surgeons may prefer to use an abdominal approach. However, experienced surgeons may remove large uteri vaginally using a variety of morcellation techniques or preoperative gonadotropin-releasing hormone analogue therapy to reduce uterine size.

It is often possible to remove an ovary after vaginal hysterectomy, but if ovarian cancer is suspected, vaginal hysterectomy is contraindicated and an abdominal approach should be undertaken. As an exception, the vaginal route may be used if the adnexal mass can be completely and safely excised laparoscopically before proceeding with vaginal hysterectomy.

It is imperative to evaluate abnormal uterine bleeding before surgery, but the presence of abnormal bleeding is not a contraindication to vaginal hysterectomy.

Dicker RC, Greenspan JR, Strauss LT, Cowart MR, Scally MJ, Peterson HB, et al. Complications of abdominal and vaginal hysterectomy among women of reproductive age in the United States. Am J Obstet Gynecol 1982;144:841–848

Kovac SR. Intramyometrial coring as an adjunct to vaginal hysterectomy. Obstet Gynecol 1986;67:131–136

Thompson JD. Hysterectomy. In: Thompson JD, Rock JA, eds. Te Linde's operative gynecology. 7th ed. Philadelphia: JB Lippincott, 1992:663–738

79

Preoperative evaluation of the elderly patient

A 72-year-old woman is diagnosed with prolapse of the vaginal vault. She underwent an abdominal hysterectomy 15 years ago without complication. She currently lives alone and does not have any complaints or symptoms. General physical examination reveals age-appropriate findings. Surgical correction of the vaginal prolapse is planned.

The test most likely to demonstrate an abnormality that might require further evaluation or alter the perioperative management of this patient is

(A) chest X-ray
(B) pulmonary function tests
(C) coagulation studies
* (D) electrocardiography (ECG)
(E) serum albumin

Surgery can be performed for both benign and cancer-related gynecologic procedures in elderly patients without excessive short-term complications. Advanced age alone is a poor predictor of surgical risk and is not a reason to withhold surgery. In patients of advanced age, a thorough history and physical examination will identify loss of physiologic reserve that accompanies the aging process and will also guide the selection of preoperative tests.

As increasing scrutiny is placed on the cost-effectiveness of laboratory tests, it is important to consider how often these tests result in a reduction of risk and how often they prompt a change in the patient management plan.

A chest X-ray is routinely ordered for most preoperative patients, although it rarely provides any information that prompts a change in the perioperative management. However, it has been argued that this test is a useful baseline for future comparison, particularly in patients with a malignancy.

Pulmonary function tests have not been shown to predict postoperative complications even in the presence of an abnormal physical examination, dyspnea, productive cough, or a history of significant cigarette smoking. However, pulmonary function tests may provide a useful baseline against which treatments to optimize respiratory function may be compared.

In the absence of a history of susceptibility to bruising or a bleeding disorder, tests of the coagulation system are invariably normal and do not add to the preoperative evaluation.

Preoperative ECG is indicated for this elderly patient, who is at increased risk of an arrhythmia and silent ischemia because of her age. One study found that only 21% of general surgical patients over the age of 65 had a normal preoperative electrocardiogram. Abnormalities detected on screening ECG often prompt further evaluation, such as with a thallium scan, echocardiography, or cardiac catheterization.

Although serum albumin may be an indirect indicator of nutritional status, it is not helpful in predicting a patient's ability to tolerate surgery.

Capen CV. Gynecologic surgery: preoperative evaluation. Clin Obstet Gynecol 1988;31:673–685

Cheng EY, Wang-Cheng RM. Impact of aging on preoperative evaluation. J Clin Anesth 1991;3:324–343

Johnson JC. Surgical assessment in the elderly. Geriatrics 1988;43:83–90

Lawton FG, Hacker NF. Surgery for invasive gynecologic cancer in the elderly female population. Obstet Gynecol 1990;76:287–289

80

Management of cervical intraepithelial neoplasia in pregnancy

A 25-year-old nulliparous woman presents to you for the first time at 16 weeks of gestation. During the course of her prenatal evaluation, a Pap test is taken, with the report of high-grade squamous intraepithelial lesion (SIL). Colposcopy reveals an abnormal transformation zone showing coarse punctation and mosaicism, with the limits of the lesion extending into the endocervical canal. Several colposcopically directed biopsies confirm high-grade SIL. The most appropriate management is

(A) cold knife cone biopsy
* (B) repeat colposcopy and Pap test during each trimester
(C) repeat colposcopy and biopsy during each trimester
(D) loop electrode excision of the transformation zone
(E) pregnancy termination followed by definitive treatment

Reports of high-grade SIL or an invasive squamous cell carcinoma of the cervix in pregnancy are rare. In a study of 95,000 deliveries, the prevalence of SIL was 0.14% and that of invasive squamous cell carcinoma of the cervix was 0.07%.

Cytologic evaluation in pregnancy can be difficult because of immature metaplasia and the acute inflammatory reaction normally seen during pregnancy. As a result, benign changes may be erroneously interpreted as atypia or dysplasia. Conversely, epithelial changes associated with pregnancy can sometimes obscure the diagnosis of SIL in Pap tests. Invasive carcinoma is not always clinically apparent; therefore, multiple punch biopsies may be necessary to rule out the presence of invasion. As pregnancy progresses, however, even a transformation zone that extends into the endocervical canal early in gestation becomes totally visible colposcopically because of the physiologic eversion of the cervix during advancing stages of gestation.

Progression of high-grade SIL to invasive carcinoma takes years. Therefore, once invasion has been ruled out in a woman who is pregnant, conservative management can be undertaken, and definitive treatment can be deferred until completion of the pregnancy. Neither a cold knife biopsy nor a loop electrode excision procedure is necessary to rule out invasion except under extraordinary circumstances. These procedures may cause extensive hemorrhage. Multiple colposcopically directed biopsies after the initial abnormal Pap test suffice. Because of the increased vascularity of the cervix during pregnancy, cervical biopsies should be carefully performed and limited to the most suspicious areas. Accordingly, after the diagnosis has been confirmed histologically, repeat colposcopy and Pap tests at each trimester are appropriate management.

After delivery, this patient should be further evaluated. Therapy may include cone biopsy or loop electrode excision of the transformation zone, depending on the results of colposcopic examination.

Averette HE, Nasser N, Yankow SL, Little WA. Cervical conization in pregnancy: analysis of 180 operations. Am J Obstet Gynecol 1970;106:543–549

Boutselis JG. Intraepithelial carcinoma of the cervix associated with pregnancy. Obstet Gynecol 1972;40:657–666

Campion MJ, Sedlacek TV. Colposcopy in pregnancy. Obstet Gynecol Clin North Am 1993;20:153–163

DePetrillo AD, Townsend DE, Morrow CP, Lickrish GM, DiSaia PJ, Roy M. Colposcopic evaluation of the abnormal Papanicolaou test in pregnancy. Am J Obstet Gynecol 1975;121:441–445

81

Management of rectal incontinence

One year ago, a healthy 24-year-old woman underwent a low-outlet forceps delivery of a 3,800-g infant over a midline episiotomy with a third-degree laceration. Her postpartum course was uncomplicated.

When the patient is seen for her annual gynecologic examination, she reports an inability to suppress the escape of flatus and liquid stool. Digital examination reveals voluntary contraction of the external anal sphincter muscles. On contraction of the puborectalis muscle, there is forward displacement of the perineal body.

In this patient, the appropriate surgical procedure is repair of

(A) the anococcygeal raphe
(B) the puborectalis muscle and the associated posterior anal angle
* (C) the external anal sphincter
(D) the transverse perineal muscle

Anal continence is a function of anatomy and neuromuscular function. In the absence of an anatomic or neuromuscular problem, continence may be impaired by dietary habits, lack of social training, insufficient exercise, medication, and diverticulosis.

Anatomic alterations of the external anal sphincter causing incontinence of flatus and stool are acquired after obstetric injuries, trauma, and prior anorectal surgery. In most series, obstetric injury is the leading cause of anal incontinence. The frequency of anal incontinence after vaginal delivery has not been firmly established, in part because the diagnosis is related to the diligence with which it is sought. After their first delivery, 13% of women develop incontinence or urgency, and 30% have structural changes of the anus. Episiotomy, the use of forceps, and a long, difficult labor are cited as predisposing factors. In one study of 38 women who underwent primary repair of third-degree lacerations, 14 were incontinent of stool or flatus 3 months after delivery. In a separate study of 34 women who underwent repairs of third-degree laceration, 50% complained of urgency or incontinence of stool or flatus.

The most effective technique to correct acquired anal incontinence is repair of the external anal sphincter muscles (Fig. 81-1). A circumlinear incision is made in the skin overlying the perineal body. By using sharp dissection, the external anal sphincter and scar tissue are mobilized. The lateral edges of the external sphincter are dissected so that reapproximation is performed without tension on the suture lines. The midline scar tissue is dissected and divided in the midline so that the edges of the cut scar can be used in the repair. The perineal body is reapproximated, and the sphincter is repaired.

Anal continence is a function of the triple-loop mechanism, which includes an upper, middle, and lower loop. The *upper loop* is created by the anococcygeal raphe, a tendonlike structure that connects the posterior rectum to the coccyx. It is seldom injured in obstetric trauma and does not contribute to incontinence in this patient. The *middle loop* of the triple-loop mechanism is created by the puborectalis muscle and is responsible for continence of solid stool. Contraction of the puborectalis muscle pulls the posterior rectal wall toward the symphysis pubis, creating a palpable posterior anal angle on rectal examination. This patient is not incontinent of solid stool, and forward pull of the puborectalis muscle is noted on physical examination; therefore, repair of the puborectalis muscle is not indicated. The *lower loop* of the triple-loop mechanism is formed by the external anal sphincter and is responsible for continence of flatus and liquid stool.

The transverse perineal muscles help achieve continence of flatus but do not contribute to the continence of stool. Because this patient is incontinent of both flatus and liquid stool, reapproximation of only the transverse perineal muscles would not correct her symptoms.

Fleshman JW, Peters WR, Shemesh EI, Fry RD, Kodner IJ. Anal sphincter reconstruction: anterior overlapping muscle repair. Dis Colon Rectum 1991; 34:739–743

Gibbs DH, Hooks VH III. Overlapping sphincteroplasty for acquired anal incontinence. South Med J 1993;86:1376–1380

Kamm MA. Obstetric damage and faecal incontinence. Lancet 1994;344:730–733

Khanduja KS, Yamashita HJ, Wise WE Jr, Aguilar PS, Hartmann RF. Delayed repair of obstetric injuries of the anorectum and vagina: a stratified approach. Dis Colon Rectum 1994;37:344–349

Moore FA. Anal incontinence: a reappraisal. Obstet Gynecol 1973;41:483–493

Shafik A. A concept of the anatomy of the anal sphincter mechanism and the physiology of defecation. Dis Colon Rectum 1987;30:970–982

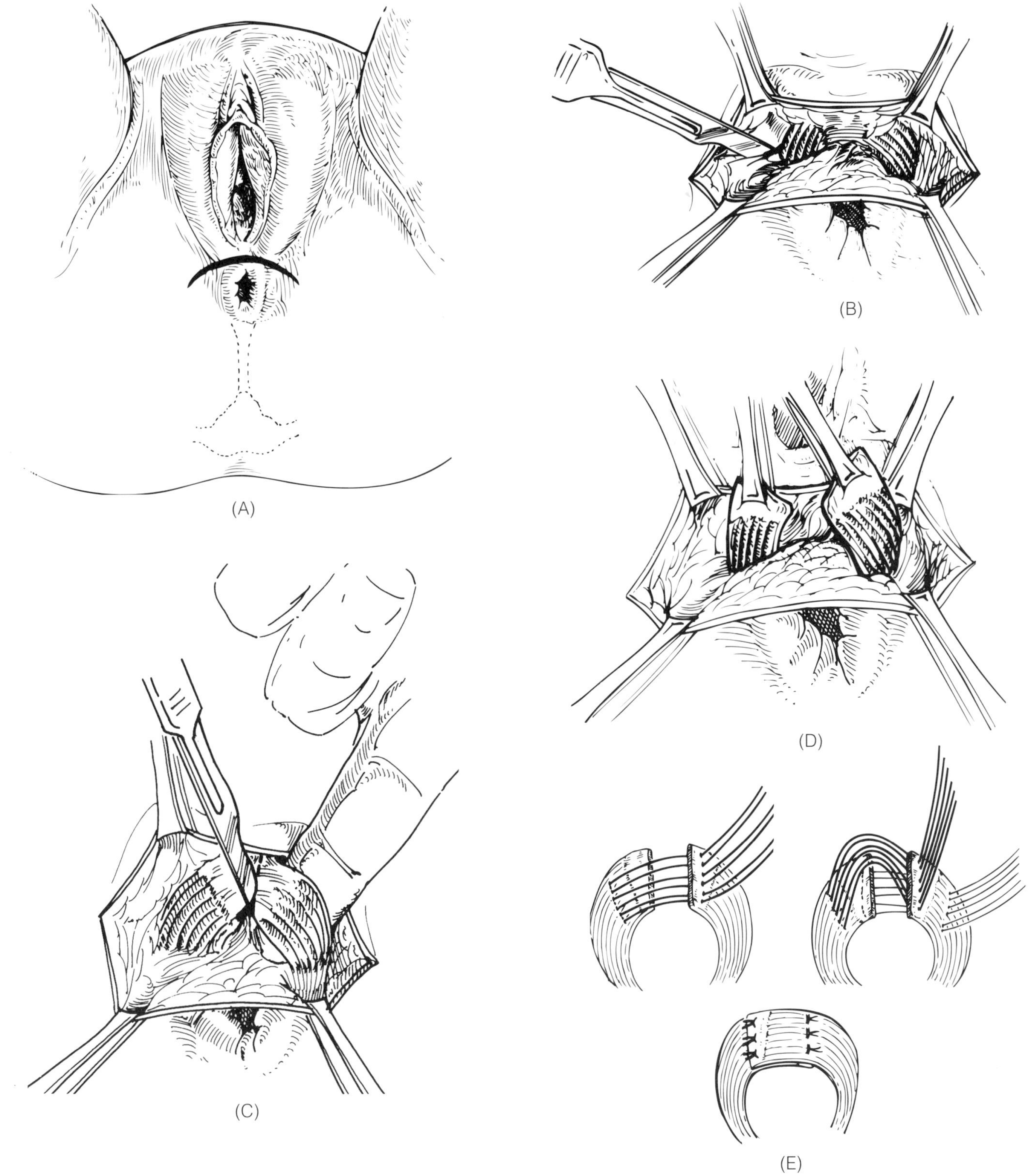

FIG. 81-1. Overlapping sphincter repair for anal incontinence. (A) The perineum before repair, showing thinning of the perineal body separating the anus from the vaginal introitus. Circumanal incision in the transverse midline projects to both right and left lateral perianal areas. (B) Skin flaps are raised superiorly and inferiorly, and an adequate length of muscle is dissected free to allow overlap without tension. (C) Scar of the muscle remaining in the anterior midline is divided. (D) Each portion is clamped with an Allis clamp. The scar on the ends of the muscle is preserved to help hold sutures. (E) Muscle ends are overlapped, and two rows of three horizontal mattress sutures (2-0 polyglactin 910 [Vicryl]) are placed. (Gibbs DH, Hooks VH III. Overlapping sphincteroplasty for acquired anal incontinence. Reprinted by permission from the SOUTHERN MEDICAL JOURNAL [86, 1377–1378, 1993])

82

Complications of laparoscopic surgery

In a patient undergoing laparoscopic tubal ligation, return of gas is audible through the Veress needle immediately after its insertion. After intraabdominal placement of the laparoscope, a puncture site is noted in the greater curvature of the stomach. The puncture site is not bleeding, and there is no visible drainage. The stomach is grossly distended. The anesthesiologist acknowledges that an endotracheal tube was not positioned and that the patient is being ventilated by mask. After intubation with an endotracheal tube and placement of a nasogastric tube, the most appropriate management is

* (A) observation
(B) single-layer laparoscopic closure with nonabsorbable suture
(C) laparotomy with single-layer interrupted closure with nonabsorbable suture
(D) laparotomy with two-layer closure with nonabsorbable suture

Penetration of the stomach with a Veress needle or trochar rarely occurs. In one large series of over 32,000 gynecologic laparoscopic procedures, 9 cases of gastric perforation were described, with an overall incidence of 0.03%. Gastric perforation is most often associated with distortion of the abdominal anatomy or gastric distention resulting from difficulty with anesthetic induction. Previous upper-abdominal surgery with gastric adhesions to the periumbilical region may predispose patients to laparoscopic injuries. Esophageal intubation and protracted mask ventilation also produce gastric distention. Less frequently, preoperative aerophagia may increase the risk of gastric perforation. If gastric distention is suspected or probable, the risk of gastric perforation can be minimized by the use of a nasogastric or oropharyngeal tube.

After gastric perforation, the injury site must be carefully inspected. Small gastric injuries can usually be managed conservatively without surgical repair by stopping oral intake and continuing nasogastric suction for 24–48 hours if there is no evidence of bleeding or gastric leakage. Histamine blockers may also be administered to decrease gastric secretion.

Laparotomy should be performed if the injury cannot be readily identified or if injury to the posterior wall is suspected. Laparotomy and primary closure are indicated for larger injuries or those associated with gastric leakage or significant bleeding. A two-layer closure with an inner continuous lock, delayed-absorbable suture is important for hemostasis. An outer inverting row of interrupted, nonabsorbable mattress sutures is recommended. The latter serves to reapproximate the serosal margins and prevent leakage. A single-layer gastric closure at laparotomy or laparoscopy would be unnecessary for the small injury described in this patient and would be insufficient for a larger injury.

After surgery, nasogastric suction should be monitored. If there is significant blood in the gastric aspirate or if serial hematocrit suggests hemorrhage, reoperation may be necessary. Additional complications include gastric leakage and abscess formation, which may later lead to subphrenic, subhepatic, or lesser sac abscess. Abscesses should be suspected in patients with significant postoperative pain, nausea, fever, and leukocytosis.

Endler GC, Moghissi KS. Gastric perforation during pelvic laparoscopy. Obstet Gynecol 1976;47:40S–42S

Loffer FD, Pent D. Indications, contraindications and complications of laparoscopy. Obstet Gynecol Surv 1975;30:407–427

Shires GT, Thal ER, Jones RC, Shires GT III, Perry MO. Trauma. In: Schwartz SI, Shires GT, Spencer FC. Principles of surgery. 6th ed. New York: McGraw-Hill, 1994:175–224

83

Ovarian tumor of low malignant potential

A 25-year-old nulligravid woman is found to have a 6-cm right ovarian cyst on routine pelvic examination. It persists during observation through one menstrual cycle. Pelvic ultrasonography reveals a mostly cystic, complex right ovarian mass measuring 6 × 7 cm. Laparoscopic right ovarian cystectomy of a single cyst is carried out without morcellation or intraperitoneal spill. There is no other evidence of disease in the abdomen or pelvis, and the left ovary appears normal. The final pathology report reveals a serous tumor of low malignant potential (serous borderline tumor) of the right ovary without apparent involvement of the resection margin. Appropriate management for this patient is

* (A) semiannual follow-up
(B) laparoscopy with right salpingo-oophorectomy
(C) laparotomy with right salpingo-oophorectomy and biopsy of the left ovary
(D) laparotomy with right salpingo-oophorectomy, biopsy of the left ovary, omentectomy, lymph node biopsies, and peritoneal biopsies and washings for staging
(E) adjuvant chemotherapy for 6 months

Borderline tumors (tumors of low malignant potential) of the ovary represent 15% of all epithelial ovarian tumors. Fifty to sixty-five percent of borderline tumors are serous. Of these, three fourths are confined to the ovary (stage I) at diagnosis, although 30% are bilateral. The typical stage I serous borderline tumor is a unilocular cyst with intracystic, papillary growths that cannot on gross examination be readily distinguished from benign or malignant serous tumors. Histologically, the characteristic features are no stromal invasion, complex branching papillae, and stratified, atypical serous epithelium that forms tufts without a connective tissue core. Psammoma bodies are common.

Because most borderline serous tumors of the ovary occur in reproductive-age women and are classified as stage I at the time of diagnosis, treatment is usually conservative. Most patients can be managed with cystectomy or oophorectomy. Cystectomy may be adequate treatment when the resection margin is uninvolved histologically, only one cyst is present on the ovary, and the opposite ovary appears normal. Based on a small series of patients, the recurrence or persistence rate in the involved ovary is 5–10%, and recurrence is not associated with disease spread elsewhere. Cystectomy is the treatment of choice in the presence of bilateral borderline ovarian cystic tumors or when only one ovary remains, if preservation of fertility is desired.

Unilateral salpingo-oophorectomy is also an option for treatment of stage IA borderline serous tumors and eliminates the possibility of incomplete resection with recurrence in the same ovary. It should also be performed if residual disease is thought to be present in the ovary after cystectomy. Biopsy of the contralateral ovary is not indicated.

If the patient is perimenopausal or postmenopausal or has no interest in fertility, hysterectomy with bilateral salpingo-oophorectomy is recommended. If an intraoperative diagnosis of borderline tumor of the ovary is made, staging procedures should be carried out including peritoneal biopsies and washings, partial omentectomy, and lymph node sampling, in the event that permanent histologic sections reveal an invasive ovarian cancer. When a postoperative diagnosis of borderline ovarian tumor is made, reoperation for staging is not indicated.

Recurrences in stage I borderline tumors are rare and are usually limited to retained ovaries. There is no good evidence for currently recommending removal of retained ovaries after completing childbearing, because survival approaches 100% in these patients. No postoperative therapy is recommended for stage IA borderline ovarian tumors. Semiannual follow-up should be performed, paying special attention to any ovarian enlargement or cysts in retained ovaries that may require surgical assessment.

Chambers JT, Merino MJ, Kohorn EI, Schwartz PE. Borderline ovarian tumors. Am J Obstet Gynecol 1988;159:1088–1094

Kærn J, Tropé CG, Abeler VM. A retrospective study of 370 borderline tumors of the ovary treated at the Norwegian Radium Hospital from 1970 to 1982. Cancer 1993;71:1810–1820

Lim-Tan SK, Cajigas HE, Scully RE. Ovarian cystectomy for serous borderline tumors: a follow-up study of 35 cases. Obstet Gynecol 1988;72:775–781

Tazelaar HD, Bostwick DG, Ballon SC, Hendrickson MR, Kempson RL. Conservative treatment of borderline ovarian tumors. Obstet Gynecol 1985;66:417–422

84

Effect of tamoxifen on the endometrium

A 50-year-old menopausal woman was diagnosed with a 1.5-cm infiltrating ductal carcinoma of the breast, stage I (nodes negative), and was treated with a lumpectomy and radiation therapy. The tumor was estrogen- and progesterone-receptor positive. Her medical oncologist has advised her to begin adjuvant therapy with tamoxifen citrate (Nolvadex). The patient is concerned because she recently read that tamoxifen has been associated with endometrial cancer. Your recommendation for her is

(A) prophylactic total abdominal hysterectomy and bilateral salpingo-oophorectomy
(B) periodic endometrial sampling
* (C) endometrial sampling if uterine bleeding occurs
(D) periodic endovaginal ultrasonography
(E) periodic hysteroscopy

Tamoxifen is the most widely prescribed antineoplastic drug. Its actions are tissue specific. In some organs (eg, the breast) it acts like an antiestrogen, whereas in other organs (eg, the uterus) it acts like a weak estrogen. Overall, it is well tolerated by most patients. Hot flushes and vaginal discharge are the most frequent side effects.

Tamoxifen has a proliferative effect on the endometrium (Figs. 84-1 to 84-4). The ratio of proliferative to atrophic endometrium in postmenopausal women is higher in patients treated with tamoxifen than in control subjects. Endometrial polyps, growth of leiomyoma, and activation of endometriosis have been reported in patients receiving tamoxifen. In a small prospective study, almost 30% of patients on tamoxifen developed endometrial hyperplasia as documented by serial endometrial biopsies. Case reports and randomized clinical trials reveal a two- to threefold increase in endometrial cancer in patients treated with tamoxifen. Some reports

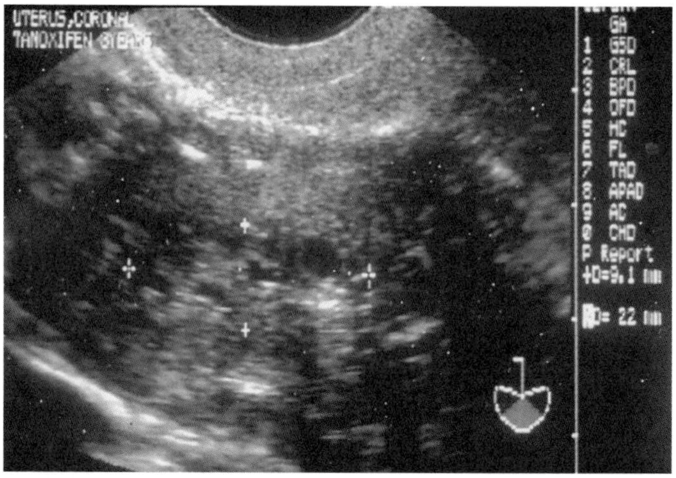

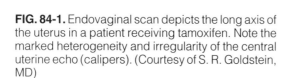

FIG. 84-1. Endovaginal scan depicts the long axis of the uterus in a patient receiving tamoxifen. Note the marked heterogeneity and irregularity of the central uterine echo (calipers). (Courtesy of S. R. Goldstein, MD)

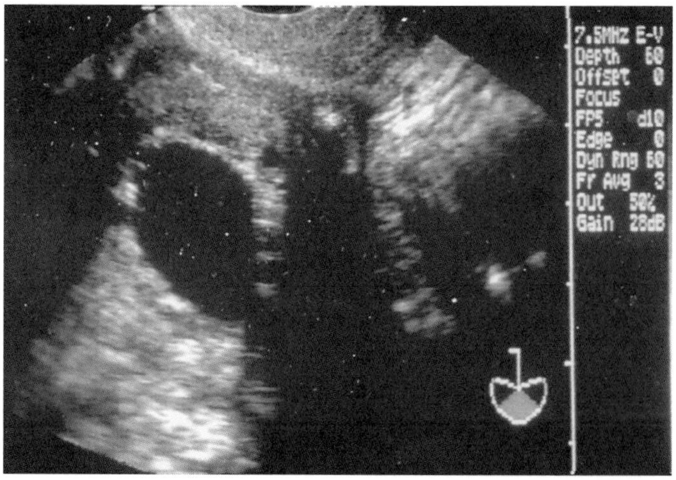

FIG. 84-2. After instillation of sterile saline (sonohysterogram), the endometrium is seen to be thin, and in the proximal myometrium are small, sonolucent microcysts, which represent reactivation of foci of adenomyosis. (Courtesy of S. R. Goldstein, MD)

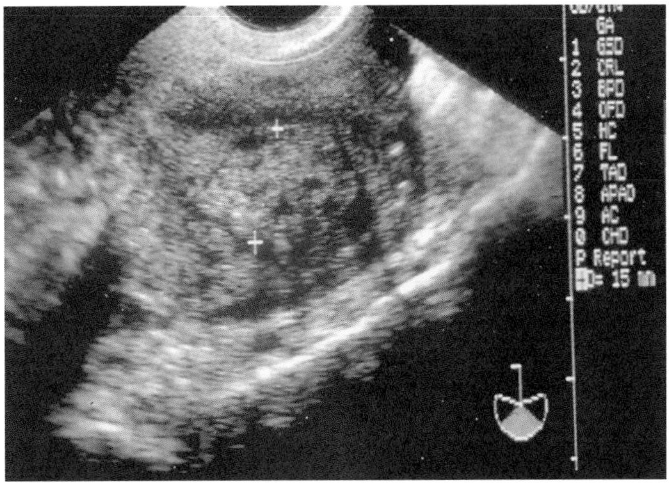

FIG. 84-3. Long-axis view of the uterus reveals a markedly heterogeneous central location with multiple small sonolucent cystic spaces. (Courtesy of S. R. Goldstein, MD)

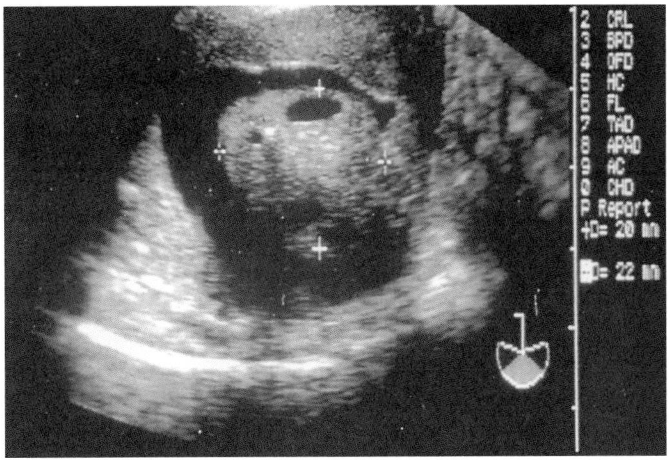

FIG. 84-4. Sonohysterogram for the patient depicted in Fig. 84-3 clearly depicts thin endometrium surrounding the fluid instillation and the presence of a large polypoid mass containing microcysts. The pathology report was that of adenomyoma. (Courtesy of S. R. Goldstein, MD)

have described virulent tumors and deaths from endometrial cancer attributable to tamoxifen, whereas other reports have not verified aggressive tumors in association with tamoxifen administration. Because of the relatively low frequency of endometrial cancer, a prophylactic total abdominal hysterectomy and bilateral salpingo-oophorectomy is not indicated for patients on tamoxifen therapy.

A patient who experiences uterine bleeding while receiving tamoxifen should undergo an adequate endometrial biopsy. However, the efficacy of screening in asymptomatic patients receiving tamoxifen and of the tests used in screening is unknown. In the ongoing Breast Cancer Prevention Trial, supported by the National Cancer Institute, the use of tamoxifen is being studied as a method of preventing breast cancer in high-risk women (chemoprevention). A subgroup of these women will have baseline and periodic endometrial sampling. The results of this trial will clarify the role of endometrial biopsy in the early detection of endometrial abnormalities in asymptomatic women.

An ever-expanding body of literature describes the role of endovaginal sonography as a means of measuring the endometrial stripe, myometrium, and adnexa. Most studies agree that an endometrial thickness of 4–5 mm or less in postmenopausal women correlates with atrophic histologic changes. However, the thickness of the endometrial stripe has not been well documented in postmenopausal women receiving either hormone replacement therapy or tamoxifen. A recent study reported an endometrial thickness of greater than 12 mm in four asymptomatic patients receiving tamoxifen. Hysteroscopy and dilation and curettage revealed only atrophic endometrium in these patients. Hysterography with instillation of 3–10 ml of sterile saline into the uterine cavity under sonographic guidance has demonstrated that the increased thickness is due to subendometrial cystic spaces. Until larger trials are reported, definitive sonographic criteria for endometrial thickness will not be available for women receiving tamoxifen.

Although endometrial sampling and sonography are intuitively attractive screening options, their role in asymptomatic patients receiving tamoxifen awaits more data. Similarly, the role of hysteroscopy and hysterosonography in determining the response of the endometrium to tamoxifen requires further evaluation. The gynecologist should encourage an asymptomatic patient receiving tamoxifen to seek semiannual or annual examinations. If a patient develops uterine discharge or bleeding, an adequate endometrial sampling with or without hysteroscopy should be performed immediately.

Anteby E, Yagel S, Zacut D, Palti Z, Hochner-Celnikier D. False sonographic appearance of endometrial neoplasia in postmenopausal women treated with tamoxifen. Lancet 1992;340(8816):433–434

Gal D, Kopel S, Bashevkin M, Lebowicz J, Lev R, Tancer ML. Oncogenic potential of tamoxifen on endometria of postmenopausal women with breast cancer—preliminary report. Gynecol Oncol 1991;42:120–123

Goldstein SR. Unusual ultrasonographic appearance of the uterus in patients receiving tamoxifen. Am J Obstet Gynecol 1994;170:447–451

Lahti E, Blanco G, Kauppila A, Apaja-Sarkkinen M, Taskinen PJ, Laatikainen T. Endometrial changes in postmenopausal breast cancer patients receiving tamoxifen. Obstet Gynecol 1993;81:660–664

Wolf DM, Jordan VC. Gynecologic complications associated with long-term adjuvant tamoxifen therapy for breast cancer. Gynecol Oncol 1992;45:118–128

85

Recommendations for mammography

Various organizations have made differing recommendations for screening mammography based on their interpretation of the existing data. If in your practice you use the 1994 guidelines of the American College of Obstetricians and Gynecologists for screening mammography, which of the following would you recommend to your patients?

		Serial Screening	
	Age for Initial Study	Age (y)	Screening Interval (y)
* (A)	40	40–50	1–2
		>50	1
(B)	40–45	45–50	2
		>50	1
(C)	40–45	45–50	2
		50–70	1
(D)	50	50–70	1

To reach consensus on national screening mammography guidelines, in 1989 the American Cancer Society and the American Medical Association revised their guidelines and dropped their prior recommendation of a baseline (initial) mammogram for women between the ages of 35 and 40. Subsequently, the American College of Obstetricians and Gynecologists similarly dropped its recommendation for a baseline mammogram and now recommends that mammography be performed every 1–2 years for women aged 40–50 years and annually for women over 50 years of age.

Some question has been raised regarding the value of screening mammography between the ages of 40 and 50 years. Published data on screening mammography do not consistently demonstrate statistically decreased mortality from breast cancer with screening mammography below the age of 50 years. Several population-based randomized prospective studies show a trend of decreased mortality from breast cancer with mammography for women aged 40–49 years. Because of the relatively low incidence of invasive breast cancer in this age group, it is estimated that a prospective randomized study would require more than 250,000 participants to be followed for 20 years to reach statistical significance. Furthermore, denying mammography to the control group of women in such a study would raise an ethical issue.

Most screening mammography studies document statistically significant decreased mortality from breast cancer between the ages of 50 and 69 years. Few studies include large enough numbers of women over the age of 70 to be able to draw conclusions. Unfortunately, patient compliance with screening mammography recommendations decreases progressively after age 70, even though

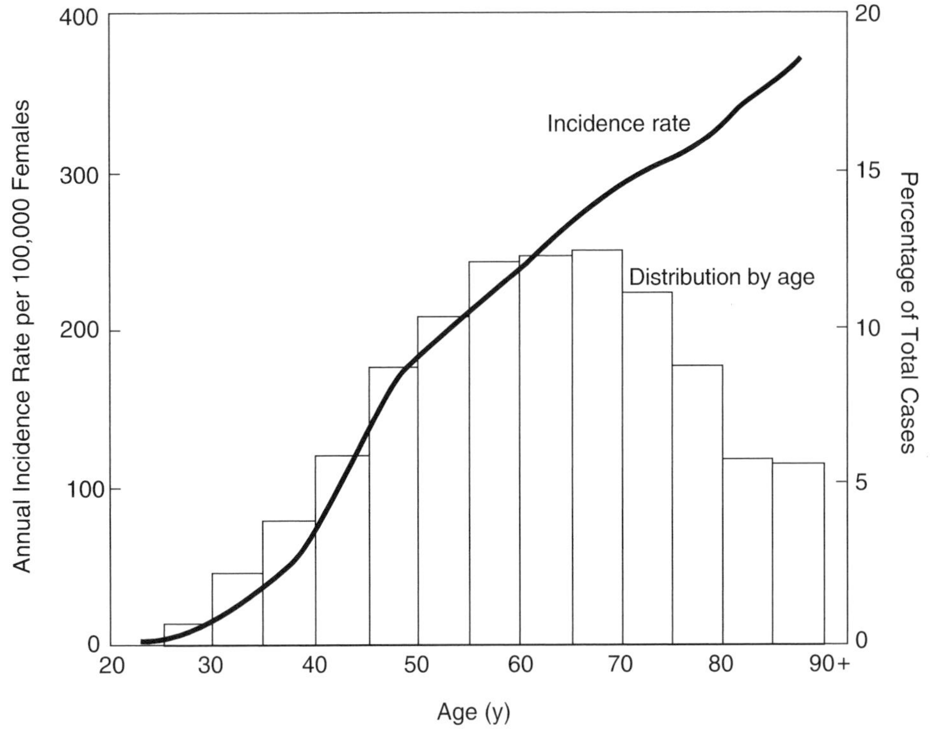

FIG. 85-1. Breast cancer incidence rates in women and distribution of cases by age. Carcinoma in situ is excluded. (Feig SA, McLelland R, eds. American College of Radiology [ACR]. Breast carcinoma: current diagnosis and treatment. Reston, Virginia: American College of Radiology, 1983:13)

the risk continues to rise. Figure 85-1 shows the incidence and frequency of invasive breast cancer as a function of a woman's age.

American College of Obstetricians and Gynecologists. Routine cancer screening. ACOG Committee Opinion 128. Washington DC: ACOG, 1993

Breast cancer screening guidelines agreed on by AMA, other medically related organizations. JAMA 1989;262:1155

Feig SA. Decreased breast cancer mortality through mammographic screening: results of clinical trials. Radiology 1988;167:659–665

Feig SA, McLelland R, eds. Breast carcinoma: current diagnosis and treatment. Chicago: Year Book Medical Publishers, 1983

Fletcher SW, Black W, Harris R, Rimer BK, Shapiro S. Report of the International Workshop on Screening for Breast Cancer. J Natl Cancer Inst 1993;85:1644–1656

Kattlove H, Liberati A, Keeler E, Brook RH. Benefits and costs of screening and treatment for early breast cancer: development of a basic benefit model. JAMA 1995;273:142–148

Kerlikowske K, Grady D, Rubin SM, Sandrock C, Ernster VL. Efficacy of screening mammography: a meta-analysis. JAMA 1995;273:149–154

NCI Breast Cancer Screening Consortium. Screening mammography: a missed clinical opportunity? Results of the NCI Breast Cancer Screening Consortium and National Health Interview Survey studies. JAMA 1990;264:54–58

Nyström L, Rutqvist LE, Wall S, Lindgren A, Lindqvist M, Rydén S, et al. Breast cancer screening with mammography: overview of Swedish randomized trials. Lancet 1993;341:973–978

Smart CR. Highlights of the evidence of benefit for women aged 40-49 years from the 14-year follow-up of the Breast Cancer Detection Demonstration Project. Cancer 1994;74:296–300

Stacey-Clear A, McCarthy KA, Hall DA, Pile-Spellman E, White G, Hulka C, et al. Breast cancer survival among women under age 50: is mammography detrimental? Lancet 1992;340:991–994

Tabar L, Fagerberg G, Duffy SW, Day NE. The Swedish two county trial of mammographic screening for breast cancer: recent results and calculation of benefit. J Epidemiol Community Health 1989;43:107–114

86

Management of the obese patient

A 30-year-old woman, gravida 2, para 2, who underwent a bilateral tubal ligation 5 years ago, is considering undergoing microsurgical tubal anastomosis and attempting conception with her new partner. She is 165 cm (65 in) tall and weighs 113 kg (250 lb), approximately 75% above ideal body weight. She would like to lose weight before achieving pregnancy. After a discussion of the risks of surgery and pregnancy for obese patients, you prescribe a 1,200-calorie diet. The most appropriate and effective additional step is

(A) referral to a lay weight loss group
(B) use of an appetite suppressant such as fenfluramine hydrochloride (Pondimin)
* (C) ongoing medical supervision for behavior modification
(D) referral for gastric stapling procedure
(E) jejunoileal bypass procedure

Approximately 35% of adult women in the United States are considered obese. Individuals who are 20–40% overweight are mildly obese, and those 41–100% overweight are moderately obese. Severe obesity denotes individuals who are more than 100% over their ideal weight. The 1983 Metropolitan Life Insurance Company height and weight tables facilitate these determinations (Table 86-1). The body mass index may also be also used for this determination. Over 90% of obese women are classified as having mild obesity, 9% have moderate obesity, and 0.5% have severe obesity.

Motivated patients with mild obesity frequently benefit from diet and behavior modification offered by lay dietary management groups such as Weight Watchers and Take Off Pounds Sensibly. Patients with moderate obesity are less likely to benefit from such programs. These patients will lose weight with diets of 1,200–1,500 calories. More rapid weight loss can be achieved with 400–700-calorie diets, but few patients are able to stay on these diets for a long period of time. Furthermore, their ultimate success will depend on permanent dietary and behavior modification, which includes dietary portion control and avoiding a sedentary lifestyle.

TABLE 86-1. Height and Weight Table for Women*

Height		Weight (lb)		
Feet	Inches	Small Frame	Medium Frame	Large Frame
4	10	102–111	109–121	118–131
4	11	103–113	111–123	120–134
5	0	104–115	113–126	122–137
5	1	106–118	115–129	125–140
5	2	108–121	118–132	128–143
5	3	111–124	121–135	131–147
5	4	114–127	124–138	134–151
5	5	117–130	127–141	137–155
5	6	120–133	130–144	140–159
5	7	123–136	133–147	143–163
5	8	126–139	136–150	146–167
5	9	129–142	139–153	149–170
5	10	132–145	142–156	152–173
5	11	135–148	145–159	155–176
6	0	138–151	148–162	158–179

* Weights at ages 25 to 59 are based on lowest mortality. Weight is given in pounds according to frame (in indoor clothing weighing 3 lb; shoes with 1-inch heels).

Metropolitan Life Insurance Company, Health and Safety Division

Studies comparing patients who followed diets accompanied by behavior modification with a second group of dieters receiving the appetite suppressant fenfluramine hydrochloride and a third group of dieters receiving both behavior modification and the appetite suppressant found that the group receiving both behavior modification and the appetite suppressant lost the most weight, but they also regained the most weight during the follow-up period. The group that received medically supervised behavior modification experienced the greatest long-term weight loss. This latter approach is most likely to be successful for the patient described, who is by definition moderately obese.

Patients with severe obesity frequently have coexisting complicating factors such as hypertension, diabetes, hyperlipidemia, arthritis, and impaired pulmonary function. Many of these patients have failed previous attempts at weight loss via diet; for them, the best results have been achieved with gastric reduction procedures. The jejunoileal bypass procedure has been largely replaced by procedures that reduce gastric size or narrow the stomach outlet, such as the gastric stapling procedure. Use of these procedures should be limited to patients with severe obesity.

Craighead LW, Stunkard AJ, O'Brien RM. Behavior therapy and pharmacotherapy for obesity. Arch Gen Psychiatry 1981;38:763–768

Stenchever MA. Counseling the patient. In: Herbst AL, Mishell DR Jr, Stenchever MA, Droegemueller W, eds. Comprehensive gynecology. 2nd ed. St Louis: Mosby Year Book, 1992:185–212

Stunkard AJ. The current status of treatment for obesity in adults. In: Stunkard AJ, Stellar E, eds. Eating and its disorders. New York: Raven Press, 1984:157–173

87

Diagnosis of hydatidiform mole

A 16-year-old woman presents with a 14-week history of amenorrhea, a positive urine pregnancy test, and vaginal spotting. Pelvic examination reveals a 14-week-size uterus, a closed cervical os, and dark blood in the vagina. No fetal heart tones are heard with Doppler. No discrete fetal structures are seen on ultrasound examination of the uterus (Fig. 87-1). Suction curettage is performed; the photomicrograph from the permanent pathology is shown in Fig. 87-2 (see color plate).

The diagnosis is

(A) partial mole
* (B) complete mole
(C) choriocarcinoma
(D) missed abortion with hydropic degeneration

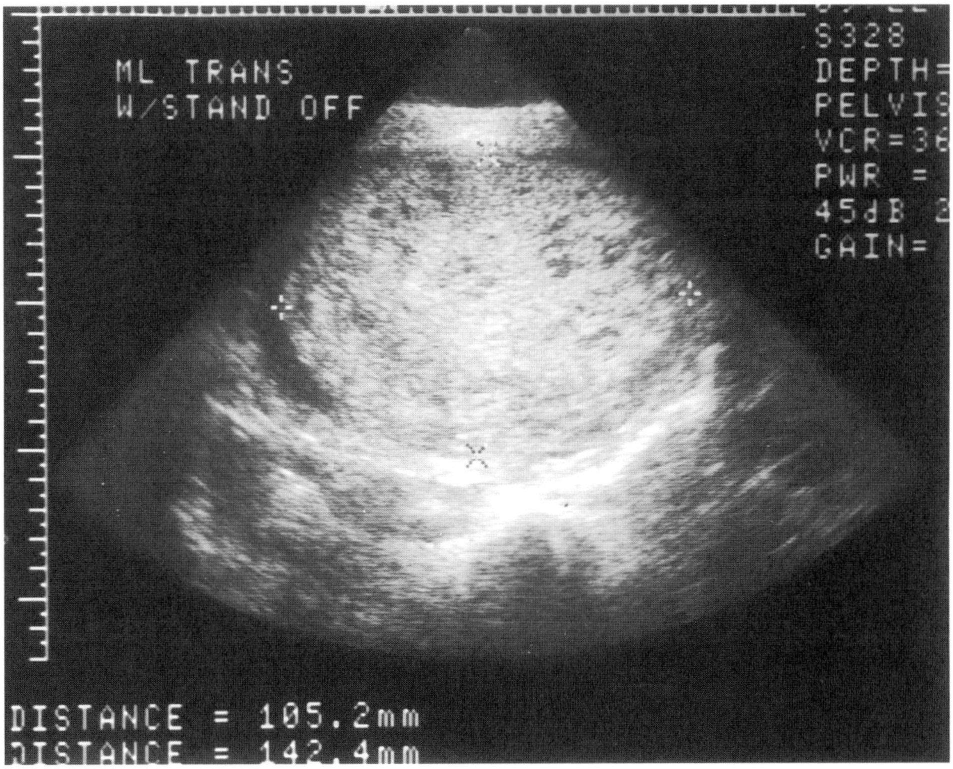

FIG. 87-1. Transverse sonogram showing areas of relative hypoechogenicity and hyperechogenicity (ie, the snowstorm pattern) characteristic of hydatidiform mole.

A complete hydatidiform mole exhibits diffuse and inhomogeneous intrauterine cysts on ultrasound examination. A fetus or gestational sac is not present (Fig. 87-1). A partial hydatidiform mole may also exhibit inhomogeneous cysts, but a fetus or gestational sac is also present. The diagnosis of partial mole cannot, however, be made preoperatively.

In contrast to a partial or complete mole, choriocarcinoma does not have any characteristic features that permit ultrasonographic diagnosis.

When the uterus is less than 14 weeks' size, a missed abortion should be part of the differential diagnosis. In Fig. 87–1 there is no fetus or sac to suggest this diagnosis. The reliability of ultrasonographic prediction of a molar pregnancy is increased when the maternal serum human chorionic gonadotropin value is greater than 80,000 mIU/ml.

Although molar pregnancies can often be diagnosed by their ultrasonographic and gross characteristics, the definitive diagnosis is established by microscopic examination of the tissue removed by suction curettage (Table 87-1). For the patient described, the photomicrograph from the permanent pathology (Fig. 87-2) establishes the diagnosis of complete hydatidiform mole. Prominent hyperplasia of the trophoblasts, hydropic swelling, and the absence of fetal vessels are noted.

TABLE 87-1. Microscopic Characteristics Differentiating Complete Hydatidiform Mole, Partial Hydatidiform Mole, Choriocarcinoma, and Hydropic Degeneration

Characteristics	Complete Mole	Partial Mole	Choriocarcinoma	Hydropic Degeneration
Cytotrophoblasts	Prominent hyperplasia	Focal hyperplasia	Poorly differentiated	Decreased or absent
Syncytiotrophoblasts	Prominent hyperplasia	Focal hyperplasia	Poorly differentiated	Normal or decreased
Villi	Hydropic swelling	Focal enlargement	Absent	Hydropic swelling
Fetal vessels	Absent or extremely immature	Present and normal	Absent	Present and normal

Buschi AJ, Brenbridge NAG, Cochrane JA, Teates CD. Hydropic degeneration of the placenta simulating hydatidiform mole. J Clin Ultrasound 1979;7:60–61

Munyer TP, Callen PW, Filly RA, Braga CA, Jones HW III. Further observations on the sonographic spectrum of gestational trophoblastic disease. J Clin Ultrasound 1981;9:349–358

Reid MH, McGahan JP, Oi R. Sonographic evaluation of hydatidiform mole and its look-alikes. AJR Am J Roentgenol 1983;140:307–311

Romero R, Horgan JG, Kohorn EI, Kadar N, Taylor KJW, Hobbins JC. New criteria for the diagnosis of gestational trophoblastic disease. Obstet Gynecol 1985;66:553–558

Santos-Ramos R, Forney JP, Schwarz BE. Sonographic findings and clinical correlations in molar pregnancy. Obstet Gynecol 1980;56:186–192

88

Surgery for endometrial cancer

A 77-year-old woman presents with a 3-month history of vaginal bleeding. Physical examination is unremarkable. Endocervical and endometrial biopsies both show a grade 3 endometrial adenocarcinoma with squamous differentiation. Chest X-ray, complete blood count, and serum chemistries are normal. The best surgical therapy for this patient is

(A) pelvic and intracavitary irradiation followed by total abdominal hysterectomy and bilateral salpingo-oophorectomy
(B) radical hysterectomy, bilateral salpingo-oophorectomy, and complete pelvic lymphadenectomy
(C) total abdominal hysterectomy, bilateral salpingo-oophorectomy, and complete pelvic lymph node dissection
* (D) total abdominal hysterectomy, bilateral salpingo-oophorectomy, and pelvic and paraaortic lymph node sampling
(E) total abdominal hysterectomy, bilateral salpingo-oophorectomy, and partial omentectomy

The mainstay of treatment for carcinoma of the endometrium is surgery (ie, total abdominal hysterectomy and bilateral salpingo-oophorectomy). In recognition of the importance of surgery in the management of endometrial cancer, the International Federation of Gynecology and Obstetrics changed from clinical to surgical staging in 1988. Therefore, patients with clinical stage I and occult stage II (positive endocervical curettage but no gross evidence of cervical involvement) endometrial carcinoma of any grade or histopathology should undergo an exploratory laparotomy as the first step in the treatment program. This approach is based on the following observations:

- Preoperative radiation therapy may obscure important surgical–pathologic information about the cancer.
- Many patients do not require adjuvant radiation therapy.
- Radiotherapy can be individualized to treat disease

that has extended beyond the operative field or to prevent local recurrence in selected high-risk patients.

- Postoperative radiotherapy is as effective and safe as preoperative radiotherapy.

The objective of the initial operative procedure is to obtain information that is as accurate as possible about the spread of disease, concurrent with removal of the uterus, tubes, and ovaries.

The abdomen should be opened through an adequate incision and peritoneal washings taken from the paracolic gutters and pelvis. Careful exploration is then carried out, looking and feeling for evidence of omental, liver, peritoneal, and adnexal metastasis as well as enlarged pelvic and paraaortic lymph nodes. An extrafascial, total hysterectomy and bilateral salpingo-oophorectomy are then performed. There is no benefit to performing a radical hysterectomy in this setting. Removal of the adnexa is part of the therapy, because they may contain microscopic metastases or a synchronous primary ovarian tumor. It is not necessary to remove a margin of vaginal cuff around the cervix.

The uterus should be opened in the operating room to determine the extent of the endometrial cancer. At a minimum, high common iliac and paraaortic lymph node dissections should be performed if there is adnexal or cervical involvement, a large tumor (>2 cm), deep (≥50%) myometrial invasion, or a poorly differentiated endometrial, papillary serous, or clear cell tumor. Some authorities do not perform pelvic lymph node biopsies in patients with these adverse risk factors, because most of these patients will be treated postoperatively with whole-pelvis radiation therapy. Lymph node biopsies do not need to be obtained in patients with small (≤2 cm) grade 1 and 2 endometrial cancers with only superficial myometrial invasion because of the very low risk of nodal metastasis in this group. Partial omentectomy should be considered in some high-risk patients, especially those with papillary serous and mixed müllerian tumors, which have a propensity for intraabdominal spread and upper-abdominal recurrence. Omentectomy is not routine in patients such as the woman described.

An initial surgical approach to most patients with endometrial cancer not only accomplishes removal of the primary tumor by hysterectomy, but also provides the best opportunity to ascertain the full extent of disease, determine prognosis, and plan appropriate postoperative therapy by obtaining specimens for cytologic and histologic evaluation from sites of known predilection for metastasis. Extended surgical staging, including lymph node biopsies, can be performed with only minor increases in perioperative morbidity, such as lymphocysts, hematomas, and blood loss, as well as slightly increased operating time and hospital stay. Whether this initial surgical approach to treatment and staging will translate into improved survival awaits further analysis and investigation.

Larson DM, Johnson K, Olson KA. Pelvic and para-aortic lymphadenectomy for surgical staging of endometrial cancer: morbidity and mortality. Obstet Gynecol 1992;79:998–1001

Moore DH, Fowler WC Jr, Walton LA, Droegemueller W. Morbidity of lymph node sampling in cancers of the uterine corpus and cervix. Obstet Gynecol 1989;74:180–184

Morrow CP, Bundy BN, Kurman RJ, Creasman WT, Heller P, Homesley HD, et al. Relationship between surgical-pathological risk factors and outcome in clinical stage I and II carcinoma of the endometrium: a Gynecologic Oncology Group study. Gynecol Oncol 1991;40:55–65

Orr JW Jr, Holloway RW, Orr PF, Holimon JL. Surgical staging of uterine cancer: an analysis of perioperative morbidity. Gynecol Oncol 1991;42:209–216

Vardi JR, Tadros GH, Anselmo MT, Rafla SD. The value of exploratory laparotomy in patients with endometrial carcinoma according to the new International Federation of Gynecology and Obstetrics staging. Obstet Gynecol 1992;80:204–208

89

Tumor markers associated with ovarian germ cell tumors

An 18-year old woman, gravida 1, para 0, abortus 1, is referred for evaluation of a 6-cm solid right adnexal mass. Her medical history is significant for an uncomplicated molar pregnancy 1.5 years ago. Laboratory studies are as follows:

Test	Patient's Results	Normal Values
Carcinoembryonic antigen (CEA)	2 ng/ml	<5 ng/ml
Quantitative beta subunit of human chorionic gonadotropin (β-hCG)	<5 mIU/ml	<5 mIU/ml
Alpha-fetoprotein (AFP)	940 ng/ml	<10 ng/ml
CA 125	60 U/ml	<35 U/ml
Lactic dehydrogenase (LDH)	140 IU/L	≤240 IU/L

The complete blood count, serum electrolytes, and chest X-ray are normal. The most likely diagnosis is

(A) dysgerminoma
* (B) endodermal sinus tumor
(C) immature teratoma
(D) choriocarcinoma

In a patient with a suspected malignancy, elevations of specific tumor markers may help narrow the differential diagnoses and prompt referral to a gynecologic oncologist for surgical staging and postoperative management. Postoperatively, serum tumor markers are monitored to assess response to therapy and determine disease status. Pure germ cell tumors (ie, those consisting of one type of germ cell element) of the ovary are often associated with elevations of specific tumor markers (Table 89-1).

Dysgerminoma is associated with elevations of LDH in over 75% of cases. It is rarely associated with increased CA 125 values.

It has been long recognized that endodermal sinus tumor is associated with elevated AFP levels, but recently other serum tumor markers have been studied as well. Elevated levels of CA 125 and LDH occur in over 75% of these patients.

Immature teratoma is usually not associated with elevated CA 125 or AFP levels. Although hCG, CEA, and LDH levels may be elevated, this elevation occurs in fewer than 25% of patients. Choriocarcinoma is associated with elevated serum hCG levels.

Mixed germ cell tumors consist of two or more histologic components. When each component secretes a tumor marker, the preoperative tumor marker profile is difficult to interpret, and the predictive value of these tests to correctly identify the germ cell neoplasm declines.

TABLE 89-1. Tumor Markers Associated with Germ Cell Neoplasms*

	Likelihood of Elevation				
Neoplasm	AFP (Normal, <10 ng/ml)	CA 125 (Normal, <35 U/ml)	CEA (Normal, <5 ng/ml)	hCG (Normal, <5 mIU/ml)	LDH (Normal, ≤240 IU/L)
Endodermal sinus tumor	Always	Usually	May be	May be	Usually
Immature teratoma	May be	May be	May be	May be	May be
Dysgerminoma	Not elevated	Rarely	Not elevated	Rarely	Usually
Choriocarcinoma	Not elevated	Not elevated	Not elevated	Always	Not elevated

* AFP indicates alpha-fetoprotein; CEA, carcinoembryonic antigen; hCG, human chorionic gonadotropin; LDH, lactate dehydrogenase.

Awais GM. Dysgerminoma and serum lactic dehydrogenase levels. Obstet Gynecol 1983;61:99–101

Ihara T, Ohama K, Satoh H, Fujii T, Nomura K, Fujiwara A. Histologic grade and karyotype of immature teratoma of the ovary. Cancer 1984;54:2988–2994

Kawai M, Kano T, Kikkawa F, Morikawa Y, Oguchi H, Nakashima N, et al. Seven tumor markers in benign and malignant germ cell tumors of the ovary. Gynecol Oncol 1992;45:248–253

Lui TL, Lian IJ, Deppe G. Serum lactic dehydrogenase (SLDH) in germ cell malignancies of the ovary. Gynecol Oncol 1984;19:355–357

Sheiko MC, Hart WR. Ovarian germinoma (dysgerminoma) with elevated serum lactic dehydrogenase: case report and review of the literature. Cancer 1982;49:994–998

90

Necrotizing fasciitis

A 51-year-old postmenopausal diabetic woman underwent total abdominal hysterectomy and bilateral salpingo-oophorectomy for endometrial adenocarcinoma. The first postoperative day was uneventful except that the patient's temperature was 38.7° (101.7°F).

On the morning of the second postoperative day, the patient experiences pain from the abdominal incision, and a small amount of purulent drainage is noted. There is erythema at the incision margins and some ecchymoses and edema laterally. The wound is opened, irrigated, and packed after the fascia is determined to be intact. As the day continues, the patient experiences increasing incisional pain, increasing amounts of foul-smelling serosanguinous drainage from a pale wound, abdominal distention, and an episode of explosive watery diarrhea. A repeat temperature is 38.3°C (101.0°F). The patient has tachycardia and concentrated urine. The action that will most affect this patient's prognosis is

(A) intravenous broad-spectrum antibiotics
(B) Gram stain of wound fluid
(C) culture of wound fluid with determination of sensitivities
(D) wound biopsy with frozen section
* (E) radical wound debridement

Necrotizing fasciitis is a rare but life-threatening postoperative infection of soft tissues above deep fascia and muscle. It may be caused by a single microbe (*Streptococcus pyogenes*, *Staphylococcus aureus*, *Streptococcus agalactiae*, or *Clostridium* species), or it may be due to a mixture of aerobic and anaerobic streptococci or *Bacteroides/Prevotella* species. This infection has a 1- to 4-day incubation period, and it spreads rapidly along fascial planes as a result of bacterial production of hyaluronidase, deoxyribonuclease, coagulase, catalase, hemolysin, or collagenase. Hemolytic, antiphagocytic, lethal, or cardiotoxic toxins or exotoxin may be produced as well. Diabetes is a common predisposing variable, as are age over 50 years, poor nutritional status, alcoholism, decreased blood supply, cardiovascular disease, and previous irradiation.

Incisional pain is out of proportion to the degree of wound findings, and the temperature is usually greater than 38.3°C (101°F). Edema around the erythematous incision differentiates necrotizing fasciitis from a typical superficial wound infection. Skin tenderness is succeeded by anesthesia as nerves become ischemic because of thrombosed nutrient vessels. Tissue becomes necrotic, and the result is production of a large amount of foul-smelling serosanguinous fluid. By the time gangrenous tissue changes are obvious, systemic symptoms are common. Adult respiratory distress syndrome, renal and other organ failure, and disseminated intravascular coagulopathy may develop.

Because this infection is rare, diagnosis is often delayed. Radical surgical debridement to viable tissue is necessary, and a delay in surgery is directly related to decreased patient survival. Antibiotics are sufficient to treat the bacteria responsible for this infection, but surgical removal of the infected gangrenous tissue that cannot be penetrated by antibiotics is required for a cure. Mortality with broad-spectrum antibiotic therapy alone, or with antibiotics plus incision and drainage without resection of necrotic tissue, has been 100%. Gram stain of the wound fluid may allow adequate identification of bacteria responsible for the infection, but the finding would be insufficient to alter patient outcome. Culture with sensitivities allows exact bacterial identification, but the results are not available for up to 72 hours.

Tissue edema and third spacing of fluid with intravascular volume depletion may be extreme, resulting in hemoconcentration, hypotension, and shock. Tachypnea with pulmonary involvement and hyperglycemia with resultant osmotic diuresis may compound the hypovolemia. Replacement with both crystalloids and colloids must be immediate and in concert with broad-spectrum antimicrobial and surgical therapy. Patients with necrotizing fasciitis are best managed in an intensive-care unit with central monitoring.

The use of a frozen-section biopsy allows possible early diagnosis if good historic information is provided to the pathologist. Most histologic findings are nonspecific and include infiltration of the dermis and fascia by polymorphic neutrophils and bacteria, thrombosis of subcutaneous arteries and veins, necrosis of superficial fascia, angiitis and fibrinoid necrosis of arterial and venous walls, bacteria in the fascia and dermis, and absence of muscle involvement. Wound biopsy is not routine but may contribute to early diagnosis, because tissue necrosis is not usually seen with routine infection in an abdominal incision.

Deaths are most commonly due to overwhelming sepsis with multiple organ failure. The mean time interval from onset of symptoms to treatment for survivors in most series is 4 days, whereas that for nonsurvivors is 7 days. Awareness is the key to early diagnosis and therapy.

Livengood CH III, Soper JT, Clarke-Pearson DL, Addison WA. Necrotizing fasciitis in irradiated tissue from diabetic women. A report of two cases. J Reprod Med 1991;36:455–458

Nolan TE, King LA, Smith RP, Gallup DC. Necrotizing surgical infection and necrotizing fasciitis in obstetric and gynecologic patients. South Med J 1993; 86:1363–1367

Stamenkovic I, Lew PD. Early recognition of potentially fatal necrotizing fasciitis. The use of frozen-section biopsy. N Engl J Med 1984;310:1689–1693

Stephenson H, Dotters DJ, Katz V, Droegemueller W. Necrotizing fasciitis of the vulva. Am J Obstet Gynecol 1992;166:1324–1327

91

Diagnosis of vulvar lesion

A 52-year-old woman has had vulvar itching for several months. She recently noticed an erythematous lesion on the labia majora (Fig. 91-1; see color plate). Appropriate management is

(A) observation
(B) treatment with hydrocortisone cream followed by repeat examination
(C) colposcopy
* (D) punch biopsy

Vulvar pruritus is a common and nonspecific symptom that may be associated with a variety of vulvar lesions. Before one embarks on a treatment plan, it is important to establish the diagnosis. Observation would be incorrect management because it would not provide a diagnosis. Failure to establish the diagnosis is also the reason that empiric treatment with hydrocortisone cream followed by repeat examination would be inappropriate.

The appearance of the lesion is not a reliable way to make the diagnosis because different diseases of the vulva often exhibit a similar appearance. It is not always possible to differentiate benign and malignant conditions of the vulva solely on the basis of appearance, even when colposcopy is used. The differential diagnosis of the erythematous vulvar lesion in this 52-year-old patient includes early invasive cancer, vulvar intraepithelial neoplasia, and squamous hyperplasia.

The appropriate recommendation for this patient is a punch biopsy. Punch biopsy of vulvar lesions is well tolerated by patients, can easily be performed in the office, and often provides an accurate diagnosis on which a subsequent management plan can be formulated. The biopsy is usually taken from the periphery of the lesion to avoid areas of necrosis or infection. To maximize diagnostic accuracy of the punch biopsy and to minimize sampling error, tissue is often taken from several sites of the lesion.

To perform a punch biopsy, the skin is infiltrated with 1% lidocaine. A cutaneous punch biopsy instrument is used to remove a core of tissue. The biopsy specimen may be placed on a small piece of cardboard or paper to maintain proper orientation during fixation and embedding.

Chafe W, Richards A, Morgan L, Wilkinson E. Unrecognized invasive carcinoma in vulvar intraepithelial neoplasia (VIN). Gynecol Oncol 1988;31:154–162

Rock B. Pigmented lesions of the vulva. Dermatol Clin 1992;10:361–370

Roman LD, Mitchell MF, Burke TW, Silva EG. Unsuspected invasive squamous cell carcinoma of the vulva in young women. Gynecol Oncol 1991;41:182–185

92

Endometrial cancer risk and hormone replacement therapy

A 52-year-old recently menopausal woman requests information about various hormone replacement therapy (HRT) regimens. She is particularly concerned about her risk of endometrial cancer. She is in good health but is obese, weighing 85 kg (187 lb). Which of the following statements regarding HRT is correct?

(A) Daily estrogen administration confers a greater risk of endometrial cancer than does interrupted therapy with 3 weeks on and 1 week off.
(B) There is no difference in the frequency of endometrial hyperplasia associated with estrogen replacement therapy when the duration of progestin therapy is increased from 10 to 12 days.
* (C) It is possible to use a 19-nortestosterone–derived progestin at a dose adequate to induce endometrial regression without adversely affecting lipoproteins.
(D) Continuous combined estrogen and progestin therapy confers a greater risk of endometrial adenocarcinoma than does cyclic therapy (1 therapy-free week each month).
(E) Obesity will significantly increase this patient's risk of endometrial adenocarcinoma on estrogen replacement therapy.

Endometrial adenocarcinoma is the primary risk of unopposed estrogen replacement therapy. Although endometrial cancer associated with estrogen replacement therapy is usually well differentiated and has a high cure rate, the potential for morbidity and mortality exists. Risk is closely correlated with dose and duration of therapy. Risk of atypical endometrial hyperplasia, the endometrial adenocarcinoma precursor, is not decreased by giving estrogen cyclically with 1 treatment-free week each month instead of continuously on a daily basis.

The addition of a progestin to HRT does confer protection. A frequency of endometrial hyperplasia of 18–32% was reported during a 2-year period with estrogen-only therapy. The frequency was decreased to 3–4% when progestins were added for 7 days each month. When progestin administration was extended further, a 2% frequency of hyperplasia was encountered with 10 days of treatment; no cases were noted with 12–13 days of progestin exposure.

Considerable concern exists regarding both the appropriate dosage of progestin needed to induce endometrial regression and the possible deleterious effects of progestin on lipoprotein profiles. According to one study, the following minimal daily progestin dosages are adequate to induce complete endometrial regression: 10 mg of medroxyprogesterone acetate, 0.7 mg of norethindrone, 75 µg of levonorgestrel, 300 mg of oral progesterone, and 10–20 mg of dydrogesterone. These data were derived by endometrial sampling and transmission electron microscopy of ultrastructural elements.

Progestin therapy has been reported to have disadvantageous effects on lipoprotein profiles, including elevation of total cholesterol, reduction of the high-density lipoprotein fraction, and elevation of the low-density lipoprotein fraction. However, these effects were observed with doses much greater than those required to induce endometrial regression. In a study comparing the effects of 10 mg of medroxyprogesterone acetate with those of 500 µg of D, L-norgestrel or 10 mg of norethindrone, medroxyprogesterone acetate did not adversely affect the lipoprotein fractions, whereas the others did. However, lower doses of the other progestins that are adequate for endometrial protection (eg, 1 mg of norethindrone) produced no change in high-density lipoprotein cholesterol values. No data regarding cholesterol values are available for the minimum doses of dydrogesterone and levonorgestrel. In addition, alterations in lipoprotein fractions may be a less important determinant of cardiovascular risk than other vascular effects of estrogen.

Continuous combined estrogen and progestin is a therapeutic option for patients who object to cyclic monthly bleeding. A frank discussion before treatment regarding benefits and side effects is important to promote compliance. Patients on combined continuous estrogen and progestin frequently have erratic bleeding during the first 3 months of therapy, but usually become amenorrheic thereafter. The incidence of proliferative endometrium and endometrial hyperplasia after 1 year of therapy is no higher than that with sequential treatment. The long-term metabolic and histologic implications of this treatment regimen have not been fully assessed.

Several studies have suggested that obese women on estrogen replacement therapy are already at increased risk for endometrial cancer and that this risk is not further increased by estrogen replacement therapy. In contrast, nonobese women have an increased risk of endometrial cancer with estrogen replacement therapy.

Hargrove JT, Maxson WS, Wentz AC, Burnett LS. Menopausal hormone replacement therapy with continuous daily oral micronized estradiol and progesterone. Obstet Gynecol 1989;73:606–612

Peterson HB, Lee NC, Rubin GL. Genital neoplasia. In: Mishell DR Jr, ed. Menopause: physiology and pharmacology. Chicago: Year Book Medical Publishers, 1987:275–298

Schiff I, Sela HK, Cramer D, Tulchinsky D, Ryan KJ. Endometrial hyperplasia in women on cyclic or continuous estrogen regimens. Fertil Steril 1982;37:79–82

Studd JWW, Thom MH, Paterson MEL, Wade-Evans T. The prevention and treatment of endometrial pathology in postmenopausal women receiving exogenous estrogens. In: Pasetto N, Paoletti R, Ambrus JL, eds. The menopause and postmenopause. Lancaster, England: MTP Press Limited, 1980:127–139

Whitehead MI, Siddle N, Lane G, Padwick M, Ryder TA, Pryse-Davies J, et al. The pharmacology of progestogens. In: Mishell DR Jr, ed. Menopause: physiology and pharmacology. Chicago: Year Book Medical Publishers, 1987:317–334

93

Treatment of nonmetastatic gestational trophoblastic tumor

A 45-year-old woman, gravida 4, para 3, has weekly serum quantitative human chorionic gonadotropin (hCG) levels obtained after suction evacuation of a complete hydatidiform mole. The hCG levels progressively decrease from a preevacuation level of 118,000 mIU/ml to 630 mIU/ml by 6 weeks after evacuation. Over the next 3 weeks, however, the hCG levels rise to 760, 1,580, and 5,290 mIU/ml, respectively. The patient is asymptomatic. She is taking oral contraceptives and does not desire future fertility. Physical examination is within normal limits except that the uterus is twice normal size. You make the diagnosis of postmolar gestational trophoblastic tumor.

A chest X-ray is negative. Pelvic ultrasonography with color Doppler reveals a tumor apparently within the uterine wall and demonstrates blood flow (Fig. 93-1; see color plate). Computed tomography (CT) of the chest, abdomen, and pelvis is normal with the exception of an enlarged uterus. The most appropriate management for this patient is

(A) methotrexate chemotherapy
(B) methotrexate, dactinomycin, and cyclophosphamide chemotherapy
(C) etoposide (VePesid), methotrexate, dactinomycin, cyclophosphamide, and vincristine sulfate (Oncovin) chemotherapy
(D) hysterectomy
* (E) hysterectomy and methotrexate chemotherapy

After evacuation of a hydatidiform mole, approximately 20% of patients require treatment for a trophoblastic tumor. Of this group of patients with trophoblastic tumor, 85% have nonmetastatic disease. The symptom most suggestive of postmolar gestational trophoblastic tumor is continued uterine bleeding after hydatidiform mole evacuation. Signs suggestive of postmolar trophoblastic tumor are an enlarged, irregular uterus and persistent, bilateral ovarian enlargement (theca–lutein cysts). The diagnosis is most commonly made, however, by the finding of rising or plateauing hCG levels after evacuation of a molar pregnancy.

Once a gestational trophoblastic tumor is diagnosed, it is necessary to determine the extent of disease. After a thorough history and physical examination, the clinician should obtain a chest X-ray and CT scans of the chest, abdomen, and pelvis. Computed tomography or magnetic resonance imaging of the brain is indicated if pulmonary or other metastases are discovered. Metastases are seen on chest CT scan in 30–40% of patients with normal chest X-rays. In asymptomatic patients, spread to other sites rarely occurs in the absence of demonstrable pulmonary metastases or an abnormal physical examination.

Single-agent chemotherapy with methotrexate or dactinomycin is the treatment of choice for nonmetastatic gestational trophoblastic tumor in patients who wish to preserve their fertility. Several different single-agent chemotherapy protocols in use have yielded excellent and comparable results, producing cures in virtually all patients without resorting to multiagent chemotherapy. Methotrexate can be given at a dosage of 0.4 mg/kg/d (maximum of 25 mg) intramuscularly (IM) or intravenously (IV) for 5 days every 2 weeks, or at slightly higher dosages of 1.0–1.5 mg/kg IM every other day for four doses plus folinic acid 0.1–0.15 mg/kg IM 24 hours after each methotrexate dose every 2 weeks. The advantage of the latter protocol, decreased toxicity (especially stomatitis), may be offset by the disadvantages of increased cost, patient inconvenience, and an increased need for a change in chemotherapy to achieve remission.

For treatment of nonmetastatic postmolar disease only, methotrexate may also be given in single weekly

IM doses of 30–50 mg/m^2. Dactinomycin, 10–13 μg/kg IV daily for 5 days or 1.25 mg/m^2 IV as a single dose, may also be given for treatment of nonmetastatic postmolar disease, and it is appropriate therapy for patients with liver or renal disease or effusions contraindicating methotrexate use. Multiagent chemotherapy with methotrexate, dactinomycin, and cyclophosphamide or with etoposide, methotrexate, dactinomycin, cyclophosphamide, and vincristine sulfate is not indicated for treatment of nonmetastatic gestational trophoblastic tumors.

Hysterectomy is advisable as primary therapy for nonmetastatic trophoblastic tumors in patients who no longer wish to preserve fertility. Hysterectomy is usually the treatment of choice for those with placental-site trophoblastic tumors. The use of hysterectomy to treat nonmetastatic disease results in a reduced number of courses and duration of chemotherapy.

Adjuvant single-agent chemotherapy at the time of operation may eradicate occult metastases and reduce the likelihood of tumor dissemination. Hysterectomy is usually performed midway through the chemotherapy protocol. No increase in postoperative morbidity has been reported with this sequence.

Hammond CB, Soper JT. Gestational trophoblastic diseases. In: Sciarra JJ, ed. Gynecology and obstetrics. Vol 4. Philadelphia: JB Lippincott, 1993:chapter 48, 1–42

Hammond CB, Weed JC Jr, Currie JL. The role of operation in the current therapy of gestational trophoblastic disease. Am J Obstet Gynecol 1980;136: 844–858

Lurain JR. Chemotherapy of gestational trophoblastic disease. In: Deppe G, ed. Chemotherapy of gynecologic cancer. 2nd ed. New York: Alan R Liss, 1990:273–301

94

Critical care

A 35-year-old woman underwent an exploratory laparotomy and right salpingectomy for a ruptured ectopic tubal pregnancy. Estimated blood loss during the procedure was 2,500 ml. She received 6 units of packed red blood cells and 4 L of crystalloids as part of the fluid resuscitation for hemorrhagic shock.

Postoperatively the patient develops dyspnea and hypoxemia. Vital signs are as follows: heart rate, 145 beats per minute; temperature, 99°F; respiratory rate, 40/min; blood pressure, 130/90 mm Hg. Her physical examination is unremarkable except for the presence of bilateral, diffuse inspiratory and expiratory wheezes and trace pitting edema in her lower extremities. Laboratory values reveal normal electrolytes, hematocrit 30%, and a normal coagulation profile. Her electrocardiogram, taken at the time of presentation, is shown in Fig. 94-1. The chest X-ray is shown in Fig. 94-2. Arterial blood gases, achieved with a 40% fraction of inspired oxygen face mask, reveal a pH of 7.47, a partial CO_2 pressure of 32, and a partial O_2 pressure of 58. A pulmonary artery balloon (Swan–Ganz) catheter is placed. The tracing that is obtained shows a pulmonary capillary wedge pressure (PCWP) of 27 (Fig. 94-3).

Your initial intervention should be

* (A) diuretic therapy with furosemide (Lasix)
(B) intravenous corticosteroids and epinephrine therapy
(C) inhaled beta-agonist therapy with albuterol
(D) positive end-expiratory pressure therapy

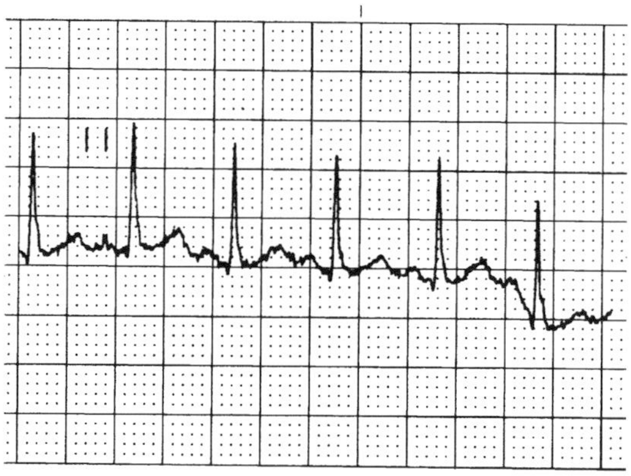

FIG. 94-1. Electrocardiogram tracing taken when the patient presented.

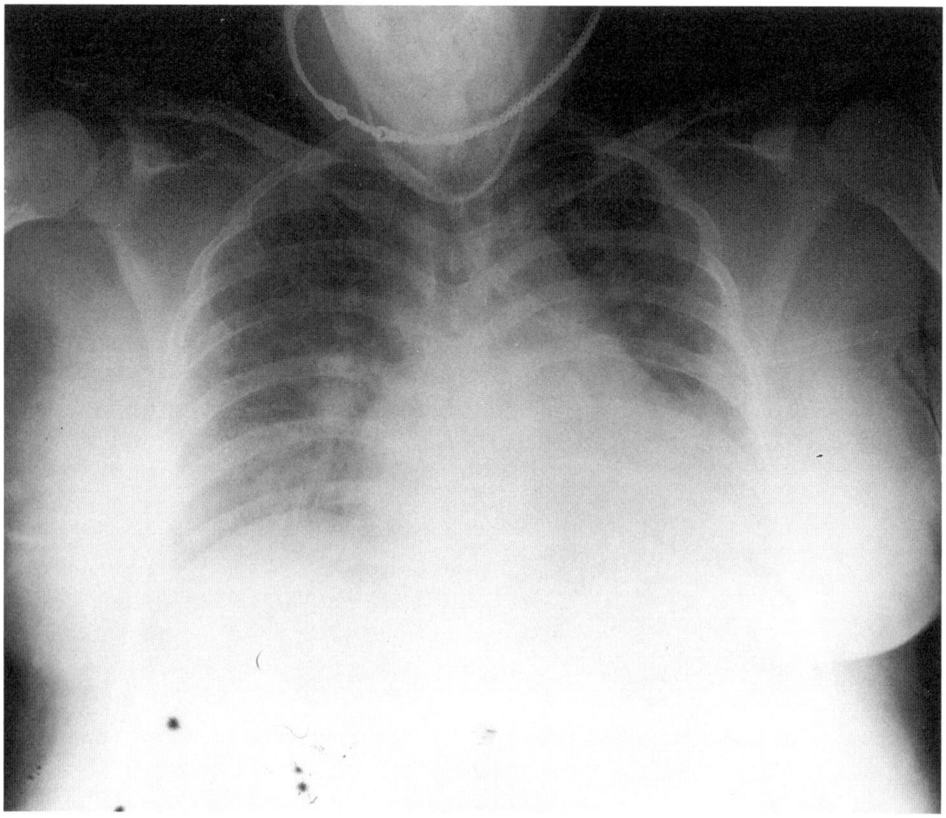

FIG. 94-2. Chest X-ray showing diffuse bilateral fluffy infiltrates and normal heart size.

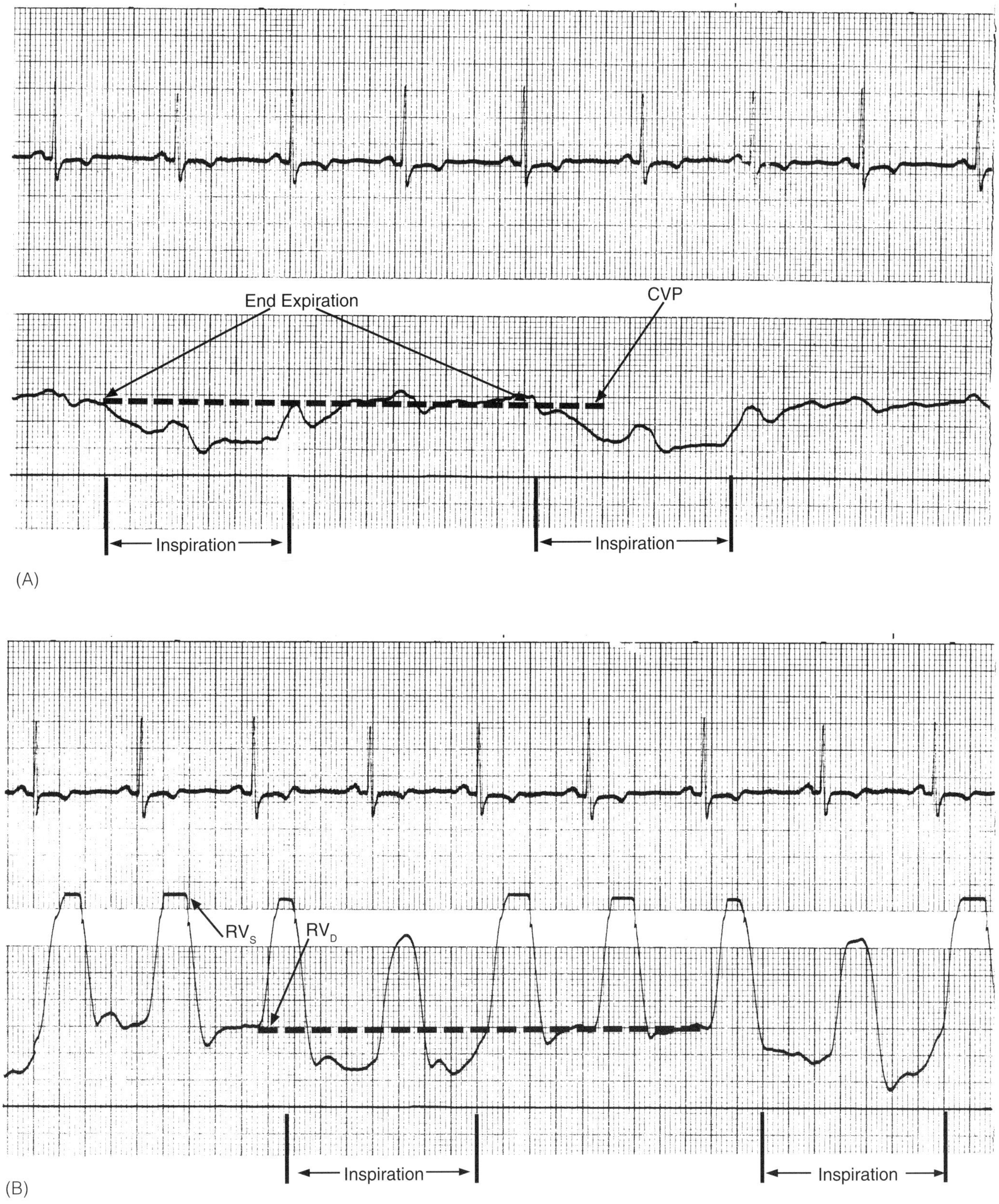

FIG. 94-3. Pulmonary capillary wedge pressure (PCWP) tracing. The baseline tracing represents a pressure of 0. Each large block (5 mm) represents 5 cm water pressure (standard scale). The heart rate at the time of pulmonary artery catheter placement has decreased since the time the patient first presented. (A) Right atrial tracing. CVP indicates central venous pressure. (B) Tracing at the time of catheter passage through the right ventricle. RV_S indicates systolic pressure in the right ventricle; RV_D, diastolic pressure in the right ventricle. (C) Tracing after passage of the catheter into the pulmonary artery. PA_S indicates systolic pressure in the pulmonary artery; PA_D, diastolic pressure in the pulmonary artery. (D) Tracing with the catheter in the distal pulmonary artery with the balloon inflated to a wedge position.

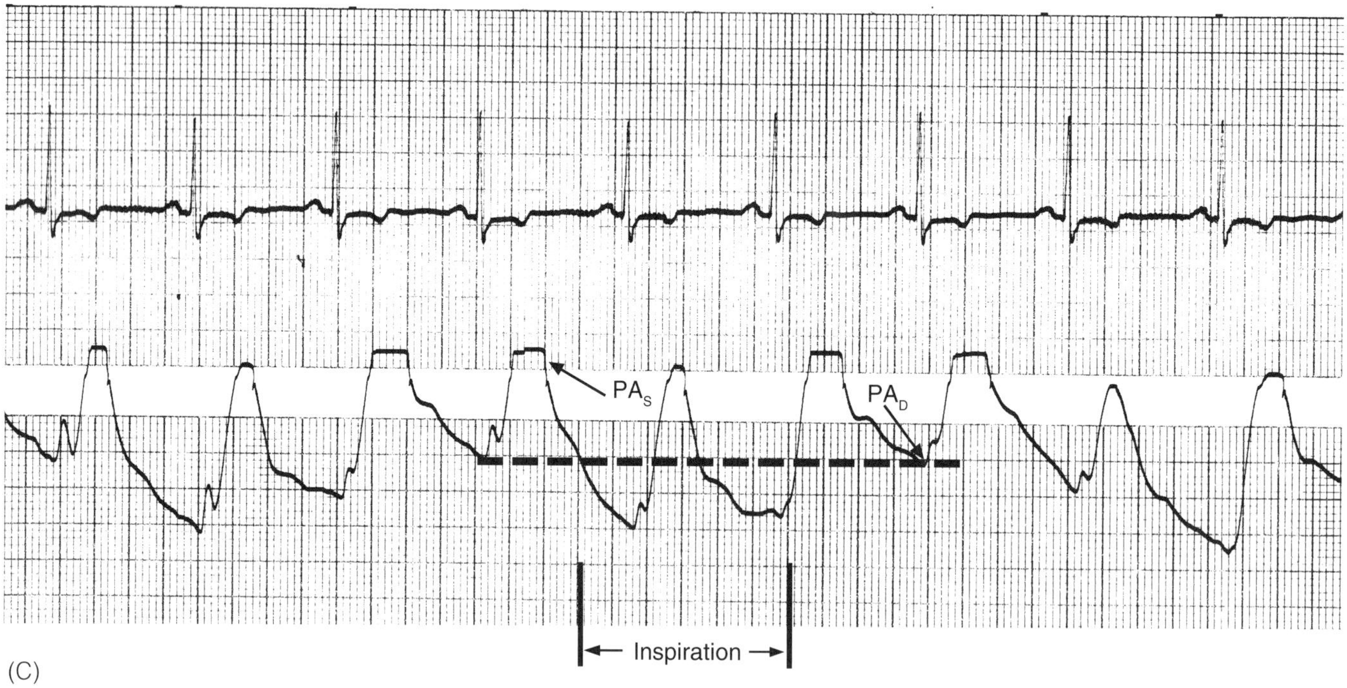

(C)

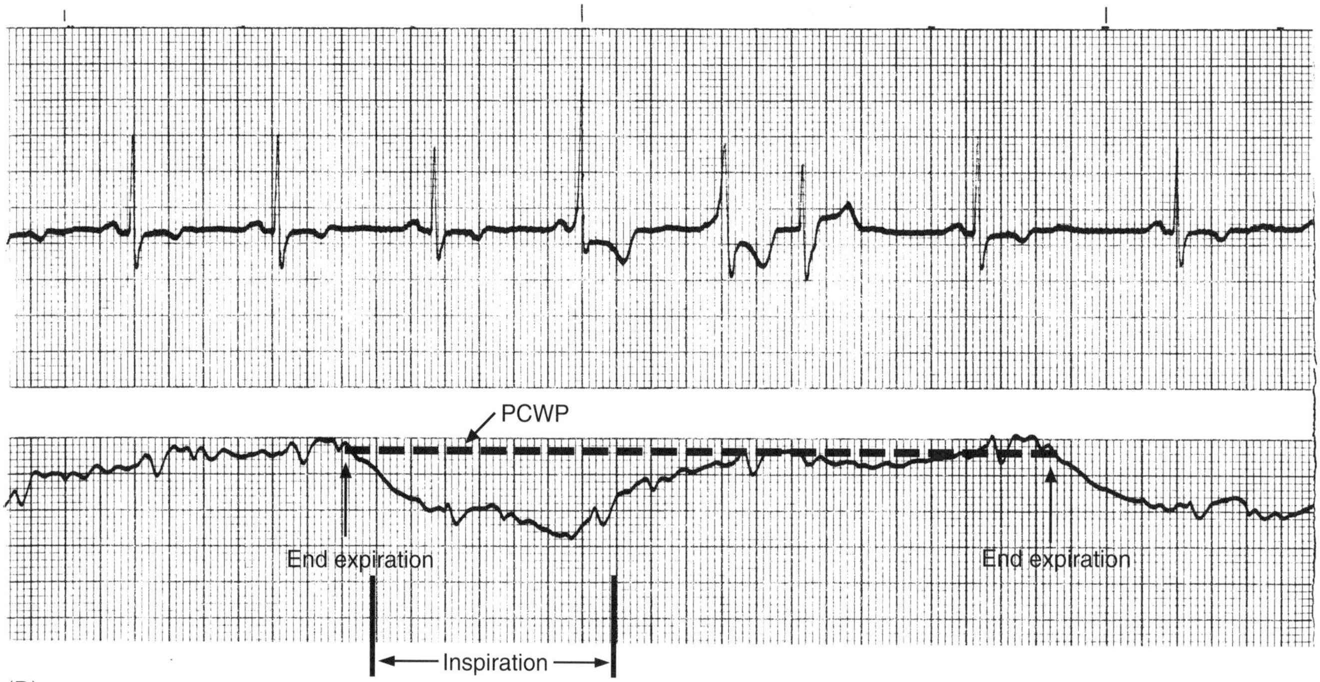

(D)

FIG. 94-3. *Continued*

This patient has pulmonary edema resulting from fluid overload. The correct therapy for her is diuresis with a potent diuretic such as furosemide. The diagnosis is made by the presence of diffuse alveolar infiltrates on chest X-ray and the PCWP reading of 27. Although pulmonary edema is frequently referred to as congestive heart failure, the pathophysiology of this disorder is a pulmonary capillary hydrostatic pressure sufficient to overcome the resorptive force of the plasma colloid osmotic pressure. Cardiac failure need not be present for pulmonary edema to occur, as is demonstrated in the case of this previously healthy patient with normal cardiac function who exhibits evidence of fluid overload. The wheezing, also called cardiac asthma, is thought to result from bronchiolar edema leading to airway narrowing and obstruction.

Pulmonary capillary wedge pressure readings are taken at the end of expiration, when the contribution of the respiratory muscles to the intrathoracic pressure is negligible. Figure 94-4 illustrates the placement of a

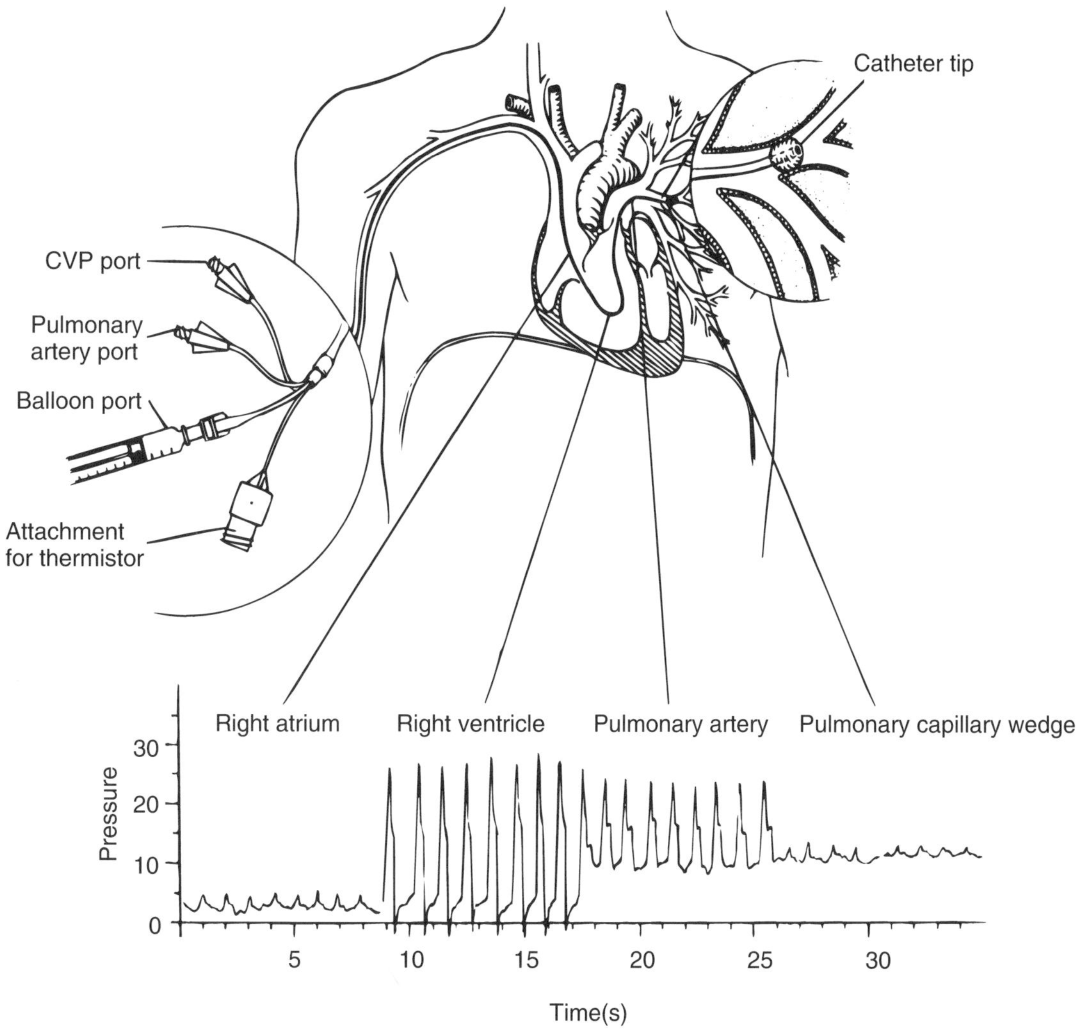

FIG. 94-4. Swan–Ganz catheter placement. Shown is a Swan–Ganz catheter (7 French) depicting central venous pressure (CVP) port, pulmonary artery and balloon port, and attachment for thermistor. During advancement through the right side of the heart, characteristic pressure tracings are recorded from the right atrial, right ventricular, pulmonary artery, and pulmonary capillary wedge positions. (Gibson RS, Kistner JR. Swan-Ganz catheter insertion. In: Suratt PM, Gibson RS, eds. Manual of medical procedures. St Louis: CV Mosby, 1982:61)

Swan–Ganz catheter. During spontaneous inspiration, the intrathoracic pressure becomes negative because of the downward movement of the diaphragm and the outward movement of the rib cage. This negative pressure causes air to move from the surrounding atmosphere into the lungs. This negative intrathoracic pressure is transmitted throughout the thorax, including the vascular spaces, and results in a decrease in the pressure recorded by the PCWP catheter. During expiration, there is a passive return to atmospheric pressure. At *end expiration,* the intrathoracic pressure equals the atmospheric pressure, and the pressure recorded by the catheter represents the intravascular (PCWP) reading only (Fig. 94-3).

The physical findings and hypoxia demonstrated in this patient could raise the question of asthma. The American Thoracic Society defines asthma as "a disease characterized by increased responsiveness of the trachea and bronchi to a variety of stimuli and manifested by widespread narrowing of the airways that changes in severity either spontaneously or as a result of appropriate therapy." Narrowing of the airways in asthma is the result of bronchiolar smooth muscle constriction, mucus hypersecretion, and inflammation of the airways. Inhalation of a beta agonist such as albuterol is currently the mainstay of asthma therapy. Corticosteroids are frequently included, but there is some controversy as to their role in the treatment of early or mild asthma. The chest X-ray in a patient with an acute asthma exacerbation would show clear and hyperinflated lungs. The PCWP would be normal. Additionally, this patient did not give a history of asthma. Therefore, therapy with corticosteroids, epinephrine, or a beta agonist would be inappropriate.

A transfusion reaction resulting from ABO incompatibility would result in circulatory collapse and disseminated intravascular coagulopathy. The associated respiratory distress would be due to the development of adult respiratory distress syndrome (ARDS). The transfusion should be stopped as soon as the problem is identified, and supportive therapy including vasopressors should be given. Treatment for ARDS includes mechanical ventilation with oxygen and PEEP therapy.

Adult respiratory distress syndrome is a clinical syndrome consisting of moderate to severe hypoxemia, diffuse alveolar infiltrates in the absence of pulmonary infection, and normal filling pressures (pulmonary capillary hydrostatic pressure). The PCWP would not be elevated in a patient with ARDS. The chest X-ray is often indistinguishable from that of a patient with cardiogenic pulmonary edema, and diagnosis often requires insertion of a pulmonary artery catheter. There are many mechanisms for the development of ARDS. All have in common the occurrence of diffuse alveolar injury or inflammation with resultant capillary leaks and decrease in pulmonary surfactant. Treatment is directed at the underlying cause and includes supportive care with mechanical ventilation and positive end-expiratory pressure therapy. This patient does not have ARDS.

Bernard GR, Brigham KL. Pulmonary edema. In: Stein JH, ed. Internal medicine. 4th ed. St Louis: CV Mosby, 1994:1649–1655

Holcroft JW, Blaisdell FW. Shock: causes and management of circulatory collapse. In: Sabiston DC Jr, ed. Textbook of surgery: the biological basis of modern surgical practice. 14th ed. Philadelphia: WB Saunders, 1991:34–56

Ingbar DH, Marcy TW. Respiratory therapy and monitoring. In: Stein JH, ed. Internal medicine. 4th ed. St Louis: CV Mosby, 1994:1655–1660

Leatherman JW, Marini J. Clinical use of the pulmonary artery catheter. In: Hall JB, Schmidt GA, Wood LDH, eds. Principles of critical care. New York: McGraw-Hill, 1992:323–342

Rinaldo JE. Multiple organ dysfunction syndrome (MODS) in the context of ARDS. In: Stein JH, ed. Internal medicine. 4th ed. St Louis: CV Mosby, 1994:1646–1649

95

Surgical therapy for vaginal prolapse

A 43-year-old woman who has delivered six large singleton infants vaginally presents with uterovaginal prolapse 24 months after the last delivery. She asks your recommendation for therapy that will cure her prolapse and restore her ability to be sexually active. You recommend a hysterectomy and

(A) posterior culdoplasty and posterior colporrhaphy
(B) posterior culdoplasty and sacrospinous colpopexy
(C) posterior colporrhaphy and sacral colpopexy
* (D) posterior culdoplasty, posterior colporrhaphy, and sacrospinous colpopexy
(E) posterior culdoplasty, posterior colporrhaphy, and sacral colpopexy

Three principal sources of damage may predispose a patient to vaginal prolapse:

- Weakness associated with neuropathy, either congenital (spina bifida) or acquired (disk herniation)
- Trauma (obstetric origin)
- Aging (damage resulting from estrogen loss with a resultant loss of collagen and supporting tissue)

Optimum surgical repair is individualized: one must identify both the primary site of damage and structures and sources of strength, including:

- The upper vaginal portion of the cardinal ligament
- The connective tissue and retinaculum of the round ligaments and peritoneum
- The pubourethral ligaments
- The fusion of the pubococcygeus musculature (the postrectal levator plate, as opposed to the insignificant fibers meeting between the rectum and the vagina)
- The rectovaginal septum (the fascia of Denonvilliers)

Reestablishing the integrity of the levator plate in a horizontal axis is the key to restoration of support and function of the vagina. Thus, this patient needs a posterior colporrhaphy, which is a vaginal procedure. Most surgeons prefer to do the entire procedure either vaginally or abdominally unless there is a compelling reason to use both approaches. For this reason, posterior culdoplasty, posterior colporrhaphy, and sacrospinous colpopexy are the preferred procedures for this patient.

It has been determined that most women are sexually active after surgical repair of vaginal prolapse. In some postmenopausal women, the vagina will be narrowed after the repair, independent of sexual activity. By comparison, a narrowed vagina after surgical repair is a most unusual finding in premenopausal women.

There is little difference in vaginal length and function after posterior culdoplasty or sacrospinous fixation. The greatest vaginal length is obtained with sacral colpopexy; however, normal vaginal length is restored with each type of repair, and sexual function afterward is comparable. In instances where there has been shortening of the prolapsed vagina, sacral colpopexy is recommended to optimize vaginal length.

Given FT Jr, Muhlendorf IK, Browning GM. Vaginal length and sexual function after colpopexy for complete uterovaginal eversion. Am J Obstet Gynecol 1993;169:284–288

Nichols DH. Surgery for pelvic floor disorders. Surg Clin North Am 1991;71:927–946

96

Needle aspiration of a breast lesion

A 38-year-old woman presents with a palpable mass in her left breast. She found the mass while doing her first breast self-examination 2 weeks ago. Clinical breast examination reveals a dominant mass at the 10-o'clock position, 3 cm from the edge of the areola. The mass is firm, smooth, nontender, and mobile.

Fine-needle aspiration of the mass is performed, and no gross fluid is obtained. However, an adequate cell sample for cytology is procured by multiple short thrusts of the needle tip within the mass. Which of the following can be definitively diagnosed by cytopathology?

* (A) Fibroadenoma
(B) Fibrocystic change
(C) Lipoma
(D) Sclerosing adenosis
(E) Ductal carcinoma in situ

Fibroadenoma can be definitively diagnosed by fine-needle aspiration cytology (Figs. 96-1 and 96-2) when sheets of benign ductal cells, normal stroma, and "naked" or "nude" bipolar nuclei are identified in an abundant cell sample (Fig. 96-3; see color plate). The histology of a breast fibroadenoma is shown in Fig. 96-4 (see color plate).

Although cytology of fibrocystic change, lipoma, and sclerosing adenosis can be suggestive of or consistent with these diagnoses, tissue biopsy is required for definitive histopathologic diagnosis. Malignant cells can be identified by fine-needle aspiration cytology, and the cytologic criteria are established for differentiating the various types of breast cancer. However, tissue biopsy with histologic evaluation is required for definitive diagnosis of invasion or to confirm in situ cancer.

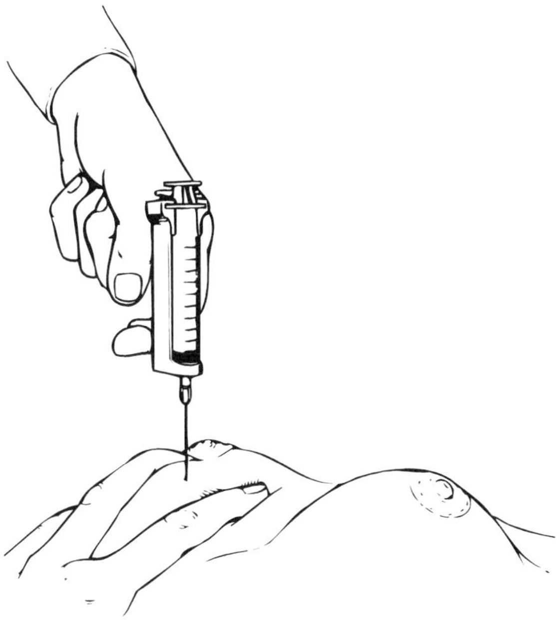

FIG. 96-1. Stabilization of a breast mass over a rib for fine-needle aspiration with a pistol-type syringe holder. (Hindle WH. Contemporary management of breast disease, I: benign disease. The diagnostic evaluation. Obstet Gynecol Clin North Am 1994:21:510)

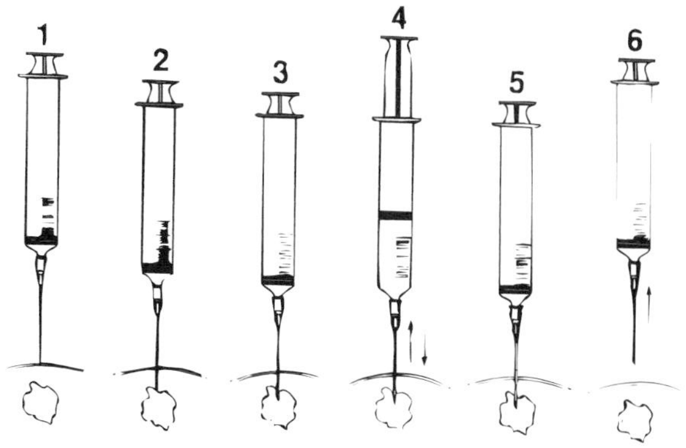

FIG. 96-2. Sequential steps of fine-needle aspiration of a solid mass for cytology. Negative pressure in the syringe is applied only during step 4, when the needle tip is thrust back and forth within the breast mass. (Hindle WH. Contemporary management of breast disease, I: benign disease. The diagnostic evaluation. Obstet Gynecol Clin North Am 1994:21:511)

Bell DA, Hajdu SI, Urban JA, Gaston JP. Role of aspiration cytology in the diagnosis and management of mammary lesions in office practice. Cancer 1983;51:1182–1189

Frable WJ. Needle aspiration of the breast. Cancer 1984;53:671–676

Hindle WH, Alonzo LJ. Conservative management of breast fibroadenomas. Am J Obstet Gynecol 1991;164:1647–1651

Hindle WH, Payne PA, Pan EY. The use of fine-needle aspiration in the evaluation of persistent palpable dominant breast masses. Am J Obstet Gynecol 1993;168:1814–1819

Oertel YC. Fine needle aspiration of the breast. Boston: Butterworths, 1987

97

Screening for colorectal cancer

A 50-year-old asymptomatic woman presents for a well-woman checkup. In addition to the pelvic and digital rectal examination, recommended colon cancer screening for this patient includes annual fecal occult blood testing and

(A) annual carcinoembryonic antigen testing
(B) annual sigmoidoscopy
* (C) sigmoidoscopy every 3–5 years
(D) colonoscopy every 3–5 years
(E) air-contrast barium enema every 3–5 years

More women die from colorectal cancer than from all types of gynecologic cancers. Colorectal cancer is the second most common cancer in the United States, with an overall mortality rate of approximately 60%. The incidence in men and women is almost equal. Approximately 138,000 new cases are estimated to occur annually, with more than 55,000 projected deaths. Early lesion detection, when the disease is confined to the colon and there is no lymph node involvement or metastasis, is associated with a mortality rate of 20% or lower.

Autopsy studies indicate that of asymptomatic persons 50 years of age or older, 36–53% have at least one colonic adenoma. Most experts believe that more than 95% of colorectal cancers derive from adenomatous polyps. Detection and removal of adenomatous polyps reduce the incidence of colorectal cancer by 76–90%.

Current strategies for prevention of colon cancer focus on detection of premalignant polyps and early diagnosis of malignant lesions, particularly in asymptomatic patients. There is a dramatic increase in the incidence of colorectal cancer beginning at age 50, justifying age-based screening in those at average risk. Screening women between the ages of 50 and 75 years should reduce their risk of colorectal cancer by 10–75%, depending on the screening technique.

Screening techniques for colon cancer include digital rectal examination, fecal occult blood testing, sigmoidoscopy, colonoscopy, and double-contrast barium enema. Although the ideal screening regimen remains controversial, national agencies have made recommendations. In 1992, the American Cancer Society recommended that persons with average risk for the development of colorectal cancer undergo flexible sigmoidoscopy every 3–5 years beginning at age 50, along with annual fecal occult blood testing. The American College of Obstetricians and Gynecologists and the American Cancer Society recommend annual fecal occult blood testing, annual digital rectal examination, and sigmoidoscopy every 3–5 years for asymptomatic women after age 50. Sigmoidoscopy more frequently than every 3 years is not cost-effective in asymptomatic women not at increased risk; every 10 years may be nearly as efficacious as every 3–5 years, according to one study.

Approximately 10% of large bowel adenomas and cancers are within the potential reach of an examining finger at rectal examination. There is no direct evidence, however, that detection of a tumor by rectal examination reduces mortality from colorectal cancer.

Fecal occult blood testing is an inexpensive test that has the capability of detecting adenomas and cancers in asymptomatic patients. It is designed to identify peroxidase, an enzyme present in human hemoglobin. Causes of false-positive and false-negative tests are presented in the box.

The most commonly recommended screening protocol for this test is to sample two areas of stool on 3 different days for a total of six samples; compliance is as low as 50% in controlled trials. A high-fiber diet for several days before testing is recommended to induce bleeding from polyps or cancers that may be present. Between 1% and 5% of unselected asymptomatic patients will have positive tests. Of those, 10% will have cancer, and 20–30% will have adenomas. In one recent clinical trial, annual fecal occult blood testing of rehydrated samples decreased the 13-year cumulative mortality rate from colorectal cancer by 33%. If testing of the sample is delayed and cards are stored, rehydration with a drop of water is indicated before testing.

Variables for five different invasive screening techniques used for the detection of colon cancer are presented in Table 97-1. Over 40% of benign and malignant

Fecal Occult Blood Test Variables

Causes of False-Positive Tests

High peroxidase activity in *uncooked* foods
- Turnips
- Broccoli
- Cauliflower
- Radishes
- Cabbage
- Potatoes
- Cucumbers
- Mushrooms
- Artichokes
- Rare red meat

Medications
- Oral iron
- Aspirin and other nonsteroidal antiinflammatory drugs

Specimen rehydration

Causes of False-Negative Tests

Insufficient or intermittent bleeding
Technical error
Specimen dehydration
Sampling error

neoplasms are proximal to the splenic flexure. Polyps are found 3.1-fold and cancer 3.5-fold more often by flexible than by rigid sigmoidoscopy. Use of the flexible instrument increases patient compliance because of decreased pain and discomfort. Principal drawbacks of colonoscopy and air-contrast barium enema are increased cost and discomfort; sedation is usually required for colonoscopy. False-positive results are negligible for all of these techniques; with air-contrast barium enema, false-positive results may occur with incomplete colon preparation. A complete colonoscopy is the most sensitive test. It is also the most expensive test. Annual serum carcinoembryonic antigen testing is not an acceptable screening method for colon cancer because of the low sensitivity and specificity of the test.

American College of Obstetricians and Gynecologists. Routine cancer screening. ACOG Committee Opinion 128. Washington, DC: ACOG, 1993

Eddy DM. Screening for colorectal cancer. Ann Intern Med 1990;113:373–384

Mandel JS, Bond JH, Church TR, Snover DC, Bradley GM, Schuman LM, et al. Reducing mortality from colorectal cancer by screening for fecal occult blood. N Engl J Med 1993;328:1365–1371

Selby JV, Friedman GD, Quesenberry CP Jr, Weiss NS. A case-control study of screening sigmoidoscopy and mortality from colorectal cancer. N Engl J Med 1992;326:653–657

Toribara NW, Sleisenger MH. Screening for colorectal cancer. N Engl J Med 1995;332:861–867

TABLE 97-1. Variables Associated With Invasive Screening Techniques for Colon Cancer

Screening Technique	Sensitivity (%)	Cancers Reached (%)	Perforation (%)	Cost
Rigid sigmoidoscopy (< 35 cm)	85	30	0.01	*X**
Flexible sigmoidoscopy (35 cm)	85	30	0.02	1.5*X*
Flexible sigmoidoscopy (60 cm)	85	40–60	0.045	2*X*
Colonoscopy	95	100	0.2	7*X*
Air-contrast barium enema	85	100	0.02	3*X*

* *X* indicates baseline values.

98

Second-look surgery for ovarian cancer

A 49-year-old woman has just completed six cycles of chemotherapy with cyclophosphamide and carboplatin (Paraplatin) for a stage III ovarian cancer. By physical examination, radiographic studies, and tumor markers, she is in complete clinical remission. She comes to your office to discuss her treatment options. In discussing second-look surgery, you inform her that:

(A) No further therapy is necessary, as she is cured.
(B) The retroperitoneum is not accessible at laparoscopy.
(C) Second-look surgery has greater benefit in patients with early disease.
* (D) Second-look surgery is investigational.
(E) Second-look surgery has improved overall survival.

During the 1970s, second-look laparotomy was incorporated into the overall treatment scheme for patients with ovarian cancer. Given the lack of precision of noninvasive techniques (physical examination, radiographic studies, tumor markers) in predicting the presence or absence of clinically occult disease, a surgical reassessment can avert the premature discontinuation of therapy in patients with persistent disease. Critics of second-look laparotomy cite the recognized 20–50% recurrence rates after a negative procedure as evidence of its severe limitations in predicting a disease-free state. These recurrence rates reflect surgical limitations associated with scarring and the number of biopsies taken, as well as the biology of ovarian cancer.

Second-look surgery conducted strictly for diagnostic purposes is not likely to influence survival unless accompanied by changes in postoperative management. Historically, "salvage" chemotherapy regimens have not been successful in most patients. With the advent of intraperitoneal chemotherapies, biologic response modifiers, and new chemotherapies, end-staging surgical reassessment may eventually be proven beneficial for advanced disease, whereas it is probably not beneficial for early-stage disease.

Despite the absence of identifiable tumor by clinical imaging examinations after completion of adjuvant cytotoxic therapy, approximately 40–60% of patients with advanced disease at diagnosis will be found to have persistent disease at second-look surgery. With the technologic advances of laparoscopic surgery, it is now possible to visualize the retroperitoneum and to sample lymph nodes, as well as to completely explore the peritoneal cavity. The older literature documented a false-negative rate of 20–55% for second-look laparoscopy. In these studies, laparoscopy was immediately followed by laparotomy. This high rate reflected the lack of modern instruments and optics and limitations in surgical laparoscopic techniques.

Second-look laparotomy is major surgery. The most frequently reported complication is prolonged ileus. Other less common complications include infections of the wound, urinary tract, or pulmonary tract.

Second-look surgery provides an opportunity to resect residual tumor and perhaps tailor subsequent therapy. The benefit of tumor resection in such patients is controversial. Recent reports have noted improved survival when residual disease was completely resected at second-look surgery. The theoretical survival benefit of tumor resection lies in reducing the tumor mass to a point at which subsequent therapy can exert a maximal effect. A large randomized trial is needed to determine whether second-look laparoscopy or laparotomy, or both, followed by optimum therapy (salvage and consolidation) has an effect on prognosis and long-term survival. Second-look surgery remains an investigational procedure.

Friedman JB, Weiss NS. Second thoughts about second-look laparotomy in advanced ovarian cancer. N Engl J Med 1990;322:1079–1082

Hoskins WJ, Rubin SC, Dulaney E, Chapman D, Almadrones L, Saigo P, et al. Influence of secondary cytoreduction at the time of second-look laparotomy on the survival of patients with epithelial ovarian carcinoma. Gynecol Oncol 1989;34:365–371

Podratz KC, Kinney WK. Second-look operation in ovarian cancer. Cancer 1993;71:1551–1558

Runowicz CD. A critical assessment of the role of second-look surgery in ovarian carcinoma. Cancer Invest 1987;5:479–485

99

Indications for breast biopsy

A 52-year-old woman is seen for a routine examination. A physical examination, including breast and pelvic examination, is normal. A mammogram reveals a developing density in the upper outer quadrant of the left breast compared with previous mammograms. A compression-spot film demonstrates persistence of the density (Fig. 99-1). As the next step in management, you recommend

(A) breast ultrasonography
(B) office needle aspiration
* (C) mammographically guided stereotactic biopsy
(D) excision biopsy
(E) follow-up mammography in 6 months

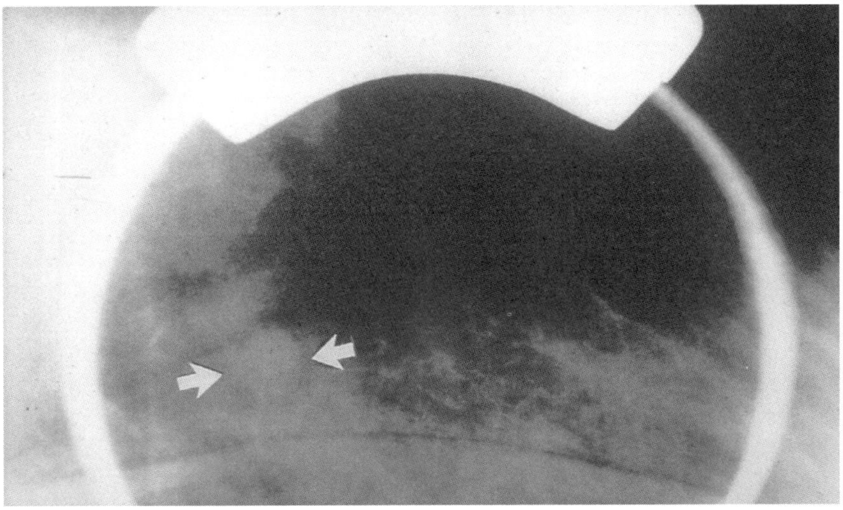

FIG. 99-1. Compression-spot mammography film demonstrating density (arrows).

Breast cancer accounts for 32% of all cancers in women and is the leading cause of death from cancer in women age 35–54 years. The value of mammography as a screening tool in the early detection of breast cancer is well established for women age 50 and beyond. Several features of mammographic nodules allow a level of suspicion to be assigned. These include irregular shape, number of microcalcifications in a cluster, definition of the margins, and interval change. Regardless of the features of a lesion on a single examination, if the lesion is known to represent an interval change from previous studies, the risk of malignancy is generally higher than that of an identical lesion seen on a patient's first mammogram and not known to be an interval change.

Classic mammographic signs of malignancy include an irregular stellate mass or more than five clustered ductal microcalcifications. However, in large studies, fewer than 40% of cancers presented with classic signs. Most cancers presented with more subtle signs, including developing density, focal asymmetry, or presence of a focally dilated duct.

A developing density is not pathognomonic of malignancy. Breast tissue can undergo changes as a result of varying hormonal stimulation. Furthermore, tissue may appear changed on mammography because of inhomogeneous involution of the surrounding tissue as well as differences in positioning or technique. Special views on compression-spot films will help demonstrate whether the density persists (implying pathology) or effaces (implying overlapping fibroglandular tissue). In this patient, spot films have confirmed a change from previous mammograms (Fig. 99-1). A repeat mammogram would not add additional information in the management of this patient.

Ultrasonography is most useful in determining whether a lesion is cystic or solid. Ultrasonography is generally not considered to be predictive of the histologic diagnosis of solid tissue in the breast. This patient's mammographic findings suggest that ultrasonography would not be useful, because the lesion is not discrete.

With newer technologies for breast biopsy, less invasive procedures are now being performed to evaluate and diagnose breast lesions. For nonpalpable lesions, outpatient or office needle aspiration or biopsy can be performed under mammographic stereotactic guidance. A core biopsy is preferred to needle aspiration at some centers because the tissue sample can be obtained for histologic rather than cytologic analysis.

The advent of stereotaxis for mammography has greatly increased the accuracy of needle placement into small, nonpalpable lesions. Stereotactic fine needle aspiration biopsy or cyst puncture can be performed for nodules as small as 3 mm. The ability of the X-ray tube to move independently of the breast compression device and the cassette holder allows two views of the breast to be taken at a fixed degree of shallow obliquity. The X, Y, and Z coordinates of the lesion are calculated by the computer according to the basic principle of stereotaxis. The radiologist selects the length of the needle to be used. The procedure is performed in the radiologist's office rather than in an operating room suite.

If the lesion is not satisfactorily diagnosed by percutaneous biopsy or aspiration, open excision biopsy is required. For a nonpalpable lesion, preoperative localization with mammographic guidance is required. After placement of a needle under radiographic guidance, the specimen is removed. Specimen radiography is performed to confirm removal of the lesion.

American College of Obstetricians and Gynecologists. Carcinoma of the breast. ACOG Technical Bulletin 158. Washington, DC: ACOG, 1991

American College of Obstetricians and Gynecologists. Nonmalignant conditions of the breast. ACOG Technical Bulletin 156. Washington, DC: ACOG, 1991

Atamdede FI, Isaacs JH. The role of fine-needle aspiration in the diagnosis of breast lesions. Gynecol Oncol 1993;50:159–163

Langer TG, de Paredes ES. Breast disease: the radiologist's expanding role. Curr Probl Diagn Radiol 1993;22:189–227

100

Surgical management of early germ cell tumor

A 29-year-old nulliparous woman undergoes surgery for a complex pelvic mass. During the procedure you note a 7-cm unilateral solid ovarian mass. Frozen pathologic evaluation reveals a dysgerminoma. Examination of the contralateral ovary, the fallopian tubes, and the uterus reveals normal pelvic organs. The remainder of the abdomen is unremarkable. The best operative procedure for this patient is

* (A) unilateral salpingo-oophorectomy, omentectomy, pelvic and paraaortic lymph node sampling
(B) bilateral salpingo-oophorectomy, omentectomy, pelvic and paraaortic lymph node sampling
(C) total abdominal hysterectomy, bilateral salpingo-oophorectomy, omentectomy, pelvic and paraaortic lymph node sampling
(D) unilateral salpingo-oophorectomy and bivalving or biopsy of the remaining ovary

Most malignant germ cell tumors are unilateral. Bilateral ovarian involvement with tumor is rare, except in the case of dysgerminoma, in which the frequency of bilaterality is 10–15%. Approximately 60–70% of patients with ovarian germ cell tumors have stage I disease at diagnosis; 75–80% of patients with a dysgerminoma have stage I disease at diagnosis. A decision about therapy is based on the permanent pathology sections.

Unilateral salpingo-oophorectomy with preservation of the contralateral ovary and the uterus is the correct surgical treatment for most patients with malignant germ cell tumors. A complete staging procedure should also be performed to define the surgical stage. An omentectomy, selected pelvic and paraaortic lymphadenectomy, cytologic washings, and diaphragmatic scrapings complete a surgical staging. A hysterectomy or removal of the other ovary is not necessary, except in rare circumstances when the uterus is involved with disease. Because of the potential for adhesions and subsequent infertility, bivalving or biopsy of the normal-appearing ovary is not recommended. Intraoperative ultrasonography may be useful in evaluating the other ovary. If a bilateral salpingo-oophorectomy is required, a hysterectomy need not be done. With the assisted reproductive technologies, pregnancy may still be possible.

Benign cystic teratoma is found in 5–10% of patients with malignant germ cell tumors. Therefore, if a dermoid cyst is discovered, removal by ovarian cystectomy with preservation of normal ovarian tissue is recommended.

In approximately 85% of patients with endodermal sinus tumor or embryonal carcinoma, disease will recur if no postoperative therapy is given. The recurrence rate in patients with immature teratoma is related to grade: 100% of patients with stage IA1 tumors remain disease free after surgery alone. In patients with surgical stage IA dysgerminoma, postoperative therapy is not required. If the disease recurs, virtually all patients with germ cell tumors can be effectively treated with chemotherapy.

For patients with stage II, III, IV, and recurrent tumor, chemotherapy with bleomycin sulfate (Blenoxane), etoposide (VePesid), and cisplatin (Platinol) is administered for three courses. Even though these tumors are radiosensitive, radiation therapy is rarely used because of long-term complications and loss of fertility.

Gershenson DM. Update on malignant ovarian germ cell tumors. Cancer 1993;71:1581–1590

Williams SD. Treatment of germ cell tumors of the ovary. Semin Oncol 1991;18:292–296

Williams SD, Loehrer PJ, Nichols CR, Einhorn LN. Chemotherapy of male and female germ cell tumors. Semin Oncol 1992;19(5 suppl):19–24

101

Prognosis of malignant mixed mesodermal tumor

A 67-year-old woman presents with vaginal bleeding and uterine enlargement corresponding to a 10-week-size gestation. Endometrial curettage is performed, and the pathologist reports a diagnosis of a mixed mesodermal tumor (MMT). In discussing this diagnosis with the patient, you bear in mind that:

* (A) Homologous mixed mesodermal tumors generally have the same prognosis as heterologous mixed mesodermal tumors.
(B) The mitotic index of the tumor is a reliable factor in predicting prognosis.
(C) Mixed mesodermal tumors grossly confined to the uterus have pelvic lymph node metastases in nearly 80% of cases.
(D) Radiation therapy appears to be ineffective in reducing the frequency of local recurrence.

Mixed mesodermal tumors of the uterus are relatively uncommon neoplasms, comprising 1–2% of all uterine malignancies. The clinical behavior of MMTs is aggressive, and the ultimate prognosis is guarded. Accurate diagnosis and appropriate therapy are important in the management of patients with this condition.

An MMT tumor containing elements native to the uterus is homologous; if the elements are foreign to the uterus, such as cartilage or striated muscle, the tumor is heterologous. Earlier reports suggested that homologous tumors, often referred to as carcinosarcoma, had a better prognosis than lesions containing heterologous elements. Evidence now indicates that this assumption was unfounded and that there is no difference in prognosis. Because there is no difference in behavior, the World Health Organization's current histologic classification uses the terms MMT and carcinosarcoma synonymously. These tumors characteristically have a high mitotic index, but in contrast to leiomyosarcomas of the uterus, the mitotic index of MMTs is not useful in predicting prognosis.

The prognosis of patients with an MMT that has spread beyond the uterus is exceedingly poor. The survival rate in such instances is 25–30%. Tumors that, on gross examination, appear to be confined to the uterus are found to have pelvic lymph node metastasis in 15–20% of cases. Only small MMTs confined to the tip of a polyp are reported to have a favorable prognosis, but even these tumors can metastasize and cause the patient's death.

The role of radiation therapy in MMTs of the uterus has been controversial. Sarcomas in general are not highly responsive to irradiation. Recent data suggest that radiation therapy is effective in reducing local pelvic recurrence of this tumor but not in improving overall survival.

Although chemotherapy remains an investigational option, current data have failed to demonstrate any improvement in either survival or progression-free interval with the use of adjuvant drug therapy. At present, chemotherapy is reserved for patients with advanced or recurrent disease.

Dinh TV, Slavin RE, Bhagavan BS, Hannigan EV, Tiamson EM, Yandell RB. Mixed müllerian tumors of the uterus: a clinicopathologic study. Obstet Gynecol 1989;74:388–392

Grosh WW, Jones HW III, Burnett LS, Greco FA. Malignant mixed mesodermal tumors of the uterus and ovary treated with cisplatin-based combination chemotherapy. Gynecol Oncol 1986;25:334–339

Nielsen SN, Podratz KC, Scheithauer BW, O'Brien PC. Clinicopathologic analysis of uterine malignant mixed müllerian tumors. Gynecol Oncol 1989;34:372–378

Silverberg SG, Major FJ, Blessing JA, Fetter B, Askin FB, Liao SY, et al. Carcinosarcoma (malignant mixed mesodermal tumor) of the uterus. A Gynecological Oncology Group pathologic study of 203 cases. Int J Gynecol Pathol 1990;9:1–19

102

Posthysterectomy management of ureterovaginal fistula

A 46-year-old woman, gravida 3, para 3, underwent vaginal hysterectomy and repair for pelvic relaxation. On the first postoperative day she experienced lower left pelvic pain and back pain localized high in the costovertebral angle. Examination revealed moderate tenderness over the costovertebral angle on the left side but no tenderness on the right side. She experienced some gradual improvement over the next 2 days. She was dismissed on the fourth postoperative day. On the ninth postoperative day she noted a watery vaginal discharge that increased over the next 24 hours, requiring four or five perineal pads over 12 hours. The leakage continued at night and soiled her bedding.

By the tenth postoperative day, the patient's back pain has improved and, other than the watery discharge, she is generally well. Methylene blue dye is instilled in the bladder and does not appear in the vagina. Intravenous pyelography (IVP) reveals dilatation of the left ureter and collecting system with flow of contrast medium from the left ureter near the bladder and left corner of the vagina. The cystoscopic examination is normal. The initial step in management is

* (A) passage of an internal double J ureteral stent in a retrograde fashion through the cystoscope
(B) percutaneous passage of a ureteral stent in an antegrade fashion
(C) left ureteroneocystostomy
(D) left ureteroureterostomy

The appearance of urine in the vagina may offer an indication of ureteral injury (Figs. 102-1 and 102-2). When a ureter has been incorporated in a ligature, 10–14 days usually pass before necrosis of the wall occurs or the suture loosens from shrinkage and retraction of the pedicle. After a total hysterectomy, urine from a ureteral defect usually enters the vagina through a small fistulous tract above the opening into the vault. If ureteral obstruction is present, the onset of vaginal drainage by the fistula may result in resolution of symptoms such as pain and fever.

When a patient presents with urine leakage, a convenient way to determine whether a bladder injury is present is to place a gauze sponge or tampon in the vagina and fill the bladder with a weak solution of methylene blue. If the sponge or tampon remains free of methylene blue after the patient ambulates, as was observed in this patient, a ureteral fistula is more probable than a vesicovaginal fistula.

Excretory urography is one of the first studies indicated after the appearance of urine in the vagina. The objective is to show whether the fistulous tract communicates with the bladder or the ureter. Hydroureteronephrosis, the most common abnormality seen on IVP resulting from a ureteral injury, suggests partial ureteral obstruction.

At cystoscopy, an attempt is made to insert an internal J ureteral stent through the ureteral orifice. It may not be

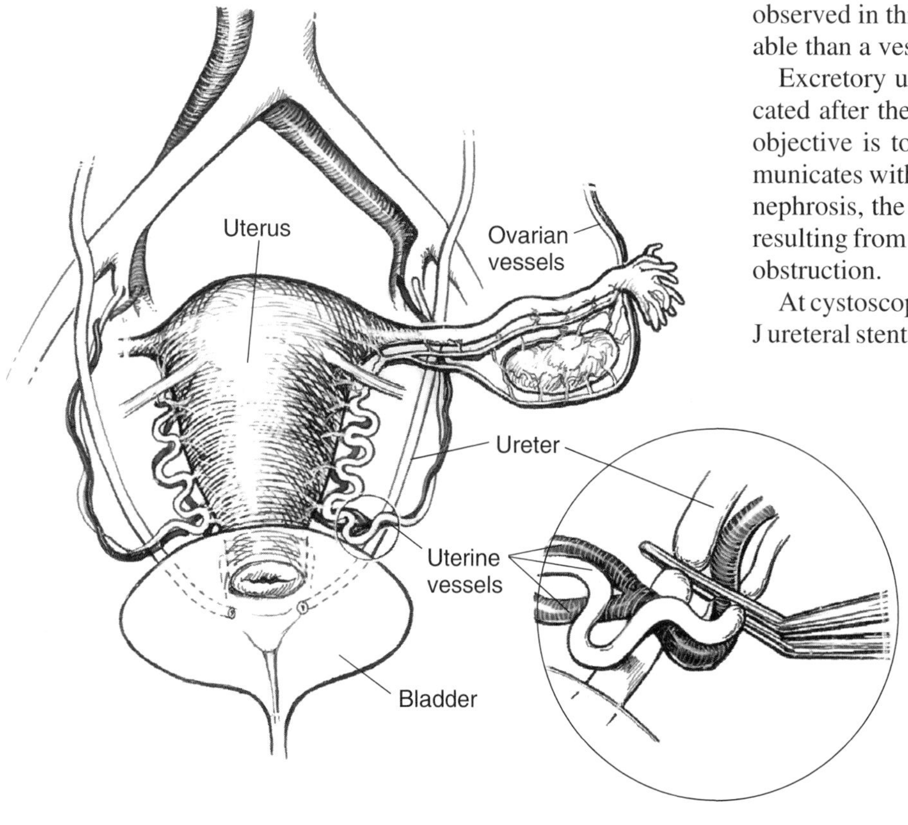

FIG. 102-1. The most common site of injury to the ureter in gynecologic surgery: the junction of the ureter and the uterine artery.

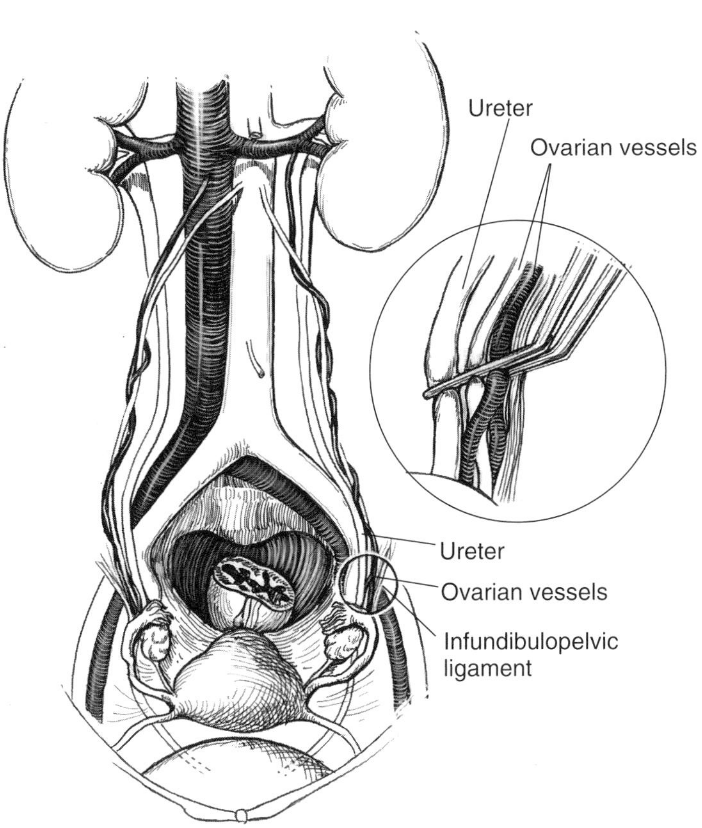

FIG. 102-2. Ureteral injury at the infundibulopelvic ligament, the second most common site of injury in gynecologic surgery.

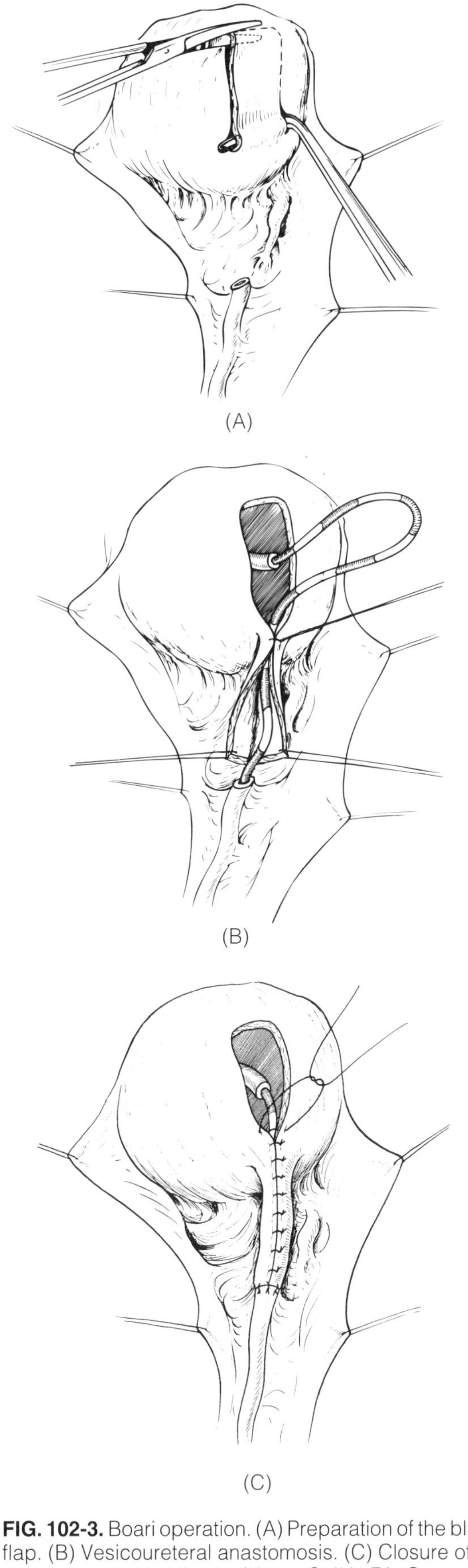

FIG. 102-3. Boari operation. (A) Preparation of the bladder flap. (B) Vesicoureteral anastomosis. (C) Closure of flaps over the ureteral catheter. (Käser O, Iklé FA. Gynecologic operations: indications, technic and results. New York: Grune and Stratton, 1967:320)

possible to advance a double J stent past the point of injury. Resistance to the passage of a ureteral catheter is usually due to the submucosal infarction, edema, stricture formation, ligation, or angulation of the ureter. If the catheter can be successfully passed through the injured area of the ureter, it should be left in the ureter for 14 days or longer, during which time the ureteral wall will usually heal. To demonstrate that the ureter is intact and that healing of the fistula is complete, IVP should be done before the stent is removed. If it is not possible to pass a stent in the retrograde direction, a percutaneous nephrostomy is performed, and an attempt is made to pass an antegrade stent. If these measures are not successful, the percutaneous nephrostomy catheter is retained for temporary drainage.

Knowledge of the function of the opposite kidney is essential to the surgeon in determining the best surgical approach to treat the injured ureter. If operation is necessary, the preferred procedure to be undertaken can only be determined after investigating the condition of the surrounding tissues. If the injury is at the level of the uterine vessels or within 4–5 cm of the ureterovesical junction, ureterovesical implantation (ureteroneocystostomy) can usually be accomplished and is preferable to ureteroureteral anastomosis. A variety of techniques, including the Boari flap (Fig. 102-3) and the psoas hitch (Fig. 102-4), can be used to mobilize the bladder to facilitate reattachment. If the ureteral injury is in the mid ureter, ureteroureterostomy may be required. Rarely, a transureteroureterostomy is necessary if an insufficient length of ureter is present for anastomosis.

Lee RA, Symmonds RE, Williams TJ. Current status of genitourinary fistula. Obstet Gynecol 1988;72:313–319

Thompson JD. Operative injuries to the ureter: prevention, recognition, and management. In: Thompson JD, Rock JA, eds. Te Linde's operative gynecology. 7th ed. Philadelphia: JB Lippincott, 1992:749–783

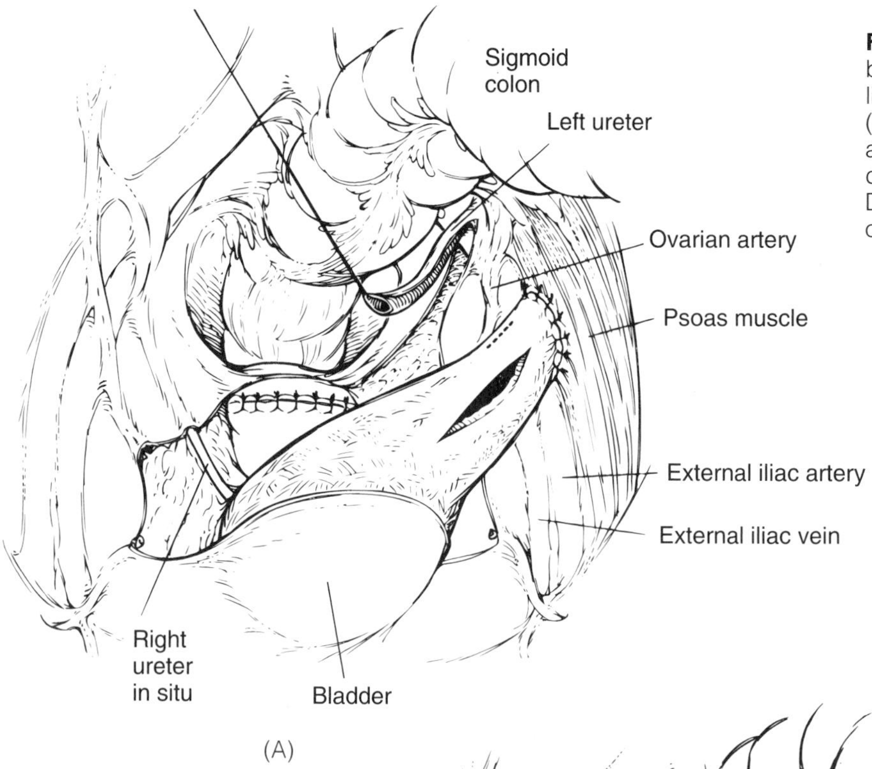

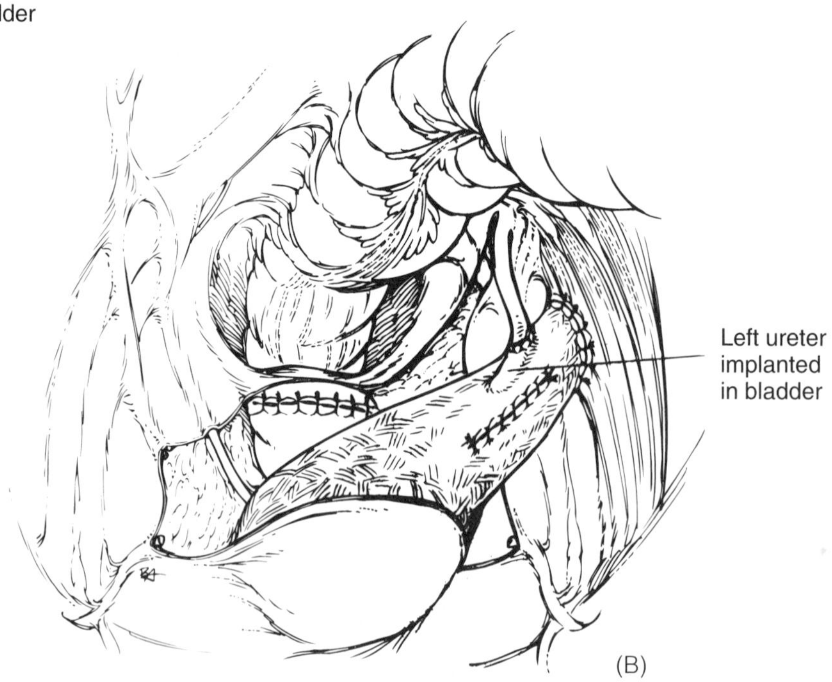

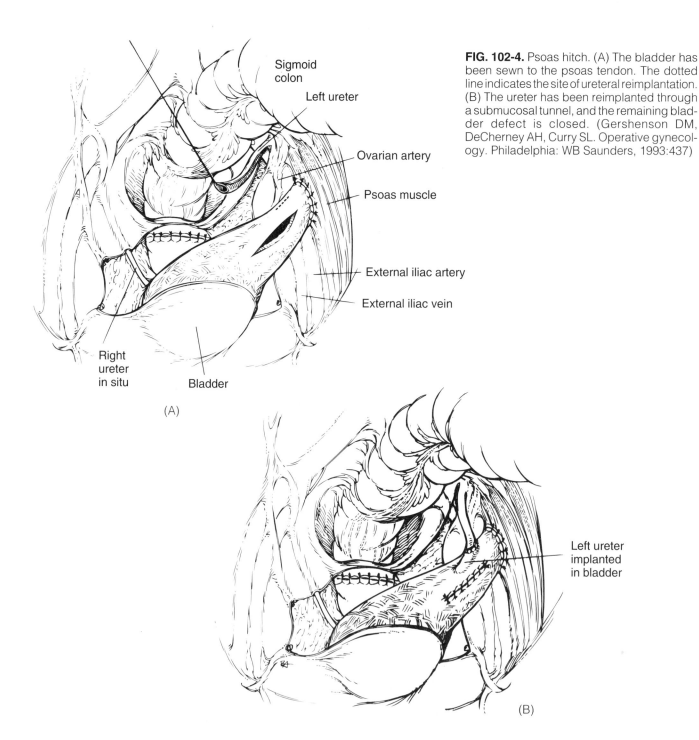

FIG. 102-4. Psoas hitch. (A) The bladder has been sewn to the psoas tendon. The dotted line indicates the site of ureteral reimplantation. (B) The ureter has been reimplanted through a submucosal tunnel, and the remaining bladder defect is closed. (Gershenson DM, DeCherney AH, Curry SL. Operative gynecology. Philadelphia: WB Saunders, 1993:437)

103

Management after abnormal Pap test

A 30-year-old woman, who has been conscientiously seeing you for the past 10 years for her annual gynecologic examination, has a Pap test interpreted as atypical squamous cells of undetermined significance (ASCUS). Previous Pap tests have always been normal. The most appropriate next step in this patient's management is

(A) immediate colposcopy and repeat Pap test
(B) repeat Pap test after treatment with intravaginal antibiotic cream
* (C) repeat Pap test in 4–6 months
(D) electroexcisional biopsy of the transformation zone
(E) cryosurgery of the transformation zone

The Bethesda System for reporting cervical and vaginal cytologic diagnoses was developed at a National Cancer Institute–sponsored workshop in 1988 to provide uniform diagnostic terminology that would facilitate communication between the laboratory and the clinician. The format of the Bethesda System report includes a descriptive diagnosis and an evaluation of specimen adequacy. The classification used is not a histogenetic one, but rather a nomenclature designed to facilitate categorization and reporting of cytologic diagnoses. Accordingly, squamous cell abnormalities are divided into three categories:

1. Atypical squamous cells of undetermined significance
2. Squamous intraepithelial lesions (SIL), which are subdivided into low grade and high grade
3. Squamous cell carcinoma

Low-grade SIL corresponds with cytologic changes produced by human papillomavirus infection, mild dysplasia, and cervical intraepithelial neoplasia (CIN 1). High-grade SIL encompasses moderate dysplasia (CIN 2) and severe dysplasia, or carcinoma in situ (CIN 3).

Atypical squamous cells of undetermined significance are defined as a cellular abnormality that is more marked than reactive changes but that quantitatively or qualitatively falls short of a definitive diagnosis of SIL. Because the cellular changes in ASCUS may reflect an exuberant benign change or a potentially serious lesion, ASCUS does not correspond with the previous class II Pap designation, which included obvious benign reactive changes only.

At times, the cytopathologist may feel sufficiently confident to qualify the ASCUS diagnosis by favoring a reactive or a neoplastic process. At other times, it is not possible to make such a determination, and the ASCUS diagnosis is not qualified further. Accordingly, the prognosis of patients with an ASCUS report can vary depending on whether the diagnosis is qualified and depending on the cytopathologist or laboratory. A diagnosis of ASCUS may be expected in no more than 5% of Pap test reports. In high-risk populations with a higher prevalence of SIL, there will be a corresponding higher prevalence of ASCUS. As a general guide, in a screened population the rate of ASCUS may be assumed to be two to three times the rate of SIL.

When a patient can be relied on to return for repeat cytologic examination at scheduled intervals (4–6 months), she can be monitored by cytology alone. A patient who receives two or more ASCUS reports should undergo a colposcopic evaluation. When patient compliance with follow-up recommendations is uncertain, colposcopic examination should be considered at the initial visit. Once the significance of the ASCUS report and the likelihood of compliance have been determined, an immediate repeat Pap test is of little value.

Because ASCUS may reflect a completely benign reactive phenomenon, electroexcisional biopsy of the transformation zone is not indicated. Cryosurgery of the transformation zone in the absence of a histologic diagnosis of SIL is not indicated in a patient with an abnormal Pap test. Treatment with intravaginal antibiotic cream in the absence of identifying specific microorganisms is not indicated.

American College of Obstetricians and Gynecologists. Cervical cytology: evaluation and management of abnormalities. ACOG Technical Bulletin 183. Washington, DC: ACOG, 1993

Kurman RJ, Henson DE, Herbst AL, Noller KL, Schiffman MH. Interim guidelines for management of abnormal cervical cytology. JAMA 1994;271:1866–1869

Kurman RJ, Solomon D. The Bethesda System for reporting cervical/vaginal cytologic diagnoses: definitions, criteria, and explanatory notes for terminology and specimen adequacy. New York: Springer-Verlag, 1994

Wright TC, Kurman RJ, Ferenczy A. Precancerous lesions of the cervix. In: Kurman RJ, ed. Blaustein's pathology of the female genital tract. 4th ed. New York: Springer-Verlag, 1994:229–277

104

Breast biopsy for a persistent mass

A 46-year-old woman has just had screening mammography with normal findings. Breast examination reveals a suspicious 1.5-cm dominant mass. There is no gross fluid on fine-needle aspiration. The cytologic specimen of the mass obtained by fine-needle aspiration is reported as hypocellular. The optimal management is

(A) repeat fine-needle aspiration in 3 months
(B) tissue core-needle biopsy in 3 months
(C) repeat mammography in 3 months
(D) ultrasonography of the breast
* (E) open surgical biopsy

A persistent dominant breast mass must be definitively diagnosed. It would be inappropriate to wait 3 months before taking further diagnostic measures, because early diagnosis correlates with increased disease-free survival.

Fine-needle aspiration with an adequate cell sample can cytologically diagnose as many as 90% of palpable breast neoplasms. If fine-needle aspiration cytology is not diagnostic of a clinically suspicious breast mass, open surgical biopsy should be performed. Open surgical biopsy is the final diagnostic procedure for a dominant breast mass.

Alternatively, a tissue core-needle biopsy, usually with ultrasound guidance, can be used to obtain material for histologic diagnosis if the fine-needle aspirate is not diagnostic. For a nonpalpable lesion, ultrasound-guided tissue core-needle biopsy can be used to obtain histologic material. Spring-loaded automated "guns" for percutaneous tissue core-needle biopsy have replaced Tru-Cut needles.

About 10% of palpable breast masses are not seen with mammography. The probability that a breast mass will be seen mammographically increases with a woman's advancing age because of fatty replacement of the glandular tissue of the breast as she grows older. Breast ultrasonography is a focused examination and is useful as an adjunct to mammography in determining whether a mammographically identified mass is cystic or solid. However, the number of false-positive and false-negative impressions is unacceptably high with ultrasonography, precluding its use as a screening technique. Open surgical biopsy provides tissue for a definitive histopathologic diagnosis and is indicated for this patient.

Baker LH. Breast Cancer Detection Demonstration project: five-year summary reports. CA Cancer J Clin 1982;32:194–225

Donegan WL. Evaluation of a palpable breast mass. N Engl J Med 1992;327:937–942

Edeiken S. Mammography and palpable cancer of the breast. Cancer 1988;61:263–265

Ennis JT. Diagnostic radiological imaging for breast disease. In: Bland KI, Copeland EM III, eds. The breast: comprehensive management of benign and malignant disease. Philadelphia: WB Saunders, 1991:426–468

Hindle WH. Breast masses: in-office evaluation with diagnostic triad. Postgrad Med 1990;88:85–94

Moore MP. Mass: lump/cyst. In: Harris JR, Hellman S, Henderson IC, Kinne DW, eds. Breast diseases. 2nd ed. Philadelphia: JB Lippincott, 1991:77–79

105

Staging of vulvar cancer

A 67-year-old woman has a 3 × 4-cm squamous carcinoma of the vulva located on the right posterior labia majora. The anus, vagina, and urethra are not involved. There are no palpable lymph nodes in either inguinal area. A modified radical hemivulvectomy and bilateral inguinofemoral lymphadenectomy are performed. Three lymph nodes from the right inguinofemoral specimen contain metastatic cancer. The International Federation of Gynecology and Obstetrics (FIGO) stage is

(A) stage I
(B) stage II
* (C) stage III
(D) stage IVA
(E) stage IVB

Before 1989, the FIGO staging for vulvar cancer was based on clinical examination. In 1989, the Cancer Committee of FIGO adopted a surgical staging classification for vulvar cancer. This classification does not rely on palpation of lymph nodes, but rather on the histologic examination of surgical specimens. In 1994, the classification was revised to include depth of stromal invasion (Appendix, Table 5). Because this patient has unilateral inguinofemoral lymph node metastases, she is classified as having stage III disease. Bilateral inguinofemoral lymph node metastases result in a classification of stage IVA disease. Distant metastases (including pelvic lymph nodes) result in a classification of stage IVB disease. Stages I and II are determined by size and location of the primary tumor and require the patient to have no nodal metastases.

The current FIGO surgical staging system provides a more accurate assessment of the true extent of disease than does the pre-1989 clinical staging classification. However, patients who cannot undergo surgery must be staged by the pre-1989 FIGO staging system. This clinical staging classification is based on the size and location of the primary lesion and the presence or absence of clinically palpable inguinofemoral lymph nodes.

Hacker NF, Eifel P, McGuire W, Wilkinson EJ. Vulva. In: Hoskins WJ, Perez CA, Young RC, eds. Principles and practice of gynecologic oncology. Philadelphia: JB Lippincott, 1992:538–539

Morrow CP, Curtin JP, Townsend DE. Synopsis of gynecologic oncology. 4th ed. New York: Churchill Livingstone, 1993:65–92

106

Therapy for granulosa cell tumor

A 20-year-old nulligravid woman has noticed progressive breast tenderness and unpredictable vaginal bleeding over the preceding 6 months. She is found to have a right adnexal mass. At surgery, a 7 × 8 × 6-cm tumor of the right ovary is found (Fig. 106-1; see color plate). There is no ascitic fluid, and the capsule is smooth and intact. The uterus, tubes, and left ovary are normal. The abdominal cavity peritoneal surfaces, omentum, bowel serosa and mesentery, pelvic and paraaortic lymph nodes, and diaphragm are clinically normal. A frozen section of the tumor is shown in Fig. 106-2. The treatment of choice for this patient is

* (A) unilateral salpingo-oophorectomy
(B) unilateral salpingo-oophorectomy with wedge resection of the contralateral ovary
(C) unilateral salpingo-oophorectomy and chemotherapy
(D) bilateral salpingo-oophorectomy
(E) bilateral salpingo-oophorectomy with total abdominal hysterectomy

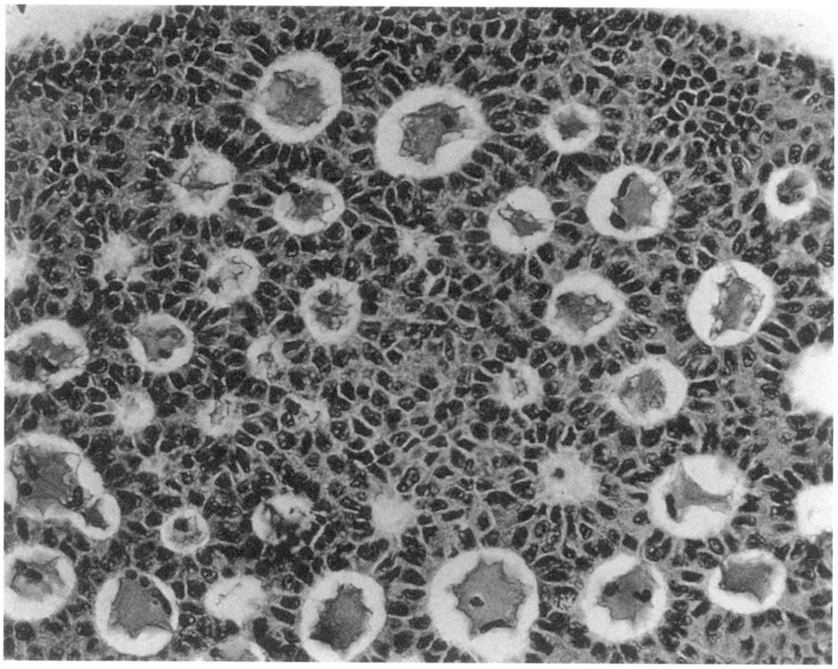

FIG. 106-2. Frozen section of the granulosa cell tumor.

Granulosa cell tumors (GCTs) comprise 1–2% of all ovarian tumors. The GCT is the most common estrogen-secreting ovarian tumor, and cystic hyperplasia is the typical endometrial response. Carcinoma is observed in up to 5% of all women with GCT but occurs more frequently in postmenopausal women.

Although women with this tumor most often present with a mass, postmenopausal or anovulatory bleeding may be a presenting symptom. About 10% of these patients present with acute abdominal pain caused by rupture and hemoperitoneum. Granulosa cell tumors are unilateral in over 95% of cases and may appear solid or solid and cystic. The cystic compartments are characteristically filled with fluid or clotted blood. The tumors vary in size from microscopic to large but have an average diameter of 12 cm. They are gray-white or yellow in color, may be firm or soft, and may have areas of necrosis or hemorrhage.

Stage of tumor has the greatest prognostic significance. Ninety percent of tumors are classified as stage I at diagnosis. Recurrent tumors and tumors of stage II and above are usually fatal.

Tumor size is directly related to prognosis. In patients with tumors of no larger than 5 cm, survival is 73–100%; with tumors of 6–15 cm, survival is 50–92%; and with tumors over 15 cm, survival is only 34%. Rupture adversely affects prognosis, decreasing survival at 25 years by 25% compared with cases in which tumor rupture did not occur. Recurrence is most common within 5 years, but it is not unusual up to 3 decades after initial therapy.

The cornerstone of treatment in perimenopausal and postmenopausal women is surgical removal of the uterus, fallopian tubes, and ovaries with maximal tumor resection. Most gynecologic oncologists support conservative surgery (unilateral salpingo-oophorectomy) in young women with tumor confined to one ovary, as is the case with the patient described. Wedge resection or excision of a normal contralateral ovary is not justified, because the rate of bilaterality is less than 5%.

Removal of the uterus and remaining tube and ovary after completion of childbearing in a patient treated conservatively is controversial. Irradiation or chemotherapy is adjuvant, and one or both may be added to surgical excision in cases of more advanced (stage II and above) disease or when disease recurs.

Inhibin, a peptide hormone normally produced by ovarian granulosa cells, may be a useful marker for this tumor. It has been elevated in some patients with recurrent disease from 5 to 20 months before there is clinical evidence of recurrence.

Colombo N, Sessa C, Landoni F, Sartori E, Pecorelli S, Mangioni C. Cisplatin, vinblastine, and bleomycin combination chemotherapy in metastatic granulosa cell tumor of the ovary. Obstet Gynecol 1986;67:265–268

Evans AT III, Gaffey TA, Malkasian GD Jr, Annegers JF. Clinicopathologic review of 118 granulosa and 82 theca cell tumors. Obstet Gynecol 1980;55:231–238

Lappöhn RE, Burger HG, Bouma J, Bangah M, Krans M, de Bruijn HWA. Inhibin as a marker for granulosa-cell tumors. N Engl J Med 1989;321:790–793

Stenwig JT, Hazekamp JT, Beecham JB. Granulosa cell tumors of the ovary. A clinicopathological study of 118 cases with long-term follow-up. Gynecol Oncol 1979;7:136–152

107

Control of bleeding in cervical carcinoma

A 48-year-old woman presents with profuse vaginal hemorrhage 3 months after completing a course of radiation therapy for squamous cell carcinoma of the cervix (International Federation of Gynecology and Obstetrics stage IIB). Initial efforts toward hemostasis, including vaginal packing, have been unsuccessful. The patient has received four units of packed red blood cells, and her hemoglobin level is 7.5 g/dl. On examination, arterial bleeding is evident from an exophytic lesion on the cervix. The most appropriate next step is

(A) vaginal packing with a large gauze roll soaked in ferric subsulfate (Monsel solution)
(B) suture ligation of the bleeder
(C) bilateral hypogastric artery ligation
* (D) arteriography and transcatheter embolization with surgical-type gelatin sponge (Gelfoam)
(E) arteriographic administration of vasopressin (Pitressin)

Patients with locally recurrent cervical carcinoma after radiation therapy may present with massive bleeding resulting in hypovolemia and hypotension. These patients usually have large, exophytic lesions and obvious arterial bleeding from the tumor mass. Conservative initial management may include topical application of sclerosing agents such as ferric subsulfate or a vaginal pack soaked in acetone. A vaginal pack should not be soaked with ferric subsulfate, because this may result in general sloughing of the normal epithelium of the lower genital tract. If a vaginal pack is used, an indwelling catheter should be placed in the bladder; both can be left in place for 24–48 hours. If the pack is not freshly blood soaked, it can usually be removed after 48 hours without provoking additional bleeding. Placing sutures in the tumor mass is rarely successful and is not recommended.

This patient has significant anemia after blood transfusion and continuing hemorrhage despite vaginal packing. She needs more aggressive therapy.

Bilateral hypogastric artery ligation is often effective in controlling bleeding. However, this procedure requires retroperitoneal dissection, is often less effective secondary to tumor-induced collateral circulation, and is complicated by radiation-induced fibrosis. Hypogastric artery ligation is associated with significantly increased surgical risk in an already compromised patient.

Recent advances in selective arteriography have provided valuable adjuncts in controlling gynecologic and gastrointestinal hemorrhage. Arterial bleeding sites can usually be identified and treated by embolization (Fig. 107-1). Because bleeding from more than one artery is often present, a diligent search for multiple bleeding sites must be undertaken.

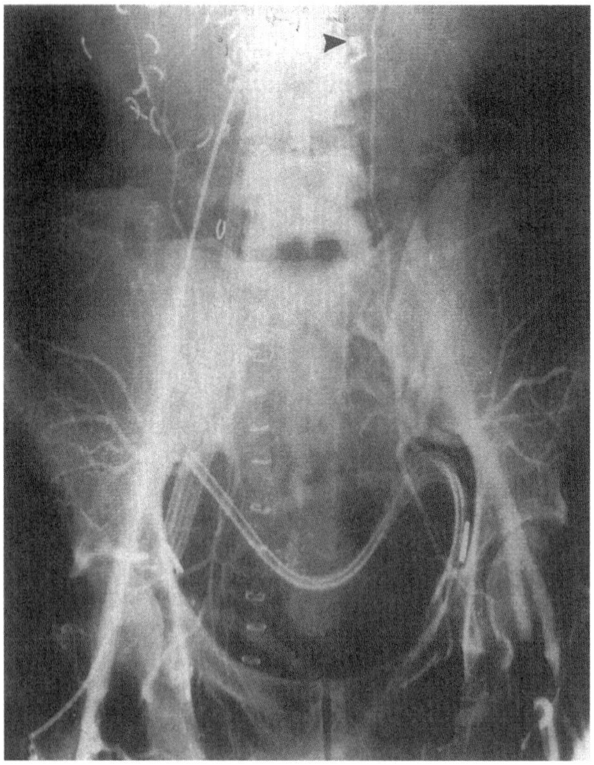

FIG. 107-1. Capillary phase aortogram demonstrating contrast extravasation to the left of the aortic bifurcation (arrowhead) in the region of the paraaortic node dissection. This bleeding site can be selectively embolized. (O'Hanlan KA, Trambert J, Rodriguez-Rodriguez L, Goldberg GL, Runowicz CD. Arterial embolization in the management of abdominal and retroperitoneal hemorrhage. Gynecol Oncol 1989;34:134)

Vasopressin infusion via arteriography is effective in controlling bleeding at some sites, particularly the gastrointestinal tract. Infusion may take several hours to be effective. The catheter should be left in place for at least 12–24 hours after hemostasis is achieved. Vasopressin infusion is usually ineffective in controlling bleeding from tumor vessels, large vessels, arteriosclerotic vessels, and lesions with dual blood supply.

Embolization with surgical-type gelatin sponge provides an effective means of achieving hemostasis. Gelatin sponge provokes little tissue reaction and persists for 20–50 days after embolization. Patients with arterial hemorrhage from gynecologic malignancies frequently have difficulties forming an adequate clot unless thrombin and platelets or ε-aminocaproic acid are added to maintain the clot.

Additional materials that may be used for embolization include polyvinyl alcohol, oxidized cellulose (Oxycel), and autologous blood clot. Arterial balloon catheters have been used to effectively tamponade major blood vessels. Recently, special stainless steel coils containing multiple strands of Dacron have been developed in a variety of widths for intravascular placement. Complications of transcatheter embolization include sepsis, inadvertent embolization to other arteries including the bowel and gluteal tissues, and transient acute tubular necrosis.

DiSaia PH, Creasman WT. Clinical gynecologic oncology. 4th ed. St Louis: Mosby Year Book, 1993:643–647

Harima Y, Shiraishi T, Harima K, Sawada S, Tanaka Y. Transcatheter arterial embolization therapy in cases of recurrent and advanced gynecologic cancer. Cancer 1989;63:2077–2081

Pisco JM, Martins JM, Correia MG. Internal iliac artery: embolization to control hemorrhage from pelvic neoplasms. Radiology 1989;172:337–339

Schwartz PE. Arterial hemorrhage in gynecologic malignancies. In: Delgado G, Smith JP, eds. Management of complications in gynecologic oncology. New York: John Wiley & Sons, 1982:35–44

108

Management of gestational trophoblastic disease

An 18-year-old primigravid woman had a complete hydatidiform mole evacuated by suction curettage. Her preevacuation serum human chorionic gonadotropin (hCG) level was 125,000 mIU/ml, and her uterus was 22 weeks' gestational size. Follow-up serum quantitative hCG levels were obtained every 2 weeks. Her hCG level decreased to 45,000 mIU/ml at 2 weeks and is now 32,000 mIU/ml after 4 weeks. Physical examination is within normal limits except for a slightly enlarged, boggy uterus. Your next step in management is

(A) weekly hCG testing
(B) hCG testing every 2 weeks
(C) repeat dilation and curettage (D&C)
* (D) metastatic workup

Follow-up of patients after evacuation of a hydatidiform mole indicates that evacuation alone is curative in over 80% of patients. At postoperative examination, the clinical findings of prompt uterine involution, ovarian cyst regression, and cessation of bleeding are reassuring signs. Definitive follow-up, however, requires serial hCG testing with a sensitive assay. Quantitative serum hCG levels should be obtained every 1–2 weeks until three consecutive determinations are negative; thereafter, hCG levels should be obtained every 3 months for 1 year. Contraception is recommended during this follow-up period, preferably with oral contraceptives.

Patients at highest risk for postmolar trophoblastic tumors are those with 1) a preevacuation uterus that is larger than expected for the gestational duration or is more than 20 weeks' size; 2) bilateral ovarian enlargement (theca–lutein cysts); 3) age more than 40 years; 4) hCG levels greater than 100,000 mIU/ml; 5) medical complications of molar pregnancy such as toxemia, hyperthyroidism, and trophoblastic embolization; and 6) previous hydatidiform mole.

Indications for treatment of postmolar trophoblastic tumor include 1) plateauing hCG levels for three consecutive determinations, 2) rising hCG levels for two consecutive determinations, 3) hCG levels greater than 20,000 mIU/ml 4 or more weeks after evacuation (as in this patient), 4) persistently elevated hCG levels 6 months after evacuation, 5) detection of metastases, or 6) histopathologic diagnosis of choriocarcinoma.

A repeat D&C is rarely indicated for the management of postmolar trophoblastic disease. Repeat D&C in patients with persistently elevated or rising hCG levels after molar evacuation usually does not lead to spontaneous remission when used without chemotherapy and may result in uterine perforation, which might require laparotomy or hysterectomy. Although histologic evaluation of tissue obtained at D&C may yield prognostic information, the result rarely affects the management of postmolar trophoblastic disease. Therefore, repeat D&C should be reserved for patients who experience significant uterine bleeding or who have ultrasonographic evidence of a large volume of molar tissue remaining within the cavity of the uterus.

In this patient, the diagnosis of postmolar gestational trophoblastic tumor has been confirmed by an hCG level greater than 20,000 mIU/ml 4 weeks after evacuation. The extent of disease should be determined before selecting treatment. This requires a metastatic workup. Staging, scoring, and classification systems for gestational trophoblastic tumors are shown in Table 6, Table 7, and Table 8 of the Appendix. If there is no evidence of metastatic disease or only pulmonary or vaginal metastases without high-risk factors, single-agent chemotherapy with either methotrexate or actinomycin D is the appropriate treatment. This patient does not have high-risk metastatic disease, which would require multiagent chemotherapy.

Lurain JR, Brewer JI, Torok EE, Halpern B. Natural history of hydatidiform mole after primary evacuation. Am J Obstet Gynecol 1983;145:591–595

Morrow CP, Kletzky OA, DiSaia PJ, Townsend DE, Mishell DR, Nakamura RM. Clinical and laboratory correlates of molar pregnancy and trophoblastic disease. Am J Obstet Gynecol 1977;128:424–429

Schlaerth JB, Morrow CP, Rodriguez M. Diagnostic and therapeutic curettage in gestational trophoblastic disease. Am J Obstet Gynecol 1990;162:1465–1471

World Health Organization Scientific Group. Gestational trophoblastic diseases. Technical Report Series 692. Geneva: WHO, 1983

109
Autologous transfusion

A healthy 29-year-old woman is diagnosed with stage IB cervical carcinoma. In counseling her regarding radical hysterectomy and pelvic lymph node dissection, you explain that she may require a blood transfusion. The patient tells you that she is concerned about acquiring the human immunodeficiency virus (HIV) through a blood transfusion. You tell her that the risk from infection is LEAST with

* (A) autologous donation of two units of blood
(B) directed donation by relatives or friends
(C) use of frozen stored packed donor red blood cells
(D) use of stored packed donor red blood cells
(E) use of washed donor red blood cells

For patients who are undergoing major abdominal surgery in which there is a reasonable chance that a blood transfusion may be required, autologous donation is an important option. Accurately administered autologous transfusion eliminates questions of compatibility and induced infection with hepatitis or HIV. Although blood may become contaminated by bacteria during processing, this risk is extremely low, and there is no risk of sensitization from foreign proteins.

This patient's surgery can probably be delayed for 3 weeks to allow time for autologous donation, if there are no contraindications to this procedure. Gynecologic cancer in general is not a contraindication to autologous blood donation. In cases where extensive chemotherapy is planned, autologous donation may be of limited benefit, because subsequent transfusions may be needed.

There is no evidence that directed donation by friends or relatives is effective in reducing the risk from blood transfusions. Directed donor blood appears to carry the same, if not greater, risks of infection, contamination with antigens, and mismatching as that from random donors. Data from one center are shown in Table 109–1.

Use of frozen blood carries a lower risk of contamination with antigens and foreign proteins simply because over 95% of the plasma, leukocytes, and platelets are removed in the process of freezing. However, the process does not eliminate viral agents, and the risk of infection remains. Other disadvantages of frozen blood are the expense of the process and the need to thaw and wash the erythrocytes, which must then be used within 24 hours. Simply storing blood without additional processing does not provide any benefit, because infectious agents and foreign proteins will survive.

Although the greatest public concern in regard to blood transfusions is the risk of infection with HIV, posttransfusion hepatitis is a much more common cause of morbidity in transfusion recipients. Early studies recognized two types of hepatitis viruses: type A, associated with infectious hepatitis, and type B, associated with serum hepatitis. In the early 1970s, tests for hepatitis A and B with sensitive radioimmunoassay systems were instituted. Despite these tests, cases of posttransfusion hepatitis still occurred. Because these cases had no serologic markers of infection with hepatitis A or B, the term non-A, non-B hepatitis was coined for this disease with a presumed viral etiology.

In 1989, molecular techniques were used to derive clones from the genome of the agent associated with non-A, non-B posttransfusion hepatitis. The proteins derived from these clones were used to develop an enzyme-linked immunosorbent assay to detect antibodies to the virus now known as hepatitis C (HCV). In May 1990, this assay was placed in routine use in blood donor screening.

The incidence of HCV seroconversion was 3.84% before the institution of testing. Screening of donor blood for surrogate markers lowered the risk of seroconversion to 1.54%. In 1992, a second-generation HCV test was implemented that demonstrated increased sensitivity and specificity in blood donor screening. Additionally, the interval for seroconversion was significantly shortened by this new assay. This test plus additional tests that are likely to be developed as further portions of the HCV genome are characterized may further lower the incidence of HCV posttransfusion hepatitis. The current estimate of posttransfusion hepatitis, less than 1 in 3,300 units, demonstrates marked progress from the 10% incidence of the 1970s.

Human immunodeficiency virus currently poses only a remote hazard in blood transfusion because of donor selection and laboratory screening procedures. It is estimated that the risk of HIV infection from blood transfusion in the United States is between 1:40,000 and 1:100,000.

Sensitization by leukocyte antigens can cause febrile nonhemolytic transfusion reactions. Although these reactions cause no permanent sequelae, they can be difficult to distinguish from more serious transfusion reactions involving hemolysis. Subsequent reactions can be prevented by using leukocyte-poor blood components. Allergic transfusion reactions are common, and usually present as mild hives. They can be prevented with the administration of pretransfusion antihistamines. More serious cases are prevented by washing erythrocytes to remove plasma (not a standard practice). Washed erythrocytes are usually requested only after a patient has demonstrated a sensitivity to leukocyte antigens.

Given the current safety of random donor blood, the most cost-effective approach for this patient would be transfusion, if needed, with random donor blood. However, her desire to minimize the risk of acquired infection is best met by autologous donation.

Consensus Conference. Perioperative red blood cell transfusion. JAMA 1988;260:2700–2703

Dodd RY. The risk of transfusion-transmitted infection. N Engl J Med 1992;327:419–421

Kruskall MS, Leonard S, Klapholz H. Autologous blood donation during pregnancy: analysis of safety and blood use. Obstet Gynecol 1987;70:938–941

Wilmore DW, Brennan MF, Harlen AH, Holcroft JW, Meakins JL, eds (American College of Surgeons). Care of the surgical patient. Vol 1: Critical care. A publication of the Committee on Pre and Postoperative Care. New York: Scientific American, 1991

TABLE 109–1. Complications Associated with Random (Volunteer) Donor Blood as Compared with Donor-Directed Units (%)*

Blood Status	HBc	ALT	HBsAg	HCV	HTLV	Syphilis†	HIV	Total Infections
Volunteer (n = 113 units)	3 (2.6)	4 (3.5)	0 (0)	1 (0.4)	0 (0)	0 (0)	0 (0)	8 (7.1)
Donor directed (n = 466 units)	37 (7.9)	16 (3.4)	4 (0.9)	2 (0.9)	3 (0.6)	1 (0.2)	1 (0.2)	64 (13.7)
Total	40 (6.9)	20 (3.5)	4 (0.7)	3 (0.5)	3 (0.5)	1 (0.2)	1 (0.2)	72 (12.4)

*HBc indicates hepatitis B core antigen; ALT, alanine aminotransferase (liver enzyme previously known as serum glutamate pyruvate transaminase [SGPT]); HBsAg, hepatitis B surface antigen; HCV, hepatitis C virus; HTLV, human T-cell leukemia/lymphoma virus; HIV, human immunodeficiency virus.

†The rapid plasma reagin test was used.

Courtesy of K. Cash, MD, Albert Einstein College of Medicine and Montefiore Medical Center

110

Mildly atypical Pap test

A 36-year-old woman, gravida 3, para 3, presents for her annual physical examination. Although the pelvic examination is negative, cervical cytology is reported as "atypical squamous cells of undetermined significance" (ASCUS). In counseling the patient regarding this finding, you would regard each of the following statements to be correct EXCEPT:

* (A) The likelihood that a high-grade cervical neoplasia is present is less than 5%.
(B) A normal healing process of the cervix can cause these cytologic changes.
(C) Infection by the human papillomavirus (HPV) can cause these cytologic changes.
(D) Human papillomavirus viral culture and typing can identify patients who are most likely to progress to neoplastic cervical lesions including invasion.
(E) Cytologic screening for cervical adenocarcinomas is less sensitive than that for squamous lesions.

The frequency with which minimal abnormalities of cervical cytology are reported under the Bethesda System varies both with the population screened and the laboratory used. Cytologists agree that there is a subjective, human element to Pap test interpretation. In general, a reading of ASCUS is expected in no more than 5% of Pap test reports. Significant lesions, including a rare invasive carcinoma, are found on further evaluation in 15–20% of patients with a Pap test reported only as ASCUS.

With proper performance of colposcopy and biopsy, one of every six patients with ASCUS will be shown to have a high-grade cervical neoplasia. On the other hand, one half to three fourths of low-grade cytologic abnormalities will resolve spontaneously when monitored only by repeated colposcopic examinations. Expense issues and medical–legal concerns create a debate as to whether such cytologic reports require immediate investigation or repeat cytology within a year. If a patient can be counted on to return for follow-up, it is common practice to defer colposcopy and repeat the test in 3–6 months. If results of a repeat test are abnormal, colposcopy is then performed.

Cytologic changes described as ASCUS can represent metaplastic squamous epithelium, which may result from a repair process after trauma or nonspecific cervical infection. They can also be caused by HPV infection. There is an important difference between these causes, because patients with a normal repair process are at very low risk of developing neoplastic epithelial lesions. Patients with HPV infections have a variable risk for developing neoplastic lesions, depending on the specific viral type. For example, women who undergo viral typing and are discovered to have HPV type 6 have a much lower risk of developing a neoplastic lesion than do women with a type 18 infection. Routine viral typing is not, however, part of standard clinical practice.

Although cervical cytology screening has reasonable sensitivity and specificity for squamous abnormalities, especially when repeated at regular intervals, it does not have the same accuracy for adenomatous lesions, especially adenocarcinoma in situ. The clinician must be aware of this weakness in cytologic screening, especially in young women. Because adenocarcinomas more commonly escape detection by cytology, an unusual incidence of interval adenocarcinomas compared with squamous cell carcinomas is found in women who have regular Pap tests. Therefore, biopsy of visible lesions and endocervical sampling in women with unexplained bleeding are justified, even when cervical cytology is negative or shows only low-grade lesions.

Montz FJ, Monk BJ, Fowler JM, Nguyen L. Natural history of the minimally abnormal Papanicolaou smear. Obstet Gynecol 1992;80:385–388

Nasiell K, Nasiell M, Vaclavinkova V. Behavior of moderate cervical dysplasia during long-term follow-up. Obstet Gynecol 1983;61:609–614

Reid R, Greenberg MD, Lorincz A, Jenson AB, Laverty CR, Husain M. Should cervical cytology testing be augmented by cervicography of human papillomavirus deoxyribonucleic acid detection? Am J Obstet Gynecol 1991;164:1461–1469

111

Hormone therapy for breast cancer

A 58-year-old woman who has recently completed primary treatment for invasive ductal carcinoma of the breast has been advised to have tamoxifen citrate (Nolvadex) therapy for 5 years. Her cancer was stage II estrogen receptor positive, with 2 out of 19 axillary lymph nodes involved with carcinoma. Her weight is normal for her age. Her family history is noncontributory. She seeks your consultation as to the risks and benefits of tamoxifen therapy. Each of the following is associated with tamoxifen therapy EXCEPT:

* (A) Decreased high-density lipoprotein
(B) Decreased bone resorption
(C) Normal serum glucose levels
(D) Increased risk of endometrial carcinoma
(E) Increased risk of endometrial polyps

Tamoxifen therapy decreases low-density lipoprotein cholesterol levels. This metabolic change correlates with preliminary reports suggesting a decreased incidence of angina, myocardial infarction, and stroke. Tamoxifen therapy has an inconsistent effect on high-density lipoprotein cholesterol levels.

Tamoxifen therapy preserves bone mineral density and thus may decrease the incidence of osteoporosis. It has not yet been confirmed to decrease fractures, however. Serum glucose levels are not affected by tamoxifen therapy.

Tamoxifen has estrogenic and antiestrogenic tissue-specific effects. The incidence of endometrial carcinoma is increased twofold to threefold for women on tamoxifen therapy. Endometrial polyps are more frequent in postmenopausal women on tamoxifen therapy than in similar untreated women. A patient on tamoxifen who experiences any abnormal vaginal or uterine bleeding should undergo endometrial sampling.

Cuzick J, Allen D, Baum M, Barrett J, Clark G, Kakkar V, et al. Long term effects of tamoxifen: biological effects of tamoxifen working party. Eur J Cancer 1993;29A:15–21

Fisher B, Costantino JP, Redmond CK, Fisher ER, Wickerham DL, Cronin WM, et al. Endometrial cancer in tamoxifen-treated breast cancer patients: findings from the National Surgical Adjuvant Breast and Bowel Project (NSABP) B-14. J Natl Cancer Inst 1994;86:527–537

Jordan VC, ed. Long-term tamoxifen treatment for breast cancer. Madison, Wisconsin: University of Wisconsin Press, 1994

Lahti E, Blanco G, Kauppila A, Apaja-Sarkkinen M, Taskinen PJ, Laatikainen T. Endometrial changes in postmenopausal breast cancer patients receiving tamoxifen. Obstet Gynecol 1993;81:660–664

Love RR, Mazess RB, Barden HS, Epstein S, Newcomb PA, Jordan VC, et al. Effects of tamoxifen on bone mineral density in postmenopausal women with breast cancer. N Engl J Med 1992;326:852–856

Love RR, Wiebe DA, Newcomb PA, Cameron L, Leventhal H, Jordan VC, et al. Effects of tamoxifen on cardiovascular risk factors in postmenopausal women. Ann Intern Med 1991;115:860–864

Seoud MA-F, Johnson J, Weed JC Jr. Gynecologic tumors in tamoxifen-treated women with breast cancer. Obstet Gynecol 1993;82:165–169

Thangaraju M, Kumar K, Gandhirajan R, Sachdanandam P. Effect of tamoxifen on plasma lipids and lipoproteins in postmenopausal women with breast cancer. Cancer 1994;73:659–663

112

Pathology of partial mole

A 30-year-old woman at 18 weeks of gestation has a small-for-dates uterus, which has not shown growth for the past 4 weeks. A sonogram reveals a nonviable pregnancy. A dilation and evacuation is performed, identifying a small fetus and hydropic swelling in some of the placental tissue (Fig. 112-1; see color plate). Each of the following statements regarding this condition is true EXCEPT:

(A) The karyotype of the conceptus is probably 69,XXY.
(B) A preoperative diagnosis of a missed abortion is frequently made.
(C) Serum human chorionic gonadotropin (hCG) levels associated with this lesion are often in the normal range for gestational age.
* (D) This patient's risk of developing persistent gestational trophoblastic disease is 10–30%.

Two populations of chorionic villi can be seen in Fig. 112-1: one is normal in appearance and the other shows hydropic swelling. In contrast with the diffuse hydropic swelling in the complete mole, which involves almost all chorionic villi, the swelling in the lesion shown involves only a portion of the villi. Accordingly, this patient has a partial mole. Partial moles are characterized by a mixture of small to relatively normal-sized villi, some of which are edematous. Usually a fetus or embryo is present; however, demise in utero may lead to resorption, making identification of the fetus difficult. In contrast, complete moles are not associated with a fetus or embryo.

Partial moles have distinctive clinical and cytogenetic features in addition to the characteristic morphology described. In contrast to the complete mole, which has a 46,XX karyotype, the partial mole typically shows triploidy, with a 69,XXY karyotype. In the complete mole, all chromosomes including both X chromosomes are of paternal origin, whereas in the partial mole, 23 chromosomes including one X chromosome are of maternal origin and the remaining 46 chromosomes, including two sex chromosomes (X, Y), are paternally derived, usually from two separate sperm (dispermy).

Partial moles, which account for 25–43% of all molar pregnancies, characteristically are diagnosed in the early second trimester. Patients often present with a missed abortion, which can be confirmed by ultrasonography. In contrast to serum hCG levels in the complete mole, serum hCG levels in the partial mole are low or in the normal range for gestational age. It is unusual for a partial mole to show the markedly elevated hCG levels seen in association with a complete mole. Thus, the diagnosis is usually not made preoperatively.

The risk of subsequent gestational trophoblastic disease associated with a complete mole is 10–30%. In contrast, the risk of subsequent gestational trophoblastic disease associated with a partial mole is 5–10%. Although development of choriocarcinoma after a partial mole is rare, the precautions for follow-up in patients with a complete mole also apply to patients with a partial mole.

Berkowitz RS, Goldstein DP, Bernstein MR. Natural history of partial molar pregnancy. Obstet Gynecol 1985;66:677–681

Szulman AE, Surti U. The clinicopathologic profile of the partial mole. Obstet Gynecol 1982;59:597–602

Szulman AE, Surti U. The syndromes of hydatidiform mole, II: morphologic evolution of the complete and partial mole. Am J Obstet Gynecol 1978;132:20–27

113

Risk factors for radiation enteritis

A 77-year-old woman with insulin-dependent diabetes mellitus and hypertension underwent a transperitoneal staging laparotomy for a stage IIB cervical carcinoma. The paraaortic lymph nodes were negative for metastases. She received a total dose of whole-pelvis irradiation of 4,000 cGy, followed by two intracavitary cesium applications of 2,200 cGy each to point A (2 cm above and 2 cm lateral to the external os of the cervix). Additional whole-pelvis irradiation with a midline block was administered to bring the dose to the pelvic sidewalls to 6,000 cGy. Each of the following statements about this patient's risk factors for developing radiation enteritis is true EXCEPT:

* (A) The major risk factor for radiation enteritis is the cesium applications.
(B) This patient's age is a risk factor for radiation enteritis.
(C) Insulin-dependent diabetes is a risk factor for radiation enteritis.
(D) Hypertension is a risk factor for radiation enteritis.
(E) The staging laparotomy is a risk factor for radiation enteritis.

The schedule and dose of radiation therapy in this patient with a stage IIB carcinoma of the cervix are within the accepted standards of therapy. The initial 4,000-cGy dose of whole-pelvis irradiation will shrink the primary tumor and treat the nodal areas in the pelvis. The two intracavitary treatments will bring the total dose to point A (2 cm above and 2 cm lateral to the external os of the cervix) to about 8,400 cGy. Boosting the dose to the pelvic sidewalls to 6,000 cGy should control microscopic disease in lymphatics, and the midline block will help prevent excessive irradiation to the bladder and rectum. The cesium applications add little to the risk of radiation enteritis but may increase the risk of damage to the bladder and rectum. If the implants are properly placed, however, the dose of irradiation to these organs will not result in serious complications in most patients.

Radiation complications to the intestine can occur, even with optimum radiation dosimetry. This patient has several risk factors that increase the likelihood of radiation complications. Any natural factor or disease that impairs the blood supply to tissues will result in an increase in the likelihood of radiation-related injury. In this woman, advanced age is a risk factor, because there is some degree of atherosclerosis in all individuals as they become older. Although the degree of atherosclerosis varies among individuals, it is well documented that older individuals have less tolerance to irradiation. If this woman had smoked cigarettes, her risk would have been further increased.

The history of diabetes and hypertension in this woman increases her risk of radiation enteritis because of the effects of these diseases on the vasculature. In both of these conditions, there is vasculitis, and because the major damage from irradiation is also vasculitis, there is an increased risk for radiation enteritis.

The small intestine is likely to suffer significant radiation damage when the dose of irradiation exceeds 4,500 cGy. When whole-pelvis irradiation is administered, the major factor preventing serious damage to the small intestine is its mobility within the abdominal cavity. Placement of the radiation therapy table in a slight Trendelenburg position usually results in movement of the intestine out of the irradiation field. In addition, because of the normal motility of the intestine, different portions of the intestine are in the irradiation field at different treatment times, thus preventing the same area of the intestine from receiving a full dose of irradiation every day. The terminal ileum is the least mobile region of the small intestine and therefore is the most likely to suffer radiation injury.

The major danger of a transperitoneal staging laparotomy is the risk of developing an adhesion of the small intestine so that it becomes fixed in the pelvis. As a result, the loop of small intestine would receive an excessive dose of irradiation and suffer permanent injury. Another serious complication of staging laparotomy is an adhesion of the sigmoid colon to the uterus. As a result, this portion of the large intestine would receive an excessive dose of irradiation from the intracavitary therapy in addition to the whole-pelvis irradiation. Similar complications can be seen in patients who have diverticulitis or endometriosis, which may cause adhesions of the rectosigmoid colon to the uterus.

Thus, in this patient, advanced age, insulin-dependent diabetes, hypertension, and the staging laparotomy are all independent risk factors that increase her risk of radiation complications to the gastrointestinal tract. Despite the administration of a standard dose of irradiation, she is at increased risk for intestinal injury.

Hoskins WJ, Burke TW, Weiser EB, Heller PB, Grayson J, Park RC. Right hemicolectomy and ileal resection with primary reanastomosis for irradiation injury of the terminal ileum. Gynecol Oncol 1987;26:215–224

Kottmeier HL. Complications following radiation therapy in carcinoma of the cervix and their treatment. Am J Obstet Gynecol 1964;88:854–866

Perez CA, Purdy JA. Biologic and physical aspects of radiation oncology. In: Hoskins WJ, Perez CA, Young RC, eds. Principles and practice of gynecologic oncology. Philadelphia: JB Lippincott, 1992:217–288

Schofield PF, Carr ND, Holden D. Pathogenesis and treatment of radiation bowel disease: discussion paper. J R Soc Med 1986;79:30–32

114

Epidemiology of human papillomavirus

A 28-year-old woman comes to your office because she has recently detected "bumps" on her vulva. You examine her and make a diagnosis of condylomata acuminata. The patient has a number of questions concerning what the characteristics of the disease are and how she acquired it. Each of the following statements is true regarding human papillomavirus (HPV) infection EXCEPT:

(A) Human papillomavirus DNA can be detected on the vulva in up to 30% of young, sexually active women with the use of molecular biology methods.
(B) Human papillomavirus type 6 is most often associated with vulvar condyloma.
(C) Human papillomavirus type 16 is most often associated with vulvar intraepithelial neoplasia.
(D) Between 30% and 50% of women with vulvar condylomas have associated cervical HPV infection.
* (E) Infants who were delivered vaginally from women with vulvar condylomas have a high frequency of laryngeal papillomatosis.

Condylomata acuminata (genital warts) are sexually transmitted benign neoplasms that involve the vulva, vagina, cervix, perianal skin, anal canal, and urethra, in order of frequency. The prevalence of HPV infection varies greatly, depending on the population studied, but in populations of young, sexually active women, the detection rate of HPV DNA on the vulva with sensitive molecular biology techniques such as Southern blot hybridization or polymerase chain reaction can be as high as 30%.

Molecular biologic methods have identified HPV 6 in 90% of typical genital condylomas. Occasionally, HPV 16 can be identified in these lesions, but in these instances the condylomas show areas of high-grade vulvar intraepithelial neoplasia. The presence of HPV 16 in vulvar lesions is usually associated with intraepithelial neoplasia. Between 30% and 50% of women with vulvar condylomas have associated cervical HPV infection. Accordingly, in women who have external genital warts, a Pap test of the cervix should be obtained.

Although 40–60% of children with laryngeal papillomatosis were born to mothers with a history of genital HPV infection, the incidence of such an infection in newborn infants of mothers with genital papillomatosis is extremely low. No correlation has been shown between the volume of maternal wart tissue and the occurrence of infantile laryngeal papillomatosis.

Gissmann L, Wolnik L, Ikenberg H, Koldovsky V, Schnurch HG, zur Hausen H. Human papillomavirus type 6 and 11 DNA sequences in genital and laryngeal papillomas and in some cervical cancers. Proc Natl Acad Sci U S A 1983;80:560–563

Lynch PJ. Condylomata acuminata (anogenital warts). Clin Obstet Gynecol 1985;28:142–151

Majmudar B, Hallden C. The relationship between juvenile laryngeal papillomatosis and maternal condylomata acuminata. J Reprod Med 1986;31:804–807

Wright TC, Kurman RJ, Ferenczy A. Precancerous lesions of the cervix. In: Kurman RJ, ed. Blaustein's pathology of the female genital tract. 4th ed. New York: Springer-Verlag, 1994:229–277

115

Rupture of a malignant ovarian cyst

A 55-year-old woman is undergoing a laparotomy for the evaluation and treatment of a 7-cm adnexal mass. The cyst ruptures when handled. Frozen section of the cyst wall shows a grade 1 serous cystadenocarcinoma. A total abdominal hysterectomy and bilateral salpingo-oophorectomy and full staging are performed. The International Federation of Gynecology and Obstetrics classification is stage IC. Each of the following postoperative options may be recommended for this patient EXCEPT:

(A) No therapy
(B) Intraperitoneal ^{32}P
(C) Chemotherapy
(D) Abdominopelvic irradiation
* (E) Combined chemotherapy and irradiation

Management of a ruptured malignant ovarian cyst remains controversial. Recent studies of factors that influence outcome of stage I ovarian epithelial carcinoma have not consistently shown a deleterious effect of rupture of the ovarian capsule. The clinical importance of intraoperative rupture has become more relevant with the increase in laparoscopic oophorectomies and cystectomies for ovarian cysts.

Intraperitoneal ^{32}P, chemotherapy, and irradiation are adjuvant therapies for early-stage ovarian carcinoma. The option of no further therapy is supported by several studies. Combined chemotherapy and abdominopelvic irradiation is not appropriate in early-stage ovarian carcinoma.

Dembo AJ, Davy M, Stenwig AE, Berle EJ, Bush RS, Kjorstad K. Prognostic factors in patients with stage I epithelial ovarian cancer. Obstet Gynecol 1990;75:263–273

Kaldor JM, Day NE, Pettersson F, Clarke EA, Pedersen D, Mehnert W, et al. Leukemia following chemotherapy for ovarian cancer. N Engl J Med 1990;322:1–6

Monga M, Carmichael JA, Shelley WE, Kirk ME, Krepart GV, Jeffrey JF, et al. Surgery without adjuvant chemotherapy for early epithelial ovarian carcinoma after comprehensive staging. Gynecol Oncol 1991;43:195–197

Richardson GS, Scully RE, Nikrui N, Nelson JH Jr. Common epithelial cancer of the ovary (first of two parts). N Engl J Med 1985;312:415–424

Richardson GS, Scully RE, Nikrui N, Nelson JH Jr. Common epithelial cancer of the ovary (second of two parts). N Engl J Med 1985;312:474–483

Sainz de la Cuesta R, Goff BA, Fuller AF, Nikrui N, Eichhorn JH, Rice LW. Prognostic importance of intraoperative rupture of malignant ovarian epithelial neoplasms. Obstet Gynecol 1994;84:1–7

Sigurdsson K, Alm P, Gullberg B. Prognostic factors in malignant epithelial ovarian tumors. Gynecol Oncol 1983;15:370–380

Smith JP, Day TG Jr. Review of ovarian cancer at the University of Texas Systems Cancer Center, M.D. Anderson Hospital and Tumor Institute. Am J Obstet Gynecol 1979;135:984–993

Young RC, Walton LA, Ellenberg SS, Homesley HD, Wilbanks GD, Decker DG, et al. Adjuvant therapy in stage I and stage II epithelial ovarian cancer: results of two prospective randomized trials. N Engl J Med 1990;322:1021–1027

116

Treatment of stage I and II breast cancer

A 52-year-old woman with a diagnosed invasive ductal carcinoma in her right breast presents to discuss options for therapy. The cancer is 2 cm at the largest diameter with no evidence of spread (T1 N0 M0). The cancer is freely mobile and not fixed to the underlying fascia or overlying skin. She has been told that her options for treatment are modified radical mastectomy or breast-conserving therapy. Each of the following is a feature of both therapies EXCEPT:

(A) Removal of the level I and II axillary lymph nodes
(B) Total surgical removal of the local breast cancer
* (C) Necessity of radiation therapy to the anterior chest wall
(D) Ten-year disease-free survival of 70%

Radiation therapy to the anterior chest is given after lumpectomy and axillary lymph node dissection to women choosing the option of breast-conserving therapy for stage I and II breast cancer. The National Surgical Adjuvant Breast and Bowel Project B-06 clinical trial documented an unacceptable 39% rate of local recurrence, usually at the site of the lumpectomy, when irradiation was not given as part of breast-conserving therapy. Treatment by modified radical mastectomy does not usually require postoperative radiation therapy.

Both modified radical mastectomy and breast-conserving therapy remove the level I and II axillary lymph nodes. Modified radical mastectomy removes the nodes en bloc with the breast. With breast-conserving therapy the axillary lymph nodes are removed through a separate incision, usually at the time of the lumpectomy. The local breast cancer is removed with either surgical procedure.

Multiple published reports cite similar rates of local recurrence, disease-free survival, and overall survival for women with stage I and II breast cancer treated by either modified radical mastectomy or breast-conserving therapy (lumpectomy, axillary lymph node dissection, and postoperative radiation therapy). The 10-year disease-free survival rate is 70%. The local recurrence rate is 20% for lumpectomy, and the regional recurrence rate with mastectomy is about 10%. The National Institutes of Health consensus meeting in 1991 designated breast-conserving therapy as the preferred treatment for stage I and II breast cancer.

The American Joint Committee on Cancer definitions of the TNM (tumor, regional lymph nodes, distant metastasis) staging system for breast cancer are in Table 9 of the Appendix.

American Joint Committee on Cancer. Manual for staging of cancer. 4th ed. Philadelphia: JB Lippincott, 1992

Fisher B, Anderson S. Conservative surgery for the management of invasive and noninvasive carcinoma of the breast: NSABP trials. World J Surg 1994;18:63–69

Fisher B, Redmond C, Poisson R, Margolese R, Wolmark N, Wickerham L, et al. Eight-year results of a randomized clinical trial comparing total mastectomy and lumpectomy with or without irradiation in the treatment of breast cancer. N Engl J Med 1989;320:822–828

Fowble B. The role of conservative surgery and radiation in the treatment of early breast cancer. Breast Dis 1991;4:11

NIH Consensus Conference. Treatment of early-stage breast cancer. JAMA 1991;265:391–395

Primary treatment of breast cancer. In: Harris JR, Hellman S, Henderson IC, Kinne DW, eds. Breast disease. 2nd ed. Philadelphia: JB Lippincott, 1991:347–426

117

Microinvasive carcinoma of the cervix

In patients with microinvasive cervical carcinoma diagnosed by cone biopsy, factors that have been reported to increase the risk of nodal metastasis, recurrence, and death include all of the following EXCEPT:

(A) Status of the resection margin
(B) Depth of stromal invasion
(C) Presence of lymph–vascular space invasion
(D) Tumor volume
* (E) Tumor grade

The most important factor in determining the appropriate management of microinvasive cervical carcinoma is the status of the surgical margin of the conization specimen. In most studies, women with a cone margin that shows invasive disease have a significantly higher risk of residual invasive disease in the hysterectomy specimen than do women with negative margins. The residual invasion may be deeper than that found in the cone biopsy specimen.

Depth of stromal invasion is another major determining factor in the outcome of patients with microinvasive cervical carcinoma. A compilation of studies with a total of 382 women having 3 mm or less of stromal invasion revealed only two cases of lymph node metastases. With invasion between 3.1 and 5 mm, the prevalence of lymph node metastasis is 5.3%. Recurrent disease or death from cervical cancer has not been reported in women with less than 1 mm of stromal invasion who have been managed with either a cone biopsy or simple hysterectomy. In three recent long-term follow-up studies involving 403 women, not a single patient with less than 1 mm of stromal invasion treated with a cone biopsy or simple hysterectomy died of cervical cancer.

The clinical significance of lymph–vascular space involvement in patients with early invasive cervical cancer is controversial. Although several series of patients with invasive tumors of 5 mm or less reported no direct relationship between the presence of lymph–vascular space involvement and the presence of lymph node metastasis, other studies have found lymph–vascular space involvement to be an adverse prognosticator. Despite the controversy, it is the prevailing view in the United States that lymph–vascular space involvement should be assessed in women with early invasive squamous cell carcinoma and that the presence of lymph–vascular space involvement alters the treatment of microinvasive cervical carcinoma.

In recent years morphologic evaluation of the volume of disease in microinvasive cervical carcinoma has been emphasized by some authors. One study reported no pelvic node metastases in patients with 420 mm^3 of cancer or less, with the exception of one case in which vascular invasion was noted. Other investigators have used the extent of lateral spread as a surrogate for measuring tumor volume.

The grade of microinvasive cervical carcinoma or, for that matter, frankly invasive squamous cell carcinoma does not correlate with lymph node metastasis, recurrence, or death.

Burghardt E, Girardi F, Lahousen M, Pickel H, Tamussino K. Microinvasive carcinoma of the uterine cervix (International Federation of Gynecology and Obstetrics, stage IA). Cancer 1991;67:1037–1045

Copeland LJ, Silva EG, Gershenson DM, Morris M, Young DC, Wharton JT. Superficially invasive squamous cell carcinoma of the cervix. Gynecol Oncol 1992;45:307–312

Sedlis A, Sall S, Tsukada Y, Park R, Mangan C, Shingleton H, et al. Microinvasive carcinoma of the uterine cervix: a clinical-pathologic study. Am J Obstet Gynecol 1979;133:64–74

van Nagell JR Jr, Greenwell N, Powell DF, Donaldson ES, Hanson MB, Gay EC. Microinvasive carcinoma of the cervix. Am J Obstet Gynecol 1983;145:981–991

Zaino RJ, Ward S, Delgado G, Bundy B, Gore H, Fetter G, et al. Histopathologic predictors of the behavior of surgically treated stage IB squamous cell carcinoma of the cervix. Cancer 1992;69:1750–1758

118

Characteristics of fibroadenoma

A 24-year-old woman who comes to your office for the first time is concerned about a slowly growing mass in her left breast. She has been aware of the mass for 5 years. A fine-needle aspiration of the mass was performed 6 months ago, and the cytology report described the typical features of a fibroadenoma. The mass is now 2.5 cm in diameter. The characteristics of a fibroadenoma by physical examination include each of the following EXCEPT:

(A) Firm or rubbery consistency
(B) Discrete, smooth borders
(C) Mobility
(D) Lobular shape
* (E) Tenderness

By palpation, fibroadenomas are typically rubbery, firm, discrete, smooth, mobile, and lobular. Although there is usually a single lobule, several may be present. Fibroadenomas are usually nontender. The gross appearance of a fibroadenoma is shown in Fig. 118-1 (see color plate).

Rapid growth of a breast mass clinically presumed to be a fibroadenoma may be a sign of a rare phyllodes tumor. Phyllodes tumors were formerly called cystosarcoma phyllodes. According to the current World Health Organization classification, phyllodes tumors may be benign, borderline, or malignant. Although phyllodes tumors are composed of dual tissue elements of sheets of ductal cells and stroma, the indeterminate (borderline) and malignant changes occur in the stroma. When a breast mass exhibits rapid growth, it should be excised for histopathologic diagnosis.

Dent DM, Cant PJ. Fibroadenoma. World J Surg 1989;13;706–710

Hindle WH, Alonzo LJ. Conservative management of breast fibroadenomas. Am J Obstet Gynecol 1991;164:1647–1651

Smith BL. Fibroadenomas. In: Harris JR, Hellman S, Henderson IC, Kinne DW, eds. Breast diseases. 2nd ed. Philadelphia: JB Lippincott, 1991:34–37

Souba WW. Evaluation and treatment of benign breast disorders. In: Bland KI, Copeland EM III, eds. The breast: comprehensive management of benign and malignant diseases. Philadelphia: WB Saunders, 1991:715–729

Wilkinson S, Forrest APM. Fibro-adenoma of the breast. Br J Surg 1985;72:838–840

119

Symptoms of colorectal cancer

A 52-year-old woman presents with a change in bowel habits, including alternating constipation and diarrhea, usually associated with passage of blood and mucus. She also complains of tenesmus and constant lancinating rectal and lower back pain. Each of her symptoms is consistent with early carcinoma of the rectum EXCEPT:

(A) Rectal bleeding
(B) Alternating constipation and diarrhea
(C) Passage of mucus
(D) Tenesmus
* (E) Rectal and low back pain

Colorectal cancer is second only to lung cancer as the leading cause of death from cancer in the United States. It typically is found in late-middle-age and elderly patients, but is affecting an increasing number of younger individuals. The latter group has a poor prognosis because diagnosis is often delayed and tumors are more often poorly differentiated. Surgery remains the most effective treatment for early-stage disease, but there has been little change in survival over the past 40 years despite the introduction of new surgical techniques, chemotherapy, and immunotherapy.

Awareness of early symptoms of colorectal cancer is critical, and the occurrence of symptoms mandates a thorough evaluation. Carcinoma of the rectum, which often produces no symptoms initially, can be detected early by routine proctosigmoidoscopy or rectal examination. Carcinomas of the rectum and descending colon are more likely to be symptomatic than are carcinomas involving the cecum or ascending colon. The most commonly encountered symptom of rectal carcinoma is bleeding, which is often incorrectly ascribed to hemorrhoids. Profuse hemorrhage is unusual, and anemia is more often encountered with advanced disease.

Many patients acknowledge a change in bowel habits. A pattern of alternating constipation and diarrhea is common. Patients with carcinoma in the distal colon frequently experience the urge to defecate, and they may have several bowel movements in the course of the day, consisting of blood and mucus with a small amount of stool. This condition has been described as a "spurious diarrhea" because the patient may, in fact, be constipated. These episodes are often associated with tenesmus, an ineffectual effort at defecation often associated with painful spasms of the anal sphincter.

Persistent pain in the rectum and lower back are not symptoms of early rectal carcinoma, but occur late in the course of the disease when local fixation is extensive and compression or invasion of local nerve trunks has occurred. Additional symptoms of advanced colorectal cancer include dyspepsia, flatulent distention, and borborygmi. With advanced disease an abdominal mass may be palpable, and there is impairment of general health reflected by weight loss and weakness.

Clinical features and diagnosis of carcinoma of the colon and rectum. In: Goligher J, Duthie H, Nixon H, eds. Surgery of the anus, rectum, and colon. 5th ed. London: Baillière Tindall, 1984:465–484

Gordon PH. Malignant neoplasms of the rectum. In: Gordon PH, Nivatvongs S, eds. Principles and practice of surgery for the colon, rectum, and anus. St Louis: Quality Medical Publishing, 1992:591–653

Neugut AI, Garbowski GC, Waye JD, Forde KA, Treat MR, Tsai JL, et al. Diagnostic yield of colorectal neoplasia with colonoscopy for abdominal pain, change in bowel habits, and rectal bleeding. Am J Gastroenterol 1993;88:1179–1183

Walker ARP, Burkitt DP. Colon cancer: epidemiology. Semin Oncol 1976;3:341–350

120

Epidemiology of cervical cancer

You have been asked to be an expert witness in a case involving the relationship of human papillomavirus (HPV) infection and cervical cancer. Each of the following statements is true regarding the link between HPV infection and cervical neoplasia EXCEPT:

(A) Human papillomavirus DNA is found in 90% of patients with either squamous intraepithelial lesions or invasive cervical carcinoma.

* (B) Human papillomavirus DNA is rarely found integrated within the chromosomes of cervical cancers.

(C) Most women with invasive cancer of the cervix have had multiple sexual partners.

(D) Sexual partners of women with cervical cancer have a substantially higher frequency of cancer of the penis than sexual partners of women who do not have cervical cancer.

The molecular evidence linking HPV to invasive squamous cell carcinoma of the cervix is considerable. Human papillomavirus DNA has been detected in 90% of squamous cell carcinomas of the cervix and in most cervical carcinoma cell lines, as well as in 90% of all grades of squamous intraepithelial lesions.

Molecular analysis of cervical cancers reveals that HPV DNA is integrated into the host's DNA in a high proportion of cancers containing HPV 16 and in almost all cancers containing HPV 18. Recent case–control studies with various methodologies for detecting HPV DNA have found strong associations between the presence of HPV 16 and 18 and the development of preinvasive and invasive cervical squamous carcinomas.

None of the standard sexual risk factors are independently associated with the development of invasive cervical cancer after controlling for the effect of HPV, suggesting that sexual-behavioral risk factors are surrogates for HPV infection. These risk factors include early onset of heterosexual activity, early marriage, multiple sexual partners, lower socioeconomic status, and multiparity. It has been found that sexual partners of women with cervical cancer are eight times more likely to have penile cancer than sexual partners of women without cervical cancer.

Bosch FX, Munoz N, de Sanjose S, Izarzugaza I, Gili M, Viladin P, et al. Risk factors for cervical cancer in Colombia and Spain. Int J Cancer 1992;52:750–758

DeBritton RC, Hildesheim A, De Lao SL, Brinton LA, Sathya P, Reeves WC. Human papillomaviruses and other influences on survival from cervical cancer in Panama. Obstet Gynecol 1993;81:19–24

Graham S, Priore R, Graham M, Browne R, Burnett W, West D. Genital cancer in wives of penile cancer patients. Cancer 1979;44:1870–1874

Ikenberg H, Teufel G, Schmitt B, Kommoss F, Stanimirovic B, Pfleiderer A. Human papillomavirus DNA in distant metastases of cervical cancer. Gynecol Oncol 1993;48:56–60

Lorincz AT, Reid R, Jenson AB, Greenberg MD, Lancaster W, Kurman RJ. Human papillomavirus infection of the cervix: relative risk associations of 15 common anogenital types. Obstet Gynecol 1992;79:328–337

Schiffman MH, Bauer HM, Hoover RN, Glass AG, Cadell DM, Rush BB, et al. Epidemiologic evidence showing that human papillomavirus infection causes most cervical intraepithelial neoplasia. J Natl Cancer Inst 1993;85:958–964

121

Medical management of mastalgia

A 29-year-old woman presents with progressive cyclic breast pain. The pain, which is diffuse and bilateral, increases during the week before menstruation and ceases with the onset of menstruation. Physical examination reveals diffuse nodularity, thickening, and tenderness throughout both breasts. No palpable dominant mass is felt. The clinical impression is of symptomatic fibrocystic changes of both breasts. The patient requests treatment. Each of the following has been reported to be effective therapy for mastalgia EXCEPT:

(A) Bromocriptine mesylate (Parlodel)
(B) Danazol (Danocrine)
* (C) Dietary restriction of methylxanthines
(D) Oil of evening primrose
(E) Tamoxifen citrate (Nolvadex)

Multiple prospective, double-blind, crossover studies document that methylxanthines (including caffeine and theophylline) have no effect on breast pain, tenderness, or the risk of cancer. In 1981 a nonrandomized, uncontrolled clinical observation of a small number of women suggested that caffeine intake was related to breast pain. However, subsequent controlled studies revealed no scientific basis for a therapeutic response to dietary restriction of methylxanthines.

Prospective randomized, double-blind, crossover studies have documented the efficacy of bromocriptine, danazol, oil of evening primrose, and tamoxifen in the treatment of cyclic mastalgia. Gonadotropin-releasing hormone has also been shown to be effective therapy for cyclic mastalgia in limited studies. Most of these published studies have insufficient statistical power because of small sample size. Studies with sufficient statistical power from multiple institutions are needed.

Bromocriptine can alter fertility and causes adverse side effects (nausea, vomiting, edema, dizziness, and alopecia) in many patients. Tamoxifen has been associated with serious side effects including endometrial cancer. Neither bromocriptine nor tamoxifen should be prescribed as therapy for mastalgia. Oil of evening primrose contains polyunsaturated essential fatty acids (particularly γ-linolenic acid) and has been commonly prescribed for mastalgia in England. In the United States, oil of evening primrose is available in health food stores.

Of all these therapies, only danazol is approved by the U.S. Food and Drug Administration for the treatment of mastalgia. However, because of cost, masculinizing side effects (acne, weight gain, hoarseness), and poor patient tolerance, danazol therapy is infrequently prescribed for mastalgia.

Fentiman IS, Caleffi M, Brame K, Chaudary MA, Hayward JL. Double-blind controlled trial of tamoxifen therapy for mastalgia. Lancet 1986;1:287–288

Heyden S, Muhlbaier LH. Prospective study of "fibrocystic breast disease" and caffeine consumption. Surgery 1984;96:479–484

Hinton CP, Bishop HM, Holliday HW, Doyle PJ, Blamey RW. A double-blind controlled trial of danazol and bromocriptine in the management of severe cyclical breast pain. Br J Clin Pract 1986;40:326–330

Minton JP, Abou-Issa H, Reiches N, Roseman J. Clinical and biochemical studies on methylxanthine-related fibrocystic breast disease. Surgery 1981; 90:299–304

Pashby NL, Mansel, RE, Hughes LE, Hanslip J. A clinical trial of evening primrose oil in mastalgia. Br J Surg 1981;68:801

Sandrucci S, Mussa A, Festa V, Borre A, Grosso M, Dogliotti L. Comparison of tamoxifen and bromocriptine in management of fibrocystic breast disease: a randomized blind study. Ann N Y Acad Sci 1986;464:626–628

122

Lymph node metastasis in endometrial cancer

A 59-year-old nulliparous woman has an endometrial biopsy for evaluation of postmenopausal bleeding, which reveals grade 2 endometrial adenocarcinoma. Physical examination is within normal limits except for mild obesity. Chest X-ray, complete blood count, and serum chemistries are normal.

The patient undergoes an exploratory laparotomy, peritoneal washings, total abdominal hysterectomy, and bilateral salpingo-oophorectomy. On opening the uterus, a 3×4-cm tumor is found occupying the upper endometrial cavity with apparent superficial myometrial invasion but no evidence of cervical or adnexal spread. There is no evidence of disease spread within the peritoneal cavity, and lymph nodes are not suspicious for malignancy. In deciding whether to perform selective pelvic and paraaortic lymph node dissections in this patient, all of the following factors should be considered EXCEPT:

(A) Tumor grade
(B) Tumor size
(C) Depth of myometrial invasion
(D) Degree of local spread
* (E) Degree of clinical suspicion of nodes

It has long been recognized that lymphatic permeation with embolization to retroperitoneal lymph nodes is an important mode of spread of endometrial carcinoma. Of patients with clinical stage I endometrial cancer, approximately 10% will have pelvic lymph node metastases and 6% will have aortic lymph node metastases. The frequency of lymph node metastasis increases with loss of tumor differentiation, increasing tumor size, increasing depth of myometrial invasion, extension to the isthmus or cervix, lymph–vascular space invasion, and other evidence of extrauterine disease, such as adnexal spread, positive peritoneal cytology, and peritoneal tumor implants. Selective paraaortic lymph node dissection with or without pelvic lymph node biopsies should be performed in all patients with one or more of these risk factors. Almost all patients with lymph node metastases have at least one of these risk factors.

Tumor grade and depth of myometrial invasion seem to be the two most important factors in determining the risk of lymph node metastasis. Considering tumor grade alone, the overall incidence of lymph node metastasis in clinical stage I endometrial cancer is approximately 3% in grade 1, 9% in grade 2, and 18% in grade 3 tumors. Considering myometrial invasion alone, fewer than 5% of patients with no myometrial invasion or with superficial (less than one half the thickness of the myometrium) myometrial invasion have lymph node metastasis, compared with 25% of patients with deep (at least one half the thickness of the myometrium) myometrial invasion. Considering both tumor grade and myometrial invasion, pelvic lymph node metastases are present in fewer than 5% of grade 1 and 2 tumors with superficial myometrial invasion, approximately 10–20% of grade 1 and 2 tumors with deep myometrial invasion and grade 3 tumors with superficial invasion, and more than 40% of grade 3 tumors with deep myometrial invasion. Approximately one half to two thirds of patients with posi-tive pelvic lymph nodes will also have paraaortic lymph node metastasis, but the aortic nodes are seldom involved in the absence of pelvic nodal disease. The incidence of lymph node metastasis also correlates with tumor size ($\leq$2 cm = 4%, >2 cm = 15%, entire cavity = 35%).

The risk of pelvic lymph node and paraaortic lymph node metastasis increases with pathologic demonstration of lymph–vascular space invasion to 27% and 19%, respectively. Adnexal and cervical involvement are associated with an increased risk of nodal disease (32% and 16% for pelvic lymph nodes and 20% and 14% for paraaortic lymph nodes, respectively). Of patients with positive peritoneal cytology, 25% have positive pelvic nodes and 19% have positive paraaortic nodes.

Because fewer than 10% of patients with lymphatic metastasis have grossly enlarged nodes, palpation is not an acceptable alternative to lymph node biopsies. On the other hand, lymph node biopsies are not required in patients at low risk for lymphatic metastasis. This patient should have selected pelvic and paraaortic lymph node sampling because of the tumor size and grade.

Boronow RC, Morrow CP, Creasman WT, DiSaia PJ, Silverberg SG, Miller A, et al. Surgical staging in endometrial cancer: clinical-pathologic findings of a prospective study. Obstet Gynecol 1984;63:825–832

Creasman WT, Morrow CP, Bundy BN, Homesley HD, Graham JE, Heller PB. Surgical pathologic spread patterns of endometrial cancer: a Gynecologic Oncology Group study. Cancer 1987;60:2035–2041

123

Anatomy of the ureter

In the performance of pelvic surgery, the gynecologic surgeon should be aware that the ureter receives its blood supply from each of the following sources EXCEPT:

* (A) The opposite ureter at the level of the presacral area
(B) The anastomotic capillary network in the adventitia
(C) An arterial branch from the renal artery
(D) A branch from the uterine artery and the superior and inferior vesicle arteries
(E) An arterial branch from the lower aorta, common iliac artery, or external iliac artery

The ureter is a narrow, thick-walled tube that in the adult varies in length from 28 cm to 34 cm and has an external diameter of from 4 mm to 1 cm (Fig. 123-1). The ureter is composed of a fibrous outer layer, a muscular middle layer, and a mucosal inner layer (Fig. 123-2). The muscular layer is composed of an outer longitudinal layer and an inner circular layer. The mucosal layer is smooth, with only a few longitudinal folds and a transitional epithelium.

The outer, fibrous coat of the ureter (the adventitia) has a rich network of capillaries as well as a profuse lymphatic network. Therefore, the ureter can usually tolerate interruption of the blood supply to one of the segments, provided the adventitia is not damaged. When one performs pelvic surgery, it is important to attempt to preserve the adventitial coat of the ureter to prevent damage to its blood supply. This is particularly important in a patient who has had irradiation, which may damage the blood supply of the ureter.

The nerve supply to the ureter is derived from the inferior mesenteric and pelvic plexuses. It has both sympathetic and parasympathetic enervation. The afferent somatic nervous supply is via the 11th and 12th thoracic and the 1st lumbar nerves.

The blood supply to the ureter is segmental and is usually described as occurring in thirds. The upper one third of the ureter receives its blood supply from branches of the renal artery, and the distal one third receives its blood supply from various vessels in the pelvis (Fig. 123-3). Usually, this pelvic blood supply is derived from branches of the uterine artery and the superior and inferior vesicle arteries. Occasionally, the ureter receives a branch from the hemorrhoidal artery. In the

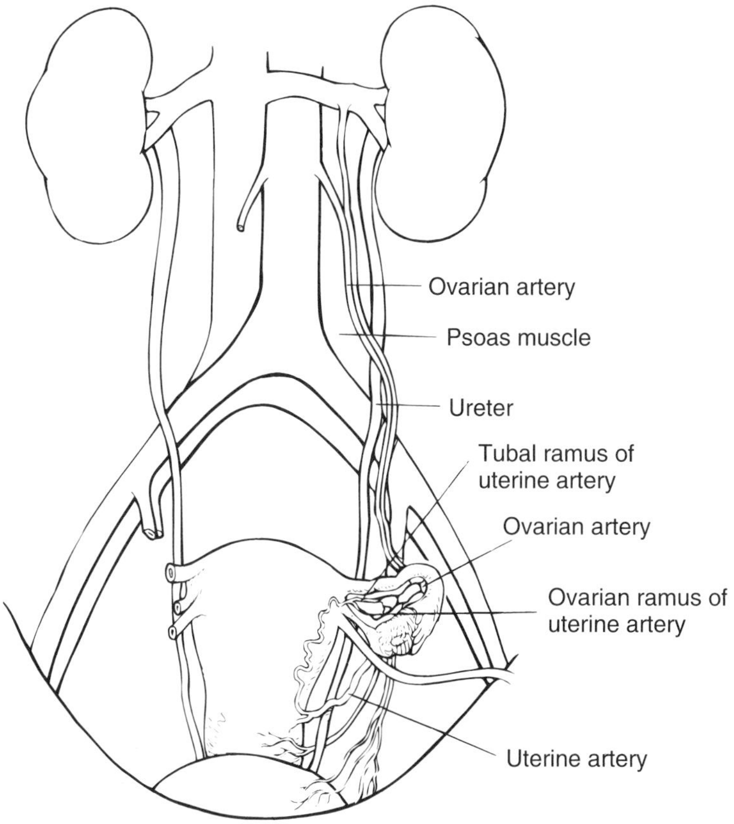

FIG. 123-1. The ureters, coursing over the common iliac artery en route to the bladder. Note the ovarian artery and ureter coursing over the surface of the psoas muscle. (Nichols DH, ed. Gynecologic and obstetric surgery. St Louis: CV Mosby, 1993:31)

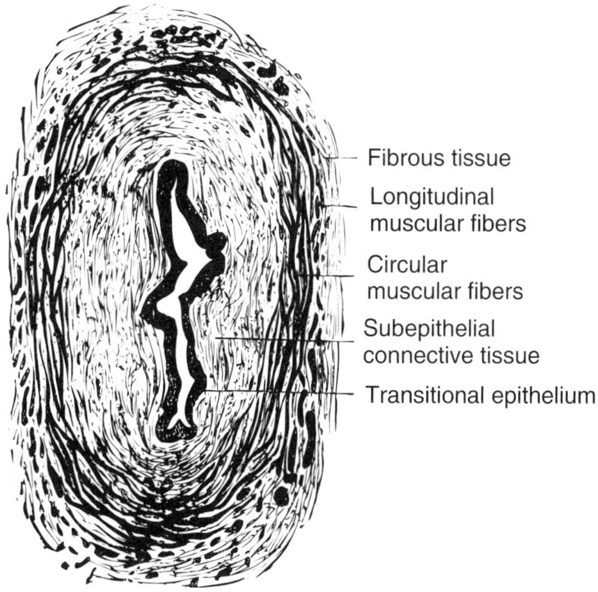

FIG. 123-2. Transverse section of the ureter. (Clemente CD, ed. Gray's anatomy. 30th American ed. Philadelphia: Lea and Febiger, 1985:1538)

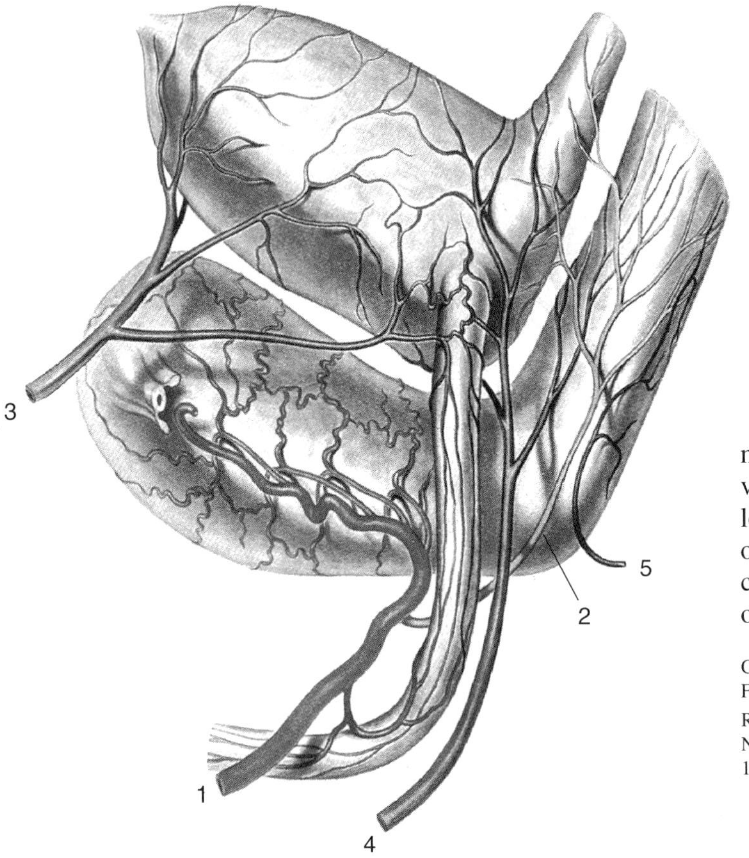

FIG. 123-3. Blood supply of the portion of the ureter near the bladder and of the uterus, as seen from the side. (1) Uterine artery; (2) vaginal artery; (3) superior vesical artery; (4) inferior vesical artery; (5) branch of the inferior rectal artery. (Reiffenstuhl/Platzer/Knapstein. Die vaginalen Operationen. 2nd edition 1994. Urban & Schwarzenberg München–Wien–Baltimore.)

middle third of the ureter, the blood supply is more variable. Branches to the ureter may arise from the lower aorta, the common or external iliac artery, and occasionally from the ovarian artery. There is no cross-connection of blood supply from one ureter to the ureter on the opposite side.

Clemente CD, ed. Gray's anatomy. 30th American ed. Philadelphia: Lea and Febiger, 1985:1537–1539

Reiffenstuhl G. Practical pelvic anatomy for the gynecologic surgeon. In: Nichols DH, ed. Gynecologic and obstetric surgery. St Louis: CV Mosby, 1993:26–71

124

Anatomy of the cervix

A 47-year-old woman is diagnosed with a stage IB squamous cell carcinoma of the cervix. Regarding spread patterns of cervical cancer, each of the following is a nodal group with primary lymphatic drainage from the cervix EXCEPT:

(A) Paracervical lymph nodes
(B) Interiliac lymph nodes
(C) External iliac lymph nodes
(D) Obturator lymph nodes
* (E) Inguinofemoral lymph nodes

The lymphatics of the cervix arise as channels that surround the endocervical glands and lie beneath the epithelium of the columnar cells that form the glands. These lymphatics form capillary channels that traverse the cervical stroma to become small lacunae at the border of the cervix and the paracervical tissues. There are several lymph nodes in the paracervical and parametrial tissues, and these nodes are the first point of direct drainage from the cervix. There is often a lymph node where the ureter crosses under the uterine artery. Some authorities have called this node the parauterine node. After traversing the paracervical tissues, the lymphatics divide into collecting trunks (Fig. 124-1).

The *upper trunks* of lymphatics drain to the interiliac and external iliac lymph nodes and from there to the common iliac artery and finally to the paraaortic lymph nodes. The *middle trunks* of lymphatics drain primarily to the obturator lymph nodes, and the *lower trunks* of lymphatics drain primarily to the hypogastric (internal iliac) lymph nodes. The *middle trunks* of lymphatics traverse the cardinal ligaments, and occasionally lymph nodes will be found before the obturator lymph nodes are reached. The *lower trunks* traverse the uterosacral ligaments on their way to the hypogastric nodal chains. These trunks also communicate with lymph nodes in the region of the inferior gluteal vessels and continue up

FIG. 124-1. A diagrammatic presentation of the major lymphatic trunks leaving the cervix. These consist of three lateral sets, which start in the cardinal ligament and reach the pelvic wall in a pattern consistent with their level of origin. The uppermost set follows the uterine artery upward, where it may be interrupted by the parauterine node, and it terminates in the uppermost interiliac nodes. The middle set takes a similar course and reaches the deeper iliac nodes, commonly referred to as obturator. The lowest set of lateral lymphatics immediately sweeps downward toward the posterior pelvic wall and discharges its lymph into all nodes of this area, including inferior and superior gluteal, common iliac, and preaortic nodes. Trunks arising from the posterior cervix follow the uterosacral ligament to drain into the gluteal, common iliac, superior rectal, and preaortic and aortic nodes. The anterior pathway to the interiliac nodes is not included in this composite picture. (Plentl AA, Friedman EA. Lymphatic system of the female genitalia: the morphologic basis of oncologic diagnosis and therapy. In: Major problems in obstetrics and gynecology. Vol 2. Philadelphia: WB Saunders, 1971:83)

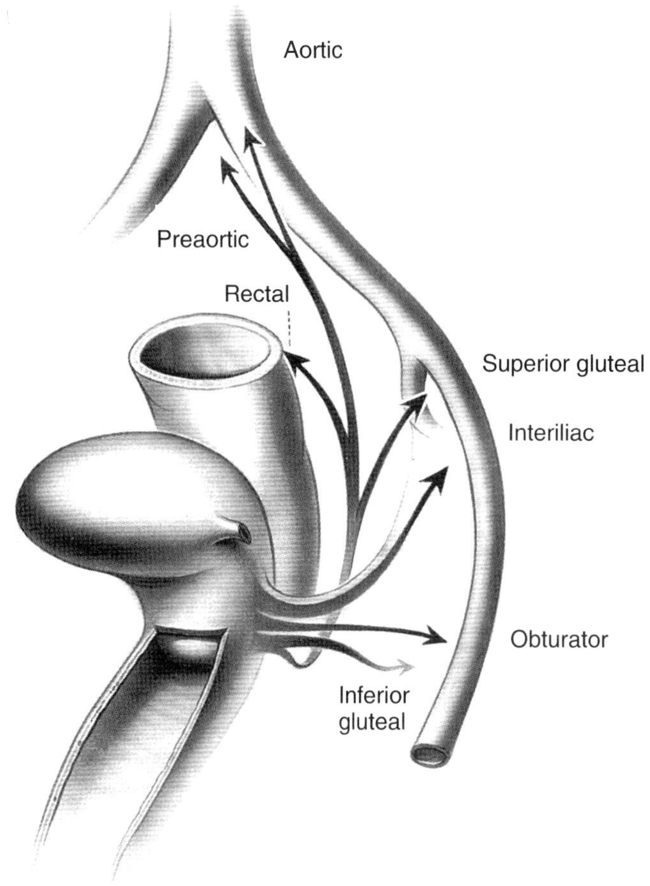

along the sacrum to the presacral lymph nodes, which then communicate with the lower paraaortic lymph nodes.

There is extensive intercommunication between the three main trunks of lymphatics. The upper trunk communicates with the upper portion of the obturator lymph nodes, and the middle trunk communicates with both the interiliac and hypogastric lymph nodes. The lower trunk anastomoses with the obturator as well as the hypogastric (internal iliac) lymph nodes. There is communication between the lymphatics of the cervix and the lower uterine (isthmus) segment. This communication with the isthmus of the uterus explains why lower-uterine-segment endometrial cancers spread like cervical cancers. In contrast, endometrial cancers that arise in the fundus of the uterus may traverse the lymphatics of the round ligament to involve the femoral and inguinal lymph nodes. There is no direct flow of lymphatics from the cervix to the inguinofemoral lymph nodes.

Clemente CD, ed. Gray's anatomy. 30th American ed. Philadelphia: Lea and Febiger, 1985:906–907

Plentl AA, Friedman EA. Lymphatic system of the female genitalia: the morphologic basis of oncologic diagnosis and therapy. In: Major problems in obstetrics and gynecology. Vol 2. Philadelphia: WB Saunders, 1971:75–115

125–128

Properties of sutures

The specific properties of each type of suture vary throughout the wound-healing process. Assuming the 28th postoperative day, for each of the descriptions (125–128), select the suture described (A–D).

(A) Synthetic polyglactin 910 (Vicryl)
(B) Chromic catgut (naturally occurring chemically treated collagen)
(C) Synthetic polydioxanone (PDS)
(D) Polypropylene (Prolene)

D **125.** Nonabsorbable suture with the greatest tensile strength

C **126.** Absorbable suture with the greatest tensile strength

B **127.** Absorbable suture with the greatest inflammatory tissue reaction

C **128.** Absorbable suture with the least inflammatory tissue reaction

The ideal suture material should be easy to handle, maintain good knot security, and have low tissue drag, lasting tensile strength (retaining this strength in the presence of infection), and a predictable absorption throughout the wound-healing process. The absorbable sutures include polyglyconate (Maxon), polyglactin 910, chromic catgut, and polydioxanone; polypropylene is a nonabsorbable suture.

When tested in a standardized laboratory setting, four sutures (of 4-0 weight) were found to have the following properties: polyglyconate and polydioxanone elicit a lower degree of chronic inflammation compared with polyglactin 910 and chromic catgut (Fig. 125–128-1). Of these, chromic catgut induces the greatest inflammation and polydioxanone the least. The tensile strengths of polyglyconate and polydioxanone significantly exceed those of polyglactin 910 and chromic catgut during the critical period of wound healing (Fig. 125–128-2). Polyglyconate and polydioxanone retain a larger percentage of tensile strength during the extended postoperative period, whereas polyglactin 910 and chromic catgut are mostly absorbed (Fig. 125–128-2). At day 28 postoperatively, polydiaxanone has the greatest tensile strength of the sutures listed.

In another study, the relative strengths of various suture materials were determined through the postoperative period (Fig. 125–128-3). Polypropylene retains tensile strength better than any absorbable suture.

The strength of wound closure is important in the prevention of wound dehiscence and later herniation. In

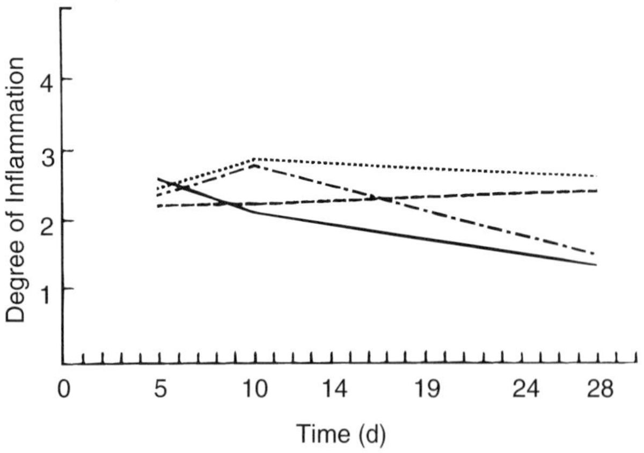

FIG. 125–128-1. Degree of wound inflammation induced at days 5, 10, and 28 for the chromic catgut (dotted line), polyglactin 910 (Vicryl; dashed line), polyglyconate (Maxon; dot-dashed line), and polydioxanone (PDS; solid line) sutures. (Sanz LE, Patterson JA, Kamath R, Willett G, Ahmed SW, Butterfield AB. Comparison of Maxon suture with Vicryl, chromic catgut, and PDS sutures in fascial closure in rats. Reprinted with permission from The American College of Obstetricians and Gynecologists [Obstetrics and Gynecology, 1988, 71, 420])

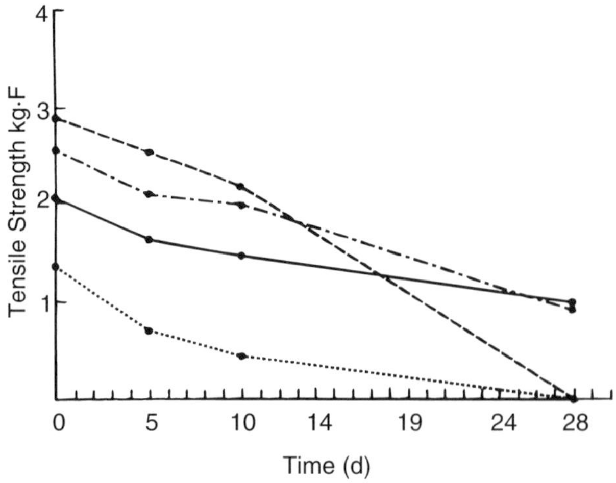

FIG. 125–128-2. Tensile strength at days 0, 5, 10, and 28 for chromic catgut (dotted line), polyglactin 910 (Vicryl; dashed line), polyglyconate (Maxon; dot-dashed line), and polydioxanone (PDS; solid line) sutures. kg·F indicates kilograms of force. (Sanz LE, Patterson JA, Kamath R, Willett G, Ahmed SW, Butterfield AB. Comparison of Maxon suture with Vicryl, chromic catgut, and PDS sutures in fascial closure in rats. Reprinted with permission from The American College of Obstetricians and Gynecologists [Obstetrics and Gynecology, 1988, 71, 420])

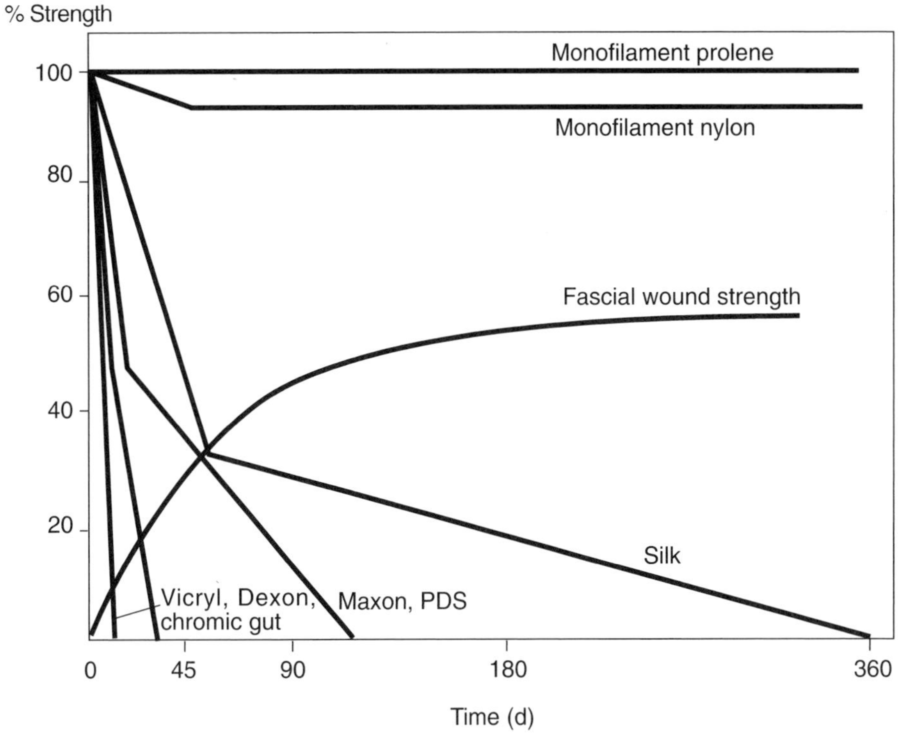

FIG. 125–128-3. Strength of suture material in relation to fascia. Vicryl indicates polyglactin 910; Dexon, polyglycolic acid; Maxon, polyglyconate; PDS, polydioxanone.

other circumstances, the functional stability of the operative repair, such as the long-term results of bladder neck elevation (as in the Pereyra procedure), is improved with nonabsorbable as opposed to absorbable suture. By contrast, in microsurgery, the major consideration may not be tensile strength but the inflammatory response and thus scar formation induced by the suture material. Choice of the correct suture material should be tailored to the required surgical outcome.

Delbeke LO, Gomel V, McComb PF, Jetha N. Histologic reactions to four synthetic microsutures in the rabbit. Fertil Steril 1983;40:248–252

Korn AP. Does use of permanent suture material affect outcome of the modified Pereyra procedure? Obstet Gynecol 1994;83:104–107

Sanz LE, Patterson JA, Kamath R, Willett G, Ahmed SW, Butterfield AB. Comparison of Maxon suture with Vicryl, chromic catgut, and PDS sutures in fascial closure in rats. Obstet Gynecol 1988;71:418–422

129–133

Screening for skin cancer

During a busy afternoon clinic, you see four women with skin lesions. For each of the descriptions below (129–133), select the corresponding lesion (A–D).

(A) Fig. 129–133-1
(B) Fig. 129–133-2
(C) Fig. 129–133-3
(D) Fig. 129–133-4

B **129.** Found more frequently in dark-complexioned patients

A **130.** Most common skin cancer in light-complexioned patients

D **131.** Most common skin cancer in Asians, African Americans, Hispanics, and American Indians

B **132.** Associated with skin scarring such as from burns and ulcers

C **133.** Can occur anywhere, but is most commonly found on the shins and upper back

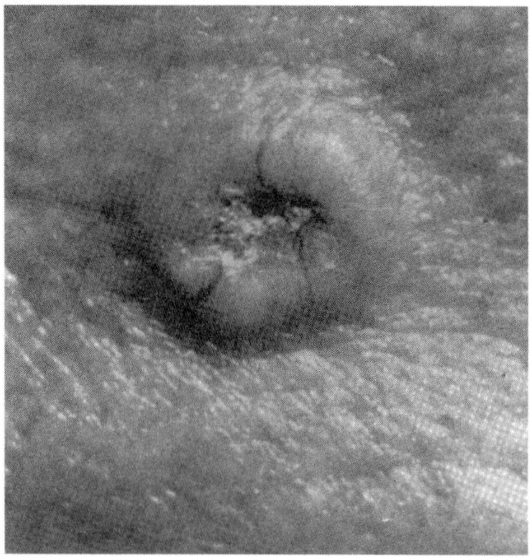

FIG. 129–133-1. Basal cell carcinoma. (Arnold HL Jr, Odom RB, James WD. Andrews' diseases of the skin: clinical dermatology. 8th ed. Philadelphia: WB Saunders, 1990:763)

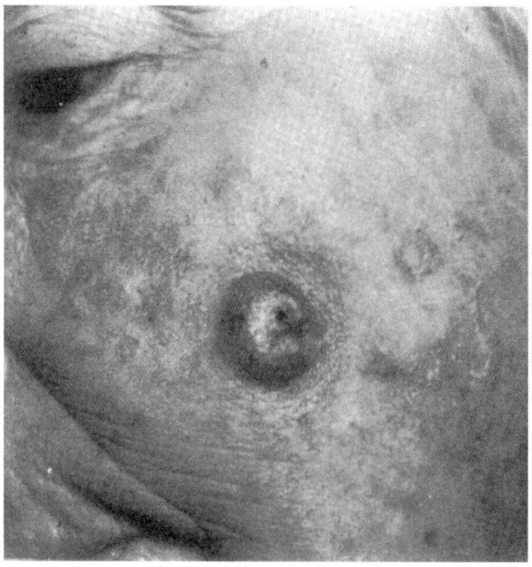

FIG. 129–133-2. Squamous cell carcinoma. (Arnold HL Jr, Odom RB, James WD. Andrews' diseases of the skin: clinical dermatology. 8th ed. Philadelphia: WB Saunders, 1990:778)

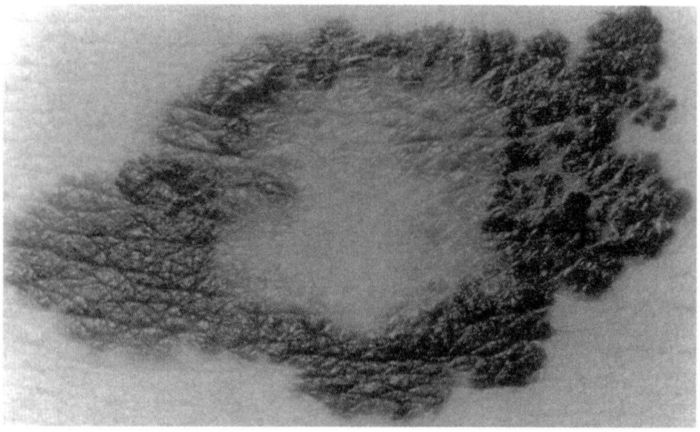

FIG. 129–133-3. Superficially spreading melanoma. (Courtesy of Dr. Axel W. Hoke)

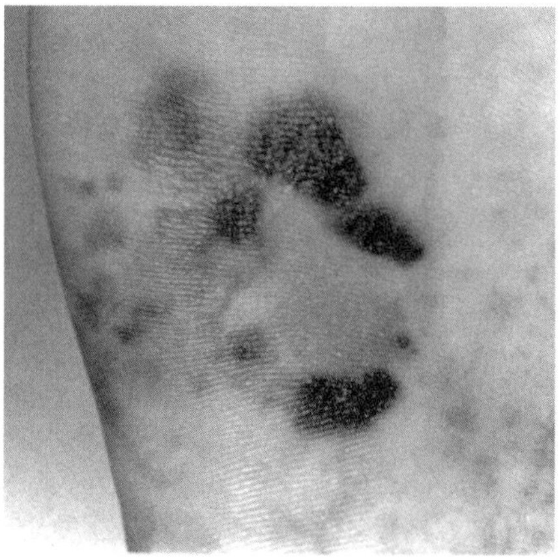

FIG. 129–133-4. Acral–lentiginous melanoma. (Courtesy of Dr. Axel W. Hoke)

The skin is the largest of the body organs, and according to recent data from the American Cancer Society, skin cancer is the most frequently diagnosed malignancy in the United States. Melanoma is the most frequent of all cancers in women aged 25–29 years.

Sun exposure plays a major role in the development of skin cancer. Avoidance of tanning parlors and direct exposure of skin to sunlight and the use of sunscreen with a protection factor of at least 15 (SPF-15) will decrease the incidence of these tumors.

Screening for skin cancer is quick, painless, and inexpensive, and early treatment reduces morbidity and mortality. Examination of the shoulders, back, and other areas that the patient cannot see is particularly important. Because these tumors are slow growing, the gynecologist providing annual examination has an ideal opportunity for early discovery and diagnosis. Patients also should be encouraged to do self-examination of the skin. Women are more likely than are men to discover their own tumors and to detect tumors in other family members.

Excessive sunlight exposure, increasing age, genetic determinants, immunosuppression, and chemical cocarcinogens are implicated in the etiology of basal cell carcinoma. It is the most common skin tumor of light-complexioned people and is seen less commonly in women than in men. The typical appearance is a ring of translucent nodules surrounding a central depression (Fig. 129–133-1). Larger lesions have a characteristic rolled border; telangiectases are common, with resultant bleeding on slight injury. These tumors may be slightly ulcerated, crusted, or pigmented. They enlarge slowly, are asymptomatic except for bleeding, and are most frequently found on the face (particularly the nose) and ears, although they can also be found on the trunk. Basal cell carcinomas rarely occur on the dorsum of the hand, one of the locations most prone to sun exposure, where actinic keratosis and squamous cell carcinoma are frequently found. They can be locally destructive but almost never metastasize. If the margins are involved, further excision is appropriate.

Squamous cell carcinoma usually begins at a site of actinic keratosis on sun-exposed areas such as the back of the hands, face, neck, and lower extremities. These lesions, which are found more frequently in African-American patients, are also associated with scarring from burns, ulcers, or hidradenitis suppurativa. Ultraviolet light exposure is a prime causative agent. Ultraviolet B rays are considered more damaging, although ultraviolet A rays appear to be potentiators. Squamous cell tumors are usually dull red with telangiectases and an elevated base or scaly plaques; ulceration is common (Fig. 129–133-2). Within a few months, lesions become larger, more nodular, and ulcerated; the ulcer may be covered by a crust, which when removed reveals a discrete hard lesion.

Superficially spreading melanoma is the most common type of melanoma, constituting 70% of these lesions (Fig. 129–133-3). Median age for diagnosis is in the 50s. The upper back and shins are the most common areas of melanoma occurrence, but it may occur anywhere. Lesions are multicolored with varying shades of tan, black, red, brown, blue, and white. The border is frequently notched. Easy bleeding, erosion, and ulceration are signs of malignancy.

Acral–lentiginous melanoma (Fig. 129–133-4) is an irregular black macule that develops on palmar and plantar surfaces as well as on distal phalanges of the toes or fingers, the thumb and great toe being the most frequently involved. It accounts for approximately 10% of all lesions and is most common in Asians, African Americans, Hispanics, and American Indians. Median age at diagnosis is 50 years, with equal sex distribution.

Koh HK, Lew RA, Prout MN. Screening for melanoma/skin cancer: theoretic and practical considerations. J Am Acad Dermatol 1989;20:159–172

McDonald CJ. Status of screening for skin cancer. Cancer 1993;72:1066–1070

134–137

Tissue injury with mechanical, cautery, and laser surgery

A variety of techniques are available for the performance of pelvic surgery. Although many of these techniques can be used interchangeably, they each have specific characteristic effects on tissue. For each of the indications listed (134–137), select the technique (A–D) that results in the least tissue injury.

(A) Sharp incision
(B) Electrocoagulation
(C) Carbon dioxide (CO_2) laser
(D) Neodymium-yttrium-aluminum-garnet (Nd-YAG) laser

A **134.** Bivalve incision of the ovary

B **135.** Hemostasis of a bleeding 3-mm blood vessel

A **136.** Incision of the fallopian tube

A **137.** Ovarian cystectomy

The choice of instruments to cut, coagulate, or obliterate tissues can have far-reaching consequences. Sharp incision is the least damaging to the tissues, as has been confirmed by histologic studies of the genital tract, especially of the ovary and fallopian tube. Animal data show that sharp incision preserves more ovarian follicles than incision by either laser or electrosurgery (Figs. 134–137-1, 134–137-2, and 134–137-3; see color plates). At the time of sharp incision, the use of interstitial dilute vasopressin solution (Pitressin) for hemostasis replaces the need for the hemostatic qualities of laser or electrosurgery. With either laser or electrosurgery, the property of hemocoagulation is due to the dispersal of thermal energy from the incision site into the adjacent tissue.

A distinction is drawn between the use of laser and electrosurgery for incisional purposes and their use for ablation of tissue. The prime example of the benefit of ablation is for endometriosis. Even this benefit is location dependent, however. Endometriosis of the uterosacral ligaments and much of the pelvic peritoneal surface can be safely and effectively destroyed by either laser or electrosurgery. The selection of instrumentation becomes key when the endometriosis is located over vital structures such as the ureter, bowel, bladder, vessels, or ovary. In these areas, the surgeon must be aware of the depth of penetration of the tissue injury. There are potential photothermal, photochemical, photoacoustic, and photodynamic tissue effects. Most lasers have been well quantified for their individual photothermal effects, as determined by tissue type, laser wavelength, and time taken to deliver a certain quantity of energy. Above 100°C, tissue vaporization and ablation occur. Pulsed delivery of the laser induces less thermal injury than a continuous wave laser.

Photochemical damage associated with the laser leads to electronic fragmentation of molecules, whereas an acoustic shock wave produces steam-mediated tissue cavitation. Under certain circumstances laser light is absorbed by a light-activated compound, and energy is transferred to molecular oxygen, with production of free oxygen radicals and resultant tissue destruction.

The thermal effects of either electrosurgery or laser induce a significantly more pronounced acute inflammatory response, and subsequently greater chronic inflammation, than sharp incision. A delayed thermal effect may result in damage to surrounding tissue, with clinical presentation of complications up to 10 days later.

Although CO_2 laser is absorbed within a 0.1-mm tissue depth, the surrounding shoulder of maximal thermal coagulation is approximately 0.5 mm. However, bleeding of any degree impedes the beam and effectiveness of the laser. The argon laser is absorbed selectively by pigmented lesions such as endometriosis, but produces greater thermal damage than the CO_2 laser. The Nd-YAG laser has good hemostatic qualities, but its depth of penetration (up to 5 mm) may lead to unrecognized injury of surrounding tissue. The potassium-titanyl-phosphate laser has good coagulative properties. Its depth of penetration is shallow (0.3–1 mm) compared with that of the Nd-YAG laser.

Based on this information, sharp incision is optimum for bivalve incision of the ovary, incision of the fallopian tube, and ovarian cystectomy. Electrocoagulation is most effective for hemostasis of a bleeding 3-mm blood vessel.

Bhatta N, Isaacson K, Bhatta KM, Anderson RR, Schiff I. Comparative study of different laser systems. Fertil Steril 1994;61:581–591

Filmar S, Gomel V, McComb P. The effectiveness of CO_2 laser and electromicrosurgery in adhesiolysis: a comparative study. Fertil Steril 1986;45:407–411

Filmar S, Jetha N, McComb P, Gomel V. A comparative histologic study on the healing process after tissue transection, I: carbon dioxide laser and electromicrosurgery. Am J Obstet Gynecol 1989;160:1062–1067

Filmar S, Jetha N, McComb P, Gomel V. A comparative histologic study on the healing process after tissue transection, II: carbon dioxide laser and surgical microscissors. Am J Obstet Gynecol 1989;160:1068–1072

McComb P. Advances in infertility surgery: can laparoscopy replace microsurgical laparotomy? Clin Prac Gynecol 1991;3:1–20

McComb PF. Infertility surgery: operative endoscopy, new instruments and techniques. Clin Obstet Gynecol 1989;32:564–575

138–142

Diagnosis of gestational trophoblastic disease

For each of the patients described below (138–142), select the gestational trophoblastic disease (A–D) that is the most likely diagnosis.

(A) Invasive mole
(B) Hydatidiform mole
(C) Choriocarcinoma
(D) Placental-site trophoblastic tumor

B **138.** A woman presents with a last normal menstrual period 10 weeks ago, uterine bleeding, a uterus of 14 weeks' gestational size, and a human chorionic gonadotropin (hCG) level of 137,000 mIU/ml.

A **139.** A woman underwent evacuation of a molar pregnancy 6 weeks ago. She has continued uterine bleeding, a persistently enlarged uterus, bilateral 6-cm theca–lutein cysts, and a plateauing hCG level of 4,500–5,000 mIU/ml.

C **140.** A women presents with shortness of breath and vaginal bleeding at 2 weeks postpartum. Chest X-ray reveals multiple metastatic tumors; an hCG level is 56,000 mIU/ml.

C **141.** A woman with a last menstrual period 9 weeks ago presents with uterine bleeding, an hCG of 6,500 mIU/ml, and a slightly enlarged uterus. Transvaginal ultrasonography reveals an empty uterus and no adnexal masses. Chest X-ray is negative. Dilation and curettage yields a few abnormal trophoblastic cells without villi.

D **142.** A woman has continued irregular uterine bleeding after a first-trimester spontaneous abortion 6 months ago. Her uterus is twice normal size, and an hCG level is 16 mIU/ml.

According to the World Health Organization, gestational trophoblastic disease encompasses four clinical–pathologic forms of trophoblast growth disturbance: hydatidiform mole, invasive mole, choriocarcinoma, and placental-site trophoblastic tumor. The latter three are termed gestational trophoblastic tumors because they may progress, invade, metastasize, and kill if untreated. The diagnosis and decision to institute treatment are often undertaken without knowledge of the precise histology.

Hydatidiform mole is an abnormal pregnancy characterized by vesicular swelling of placental villi, trophoblastic proliferation, and usually absence of an intact fetus. The outstanding clinical feature of hydatidiform mole is uterine bleeding, which occurs during the 6th to 16th week of gestation in over 95% of patients. About one quarter of patients have associated preeclampsia or hyperemesis. On physical examination, 50% of patients have uterine enlargement greater than that expected for gestational dates. Bilateral theca–lutein enlargement of the ovaries occurs in 15% of patients, and fetal heart tones are usually absent. Human chorionic gonadotropin levels are usually elevated above levels seen with normal pregnancy. The first patient described has several of these characteristics. Pelvic ultrasonography would most likely demonstrate multiple echoes and sonolucent areas within the placental mass and no fetus.

Invasive mole results from myometrial invasion by a hydatidiform mole via direct extension or through venous channels. Invasive mole is deported to the lungs or vagina in 15% of patients. It is characterized histologically by swollen placental villi and accompanying trophoblast, with hyperplasia and usually atypia located in sites outside the cavity of the uterus. Progression to invasive mole occurs with 10–17% of hydatidiform moles. Continued uterine bleeding, an enlarged, irregular uterus, and persistent bilateral ovarian enlargement after evacuation of a molar pregnancy are suggestive of invasive mole. The diagnosis is most often made clinically based on rising or persistently elevated hCG levels after hydatidiform mole evacuation. The second patient exhibits most of these findings.

Choriocarcinoma is a malignant tumor characterized histologically by abnormal trophoblastic hyperplasia and anaplasia, absence of chorionic villi, hemorrhage and necrosis, direct uterine invasion, and vascular spread to the myometrium and distant sites, most commonly the lungs, brain, liver, pelvis, vagina, spleen, intestines, and kidneys. Gestational choriocarcinoma may be associated with any type of pregnancy. Progression to choriocarcinoma is seen in 2–3% of patients with hydatidiform moles, accounting for almost 50% of all cases, whereas 25% of choriocarcinomas occur in patients after spontaneous abortion and 25% in patients after term or preterm gestation.

No characteristic symptoms or physical signs are attributable to choriocarcinoma. Abnormal uterine bleeding is a common symptom, but 25% of patients present with nongynecologic symptoms (eg, dyspnea, hemoptysis, headaches, and seizures) and signs (eg, hemiparesis and hepatomegaly) as a result of metastatic disease. Pathologic diagnosis of choriocarcinoma can sometimes be made by uterine curettage, biopsy of metastatic lesions, or examination of hysterectomy specimens or placentas. A presumptive clinical diagnosis of choriocarcinoma is usually made based on persistent hCG elevation in conjunction with the demonstration of metastases after pregnancy. Both the third and fourth patients have choriocarcinoma.

Placental-site trophoblastic tumor is an extremely rare trophoblastic tumor that arises from the placental implantation site. Histologically, tumor cells infiltrate the myometrium and grow between smooth muscle cells, and there is vascular invasion. Placental-site tumor differs from choriocarcinoma primarily in the absence of an alternating pattern of cytotrophoblast and syncytiotrophoblast; the cells are predominantly of one type (intermediate trophoblast), and hemorrhage and necrosis are less evident. Human placental lactogen is present in tumor cells, whereas immunoperoxidase staining for hCG is positive only in scattered cells. Most patients have irregular vaginal bleeding and an enlarged uterus. Serum hCG levels are relatively low with placental-site tumors, as noted in the fifth patient, compared with the higher hCG levels in patients with choriocarcinoma. Although several reports have noted a benign course for these tumors, they are relatively resistant to chemotherapy, and deaths have resulted from metastatic disease. Surgery (dilation and curettage or hysterectomy) is the mainstay of treatment.

Hammond CB, Soper JT. Gestational trophoblastic diseases. In: Sciarra JJ, ed. Gynecology and obstetrics. Vol 4. Philadelphia: JB Lippincott, 1993:1–42

Lurain JR, Brewer JI. Invasive mole. Semin Oncol 1982;9:174–180

Mazur MT, Kurman RJ. Gestational trophoblastic disease and related lesions. In: Kurman RJ, ed. Blaustein's pathology of the female genital tract. 4th ed. New York: Springer-Verlag, 1994:1049–1091

143–146

Anatomy of the vulva

The muscles of the urogenital region in the female are listed below. Match the functions or anatomic characteristics of these muscles (143–146) with the correct muscle (A–D).

(A) Transversus perinei (superficialis and profundus)
(B) Bulbocavernosus
(C) Ischiocavernosus
(D) Sphincter urethrae

B **143.** Contraction diminishes the vaginal orifice

B **144.** Covers the lateral portion of the vestibular bulb and is attached posteriorly to the central tendon of the perineum

A **145.** Contraction fixes the central tendon of the pelvis

C **146.** Surrounds the unattached surface of the body of the clitoris

The urogenital diaphragm in the female (Fig. 143–146-1) extends from the perineum to the symphysis pubis and lies between the pubic rami. It is composed of the transversus perinei muscles (superficialis and profundus), the bulbocavernosus muscle, the ischiocavernosus muscle, and the sphincter urethrae muscle.

The transversus perinei muscles arise from a small tendon from the inner and anterior tuberosity of the ischium and insert into the central tendon of the perineum. Other muscles inserting into the central tendon are the sphincter ani externus and the bulbocavernosus. The function of the transversus muscles is to fix the central tendon of the pelvis. These muscles are supplied by the perineal branch of the pudendal nerve.

The bulbocavernosus muscle (*sphincter vaginae*) is attached posteriorly to the central tendon, where its fibers blend with the sphincter ani externus and the transversus perinei muscles. Anteriorly, the bulbo-

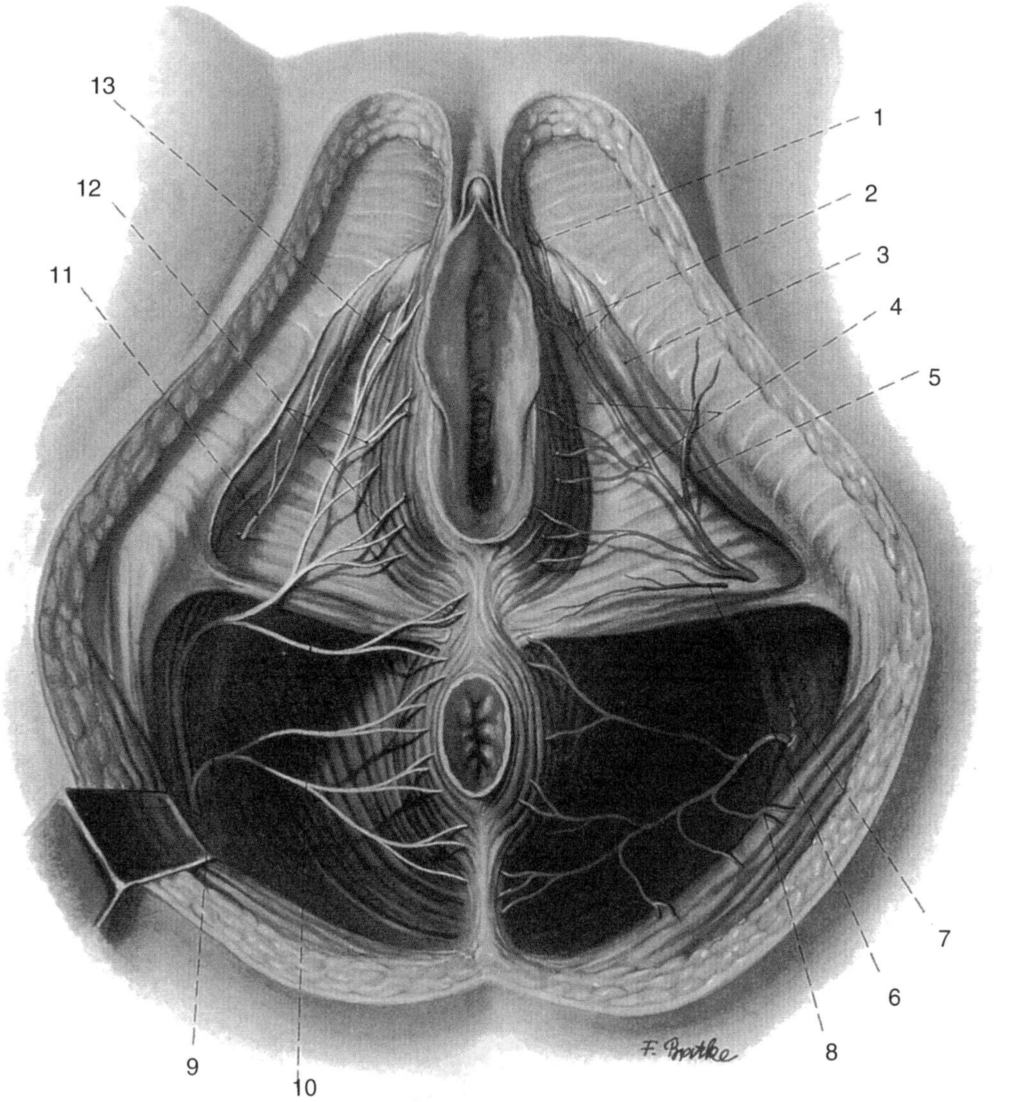

FIG. 143–146-1. The arteries and nerves of the pelvic floor as seen from below, demonstrating the branching of the internal pudendal artery and of the pudendal nerve. (1) Dorsal clitoral artery; (2) deep clitoral artery; (3) ischiocavernosus muscle; (4) bulbocavernosus muscle and the artery of the vestibular bulb; (5) posterior labial artery; (6) perineal artery; (7) internal pudendal artery in Alcock canal; (8) inferior rectal artery; (9) anal nerve; (10) perineal nerve; (11) branch innervating the ischiocavernosus muscle; (12) posterior labial nerves; (13) dorsal clitoral nerve. (Reiffenstuhl/Platzer/Knapstein. Die vaginalen Operationen. 2nd edition 1994. Urban & Schwarzenberg München–Wien–Baltimore)

cavernosus inserts into the body of the clitoris. At the point of insertion, a fasciculus of the muscle crosses the body of the clitoris and contraction compresses the dorsal vein, assisting in the maintenance of erection of the clitoris. The muscle covers the lateral part of the vestibular bulb. The major function of the muscle is to constrict the vaginal orifice. It receives its nerve supply from the perineal branch of the pudendal nerve.

The ischiocavernosus muscle (*erector clitoridis*) covers the unattached portion of the body of the clitoris. It arises from the inner surface of the tuberosity of the ischium and inserts into the sides and inferior surface of the body of the clitoris. This muscle compresses the body of the clitoris and retards venous return, serving to produce and maintain erection of the clitoris. Like the other muscles of the urogenital diaphragm, this muscle is supplied by the perineal branch of the pudendal nerve.

The sphincter urethrae consists of external and internal muscle fibers supplied by the perineal branch of the pudendal nerve. The internal sphincter surrounds the lower end of the urethra, and the external muscles arise on either side from the margin of the inferior ramus of the pubis and surround the urethra. The function of this muscle group is to constrict the urethra.

Clemente CD, ed. Gray's anatomy. 30th American ed. Philadelphia: Lea and Febiger, 1985:509–512

Reiffenstuhl G. Practical pelvic anatomy for the gynecologic surgeon. In: Nichols DH, ed. Gynecologic and obstetric surgery. St Louis: CV Mosby, 1993:26–71

147–150

Tumor markers for ovarian carcinoma

For each of the ovarian tumors listed (147–150), select the tumor marker (A–D) that is most likely to be elevated.

(A) Alpha-fetoprotein
(B) Lactic dehydrogenase
(C) Human chorionic gonadotropin (hCG)
(D) CA 125

D **147.** Epithelial carcinoma

C **148.** Nongestational trophoblastic tumor

A **149.** Endodermal sinus tumor

B **150.** Dysgerminoma

The usefulness of tumor marker findings in cases of ovarian carcinoma depends on the type of malignancy and the likelihood of that malignancy being present. Alpha-fetoprotein and hCG are found with germ cell tumors, but CA 125 is not usually significantly elevated. Alpha-fetoprotein is always elevated with endodermal sinus tumors, and hCG is always elevated with choriocarcinoma. Elevations of lactic dehydrogenase are seen in over 75% of patients with dysgerminoma, but elevations of CA 125 are rare in these patients.

Epithelial tumors do not have highly sensitive or specific circulating tumor markers. CA 125 is increasingly expressed as the disease progresses, especially in nonmucinous tumors. However, the usefulness of the CA 125 assay is limited by the finding of elevated CA 125 levels in patients with a variety of benign and malignant conditions (see the box). In one study, the CA 125 was equal to or greater than 30 U/ml in 81% of patients with malignancy and in 25% of patients with benign disease.

If the hCG alone is positive, once pregnancy is ruled out, the diagnosis of nongestational trophoblastic disease is almost certain. In the presence of mixed germ cells with choriocarcinoma elements, hCG may be elevated. Human chorionic gonadotropin may be combined with the alpha-fetoprotein assay to assist in the diagnosis and management of embryonal carcinoma and polyembryomas. Human chorionic gonadotropin is also useful for the diagnosis and management of ovarian choriocarcinoma.

Alpha-fetoprotein is associated with germ cell malignancies, immature teratomas, and mixed germ cell tumors and is a marker for the diagnosis of endodermal sinus tumors. If alpha-fetoprotein is present preoperatively in a patient with immature teratoma or mixed germ cell tumor, it is a useful tumor marker for later management.

Hilgers RD, Lewis JL Jr. Gestational trophoblastic neoplasms. Gynecol Oncol 1974;2:460–475

Diagnoses Associated with Elevated CA 125 Levels

Gynecologic Tumors
Epithelial ovarian cancer
Sertoli–Leydig cell tumors
Granulosa cell tumors
Fallopian tube carcinoma
Endometrial carcinoma
Endocervical carcinoma

Nongynecologic Tumors
Pancreatic carcinoma
Lung carcinoma
Breast carcinoma
Colon carcinoma
Lymphoma

Benign Gynecologic Conditions
Endometriosis
Adenomyosis
Leiomyomas
Normal pregnancy
Ectopic pregnancy
Pelvic inflammatory disease
Menses

Nongynecologic Conditions
Pancreatitis
Cirrhosis
Laparotomy
Peritonitis
Peritoneal tuberculosis
Congestive heart failure

Hoskins WJ, Perez CA, Young RC, eds. Principles and practice of gynecologic oncology. Philadelphia: JB Lippincott, 1992:140

Schwartz PE. Ovarian masses: serologic markers. Clin Obstet Gynecol 1991;34:423–432

Schwartz PE, Morris JMcL. Serum lactic dehydrogenase: a tumor marker for dysgerminoma. Obstet Gynecol 1988;72:511–51

151–154

Hereditary colorectal cancer

(A) Gardner syndrome (familial polyposis coli)
(B) Lynch I syndrome (site-specific colon cancer)
(C) Both
(D) Neither

C **151.** Autosomal dominant

B **152.** Predominantly right-sided colon tumors

D **153.** Several family members with one or more of these cancers: endometrial, stomach, breast, or ovarian adenocarcinoma

C **154.** Age at diagnosis usually during the 30s and 40s

Only about 6% of cases of colorectal cancer are now known to be due to heritable factors, although a variety of promoting and protecting factors may be genetically based. One percent of women with colon cancer have the rare autosomal-dominant complete penetrance inherited familial polyposis coli, or Gardner syndrome, which results from a gene line deletion of chromosomal band 5q21. The actual familial adenomatous polyposis gene was identified and has been named the *APC* gene. This genetic aberration affects predominantly the left colon, although small bowel and gastric lesions may occur. The average age of colon cancer diagnosis for these women is 39 years.

Five percent of women who develop colorectal cancer have hereditary nonpolyposis colorectal cancer (Lynch I and II syndromes). The cause was recently shown to be mutations in the *hMSH2* gene on chromosome 2p22. Other loci have been mapped to *hMLH1* on chromosome 3p21, *hPMS1* on chromosome 2q31-33, and *hPMS2* on chromosome 7p22. These tumors are predominantly (60–72%) right-sided, or transverse, colon tumors. The site-specific cancer family syndrome is the Lynch I syndrome, in which only colon cancer is inherited and the average age for diagnosis is 45 years. In contrast, Lynch II syndrome includes a subset of patients with an increased incidence of adenocarcinoma at a variety of sites (endometrium, breast, ovary, and stomach) in multiple family members. These cancers are usually diagnosed before age 40 years. It is thought that the loss of the tumor-suppressing chromosome 18q may be responsible. Both Lynch I and II syndromes are highly penetrant autosomal-dominant syndromes. Table 151–154-1 compares the Lynch I, Lynch II, and Gardner syndromes, and Table 151–154-2 compares character-

TABLE 151–154-1. Comparisons for Autosomal Dominant Heritable Colon Cancer

Variable	Gardner	HNPCC*
Colon cancers (%)	1	5
Chromosome	5q21	2p22, 3p21, 2q31-33, 7p22
Colon site	Left	Right
Average age at diagnosis (y)	39	45

* HNPCC indicates hereditary nonpolyposis colorectal cancer (Lynch I and II syndromes).

TABLE 151–154-2. Characteristics of Hereditary Nonpolyposis Colorectal Cancer and Sporadic Colorectal Cancers

Characteristic	HNPCC*	Sporadic Cases
Mean age at diagnosis (y)	44.6	67
Multiple colon cancers (%)	34.5	4–11
Simultaneous	18.1	3–6
Occurring at different times	24.3	1–5
Location proximal to the splenic flexure (%)	72.3	35
Excess rate of cancers at other sites (endometrium, stomach, ovary, urinary tract, small intestine, biliary tract)	Yes	No
Replication error (%)	79	17

* HNPCC indicates hereditary nonpolyposis colorectal cancer.

Reprinted by permission of The New England Journal of Medicine from Toribara NW, Sleisenger MH. Screening for colorectal cancer. N Engl J Med 1995;332:863; copyright 1995, Massachusetts Medical Society

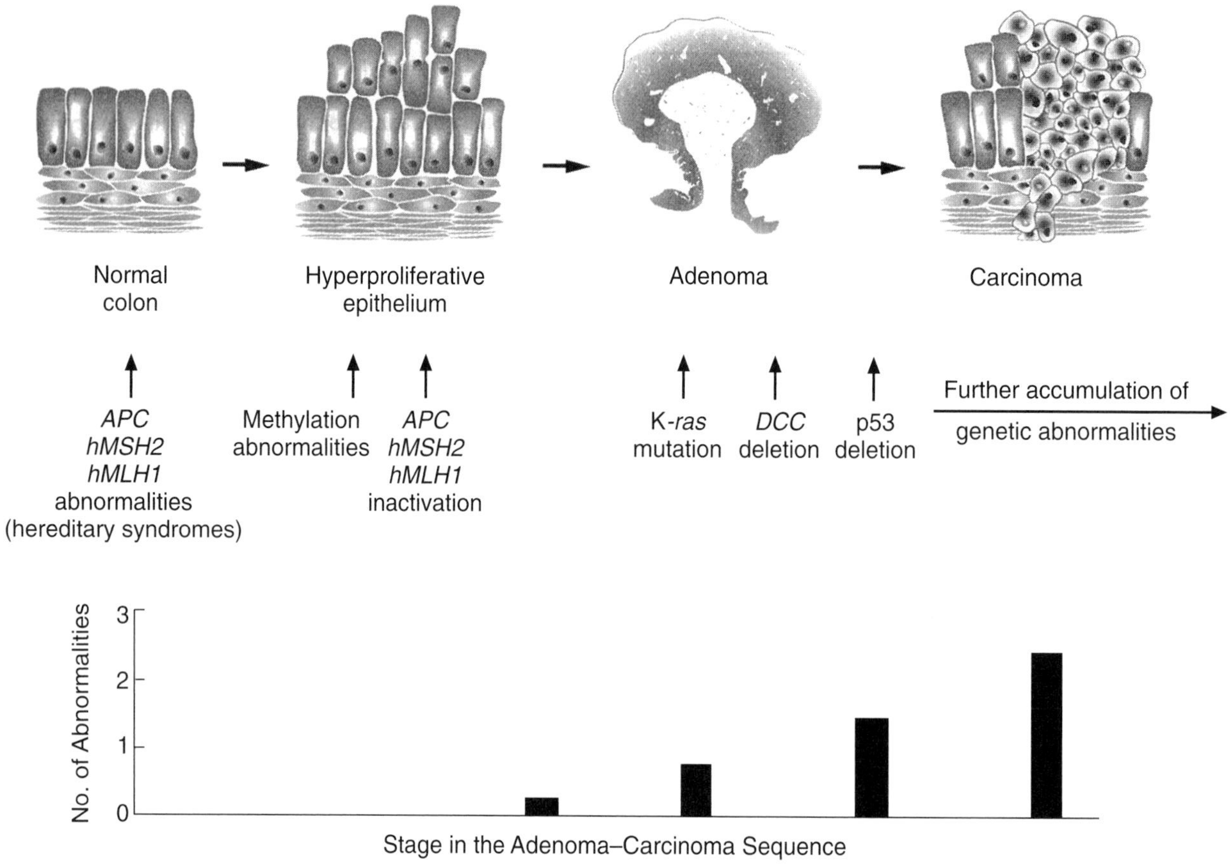

FIG. 151–154-1. Events during colorectal carcinogenesis. The molecular changes may vary in their order of occurrence; the most common sequence is shown. The average number of genetic abnormalities per tumor (shown at bottom) corresponds to the stage in the adenoma–carcinoma sequence in the diagram above. The genetic abnormalities examined were K-*ras* mutations and deletions from chromosomes 5q, 18q, and 17p (*APC*, *DCC*, and p53, respectively). (Reprinted by permission of The New England Journal of Medicine from Toribara NW, Sleisenger MH. Screening for colorectal cancer. N Engl J Med 1995;332:862; copyright 1995, Massachusetts Medical Society. Adapted from Bresalier RS, Toribara NW. Familial colon cancer. In: Eastwood GL, ed. Premalignant conditions of the gastrointestinal tract. Norwalk, Connecticut: Appleton and Lange, 1991:227–243)

istics of hereditary nonpolyposis colorectal cancer and sporadic colorectal cancer. The most common sequence of changes in colorectal carcinogenesis is shown in Fig. 151–154-1.

Approximately 19% of colon cancers develop in women with at least one first-degree relative who has had colon cancer. These women have a twofold to threefold increased risk of developing colon cancer. Partially penetrant autosomal-dominant inheritance of susceptibility to colon adenomas and cancers is more likely than recessive or sporadic occurrence in these patients.

Lynch HT, Watson P, Lanspa SJ, Marcus J, Smyrk T, Fitzgibbons RJ Jr, et al. Natural history of colorectal cancer in hereditary nonpolyposis colorectal cancer (Lynch syndromes I and II). Dis Colon Rectum 1988;31:439–444

Nyström-Lahti M, Sistonen P, Mecklin J-P, Pylkkänen L, Aaltonen LA, Järvinen H, et al. Close linkage to chromosome 3p and conservation of ancestral founding haplotype in hereditary nonpolyposis colorectal cancer families. Proc Natl Acad Sci U S A 1994;91:6054–6058

Pathak S, Hopwood VL, Hughes JI, Jackson GL. Identification of colon cancer-predisposed individuals: a cytogenetic analysis. Am J Gastroenterol 1991;86:679–684

Rustgi AK. Hereditary gastrointestinal polyposis and nonpolyposis syndromes. N Engl J Med 1994;331:1694–1702

Toribara NW, Sleisenger MH. Screening for colorectal cancer. N Engl J Med 1995;332:861–867

155–158

Treatment of early invasive cervical cancer

(A) Cone biopsy
(B) Radical hysterectomy
(C) Both
(D) Neither

B **155.** A 50-year-old woman with a stage IA2 cervical cancer with 3.1-mm stromal invasion

D **156.** A 78-year-old infirm woman (performance status 2) with a stage IA2 cervical cancer with 5-mm invasion

B **157.** A 38-year-old woman with a stage IA1 cervical cancer with 2-mm stromal invasion and lymph–vascular invasion

A **158.** A 30-year-old woman, gravida 0, with a stage IA1 cervical cancer

The management of early invasive cervical cancer (stages IA1 and IA2) requires careful patient selection and pathologic evaluation. In 1985 and 1994, the International Federation of Gynecology and Obstetrics (FIGO) redefined microinvasive squamous carcinoma of the cervix to include microscopic lesions that invade to a depth of not more than 5 mm as measured from the basement membrane and do not exceed 7 mm of horizontal (lateral) spread. Lesions that have no greater than 3 mm stromal invasion and are no wider than 7 mm are assigned to FIGO stage IA1. Lesions that have measured invasion greater than 3 mm but no greater than 5 mm and no wider than 7 mm are assigned FIGO stage IA2 (Appendix, Table 3). The functional definition of microinvasive disease, which was outlined by consensus opinion of the Society of Gynecologic Oncologists in 1974, is more restrictive in that it specifies no more than 3 mm of stromal invasion and no lymph–vascular space involvement. If a punch biopsy reveals microinvasive cervical cancer, a cone biopsy is required to firmly establish this diagnosis by ruling out invasive cervical disease. In some patients, a cone biopsy will provide definitive therapy.

Although radical hysterectomy is associated with very low mortality (<0.5%), it is costly and involves considerable patient discomfort and time lost from work. The possibility of postsurgical bladder dysfunction and sexual dysfunction must also be considered. Urinary fistulae result in 1–3% of patients. Where stromal invasion exceeds 3 mm, in the presence of lymph–vascular invasion or with disease extending to the margins of the cone biopsy specimen, the procedure of choice is radical hysterectomy and bilateral radical pelvic lymphadenectomy. For lesions with more than 3 mm of invasion, the chance of pelvic lymph node involvement is greater than 2%; it appears to be over 10% if there is vascular channel involvement in the cervical stroma. The finding of deeply invasive cancer in the surgical specimen is a distinct possibility when the cone biopsy margin is positive for microinvasive tumor.

Consideration of conization as the definitive treatment for microinvasive cervical carcinoma requires careful patient selection and pathologic evaluation. Consultation with a gynecologic oncologist may be advisable. Patients should desire fertility and meet the following criteria: 1) squamous cell histologic type, 2) no lymph–vascular space involvement, 3) unifocal lesion without extensive horizontal (lateral) spread (<7 mm), 4) negative margins for invasive cancer on the cone biopsy specimen, and 5) depth of invasion of less than 3 mm. Published reports of patients with stage IA disease managed by cone biopsy as definitive therapy suggest that recurrence rates are low in carefully selected patients. These series are small, however; larger series with longer follow-up are needed.

A patient with a cervical lesion with more than 3-mm depth of stromal invasion, such as the first patient described, requires a radical hysterectomy because of the depth of invasion. In an elderly woman with a poor performance status, such as the second patient described, radiation therapy should be selected rather than radical surgery because radiation therapy is associated with less acute morbidity and offers the same survival rate. A performance status of 2 implies that the patient

TABLE 155–158-1. Eastern Cooperative Oncology Group Performance Status Scale

Status	Description
0	Normal activity
1	Symptoms, but nearly ambulatory
2	Some bed time, but to be in bed less than 50% of normal daytime
3	Needs to be in bed more than 50% of normal daytime
4	Unable to get out of bed

Oken MM, Creech RH, Tormey DC, Horton J, Davis TE, McFadden ET, et al. Toxicity and response criteria of the Eastern Cooperative Oncology Group. Am J Clin Oncol 1982;5:654

is not fully ambulatory but is confined to bed less than 50% of the daytime hours (Table 155–158-1).

For a patient with a cervical lesion with invasion of 3 mm or less, multiple therapeutic options exist. In a patient with positive or undetermined margins on diagnostic conization or with lymph–vascular invasion, such as the third patient, a radical hysterectomy would avoid the risk of undertreatment of an undiagnosed, deeply invasive lesion. However, in a patient with less than 3 mm of stromal invasion, without lymph–vascular invasion, and with clear margins on cone biopsy, a simple hysterectomy is adequate treatment if the patient has completed childbearing. In a patient who desires to maintain fertility, such as the fourth patient described, a cone biopsy with negative margins and careful follow-up surveillance is adequate therapy. A hysterectomy does not offer a survival advantage if the tumor (<3 mm, without lymph–vascular invasion) is widely and adequately excised.

Johnson N, Lilford RJ, Jones SE, McKenzie L, Billingsley P, Songane FF. Using decision analysis to calculate the optimum treatment for microinvasive cervical cancer. Br J Cancer 1992;65:717–722

Jones WB, Mercer GO, Lewis JL Jr, Rubin SC, Hoskins WJ. Early invasive carcinoma of the cervix. Gynecol Oncol 1993;51:26–32

Morris M, Follen Mitchell M, Silva EG, Copeland LJ, Gershenson DM. Cervical conization as definitive therapy for early invasive squamous carcinoma of the cervix. Gynecol Oncol 1993;51:193–196

159–162

Antimicrobial prophylaxis at surgery

(A) Cephalosporin prophylaxis at hysterectomy
(B) Penicillin prophylaxis at hysterectomy
(C) Both
(D) Neither

B **159.** Increased recovery of *Escherichia coli* from postoperative pelvic cultures

D **160.** Decreased recovery of *Enterobacter* species from postoperative pelvic cultures

B **161.** Decreased recovery of *Enterococcus faecalis* from postoperative pelvic cultures

C **162.** Contraindicated in patients with β-lactam anaphylaxis

A wide variety of antibiotic regimens have been investigated for preventing infection after hysterectomy. In general, most of these regimens have been found to be effective.

Cephalosporins are the most widely used family of antibiotics. Cephalosporin administration results in increased recovery of *Enterococcus faecalis*, *Staphylococcus aureus*, *Streptococcus agalactiae*, and *Enterobacter* species from postoperative pelvic cultures. Administration of a penicillin prophylaxis creates an environment suitable for the overgrowth of *Escherichia coli* and other Enterobacteriaceae from such cultures but results in a reduction in *Enterococcus faecalis* recovery.

Although about 15% of patients report an allergy to penicillin, the allergic reaction is usually undocumented or vague. Avoiding administration of a penicillin to such patients is appropriate. In patients who do not report an anaphylactic reaction to penicillin, administration of another β-lactam antibiotic for prophylaxis, such as a cephalosporin, has not been associated with an increased risk of adverse effects. Conversely, an anaphylactic reaction to any β-lactam is a contraindication to the use of penicillin or cephalosporin.

Risk factors for infection differ among women undergoing hysterectomy, depending on the surgical approach used and the presence or absence of cancer. There is agreement for prophylaxis in premenopausal women undergoing vaginal hysterectomy. Risk factors include lower socioeconomic status, excessive blood loss, anemia, preceding surgery (ie, conization, dilation and curettage), and additional surgical procedures (eg, colporrhaphy, salpingo-oophorectomy).

Lower socioeconomic status is the predominant risk factor in women who develop infection after undergoing either elective abdominal hysterectomy or radical pelvic surgery. Risk factors for postoperative infection identified in various other clinical trials include older age, longer operative time, increased body weight, increased estimated blood loss, requirement for transfusion, amount of residual disease, and heparin use. The one other factor consistently associated with an increased frequency of operative-site infection after simple or radical hysterectomy is failure to administer antibiotic prophylaxis. Thorough knowledge of important risk factors for patients cared for in one's hospital or institution is imperative.

Multiple clinical trials have documented that administration of one dose of antibiotic is as effective as multiple doses in preventing major operative-site infections after pelvic surgery. Prophylactic antibiotic administration has less effect, however, on the development of other types of infections such as urinary-tract infection, pneumonia, and the enigmatic febrile morbidity of unknown origin.

Hemsell DL, Johnson ER, Heard MC, Hemsell PG, Nobles BJ, Bawdon RE. Single-dose piperacillin versus triple-dose cefoxitin prophylaxis at vaginal and abdominal hysterectomy. South Med J 1989;82:438–442

Marsden DE, Cavanagh D, Wisniewski BJ, Roberts WS, Lyman GH. Factors affecting the incidence of infectious morbidity after radical hysterectomy. Am J Obstet Gynecol 1985;152:817–821

Mittendorf R, Aronson MP, Berry RE, Williams MA, Kupelnick B, Klickstein A, et al. Avoiding serious infections associated with abdominal hysterectomy: a meta-analysis of antibiotic prophylaxis. Am J Obstet Gynecol 1993;169:1119–1124

Sevin B-U, Ramos R, Gerhardt RT, Guerra L, Hilsenbeck S, Averette HE. Comparative efficacy of short-term versus long-term cefoxitin prophylaxis against postoperative infection after radical hysterectomy: a prospective study. Obstet Gynecol 1991;77:729–734

163–167

Differences between partial and complete mole

(A) Partial hydatidiform mole
(B) Complete hydatidiform mole
(C) Both
(D) Neither

B **163.** Diploidy

A **164.** Triploidy

C **165.** May require chemotherapy after uterine evacuation

D **166.** Absence of villi

A **167.** Evidence of fetal elements present

Molar pregnancies are classified as complete or partial based on differences in histologic and genetic characteristics and biologic behavior. Both complete and partial moles have villi.

Complete molar pregnancies result from fertilization of an "empty egg" by a duplicated haploid sperm or, less commonly, by two sperm (dispermy). The DNA content is diploid (46,XX or 46,XY less commonly). Histologically, complete moles exhibit villous edema and hyperplasia of the cytotrophoblasts and syncytiotrophoblasts. Fetal vessels and fetal erythrocytes are absent. In approximately 15–20% of patients diagnosed with a complete hydatidiform mole, the human chorionic gonadotropin either fails to decline or plateaus after evacuation. These patients will require chemotherapy because of persistent disease.

Partial molar pregnancies result from fertilization of a haploid ovum by two sperm and exhibit a triploid DNA content (69,XXY or 69,XYY). Histologically, partial moles exhibit focal hydrops and variable trophoblastic hyperplasia. Fetal vessels and fetal erythrocytes are present. Because 5–7% of these patients will have persistent disease requiring chemotherapy, regression of the serum human chorionic gonadotropin values should be monitored after uterine evacuation.

Ko T-M, Hsieh C-Y, Ho H-N, Hsieh F-J, Lee T-Y. Restriction fragment length polymorphism analysis to study the genetic origin of complete hydatidiform mole. Am J Obstet Gynecol 1991;164:901–906

Lage JM, Mark SD, Roberts DJ, Goldstein DP, Bernstein MR, Berkowitz RS. A flow cytometric study of 137 fresh hydropic placentas: correlation between types of hydatidiform moles and nuclear DNA ploidy. Obstet Gynecol 1992;79:403–410

Lawler SD, Fisher RA, Dent J. A prospective genetic study of complete and partial hydatidiform moles. Am J Obstet Gynecol 1991;164:1270–1277

Rice LW, Berkowitz RS, Lage JM, Goldstein DP, Bernstein MR. Persistent gestational trophoblastic disease tumor after partial hydatidiform mole. Gynecol Oncol 1990;36:358–362

Roberts DJ, Mutter GL. Advances in the molecular biology of gestational trophoblastic disease. J Reprod Med 1994;39:201–208

168–171

Anatomy of the vagina

(A) Longitudinal vaginal septum
(B) Transverse vaginal septum
(C) Both
(D) Neither

B **168.** Usually associated with amenorrhea

D **169.** Usually a consequence of trauma

A **170.** Frequently associated with other müllerian malformations

C **171.** Frequently associated with dyspareunia

The vagina forms in utero from the union of the lower portion of the müllerian ducts after their migration and fusion and the invagination of the urogenital sinus. The vaginal plate, the anlagen of the vagina, becomes canalized and subsequently is epithelialized with cells derived from the endoderm of the urogenital sinus. The müllerian ducts form approximately the upper one third of the vagina, and the lower vagina is developed from the vaginal plate.

If a failure occurs in the development of the müllerian ducts, the vagina may fail to develop at all (vaginal agenesis, or Mayer–Rokitansky–Küster–Hauser syndrome). If müllerian duct migration is normal but the tissue between the müllerian ducts from the vaginal plate fails to resorb, a transverse vaginal septum results (Fig. 168–171-1). This septum can be of variable thickness. Transverse vaginal septum is sometimes referred to as "partial vaginal agenesis with a uterus present" or a disorder of vertical fusion. This condition is not associated with an increased risk of other müllerian anomalies.

If the lower paired müllerian ducts fail to fuse, a longitudinal septum results (Fig. 168–171-2). This failure of fusion can be partial or complete and is frequently associated with duplication of the entire reproductive tract. Patients with longitudinal vaginal septa and uterus didelphys have associated urinary-tract anomalies in 40% of cases. These patients usually have competent outflow tracts and do not typically present with amenorrhea. However, if a functioning rudimentary cornu is present on one side, the patient may have cyclic pain secondary to obstructed menstruation. Patients with a

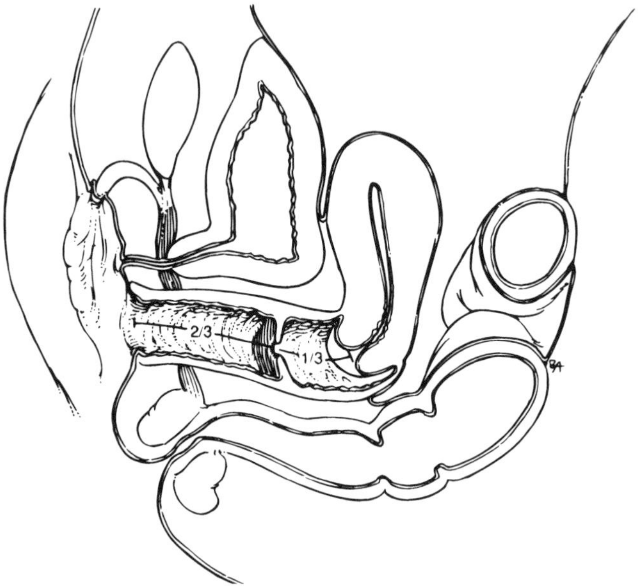

FIG. 168–171-1. Transverse vaginal septum. This anomaly results from incomplete fusion between the müllerian ducts, which form the upper third of the vagina, and the urogenital sinus, which contributes the lower two thirds of the vagina. (Elmer DB. Benign procedures for the vulva and vagina. In: Gershenson DM, DeCherney AH, Curry SL, eds. Operative gynecology. Philadelphia: WB Saunders, 1993:168)

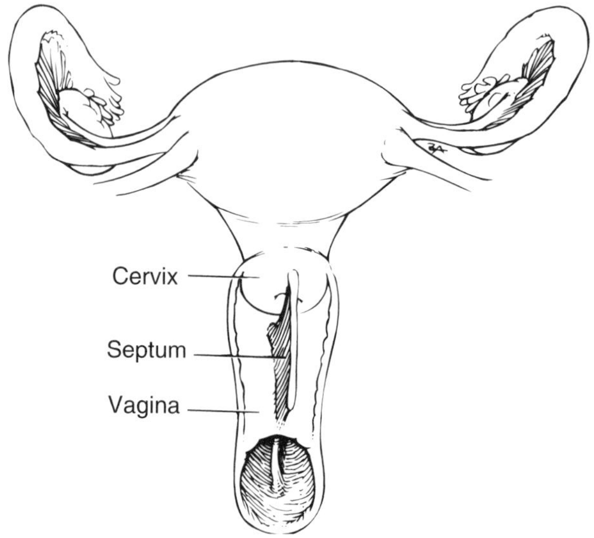

FIG. 168–171-2. Longitudinal vaginal septum, which results from incomplete fusion of the paired müllerian ducts. Other anomalies of the müllerian and mesonephric ducts should be sought. (Elmer DB. Benign procedures for the vulva and vagina. In: Gershenson DM, DeCherney AH, Curry SL, eds. Operative gynecology. Philadelphia: WB Saunders, 1993:170)

complete transverse vaginal septum do not have a functional outflow tract and typically present with amenorrhea and cyclic pelvic pain. On examination, hematometra or hematocolpos may be present.

Both longitudinal vaginal and transverse vaginal septa are developmental anomalies not associated with trauma. Both conditions may cause dyspareunia as well as infertility. In utero exposure to diethylstilbestrol increases a woman's risk for transverse vaginal septum.

Elmer DB. Benign procedures for the vulva and vagina. In: Gershenson DM, DeCherney AH, Curry SL, eds. Operative gynecology. Philadelphia: WB Saunders, 1993:159–171

Rock JA. Surgery for anomalies of the müllerian ducts. In: Thompson JD, Rock JA, eds. Te Linde's operative gynecology. 7th ed. Philadelphia: JB Lippincott, 1992:603–646

Rock JA, Zacur HA, D'Lugi AM, Jones HW Jr, Te Linde RW. Pregnancy success following surgical correction of imperforate hymen and complete transverse vaginal septum. Obstet Gynecol 1982:59:448–451

172

Human papillomavirus infection and cervical neoplasia

You have been asked by an epidemiologist to comment on the efficacy of using human papillomavirus (HPV) DNA detection in the screening of cervical cancer. Which of the following statements concerning the relationship of HPV infection to cervical neoplasia are true?

T (A) Human papillomavirus DNA can be detected in most adenocarcinomas of the cervix if sensitive molecular techniques are used.

F (B) The mean prevalence of HPV detection in women with normal cytology is 1–5%.

T (C) Either HPV type 16 or type 18 is present in 70% of invasive squamous carcinomas.

F (D) Either HPV type 16 or type 18 is detected in nearly 50% of low-grade squamous intraepithelial lesions.

F (E) Human papillomavirus types 31, 33, and 35 can be detected in nearly 40% of invasive cervical carcinomas.

The incidence and mortality of invasive cervical cancer have decreased by 75% over the last 40 years in the United States. This decrease is largely attributed to cervical cytology screening. Despite the success of screening, approximately 15,800 cases of invasive cervical carcinoma are reported annually in the United States, and 4,800 deaths result from this disease.

Sixty million Pap tests are taken in the United States annually. About 8%, or 5 million, show cytology that is "not negative" (atypical squamous cells of undetermined significance, atypical glandular cells of undetermined significance, low-grade squamous intraepithelial lesions, high-grade squamous intraepithelial lesions, etc.) Fewer than 15%, or about 0.7 million, of these cases are positive after repeated Pap tests, colposcopy, or biopsy. More than 4 million are false-positive smears based on the reference standard of biopsy or repeated smears. If no treatment or medical intervention were offered for the 0.7 million cytologically and histologically positive cases, fewer than 20,000 (3%) would develop into invasive cancer. Of the original 5 million cases that are cytologically not negative, fewer than 0.5% have the potential to develop into invasive cancer.

It has been suggested that HPV detection could assist in cervical cytology screening, because HPV DNA can be detected with sensitive molecular detection tests such as Southern blot hybridization or polymerase chain reaction. It is known that HPV DNA is found in 90% of preinvasive and invasive squamous cell neoplasms of the cervix. In addition, HPV DNA can be detected in approximately 85% of invasive adenocarcinomas of the cervix and in adenocarcinoma in situ.

Prevalence rates of HPV for women with normal cytology vary according to the population studied and the HPV detection method used, but generally range from 10% to 50%, with a mean of 25–30% in young women age 18–25 years. It has been estimated that 10–20 million women between the ages of 18 and 50 years in the United States would have HPV DNA detected in the cervix if sensitive detection methods were used. Therefore, HPV testing lacks the specificity necessary to be a useful screening test for cervical cancer or its precursors, because the vast majority of women who have HPV detected from a cervical lavage or swab would be cytologically normal.

On the other hand, 70% of invasive squamous carcinomas contain either HPV type 16 or type 18. Although these HPV types can often be detected in patients with low-grade squamous intraepithelial lesions, their prevalence is much lower in the general population and is probably less than 5%. In contrast, other HPV types such as HPV 31, 33, 35, 39, 45, 51, 52, and 56 are detected in no more than 20% of invasive carcinomas.

Currently attention is being focused on the use of HPV testing as an ancillary screening method for women with abnormal Pap tests. For example, one proposed strategy for patients with a Pap test diagnosis of atypical squamous cells of uncertain significance is to have an HPV test (for high-risk HPV types) as the next step in management. If the HPV test is negative for cancer-associated HPV types, the patient is asked to return in 4–6 months. If the HPV test is positive for cancer-associated HPV types, the patient should undergo colposcopy. Prospective clinical trials will be necessary to determine whether this strategy will be cost-effective. It was the consensus of a National Cancer Institute–sponsored workshop that HPV testing be used only by physicians who understand its present limitations.

Bauer HM, Ting Y, Greer CE, Chambers JC, Tashiro CJ, Chimera J, et al. Genital human papillomavirus infection in female university students as determined by a PCR-based method. JAMA 1991;265:472–477

Cuzick J, Terry G, Ho L, Hollingworth T, Anderson M. Type-specific human papillomavirus DNA in abnormal smears as a predictor of high-grade cervical intraepithelial neoplasia. Br J Cancer 1994;69:167–171

Lorincz AT, Temple GF, Kurman RJ, Jenson AB, Lancaster WD. Oncogenic association of specific human papillomavirus types with cervical neoplasia. J Natl Cancer Inst 1987;79:671–677

173

Risk of colorectal cancer

A 53-year-old woman presents for a yearly examination. Her medical history reveals a cholecystectomy and a bilateral tubal ligation. A review of systems is negative. Her mother developed colon cancer at age 59 and died several years later. The patient is 157 cm (62 in) tall and weighs 115 kg (254 lb). Blood pressure is 150/90 mm Hg. Her general physical and pelvic examinations are normal. A Pap test is performed. This patient's risk factors for colon cancer include

T (A) age
T (B) obesity
T (C) cholecystectomy
T (D) family history
F (E) hypertension

Colorectal cancer ranks second as a cause of death from cancer in the United States. Of women who develop colorectal cancer, more than 85% do not have a family history of colon cancer, and thus their cases are termed sporadic.

A 50-year-old woman at average risk has approximately a 5% chance of developing invasive colorectal cancer during the remainder of her life. The risk essentially doubles with each decade of life beginning at age 50 (Table 173-1). The 5-year survival rate for colon cancer was 54% in the 1980s.

The predominant pathogenic pathway in the development of colorectal cancer appears to be from adenoma to adenocarcinoma (Fig. 173-1). Exposure of genetically susceptible mucosa to environmental mutagens may initiate the formation of adenomatous polyps, which may ultimately result in colorectal cancer after multiple steps of oncogene activation and a successive allelic loss of chromosomes.

The risk for cancer in adenomatous lesions is directly related to the size, number, and histologic features of the adenomas (Table 173-2). All adenomas should be removed. In patients who have colonic polyps removed, colorectal cancer can be decreased by 75–90% compared with control subjects. Patients who have an adenoma or cancer have a fivefold to sevenfold increased risk for developing new lesions at a subsequent examination compared with the general population.

Colon cancer is multifactorial in origin (see box). Diet, life style, and exercise appear to be related to the risk of developing colorectal cancer. Mutagens are present in the stools of many people who follow a Western diet. It is unknown whether exercise is protective because it decreases the transit time for food in the colon or because those who exercise often follow a better diet (ie, increased fiber, fruits, and cruciferous vegetables). Obese individuals are less likely to exercise and are likely to consume more animal fat and less fiber in their diet. High dietary intake of animal fat results in the production of free radicals from lipid peroxidation and increased intestinal exposure to bile acids, which are believed to induce gut lumen proliferation. Cholecystectomy and increased cholesterol result in high levels of bile acids in the colon.

A high-fiber diet (cellulose and wheat bran) may decrease colon cancer risk by as much as 43%. Fiber reduces the cancer risk by increasing the transit time or by binding or diluting potential carcinogens such as bile

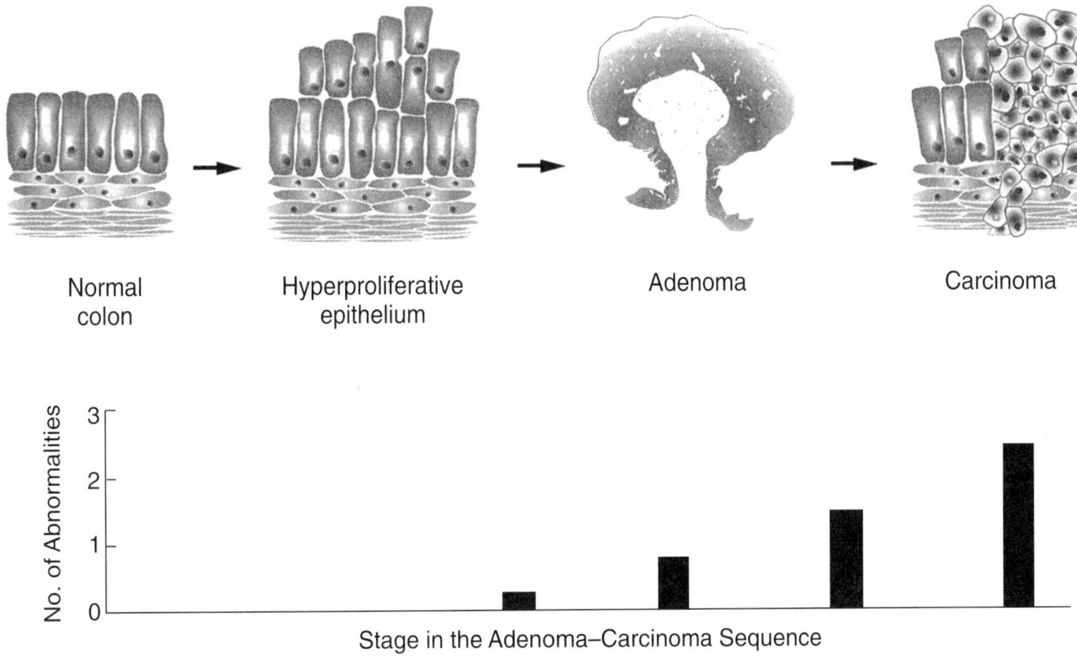

FIG. 173-1. Events during colorectal carcinogenesis. The average number of genetic abnormalities per tumor (shown at bottom) corresponds to the stage in the adenoma–carcinoma sequence in the diagram above. (Reprinted by permission of The New England Journal of Medicine from Toribara NW, Sleisenger MH. Screening for colorectal cancer. N Engl J Med 1995;332:862; copyright 1995, Massachusetts Medical Society. Adapted from Bresalier RS, Toribara NW. Familial colon cancer. In: Eastwood GL, ed. Premalignant condition of the gastrointestinal tract. Norwalk, Connecticut: Appleton and Lange, 1991:227–243)

TABLE 173-1. Age-Specific Incidence Rate for Colorectal Cancers

Age (y)	Incidence (per 100,000 women)
30–34	2.7
40–44	12.1
50–54	46.7
60–64	116.5
70–74	240.1
80–84	418.1
85+	463.4

Ries LAG, Miller BA, Hankey BF, Kosary CL, Harras A, Edwards BK, eds. SEER cancer statistics review: 1973–1991. Bethesda, Maryland: National Cancer Institute, 1994:147; NIH publication no. 93-2789.

TABLE 173-2. Cancer Risk with Adenomatous Polyp

	Cancer Risk by Polyp Size (%)		
Histologic Type	<1 cm	1–2 cm	>2 cm
Tubular adenoma	1.0	10.2	34.7
Villotubular adenoma	3.9	7.4	45.8
Villous adenoma	9.5	10.3	52.9

Adapted from Muto T, Bussey HJR, Morson BC. The evolution of cancer of the colon and rectum. Cancer 1975;36:2257

Known or Suspected Colorectal Cancer Risk Factors

Increased Risk
Prior colon adenoma or carcinoma
Family history of colon cancer
Family or personal history of endometrial, breast, ovarian, or stomach cancer
Increasing age (>40 y)
Inflammatory bowel disease
High dietary fat intake
Obesity
Cholecystectomy
Alcohol
Smoking
Sedentary life style

Decreased Risk
High-fiber diet (cellulose and wheat bran)
Increased dietary intake of fruits and cruciferous vegetables
Decreased fat intake
Nonsteroidal inflammatory drugs (aspirin)
Calcium
Active leisure time
Active occupation

acids. Several nutrients may have a therapeutic impact on the risk of colorectal cancer. Calcium appears to have a protective effect, predominantly by reducing the concentration of free bile acids through the formation of insoluble bile salt complexes. The use of antioxidants is being evaluated. Simple dietary supplementation with these agents has not proved to be of dramatic benefit. Vitamin A may afford protection by enhancing regulation of cell differentiation, and vitamins C and E appear to be protective through an antioxidant effect on free radicals. Nonsteroidal antiinflammatory medications also appear to be protective by suppression of cell proliferation through inhibition of prostaglandin synthesis. Confirmatory data from randomized prospective trials are necessary before aspirin can be recommended for this purpose, because its gastrointestinal side effects can be serious.

Three or more alcoholic drinks daily increase the risk for colon cancer threefold compared with the risk in nondrinkers. The reason for the increased risk is unknown. Cigarette smoking appears to have a significant association with the formation of colorectal adenomas and carcinomas, with the relative risk related to both the number of pack-years and the length of time of smoking. Smoking reduces protective serum carotenoids. Whether this accounts for the increased risk is unknown.

A history of colon cancer in first-degree relatives is an important predictor of the presence of adenomas. Approximately 19% of colon cancers develop in women in whom at least one first-degree relative has had colon cancer. Women who have a first-degree family member with colon cancer have a twofold to threefold increased risk of developing the disease.

Cytogenetic studies of the tumors from patients with sporadic as well as familial colorectal cancer reveal frequent structural alterations of chromosomes 2, 3, 5, 7, 12, 17, and 18. Molecular genetic studies of colonic mucosa and tumor in patients with colon cancer also have identified deletions of tumor suppressor genes (p53) that may be involved in sporadic as well as familial colonic cancers.

Women with ulcerative colitis have an increased risk (up to 30-fold) of developing colorectal cancer. The risk increases with extent of bowel involvement, age at onset, severity, and duration of disease. Women with Crohn disease also have an increased risk of developing colorectal cancer, and the risk increases with disease duration. The increased risk is less than that for women with ulcerative colitis.

For the patient described, her age, obesity, family history, and a previous cholecystectomy increase the risk of colon cancer. A history of hypertension does not increase her risk.

Burt RW, Bishop DT, Cannon-Albright L, Samowitz WS, Lee RL, DiSario JA, Skolnick MH. Hereditary aspects of colorectal adenomas. Cancer 1992;70:1296–1299

Lieberman DA. Targeted colon cancer screening: a concept whose time has almost come. Am J Gastroenterol 1992;87:1085–1093

Trock B, Lanza E, Greenwald P. Dietary fiber, vegetables, and colon cancer: critical review and meta-analyses of the epidemiologic evidence. J Natl Cancer Inst 1990;82:650–661

174

Spread pattern of ovarian cancer

A 72-year-old woman presents with bilateral ovarian masses and ascites. Her CA 125 is 1,600 units. You explain that she probably has ovarian cancer. When she asks how the disease spreads, you explain that the most common spread patterns with ovarian cancer are

T (A) metastases to lymph nodes
T (B) spread to adjacent organs
F (C) metastases to the liver and brain
F (D) blood-borne metastases
T (E) dissemination within the peritoneal cavity

To properly understand the pathophysiology of early ovarian cancer, it is necessary to understand the spread patterns of the disease (Fig. 174-1). Ovarian germ cell tumors and ovarian stromal tumors almost always begin inside the ovary. In contrast, epithelial carcinomas originate from the surface epithelium.

In most cases, spread of ovarian cancer is preceded by either rupture of the capsule or penetration of the capsule by the cancer. Malignant cells have rarely been reported in the peritoneal cavity of patients with intact ovarian carcinomas and no evidence of rupture of the capsule. After capsule rupture, the malignant tumor spreads by transperitoneal dissemination of cells into the abdominal cavity. These cancer cells have the ability to disseminate and form clones of the primary tumor. The peritoneal cavity allows cancer cells to live and implant on a variety of surfaces and grow into tumor nodules. The nodules in turn exfoliate cells, which implant on other tissues.

The normal flow of peritoneal fluid is clockwise and occurs because of respiratory movements of the diaphragm. Thus, ovarian cancer cells flow along the right pericolic gutter to the right hemidiaphragm and from there throughout the abdomen. The effect of gravity and normal daily activities, as well as peristalsis of the intestine, results in wide dissemination of the disease. The omentum is an early site of metastasis in patients with ovarian cancer, and in advanced disease it may represent the largest single site of metastasis. Ovarian cancer also extends to other surrounding structures including the bladder, rectum, and pelvic sidewall. Tumor involvement of the cul-de-sac is influenced by gravity in the upright female, usually occurs early, and may be extensive.

In addition to transperitoneal spread of cancer, spread via the lymphatic system is important in ovarian cancer, even in early disease. The lymphatic vessels of the ovarian parenchyma form a plexus of lymphatics near the hilus of the ovary. From these plexi, the three main pathways of lymphatic drainage are 1) along the ovarian vessels to the aortic nodes, 2) via the broad ligament to the pelvic lymph nodes, and 3) along the round ligament to the pelvic and inguinal lymph nodes. Table 174-1 shows the frequency of lymphatic metastases in early

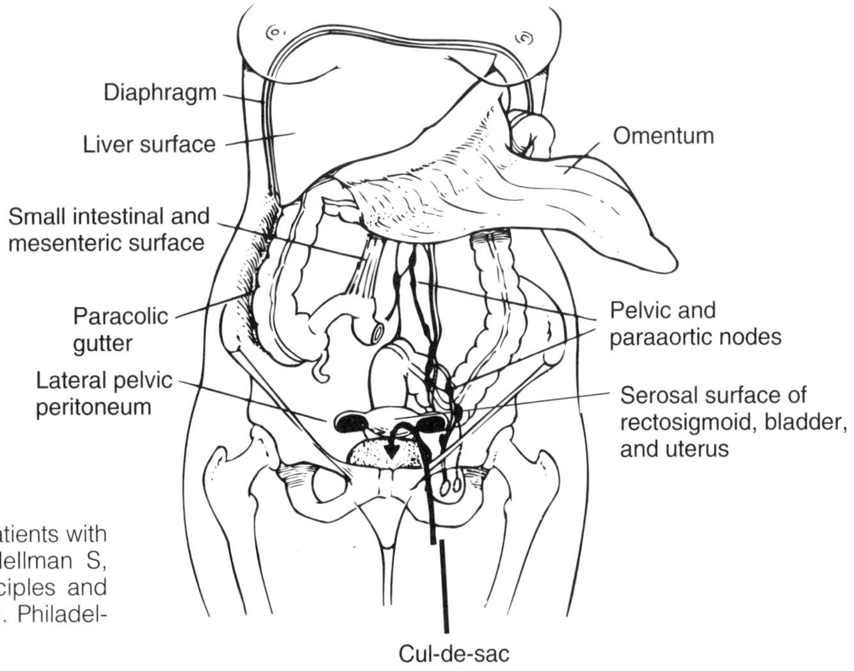

FIG. 174-1. Spread of disease in patients with ovarian cancer. (DeVita VT Jr, Hellman S, Rosenberg SA, eds. Cancer: principles and practice of oncology. Vol 1. 4th ed. Philadelphia: JB Lippincott, 1993:1227)

TABLE 174-1. Frequency of Lymph Node Metastasis in Early-Stage Ovarian Cancer

Study	Stage I	Stage II
Knapp	5/26 (19%)	—
DiRi	16/134 (12%)	—
Chen	2/11 (18%)	2/10 (20%)
Averette	1/11 (9%)	5/17 (29%)
Pickel	7/28 (23%)	4/13 (31%)
Buschbaum	4/95 (4%)	8/41 (19.5%)
Total	35/305 (11.5%)	19/81 (23.4%)

Reprinted with permission from Curtin JP. Diagnosis and staging of epithelial ovarian cancer. In: Markham M, Hoskins WJ, eds. Cancer of the ovary. New York: Raven Press, 1993:160

ovarian cancer. Nodal metastases occur in 50–70% of patients with advanced disease.

Blood-borne metastases occur rarely in ovarian cancer. Therefore, spread to the liver parenchyma and brain are uncommon. When the lung is involved, it is usually at the base of the pleura, and metastases occur by flow of malignant cells through the lymphatics of the diaphragm. Parenchymal metastases to the lungs are rare.

Burghardt E, Pickel H, Stettner H. Management of advanced ovarian cancer. Eur J Gynaecol Oncol 1984;3:155–159

Curtin JP. Diagnosis and staging of epithelial ovarian cancer. In: Markman M, Hoskins WJ, eds. Cancer of the ovary. New York: Raven Press, 1993:153–163

Feldman GP, Knapp RC. Lymphatic drainage of the peritoneal cavity and its significance in ovarian cancer. Am J Obstet Gynecol 1974;119:991–994

Piver MS, Barlow JJ, Lele SB. Incidence of subclinical metastases in stage I and II ovarian carcinoma. Obstet Gynecol 1978;52:100–104

Young RC, Perez CA, Hoskins WJ. Cancer of the ovary. In: DeVita VT Jr, Hellman S, Rosenberg SA, eds. Cancer: Principles and practice of oncology. 4th ed. Philadelphia: JB Lippincott, 1993:1227–1228

175

Adjuvant therapy for early-stage breast cancer

A woman who has just completed primary therapy for breast cancer seeks your advice about the potential benefits of adjuvant therapy (chemotherapy or hormone therapy or both). Which of the following variables will be useful in determining whether this patient will benefit from adjuvant therapy?

F (A) Age
T (B) Axillary lymph node involvement
T (C) Estrogen receptor status
T (D) Tumor size

As a group, patients with breast cancers less than 1.0 cm in size do not require adjuvant therapy and do not benefit from it. Age and menopausal status are not factors in determining who will benefit from adjuvant therapy. Although most oncologists treat women with involved (positive) axillary lymph nodes (Fig. 175-1) with adju-

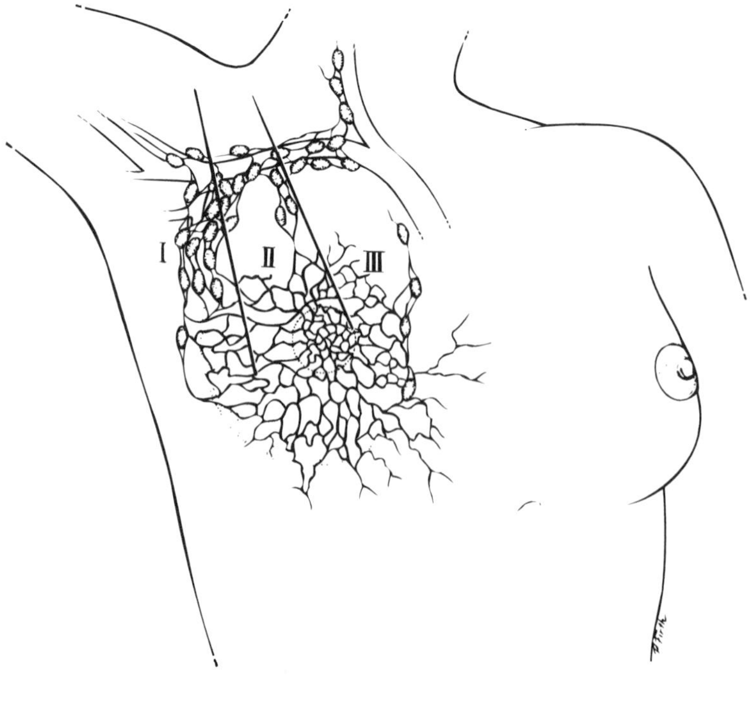

FIG. 175-1. Axillary lymph nodes. This diagram depicts the axillary and substernal lymph nodes that drain the breast. Level I (low) is lateral up to the insertion of the pectoralis minor muscle. Level II (mid) is underneath the insertion of the pectoralis minor muscle. Level III (high) is medial (deep) to the insertion of the pectoralis minor muscle.

vant therapy, women who do not have axillary lymph node involvement (node negative) may also benefit from adjuvant therapy.

Estrogen receptor status is a factor in the decision of whether to select chemotherapy or hormone therapy, because estrogen receptor–negative cancers tend to respond to chemotherapy, and estrogen receptor–positive cancers tend to respond to hormone therapy.

Flow cytometry for S phase identifies patients with a high percentage of cells in S phase, which correlates with aggressive tumor behavior, but the percentage of cells in S phase is not routinely used to predict response to adjuvant therapy.

The box contains a summary of the consensus statement from the National Institutes of Health Consensus Development Conference on the Treatment of Early-Stage Breast Cancer in 1990.

Dressler LG, Eudey L, Gray R, Tormey DC, McGuire WL, Gilchrist KW, et al. Prognostic potential of DNA flow cytometry measurements in node-negative breast cancer patients: preliminary analysis of an intergroup study (INT 0076). Monogr Natl Cancer Inst 1992;11:167–172

Early Breast Cancer Trialists' Collaborative Group. Effects of adjuvant tamoxifen and cytotoxic therapy on mortality in early breast cancer: an overview of 61 randomized trials among 28,896 women. N Engl J Med 1988;319:1681–1692

Early Breast Cancer Trialists' Collaborative Group. Systemic treatment of early breast cancer by hormonal, cytotoxic, or immune therapy. Lancet 1992; 339:1–15, 71–85

Ellis GK. Breast cancer. Prim Care Update Ob/Gyns 1994;1:17–25

Fisher B, Constantino J, Redmond C, Poisson R, Bowman D, Couture J, et al. A randomized clinical trial evaluating tamoxifen in the treatment of patients with node-negative breast cancer who have estrogen-receptor-positive tumors. N Engl J Med 1989;320:479–484

Mansour EG, Gray R, Shatila AH, Osborne CK, Tormey DC, Gilchrist KW, et al. Efficacy of adjuvant chemotherapy in high-risk node-negative breast cancer: an intergroup study. N Engl J Med 1989;320:485–490

NIH Consensus Conference. Treatment of early-stage breast cancer. JAMA 1991;265:391–395

Consensus Statement from the National Institutes of Health Consensus Development Conference, June 18–21, 1990

- 1.5 million women will develop breast cancer in the 1990s.
- Nearly 30% will ultimately die of the disease.
- Of 150,000 new cases annually, 75–80% are clinical stage I or II, and two thirds are without nodal involvement.

Recommendations

1. Breast conservation is appropriate and preferable primary therapy for stage I and II breast cancer. (Exclusions: multicentric breast malignancies, either gross multifocal disease or diffuse microcalcifications on mammography; expected unacceptable cosmetic result.)
2. Recommended technique for breast conservation treatment includes:
   - Local excision of primary tumor with clear margins
   - Level I-II axillary node dissection
   - Breast irradiation to 4,500–5,000 cGy with or without a boost
3. All patients who are candidates for clinical trials should be offered the opportunity to participate.
4. The majority of patients with node-negative breast cancer are cured by local therapy.
5. The rate of local and distant recurrence is decreased by both adjuvant combination chemotherapy and adjuvant tamoxifen. The decision to use adjuvant treatment should follow a thorough discussion with the patient regarding the likely risk of recurrence without adjuvant therapy, the expected reduction in risk with adjuvant therapy, toxicities of therapy, and its impact on quality of life.
6. Although all node-negative patients have some risk for recurrence, patients with tumors less than or equal to 1 cm have an excellent prognosis and do not require adjuvant systemic therapy outside clinical trials.

176

Evaluation of uterine serous carcinoma

A 57-year-old woman presents with scant postmenopausal bleeding. Pelvic examination discloses a small, freely movable uterus and no palpable adnexal masses. Curettage produces a small amount of tissue, which histologically shows papillary architecture and cytologic atypia (Fig. 176-1; see color plate). Which of the following are true statements about this tumor?

F (A) The lesion most likely represents metastasis from a primary ovarian carcinoma.

F (B) The likelihood of deep myometrial invasion and lymphatic–vascular permeation is low.

T (C) This tumor may metastasize widely, even if the primary carcinoma is confined to an endometrial polyp.

T (D) If the lesion recurs after therapy, the initial site of failure is often the upper abdomen.

T (E) Even when all findings indicate that the tumor is confined to the uterus, failure after appropriate treatment is approximately 50%.

The histologic variant of endometrial adenocarcinoma, shown in Fig. 176-1, is designated uterine serous carcinoma (USC). It is important to contrast this tumor with the more common endometrioid carcinoma (Fig. 176-2; see color plate), which is characterized by glandular architecture that more closely resembles proliferative endometrium. Uterine serous carcinoma comprises fewer than 10% of all uterine carcinomas. Although histologically similar to ovarian papillary serous carcinoma, USC is encountered independent of ovarian serous carcinoma and must be recognized as a distinct, highly aggressive tumor that has a poor prognosis. Even in the presence of a normal-sized uterus, deep myometrial invasion and lymphatic spread appear to be the rule rather than the exception. The tumor is often associated with malignant cells in peritoneal washings. Among 20 cases in which USC appeared to be confined to a polyp, there were 15 (75%) recurrences.

Uterine serous carcinoma spreads much like its counterpart in the ovary, and the upper abdomen is the most probable site of initial recurrence. For this reason, aggressive systemic chemotherapy has been used as an adjunct to surgery (total abdominal hysterectomy, bilateral salpingo-oophorectomy, and staging). Treatment by preoperative or postoperative pelvic irradiation is inappropriate because of frequent spread of the cancer beyond the pelvis. Current studies are evaluating whole-abdomen irradiation as adjuvant therapy. Despite aggressive treatment with either irradiation or chemotherapy, failure rates of approximately 50% have been reported for this lesion when it is confined to the uterus at diagnosis. Currently, no adjuvant therapy has been found to be effective.

Hendrickson M, Ross J, Eifel PJ, Cox RS, Martinez A, Kempson R. Adenocarcinoma of the endometrium: analysis of 256 cases with carcinoma limited to the uterine corpus. Pathology review and an analysis of prognostic variables. Gynecol Oncol 1982;13:373–392

Hendrickson M, Ross J, Eifel P, Martinez A, Kempson R. Uterine papillary serous carcinoma: a highly malignant form of endometrial adenocarcinoma. Am J Surg Pathol 1982;6:93–108

Kurman RJ, Zaino RJ, Norris HJ. Endometrial carcinoma. In: Kurman RJ, ed. Blaustein's pathology of the female genital tract. 4th ed. New York: Springer-Verlag, 1994:439–486

Sherman ME, Bitterman P, Rosenshein NB, Delgado G, Kurman RJ. Uterine serous carcinoma: a morphologically diverse neoplasm with unifying clinicopathologic features. Am J Surg Pathol 1992;16:600–610

Appendix

TABLE 1. International Federation of Gynecology and Obstetrics Staging for Ovarian Cancer

Stage	Clinical/Pathological Findings
Stage I	Growth limited to the ovaries
Stage IA	Growth limited to one ovary; no ascites. No tumor on the external surface; capsule intact.
Stage IB	Growth limited to both ovaries; no ascites. No tumor on the external surfaces; capsules intact.
Stage IC*	Tumor either stage IA or IB but with tumor on the surface of one or both ovaries; or with capsule ruptured; or with ascites present containing malignant cells or with positive peritoneal washings
Stage II	Growth involving one or both ovaries with pelvic extension
Stage IIA	Extension and/or metastases to the uterus and/or tubes
Stage IIB	Extension to other pelvic tissues
Stage IIC*	Tumor either stage IIA or IIB but with tumor on the surface of one or both ovaries; or with capsule(s) ruptured; or with ascites present containing malignant cells or with positive peritoneal washings
Stage III	Tumor involving one or both ovaries with peritoneal implants outside the pelvis and/or positive retroperitoneal or inguinal nodes. Superficial liver metastasis equals stage III. Tumor is limited to the true pelvis but with histologically verified malignant extension to small bowel or omentum.
Stage IIIA	Tumor grossly limited to the true pelvis with negative nodes but with histologically confirmed microscopic seeding of abdominal peritoneal surfaces
Stage IIIB	Tumor of one or both ovaries with histologically confirmed implants of abdominal peritoneal surfaces, none exceeding 2 cm in diameter. Nodes negative.
Stage IIIC	Abdominal implants greater than 2 cm in diameter and/or positive retroperitoneal or inguinal nodes
Stage IV	Growth involving one or both ovaries with distant metastasis. If pleural effusion is present, there must be positive cytologic test results to allot a case to stage IV. Parenchymal liver metastasis equals stage IV.

* To evaluate the impact on prognosis of the different criteria for allotting cases to stage IC or IIC, it would be of value to know whether the rupture of the capsule was spontaneous or caused by the surgeon, and whether the source of malignant cells detected was peritoneal washings or ascites.

International Federation of Gynecology and Obstetrics. Annual report on the results of treatment in gynecological cancer. Vol 21. Stockholm: FIGO, 1991:238–239

TABLE 2. International Federation of Gynecology and Obstetrics Staging for Carcinoma of the Corpus Uteri*

Stage	Clinical/Pathological Findings
Stage I	
IA G123	Tumor limited to the endometrium
IB G123	Invasion to less than one half the myometrium
IC G123	Invasion to more than one half the myometrium
Stage II	
IIA G123	Endocervical glandular involvement only
IIB G123	Cervical stromal invasion
Stage III	
IIIA G123	Tumor invades the serosa and/or adnexa, and/or positive peritoneal cytology
IIIB G123	Vaginal metastases
IIIC G123	Metastases to the pelvic and/or paraaortic lymph nodes
Stage IV	
IVA G123	Tumor invasion of bladder and/or bowel mucosa
IVB G123	Distant metastases including intraabdominal and/or inguinal lymph nodes

*Cases of carcinoma of the corpus should be classified (or graded) according to the degree of histologic differentiation as follows:
G1 = 5% or less of a nonsquamous or nonmorular solid growth pattern
G2 = 6–50% of a nonsquamous or nonmorular solid growth pattern
G3 = more than 50% of a nonsquamous or nonmorular solid growth pattern

Notes on pathologic grading:
1. Notable nuclear atypia, inappropriate for the architectural grade, raises the grade of a grade 1 or grade 2 by 1.
2. In serous adenocarcinomas, clear-cell adenocarcinomas, and squamous cell carcinomas, nuclear grading takes precedence.
3. Adenocarcinomas with squamous differentiation are graded according to the nuclear grade of the glandular component.

Rules related to staging:
1. Because corpus cancer is now staged surgically, procedures previously used for determination of stages are no longer applicable, such as the findings from fractional dilation and curettage to differentiate between stage I and stage II.
2. It is appreciated that there may be a small number of patients with corpus cancer who will be treated primarily with radiation therapy. If that is the case, the clinical staging adopted by the International Federation of Gynecology and Obstetrics in 1971 would still apply, but the designation of that staging system would be noted.
3. Ideally, width of the myometrium should be measured along with the width of tumor invasion.

International Federation of Gynecology and Obstetrics. Annual report on the results of treatment in gynecological cancer.Vol 21. Stockholm: FIGO, 1991:132

TABLE 3. International Federation of Gynecology and Obstetrics Staging for Carcinoma of the Cervix Uteri

Stage	Clinical/Pathological Findings
Stage 0	Carcinoma in situ, intraepithelial carcinoma
Stage I	The carcinoma is strictly confined to the cervix (extension to the corpus should be disregarded)
Stage IA	Invasive cancer identified only microscopically. All gross lesions even with superficial invasion are stage IB cancers. Invasion is limited to measured stromal invasion with maximum depth of 5.0 mm and no wider than 7.0 mm*
Stage IA1	Measured invasion of stroma no greater than 3.0 mm in depth and no wider than 7.0 mm
Stage IA2	Measured invasion of stroma greater than 3 mm and no greater than 5 mm and no wider than 7 mm
Stage IB	Clinical lesions confined to the cervix or preclinical lesions greater than stage IA.
Stage IB1	Clinical lesions no greater than 4.0 cm in size
Stage IB2	Clinical lesions greater than 4 cm in size
Stage II	The carcinoma extends beyond the cervix but has not extended to the pelvic wall. The carcinoma involves the vagina but not as far as the lower third
Stage IIA	No obvious parametrial involvement
Stage IIB	Obvious parametrial involvement
Stage III	The carcinoma has extended to the pelvic wall. On rectal examination, there is no cancer-free space between the tumor and the pelvic wall The tumor involves the lower third of the vagina All cases with hydronephrosis or nonfunctioning kidney are included unless they are known to be due to other causes
Stage IIIA	No extension to the pelvic wall
Stage IIIB	Extension to the pelvic wall and/or hydronephrosis or nonfunctioning kidney
Stage IV	The carcinoma has extended beyond the true pelvis or has clinically involved the mucosa of the bladder or rectum. A bullous edema as such does not permit a case to be allotted to stage IV
Stage IVA	Spread of the growth to adjacent organs
Stage IVB	Spread to distant organs

* The depth of invasion should not be more than 5 mm taken from the base of the epithelium, either surface or glandular, from which it originates. Vascular space involvement, either venous or lymphatic, should not alter the staging.

International Federation of Gynecology and Obstetrics. Annual report on the results of treatment in gynecological cancer. Vol 21. Stockholm: FIGO, 1991: 28–29;

Creasman WT. Editorial; new gynecologic cancer screening. Gynecol Oncol 1995;58:157–158

TABLE 4. International Federation of Gynecology and Obstetrics Staging for Carcinoma of the Vagina

Stage	Clinical/Pathological Findings
Stage 0	Carcinoma in situ, intraepithelial carcinoma
Stage I	The carcinoma is limited to the vaginal wall
Stage II	The carcinoma has involved the subvaginal tissue but has not extended to the pelvic wall
Stage III	The carcinoma has extended to the pelvic wall
Stage IV	The carcinoma has extended beyond the true pelvis or has clinically involved the mucosa of the bladder or rectum. Bullous edema as such does not permit a case to be allotted to stage IV.
Stage IVA	Spread of the growth to adjacent organs and/or direct extension beyond the true pelvis
Stage IVB	Spread to distant organs

International Federation of Gynecology and Obstetrics. Annual report on the results of treatment in gynecological cancer. Vol 21. Stockholm: FIGO, 1991:302

TABLE 5. International Federation of Gynecology and Obstetrics (FIGO) Staging for Vulvar Cancer

FIGO Stage	TNM*	Clinical/Pathological Findings
Stage 0	T_{is}	Carcinoma in situ, intraepithelial carcinoma
Stage I	$T_1N_0M_0$	Lesions 2 cm or less in size confined to the vulva or perineum. No nodal metastasis.
Stage IA		Lesions 2 cm or less in size confined to the vulva or perineum and with stromal invasion no greater than 1.0 mm.† No nodal metastasis.
Stage IB		Lesions 2 cm or less in size confined to the vulva or perineum and with stromal invasion greater than 1.0 mm. No nodal metastasis.
Stage II	$T_2N_0M_0$	Tumor confined to the vulva and/or perineum, >2 cm in greatest dimension, nodes are not palpable
Stage III	$T_3N_0M_0$ $T_3N_1M_0$ $T_1N_1M_0$ $T_2N_1M_0$	Tumor of any size with 1. Adjacent spread to the lower urethra or the anus 2. Unilateral regional lymph node metastasis
Stage IVA	$T_1N_2M_0$ $T_2N_2M_0$ $T_3N_2M_0$ T_4 any N M_0	Tumor invades any of the following: Upper urethra, bladder mucosa, rectal mucosa, pelvic bone, or bilateral regional node metastasis
Stage IVB	Any T, any N M_1	Any distant metastasis including pelvic lymph nodes

***TNM Classification**

T: Primary Tumor
- T_x Primary tumor cannot be assessed
- T_0 No evidence of primary tumor
- T_{is} Carcinoma in situ (preinvasive carcinoma)
- T_1 Tumor confined to the vulva and/or perineum 2 cm or less in greatest dimension
- T_2 Tumor confined to the vulva and/or perineum more than 2 cm in greatest dimension
- T_3 Tumor involves any of the following: lower urethra, vagina, anus
- T_4 Tumor involves any of the following: bladder mucosa, rectal mucosa, upper urethra, pelvic bone

N: Regional Lymph Nodes
- Regional lymph nodes are the femoral and inguinal nodes
- N_x Regional lymph nodes cannot be assessed
- N_0 No lymph node metastasis
- N_1 Unilateral regional lymph node metastasis
- N_2 Bilateral regional lymph node metastasis

M: Distant Metastasis
- M_x Presence of distant metastasis cannot be assessed
- M_0 No distant metastasis
- M_1 Distant metastasis (pelvic lymph node metastasis is M_1)

† The depth of invasion is defined as the measurement of the tumor from the epithelial–stromal junction of the adjacent most superficial dermal papilla to the deepest point of invasion.

International Federation of Gynecology and Obstetrics. Annual report on the results of treatment in gynecological cancer. Int J Gynecol Obstet 1989;28:189–190

Creasman WT. Editorial: new gynecologic cancer staging. Gynecol Oncol 1995;58:157–158

TABLE 6. International Federation of Gynecology and Obstetrics Staging for Gestational Trophoblastic Tumors*

Stage	Clinical/Pathological Findings
Stage I	Disease confined to the uterus
Stage IA	Disease confined to the uterus with no risk factors
Stage IB	Disease confined to the uterus with one risk factor
Stage IC	Disease confined to the uterus with two risk factors
Stage II	Gestational trophoblastic tumor extending outside the uterus but limited to genital structures (adnexa, vagina, broad ligament)
Stage IIA	Gestational trophoblastic tumor extending outside the uterus but limited to genital structures with no risk factors
Stage IIB	Gestational trophoblastic tumor extending outside the uterus but limited to genital structures with one risk factor
Stage IIC	Gestational trophoblastic tumor extending outside the uterus but limited to genital structures with two risk factors
Stage III	Gestational trophoblastic tumor extending to the lungs with or without known genital tract involvement
Stage IIIA	Gestational trophoblastic tumor extending to the lungs with or without genital tract involvement and with no risk factors
Stage IIIB	Gestational trophoblastic tumor extending to the lungs with or without genital tract involvement and with one risk factor
Stage IIIC	Gestational trophoblastic tumor extending to the lungs with or without genital tract involvement and with two risk factors
Stage IV	All other metastatic sites
Stage IVA	All other metastatic sites without risk factors
Stage IVB	All other metastatic sites with one risk factor
Stage IVC	All other metastatic sites with two risk factors

***Notes on staging:**

Risk factors affecting staging include the following: 1) serum human chorionic gonadotropin >100,000 mIU/ml; 2) duration of disease >6 months from termination of antecedent pregnancy.

The following factors should be considered and noted in reporting: 1) prior chemotherapy has been given for known gestational trophoblastic tumor; 2) placental-site tumors should be reported separately; 3) histologic verification of disease is not required.

International Federation of Gynecology and Obstetrics. Annual report on the results of treatment in gynecological cancer. Stockholm: FIGO, 1995:49–50

TABLE 7. World Health Organization Prognostic Scoring System for Gestational Trophoblastic Disease

	Score*			
Prognostic Factor	**0**	**1**	**2**	**4**
Age (y)	≤39	>39		
Antecedent pregnancy	Hydatidiform mole	Abortion; ectopic	Term	
Interval (mo)†	<4	4–6	7–12	>12
hCG (IU/L)	$<10^3$	10^3–10^4	10^4–10^5	$>10^5$
ABO blood groups (female / male)		O / A A / O	B AB	
Largest tumor (cm)	<3	3–5	>5	
Site of metastases		Spleen, kidney	Gastrointestinal tract, liver	Brain
Number of metastases		1–3	4–8	>8
Prior chemotherapy			Single drug	Multiple drugs

*Low risk, ≤4; intermediate risk, 5-7; high risk, ≥8.

†Interval: Time (months) between antecedent pregnancy and start of chemotherapy.

Scott JR, DiSaia PJ, Hammond CB, Spellacy WN. Danforth's obstetrics and gynecology. 7th ed. Philadelphia: JB Lippincott, 1994:1046.
Modified, by permission of WHO, from Gestational trophoblastic diseases. Report of a WHO Scientific Group. Geneva: Who, 1983 (Technical Report Series, No. 692)

TABLE 8. Clinical Classification of Gestational Trophoblastic Disease

I. Nonmetastatic GTD: no evidence of disease outside of uterus—not assigned to prognostic category

II. Metastatic GTD; any metastases
- A. Good prognosis metastatic GTD
  1. Short duration (<4 months)
  2. Low hCG level (<40,000 mIU/ml serum ß-hCG)
  3. No metastases to brain or liver
  4. No antecedent term pregnancy
  5. No prior chemotherapy
- B. Poor prognosis metastatic GTD: any high-risk factor
  1. Long duration (>4 months)
  2. High pretreatment hCG level (>40,000 mIU/ml serum ß-hCG)
  3. Brain or liver metastases
  4. Antecedent term pregnancy
  5. Prior chemotherapy

(Nichols DH, ed. Gynecologic and obstetric surgery. St. Louis: Mosby, 1993;1157. Compiled from Hammond CB, Weed JC, Currie JL. The role of operation in the current therapy of gestational trophoblastic disease. Am J Obstet Gynecol 1980;136:844–858)

TABLE 9. American Joint Committee on Cancer Staging for Breast Cancer: Definition of TNM* Staging System

Stage	Definition
Primary tumor	
TX	Primary tumor cannot be assessed
T0	No evidence of primary tumor
TIs[†]	Carcinoma in situ; intraductal carcinoma, lobular carcinoma in situ, or Paget disease of the nipple with no tumor
T1	Tumor 2 cm or less in greatest dimension
T1a	0.5 cm or less in greatest dimension
T1b	More than 0.5 cm but not more than 1 cm in greatest dimension
T1c	More than 1 cm but not more than 2 cm in greatest dimension
T2	Tumor more than 2 cm but not more than 5 cm in greatest dimension
T3	Tumor more than 5 cm in greatest dimension
T4[‡]	Tumor of any size with direct extension to the chest wall or skin
T4a	Extension to the chest wall
T4b	Edema (including peau d'orange) or ulceration of the skin of the breast or satellite skin nodules confined to the same breast
T4c	Both (T4a and T4b)
T4d	Inflammatory carcinoma
Regional lymph notes (N)	
NX	Regional lymph nodes cannot be assessed (eg, previously removed)
N0	No regional lymph node metastasis
N1	Metastasis to movable ipsilateral axillary lymph node(s)
N2	Metastasis to ipsilateral axillary lymph node(s) fixed to one another or to other structures
N3	Metastasis to ipsilateral internal mammary lymph node(s)
Pathologic classification (pN)	
pNX	Regional lymph nodes cannot be assessed (eg, previously removed or not removed for pathologic study)
pN0	No regional lymph node metastasis
pN1	Metastasis to movable ipsilateral axillary lymph node(s)
pN1a	Only micrometastasis (none larger than 0.2 cm)
pN1b	Metastasis to lymph node(s), any larger than 0.2 cm
pN1bi	Metastasis in 1 to 3 lymph nodes, any more than 0.2 cm and all less than 2 cm in greatest dimension
pN1bii	Metastasis to 4 or more lymph nodes, any more than 0.2 cm and all less than 2 cm in greatest dimension
pN1biii	Extension of the tumor beyond the capsule of a lymph node metastasis less than 2 cm in greatest dimension
pN1biv	Metastasis to a lymph node 2 cm or more in greatest dimension
pN2	Metastasis to ipsilateral axillary lymph nodes that are fixed to one another or to other structures
pN3	Metastasis to ipsilateral internal mammary lymph node(s)
Distant metastasis (M)	
MX	Presence of distant metastasis cannot be assessed
M0	No distant metastasis
M1	Distant metastasis, which includes metastasis to ipsilateral supraclavicular lymph node(s)
Stage grouping	
Stage 0	Tis, N0, M0
Stage I	T1, N0, M0
Stage IIA	T0, N1, M0 T1, N1,[§] M0 T2, N0, M0
Stage IIB	T2, N1, M0 T3, N0, M0

Continued

TABLE 9. American Joint Committee on Cancer Staging for Breast Cancer: Definition of TNM* Staging System *(continued)*

Stage	Definition
Stage grouping *(continued)*	
Stage IIIA	T0, N2, M0
	T1, N2, M0
	T2, N2, M0
	T3; N1, N2; M0
Stage IIIB	T4, any N, M0
	Any T, N3, M0
Stage IV	Any T, any N, M1

* Definitions for classifying the primary tumor (T) are the same for clinical and for pathologic classification. The telescoping method of classification can be applied. If the measurement is made by physical examination, the examiner will use the major headings (T1, T2, or T3). If other measurements, such as mammographic or pathologic, are used, the telescoped subsets of T1 can be used.

† Paget disease associated with a tumor is classified according to the size of the tumor.

‡ Chest wall includes the ribs, intercostal muscles, and serratus anterior muscle but not the pectoral muscle.

§ The prognosis of patients with pN1a is similar to that of patients with pN0.

American Joint Committee on Cancer. Manual for staging of cancer. 4th ed. Philadelphia: JB Lippincott, 1992

Index

NOTE: Numbers refer to questions, not pages, unless italicized.

NOTE: Numbers refer to questions, not pages, unless italicized.

NOTE: Numbers refer to questions, not pages, unless italicized.

NOTE: Numbers refer to questions, not pages, unless italicized.

NOTE: Numbers refer to questions, not pages, unless italicized.

NOTE: Numbers refer to questions, not pages, unless italicized.

NOTE: Numbers refer to questions, not pages, unless italicized.

NOTE: Numbers refer to questions, not pages, unless italicized.

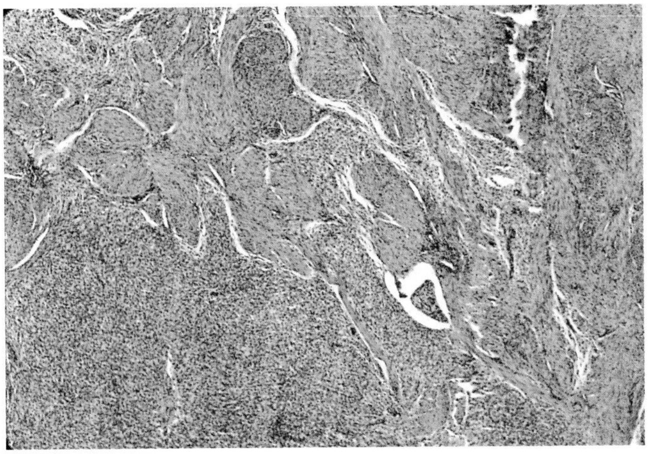

(A)

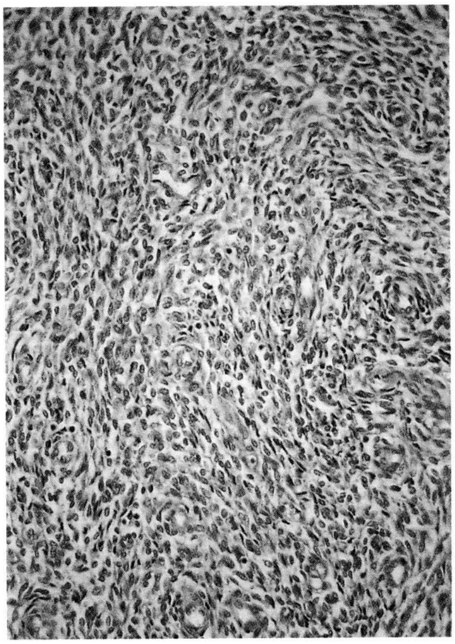

(B)

FIG. 7-1. Low-grade endometrial stromal sarcoma. (A) Irregularly shaped nests of cells are seen infiltrating the myometrium. (B) Higher magnification shows small, relatively bland cells oriented around blood vessels.

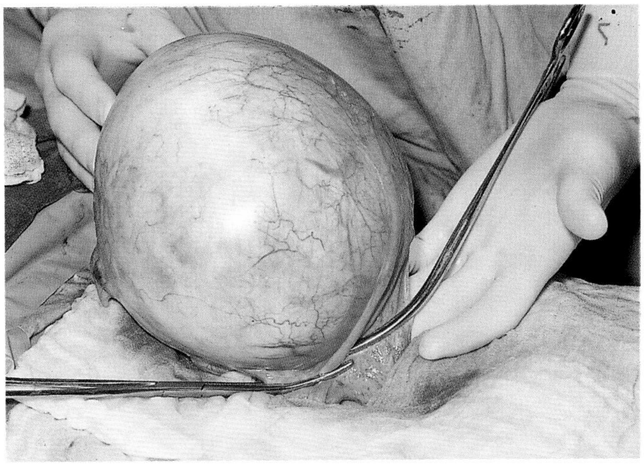

FIG. 9-1. Appearance of serous cystadenocarcinoma at initial laparotomy. The tumor was thought to be confined to the ovary.

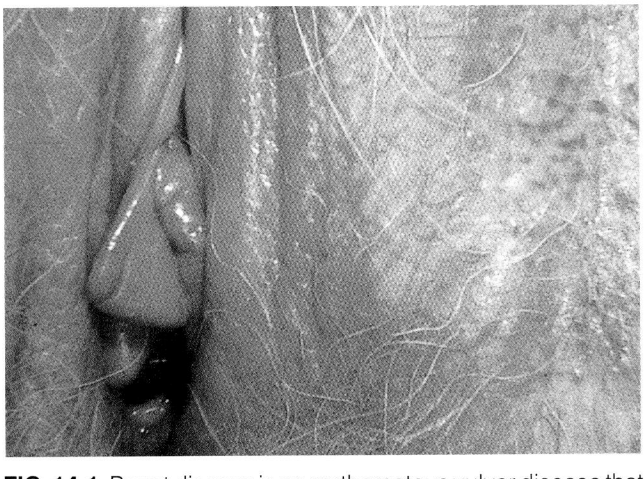

FIG. 14-1. Paget disease is an erythematous vulvar disease that may be mistaken for other vulvar conditions.

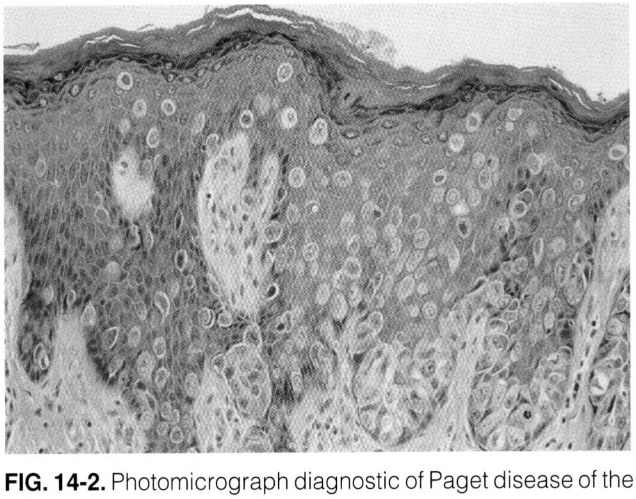

FIG. 14-2. Photomicrograph diagnostic of Paget disease of the vulva.

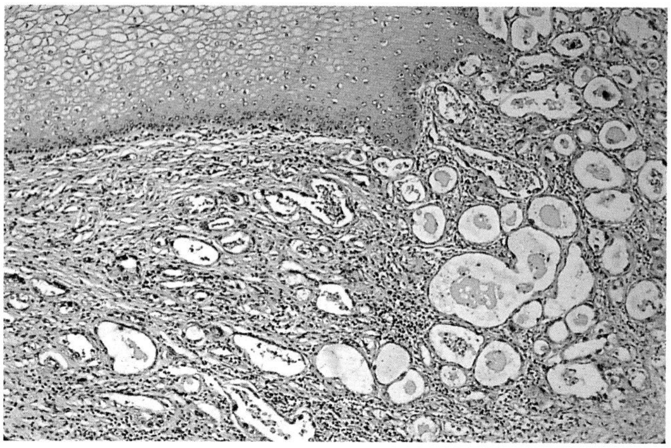

(A)

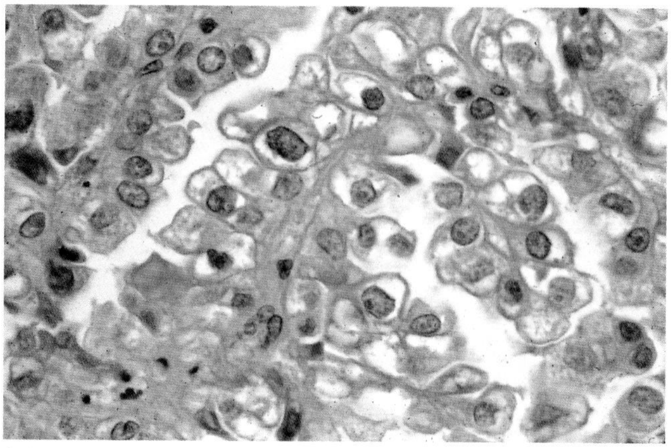

(B)

FIG. 17-1. Clear cell adenocarcinoma. (A) Low magnification reveals a tumor composed of tubules and cysts lined by flattened cells. (B) High magnification of the tumor shows cells with enlarged, atypical nuclei. The cytoplasm contains abundant glycogen, which appears clear.

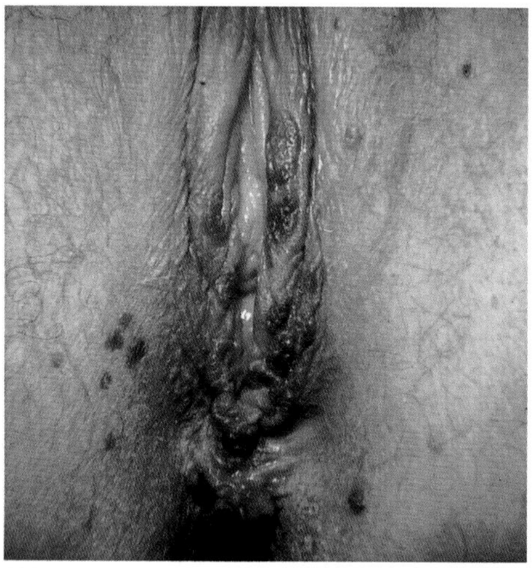

(A)

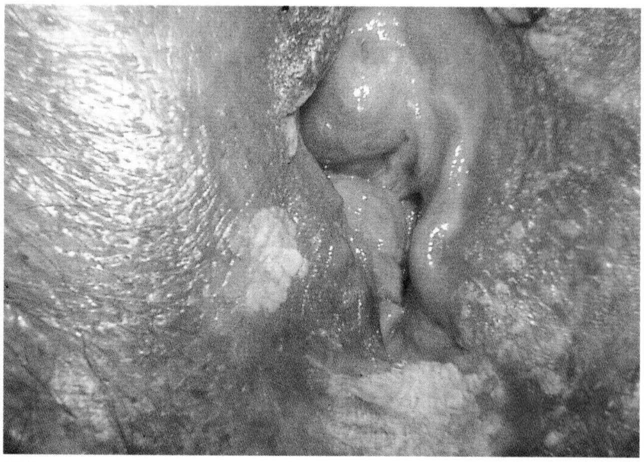

(B)

FIG. 21-1. Variable appearance of vulvar intraepithelial neoplasia. (A) Raised hyperpigmented (brown) lesions. (B) Raised white lesions.

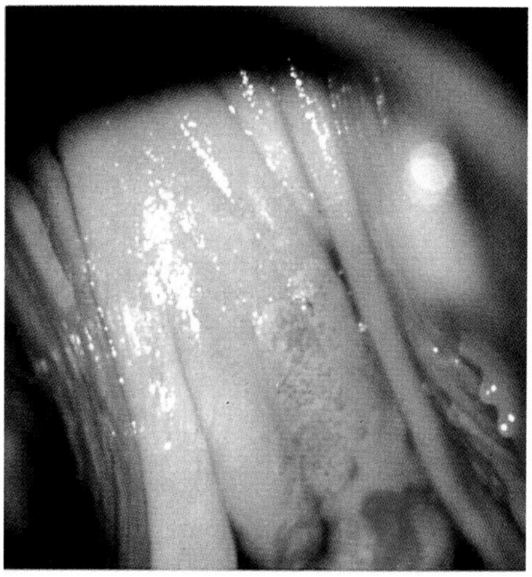

(A)

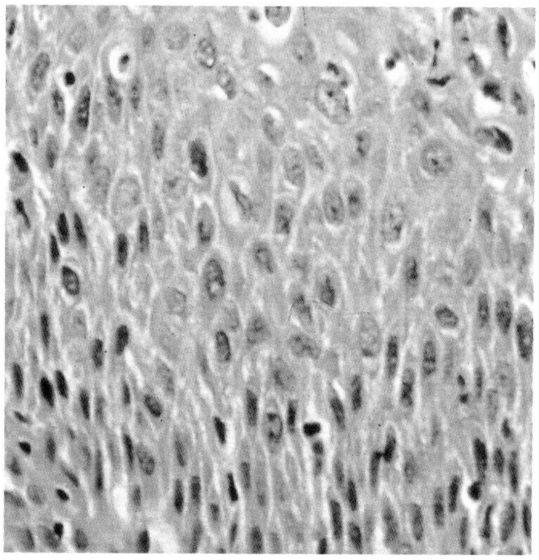

(B)

FIG. 56-1. A lesion consistent with vaginal intraepithelial neoplasia. (A) Colposcopic view showing a well-circumscribed, raised, acetowhite lesion. (B) Microscopic image showing neoplastic changes. (American College of Obstetricians and Gynecologists. Basic colposcopy. ACOG Self Learning Package, Program 26. Washington, DC: ACOG, 1991)

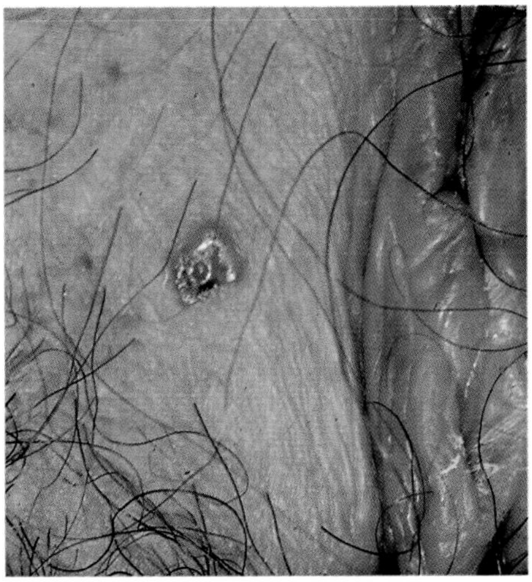

(A)

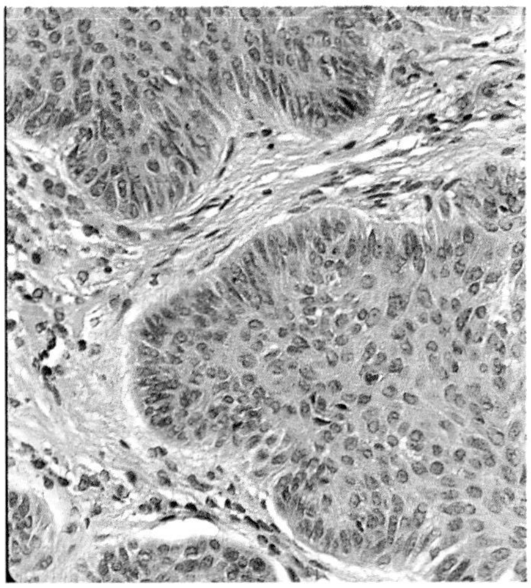

(B)

FIG. 57-1. Basal cell carcinoma of the vulva. (A) This lesion typically has central ulceration and peripheral rolled edges. (B) At microscopy, peripheral palisading tumor cells are evident.

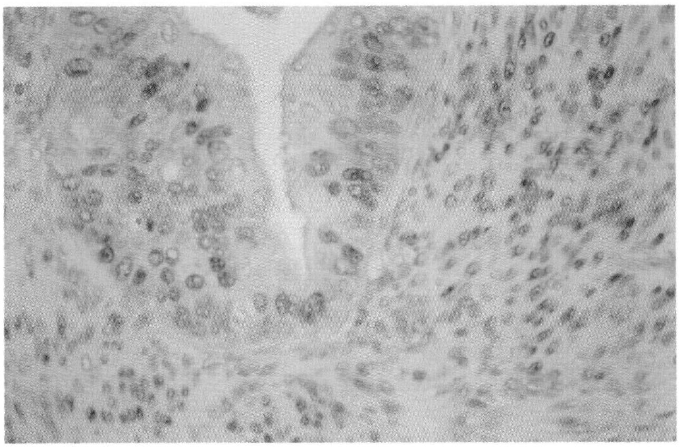

FIG. 58-1. International Federation of Gynecology and Obstetrics grade 1 endometrial adenocarcinoma of the endometrium. The nuclei of the tumor and the myometrium are strongly positive for the estrogen receptor (X400).

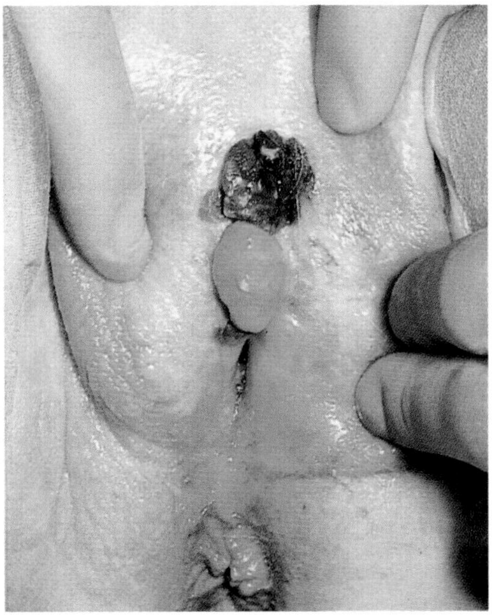

FIG. 59-1. Nodular melanoma of the vulva with clitoral lymphatic involvement.

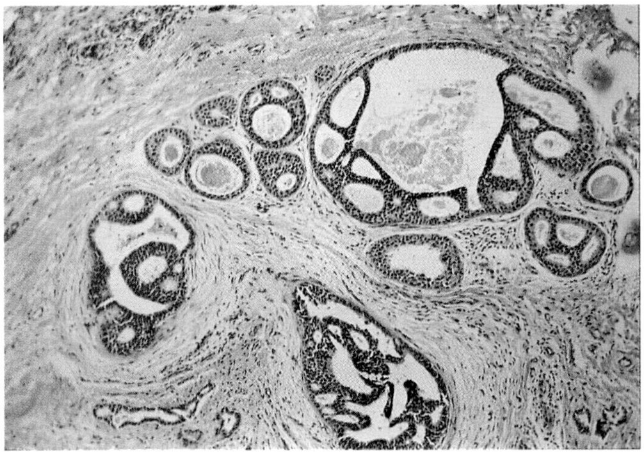

(A)

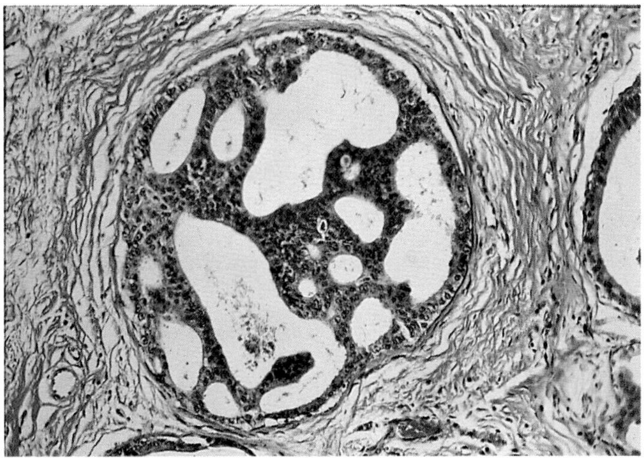

(B)

FIG. 60-1. Intraductal carcinoma. (A) At low magnification, epithelial cells bridge ducts in a cribriform pattern. (B) At high magnification, the epithelial cells are relatively small and uniform with a high nuclear to cytoplasmic ratio. Nuclei are hyperchromatic.

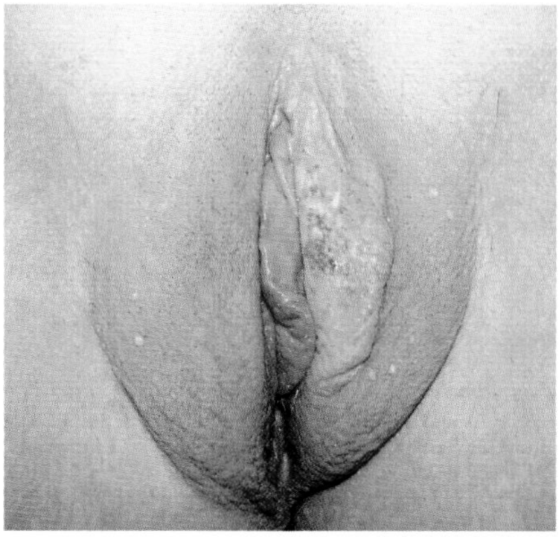

FIG. 68-1. Vulvar Paget disease.

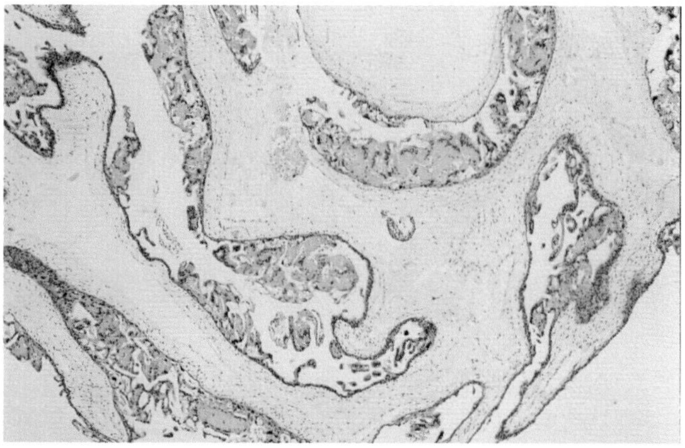

FIG. 87-2. Photomicrograph of tissue from suction curettage, which establishes the diagnosis of complete hydatidiform mole.

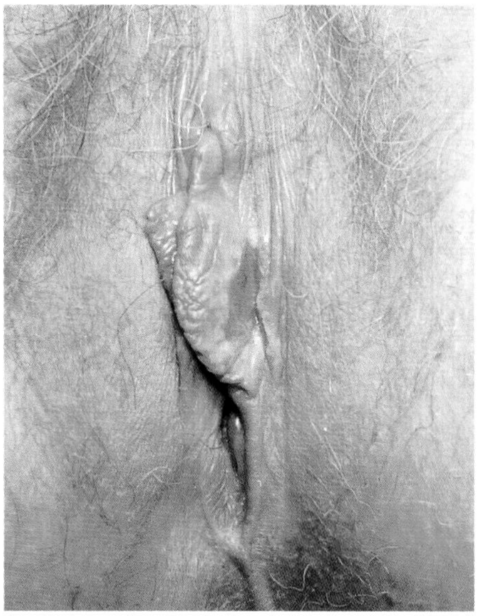

FIG. 91-1. Erythematous lesion on the labia majora.

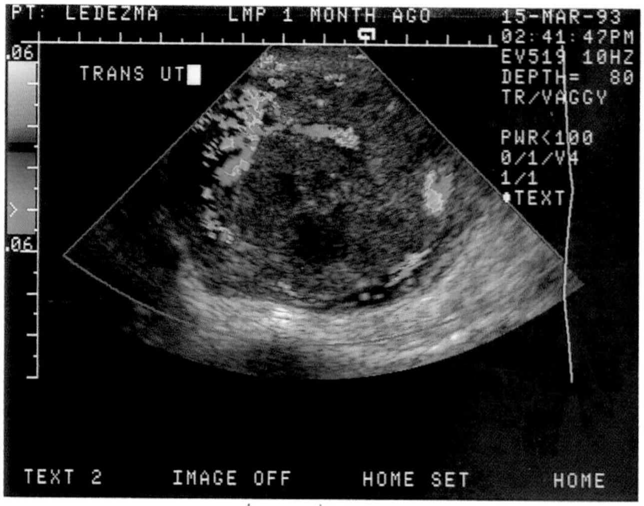

FIG. 93-1. Transvaginal ultrasonogram with color Doppler revealing gestational trophoblastic tumor within both the uterine cavity and wall with blood flow.

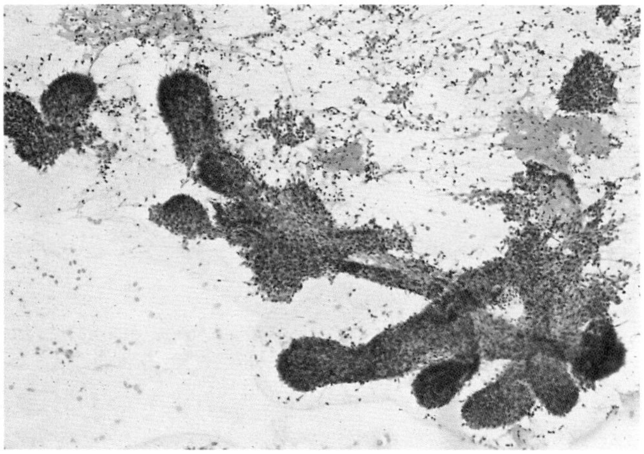

FIG. 96-3. Fine-needle aspirate of a fibroadenoma. This cytologic preparation shows the classic features of fibroadenoma. The epithelial clusters of uniform ductal cells are "staghorn" in shape. The sheets of benign ductal cells are cohesive. Fragments of benign tumor stroma and background "bipolar naked nuclei" are present.

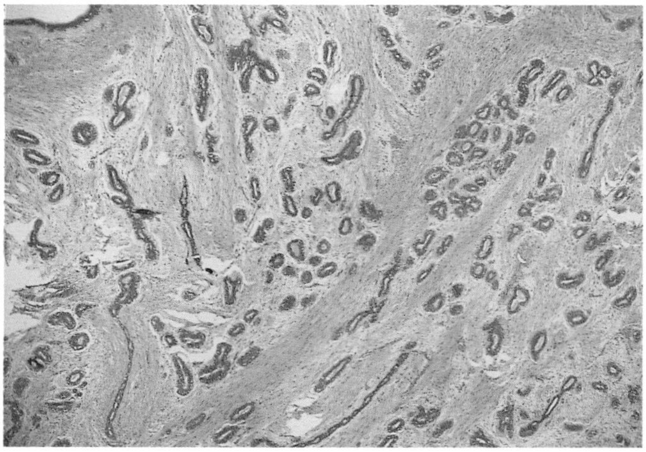

FIG. 96-4. Fibroadenoma. Histologic section shows epithelial ductal structures of various sizes with minimal foci of hyperplasia within a myoid to hyalinized stromal network.

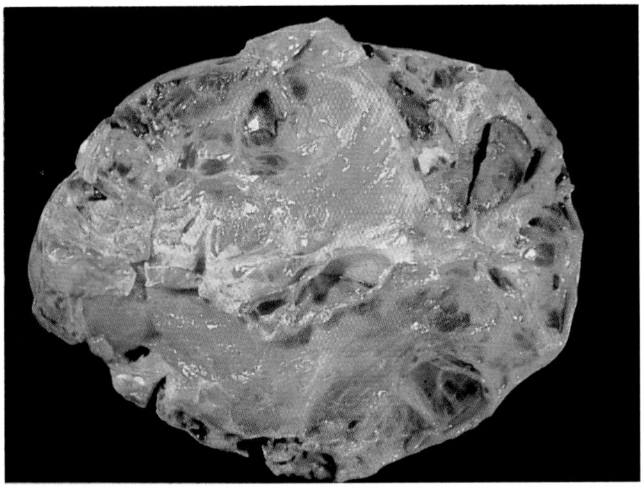

FIG. 106-1. Multicystic 7 × 8 × 6-cm granulosa cell tumor of the ovary.

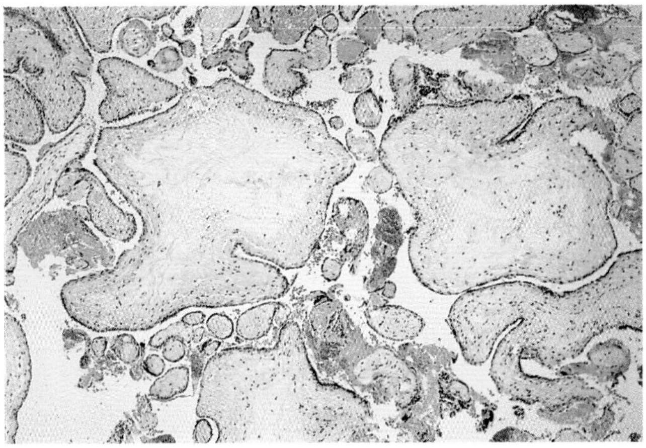

FIG. 112-1. Partial mole. Two populations of chorionic villi are present, one hydropic and one normal sized.

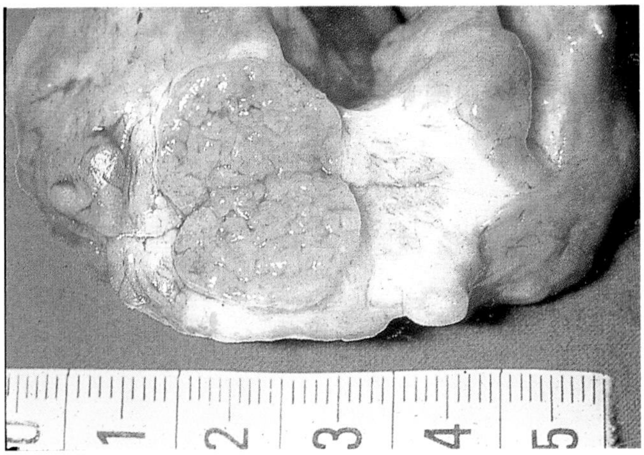

FIG. 118-1. Gross appearance of fibroadenoma. This neoplasm, which has clear demarcation from the surrounding adipose breast tissue, is lobulated and has a pale, glistening appearance on its cut surface. (Hughes LE, Mansel RE, Webster DJT. Benign disorders and diseases of the breast: concepts and clinical management. Philadelphia: Baillière Tindall, 1989:63)

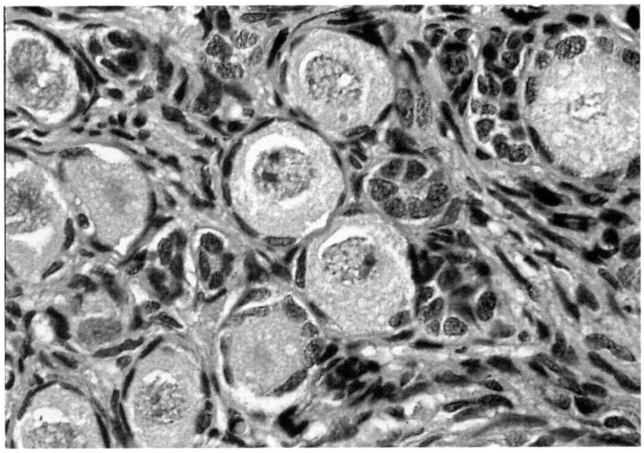

FIG. 134–137-1. Histologic section of a rabbit ovary showing normal oocytes and follicular structure.

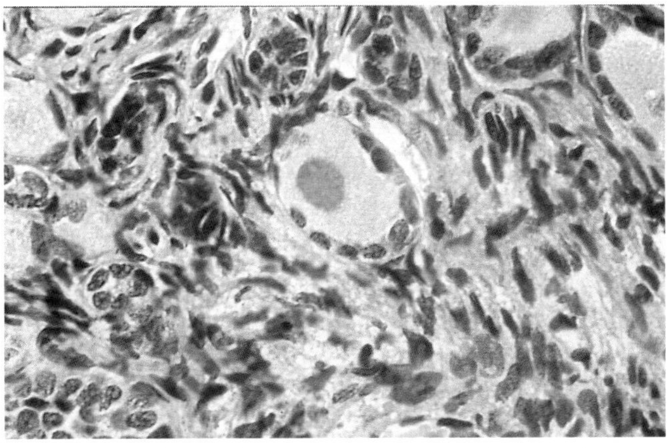

FIG. 134–137-2. Histologic section of a rabbit ovary showing abnormal oocytes and follicular structure after laser injury. The cytoplasm of the oocyte is eosinophilic and condensed. Nucleoli are not seen.

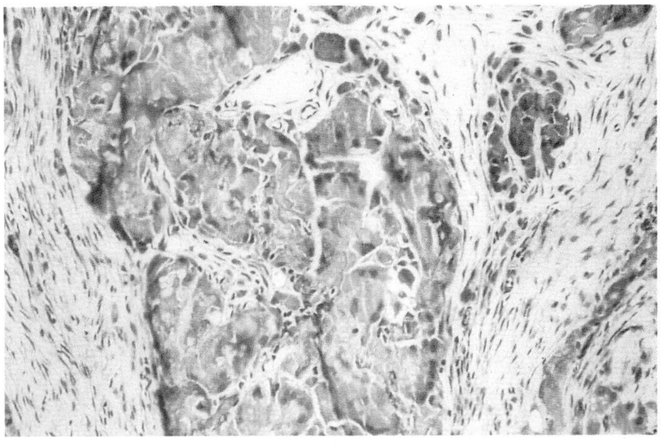

FIG. 134–137-3. Histologic section of a rabbit ovary showing granuloma formation in response to electrosurgical incision of the ovary (similar to the response to CO_2 laser incision).

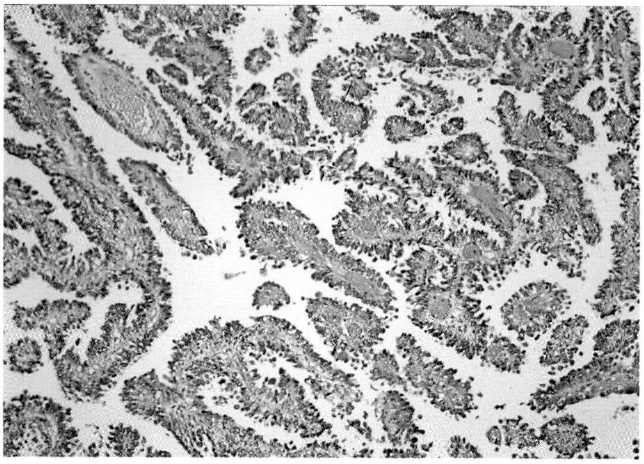

FIG. 176-1. Uterine serous carcinoma. This tumor is characterized by a papillary architecture. The cells are markedly atypical, with pleomorphic, hyperchromatic nuclei. There is abundant mitotic activity.

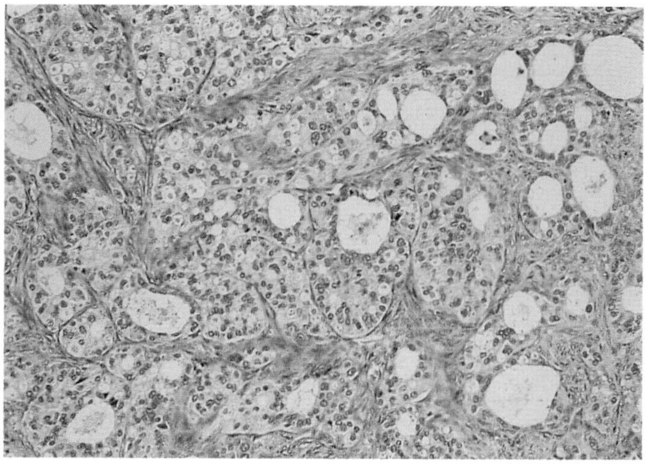

FIG. 176-2. Endometrial carcinoma. This tumor is characterized by a glandular pattern. Nuclear atypia is minimal.

SOUTH CAROLINA
Science

Reading and Writing in Science

Macmillan McGraw-Hill

Contents

LIFE SCIENCE

Contents

Contents

EARTH SCIENCE

Contents

PHYSICAL SCIENCE

Name ______________________ Date ______________

Kingdoms of Life

Complete the concept map about the classification of living things. Some parts have been done for you.

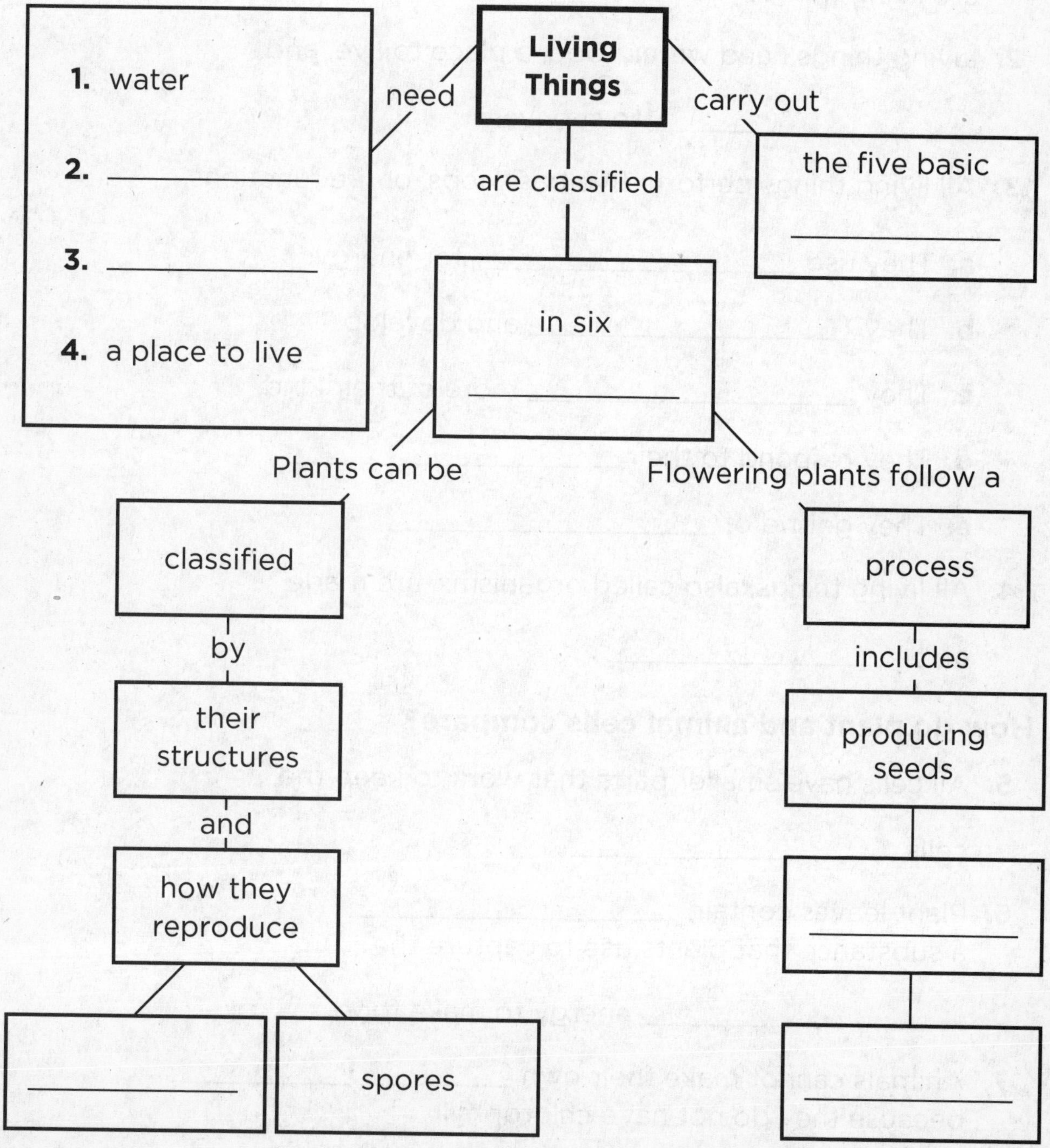

LESSON **Outline**

Name ______________________ Date ____________

Cells

Use your textbook to help you fill in the blanks.

What are living things?

1. People, ____________________, and ____________________ are living things.
2. Living things need water, food, a place to live, and ____________________ to survive.
3. All living things perform five basic jobs, or life functions.
   - **a.** They use ____________________ for energy.
   - **b.** They ____________________ and develop.
   - **c.** They ____________________ more of their kind.
   - **d.** They respond to their ____________________.
   - **e.** They get rid of ____________________.
4. All living things, also called organisms, are made of ____________________.

How do plant and animal cells compare?

5. All cells have smaller parts that work to keep the cells ____________________.
6. Plant leaves contain ____________________, a substance that plants use to capture the ____________________ energy to make food.
7. Animals cannot make their own ____________________ because they do not have chlorophyll.

Name ______________________________ Date ____________

LESSON
Outline

How are cells grouped?

8. Cells are grouped by the ____________________ they do.

9. A group of similar cells that carries out a certain job is called a(n) ____________________ .

10. Tissues in a group are called a(n) ____________________ .

11. Plants and animals have many organs that work together in an organ ____________________ .

How can you see cells?

12. A microscope works like a magnifying glass by making something ____________________ look much ____________________ .

Critical Thinking

13. Which do you think would be more harmful to an organism: a damaged cell or a damaged organ?

____

____

____

____

____

____

____

Name ______________________________ Date ____________

Cells

Use the clues to fill in the crossword puzzle.

Across

2. living thing
4. young organisms of parents
6. rigid outer covering of plant cells
7. similar cells working together

Down

1. five basic jobs of living things
2. organs working together
3. tissues working together
4. gas in the air
5. smallest part of a living thing

Name ______________________ Date ____________

LESSON
Cloze Activity

Cells

Use the words in the box to fill in the blanks.

animal	grow	offspring	oxygen
food	living	organisms	small

Everything in the world can be placed into one of two groups. There are ____________ things and nonliving things. All living things need water, food, a place to live, and ____________ . Also, all living things carry out five life functions. They need ____________ for energy. Second, living things ____________ and develop. Third, they respond to the environment. Fourth, they have ____________ . Fifth, living things get rid of wastes.

Living things, also called ____________ , are made of cells. Cells are too ____________ to see with just your eyes. A tool called a microscope is used. Plant and ____________ cells have many things in common. Plant cells also have some special cell parts.

LESSON **Outline**

Name ______________________ Date ____________

Classifying Living Things

Use your textbook to help you fill in the blanks.

How are living things classified?

1. Scientists place organisms into one of six groups, or ______________.
2. Organisms in the same kingdom share basic ______________.

How are organisms grouped within a kingdom?

3. Traits are used to sort organisms into smaller ______________.
4. The smaller groups in a kingdom include

   a. phylum

   b. ______________

   c. ______________

   d. ______________

   e. ______________

   f. species

What kinds of organisms have only one cell?

5. Kingdoms that include organisms made up of one cell are ______________, ______________, and ______________.
6. One-celled organisms are also called ______________.
7. Bacteria have no cell ______________.
8. Protists have a cell nucleus and special cell ______________ that do certain jobs.

Name ______________________ Date __________

9. Fungi have a cell nucleus and a(n) ______________, just as plants do, but they do not have chloroplasts.

How are organisms named?

10. The scientific name for an organism is made up of a genus name and ______________ name.

11. Scientists have not yet named ______________ the organisms on Earth.

Critical Thinking

12. Look at the chart on page 36 of your textbook. For each level of classification, identify a trait that the red squirrel does not have, and name an organism that would have that trait.

Name ______________________ Date ____________

Classifying Living Things

Match the correct word to its definition by writing the letter of the definition in the space provided.

1. ________ protists
2. ________ diseases
3. ________ trait
4. ________ fungi
5. ________ kingdom
6. ________ bacteria
7. ________ species
8. ________ classification

a. a group of organisms with some members that make their own food and some that eat other organisms to live

b. organisms made up of cells with a cell wall and a nucleus but without chloroplasts

c. the system used for identifying organisms

d. the group made up of one type of organism

e. a characteristic of a living thing used to identify and classify it

f. the largest group into which organisms can be classified

g. the smallest one-celled organisms

h. the harmful effects of some microorganisms

Name ______________________________ Date ____________

LESSON
Cloze Activity

Classifying Living Things

Use the words in the box to fill in the blanks.

class	genus	six
different	kingdom	species
family	similar	

Scientists study the traits of living things in order to identify and classify them. Scientists divide Earth's organisms into ____________ groups. The largest group, called a ____________, is divided into smaller groups, known as *phylum*, ____________, *order*, ____________, *genus*, and *species*.

Organisms in the same kingdom are ____________ to one another and are ____________ from organisms in the other kingdoms. Kingdoms are divided into smaller and smaller groups. The smallest group has only one type of organism and is called a ____________. Scientists use ____________ and species names to identify individual types of organisms. *Canis familiaris* is the scientific name for a dog.

Name ______________________________ Date ____________

Red Tide: A Bad Bloom at the Beach

You're ready for some fun in the Sun. But when you get to the beach, it's closed. Then you notice that the water is a strange color. You can put your swimsuit away. Your beach is a victim of red tide!

Red tide isn't actually a tide. It is ocean water that is blooming with a harmful kind of algae. These one-celled organisms are poisonous to the sea creatures that eat them. The water isn't always red, either. Sometimes it's orange, brown, or green.

An outbreak of red tide can do a lot of damage. On the coast of Florida, one killed tens of thousands of fish, crabs, birds, and other small animals within a few months. It also killed large animals like manatees, dolphins, and sea turtles. Red tides can also make people sick if they eat infected shellfish.

Scientists are working to predict where and when red tides occur. They measure the amount of algae along coastlines. They use data collected from satellites to study wind speed and direction. This information helps scientists predict where blooms may develop. With their predictions, scientists help warn local agencies about future red tides.

Write About It

Infer What could you infer about a closed beach with reddish-colored water? How could the prediction of red tides be helpful to people?

Name ______________________________ Date ____________

What I Know

Complete each statement about red tides.

- A red tide is ________________ that is blooming with harmful ________________, ________________ organisms.
- Red tides can make people sick if they ________________ infected shellfish.
- A red tide in Florida killed tens of thousands of ________________ animals.
- Scientists are using ________________ to collect data about red tides.

What I Infer

Answer the questions by making inferences about red tides.

1. What could you infer about a closed beach with reddish-colored water?

____

____

2. How could the prediction of red tides be helpful to people?

____

____

____

LESSON **Outline**

Name ______________________ Date __________

The Plant Kingdom

Use your textbook to help you fill in the blanks.

How do we classify plants?

1. We can classify plants in ______________ groups: those with and those ______________ roots, stems, and leaves.
2. One kind of plant without roots, stems, or leaves is ______________ .

How do plants get what they need?

3. Plants make their own food by using ______________ trapped from sunlight.
4. Plants take in water and nutrients from the soil through their ______________ .

Why are leaves important?

5. Plants use energy to change carbon dioxide and water into food, called ______________ .
6. Plants get carbon dioxide through openings on the undersides of their leaves, called ______________ .
7. A process called ______________ controls the amount of water stored in the leaves of a plant.
8. Photosynthesis ______________ food. Respiration ______________ energy.

What are mosses and ferns?

9. Mosses and ferns are plants that use ______________ to reproduce.

10. Spores are ______________ to the air and fall on the ground, where they begin to grow a new plant.

How do we use plants?

11. We use plants and plant parts such as bulbs, tubers,

______________, ______________,

______________, and flowers for ______________.

12. We also use plants for ______________ and

______________.

Critical Thinking

13. If your family could grow only one kind of plant, which plant would be best for your family to grow?

____

____

____

____

____

____

____

____

Name ______________________________ Date ____________

The Plant Kingdom

Match the correct word to its description by writing the letter of the word in the space provided.

a. epidermis	**d.** root	**g.** stem
b. photosynthesis	**e.** root hairs	**h.** stomata
c. respiration	**f.** spore	**i.** transpiration

1. ________ the part of a plant that carries food and nutrients to and from the roots and leaves
2. ________ a cell in a seedless plant that can grow into a new plant
3. ________ tiny holes found on the underside of a leaf
4. ________ a process that breaks down food sugars and releases energy in a plant
5. ________ threadlike cells on a root that take in water and nutrients from the soil
6. ________ a plant part that takes up water and nutrients from the ground and holds the plant in place
7. ________ the thin, protective covering on a leaf that keeps water in the leaf
8. ________ the process that a plant uses to produce plant sugars from water, carbon dioxide, and energy from sunlight
9. ________ a process that allows a plant to control how much water it has

Name ______________________ Date ____________

The Plant Kingdom

Use the words in the box to fill in the blanks.

energy	organisms	processes
food	photosynthesis	respiration
leaves	plants	

Plants have the same needs as other living things. Plants need air, water, ______________ , and a place to live. Plants get the energy they need in order to grow from the ______________ they make in their ______________ .

Photosynthesis and respiration are two very important ______________ that happen in ______________ . During ______________ , food is produced as plant sugars and then stored. During ______________ , energy is released for use by the plant. All ______________ , not just plants, depend on respiration for survival. All organisms also depend on the food made by plants.

Name ____________________ Date __________

Flowers and Seeds

Use your textbook to help you fill in the blanks.

What kinds of plants have tubes?

1. Vascular plants have ____________ or vessels that transport water, food, and waste to all parts of the plant.
2. Scientists separate vascular plants into seedless plants and ____________.
3. Scientists then divide plants with seeds into plants that produce flowers and ____________.

How are seedless and seed plants different?

4. A seed contains a(n) ____________ and stored food used to develop and grow into a new plant.
5. This new plant shares the ____________ of the two plants that produced the seed.
6. Some vascular plants do not ____________ but grow from spores.
7. Most seed plants produce ____________.
8. ____________, and almost all nuts come from flowering plants.
9. Evergreens are seed plants that ____________.
10. They produce seeds inside a(n) ____________.

Name ______________________ Date __________

LESSON
Outline

What do flowers do?

11. Flowers, the reproductive organ of flowering plants, usually have both ______________ parts.

12. Pollen grains are transferred from a flower's ______________ to the female part of the flower, the *pistil*, or to another flower's pistil.

13. This transfer is called ______________ .

14. During fertilization, the pollen and egg cell join and ______________ .

15. As the seed develops, the ovary enlarges until it becomes a(n) ______________ , which protects the seeds inside it.

16. Many flowers smell sweet or have ______________ to attract beetles and flies.

Critical Thinking

17. What are two ways scientists divide vascular plants?

____

____

____

____

____

____

Name ______________________ Date __________

Flowers and Seeds

Match the correct word to its description by writing its letter in the space provided.

a. fertilization	**c.** pistil	**e.** reproduction	**g.** stamen
b. ovary	**d.** pollination	**f.** spore	**h.** vascular

1. ________ cell used to reproduce by plants that do not have seeds
2. ________ formation of a seed by the joining of pollen and egg cells
3. ________ female part of a flowering plant, which produces eggs
4. ________ term for plants with tubes that carry water, food, and waste within the plant
5. ________ male part of a flowering plant, which produces pollen
6. ________ process used by all living things to make offspring
7. ________ female part of a flowering plant that turns into a fruit after fertilization
8. ________ movement of pollen from the stamen to the pistil, which may be done by animals

Flowers and Seeds

Use the words in the box to fill in the blanks.

evergreens	produce	spores	undeveloped
flowers	seedless	tubes	vascular

Many different kinds of plants have special features. Plants with ____________ that transport water, food, and waste to all parts of the plant are called ____________ plants. Vascular plants include ____________ plants and plants with seeds. Most common plants, such as fruits, vegetables, and herbs, ____________ seeds. Seeds contain a(n) ____________ plant and stored food.

Some vascular plants, such as horsetails, spike mosses, and ferns, do not produce seeds. Instead, these plants grow from ____________ . Some plants with seeds produce ____________ , which are the reproductive organ of some plants. ____________ are seed plants that do not produce flowers. These plants produce seeds inside a cone.

Name ______________________ Date ____________

Dandelions and Me

Write About It

Personal Narrative Think about a time you saw seeds being carried from place to place. Write a personal narrative about the event. Tell how it made you feel.

Getting Ideas

Picture the event in your mind. Jot down what happened in the chart below. Start with what happened first.

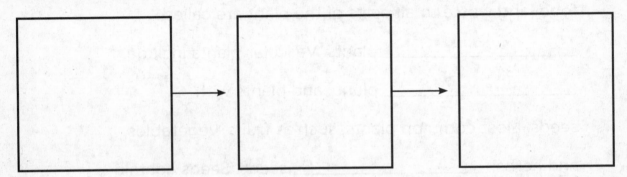

Planning and Organizing

Zoe wanted to write about the time she saw squirrels raiding the birdfeeder for sunflower seeds. Below are three sentences she wrote. Write "1" in front of the sentence that should be first. Write "2" in front of the sentence that should come next. Write "3" in front of the sentence that should be last.

_______ At first, some chickadees and blue jays came to the feeder and ate the seeds.

_______ After a few days, squirrels raided the feeder and carried seeds away.

_______ Last spring, we filled the birdfeeder in our backyard with sunflower seeds.

Revising and Proofreading

Here is a part of Zoe's personal narrative. Proofread it. She made five errors. Find the errors and correct them.

I laughed when I saw that Rascal of a squirrel run off with some seeds. I watched as the squirrel planted them. It would be fantastic if they grew? I waited about a weak. Every day, I looked to see if the seeds had sprooted. Finally, there was a little seedling, I was so excited.

Drafting

Write a sentence to begin your personal narrative. Use "I" to identify youself. Make sure your sentence will grab your readers' attention so that they will want to read your story.

____

Now write the first draft of your story. Use a separate piece of paper. Remember to tell what happened in sequence and to use time-order words.

Revising and Proofreading

Now revise and proofread your writing. Ask yourself:

- ▶ Did I use the pronoun "I" to tell my story?
- ▶ Did I tell what happened in sequence?
- ▶ Did I use time-order words?
- ▶ Did I correct all of the mistakes?

Name ______________________ Date ____________

Kingdoms of Life

Circle the letter of the best answer.

1. A group of cells that do the same job forms

a. an organ system.

b. an organ.

c. a cell.

d. a tissue.

2. The protective covering on a leaf is its

a. epidermis.

b. stomata.

c. root hairs.

d. seed covering.

3. Into how many kingdoms do scientists place organisms?

a. five

b. six

c. seven

d. eight

4. The tiny holes on the underside of a leaf are the

a. chlorophyll.

b. epidermis.

c. stomata.

d. seeds.

5. How many basic jobs do living things perform?

a. two

b. three

c. four

d. five

6. A single cell that can grow into a new plant is called a

a. spore.

b. cone.

c. stem.

d. root.

7. What are the threadlike cells on a root?

a. seeds

b. root hairs

c. runners

d. cuttings

8. Tissues that form a group are called

a. an organ.

b. a cell.

c. an organ system.

d. a cell wall.

Circle the letter of the best answer.

9. What process allows extra water to escape from a leaf?

a. fertilization

b. pollination

c. germination

d. transpiration

10. The smallest group in a kingdom is called

a. a phylum.

b. a species.

c. an order.

d. a class.

11. The process by which plants release energy stored as food sugars is called

a. transpiration.

b. respiration.

c. germination.

d. pollination.

12. Which of the following do scientists use to name individual organisms?

a. genus and species

b. phylum and class

c. family and order

d. order and genus

13. How is a plant cell different from an animal cell?

a. Only plant cells contain cytoplasm.

b. Only animal cells contain a nucleus.

c. Only plant cells contain chloroplasts.

d. Only animal cells contain mitochondria.

14. What do scientists use to see one-celled organisms?

a. microscope

b. test tube

c. balance scale

d. tongs

15. The joining of male cells and female cells in a plant is called

a. pollination.

b. germination.

c. respiration.

d. fertilization.

Name ______________________ Date ____________

Animal Kingdom

Complete the concept map about the animal kingdom. Some parts have been done for you.

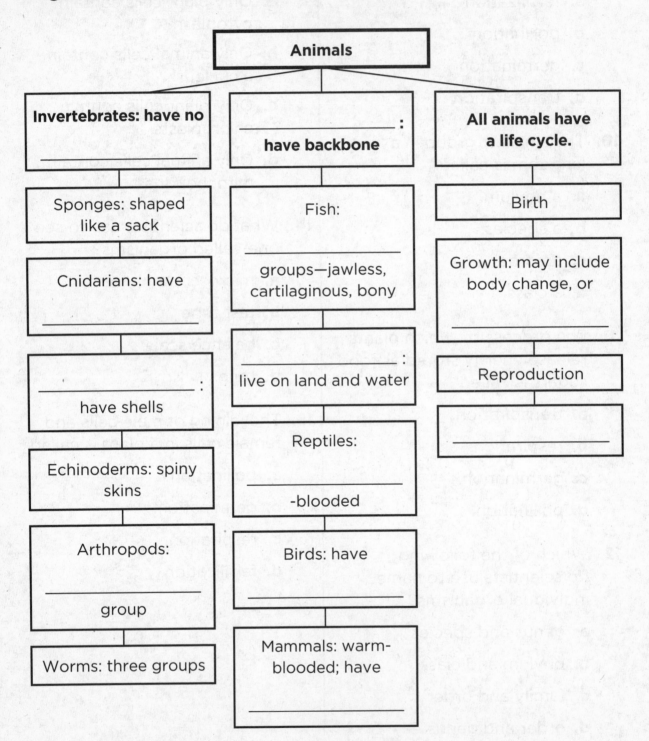

Animals

- **Invertebrates: have no ______________**
  - Sponges: shaped like a sack
  - Cnidarians: have ______________
  - ______________: have shells
  - Echinoderms: spiny skins
  - Arthropods: ______________ group
  - Worms: three groups
- **______________: have backbone**
  - Fish: ______________ groups—jawless, cartilaginous, bony
  - ______________: live on land and water
  - Reptiles: ______________ -blooded
  - Birds: have ______________
  - Mammals: warm-blooded; have ______________
- **All animals have a life cycle.**
  - Birth
  - Growth: may include body change, or ______________
  - Reproduction
  - ______________

Name ______________________ Date ____________

LESSON **Outline**

Invertebrates

Use your textbook to help you fill in the blanks.

What are invertebrates?

1. Scientists keep track of Earth's animal species by observing their similarities and ________________ .
2. An animal with symmetry has body parts that match other body parts around a point or central ________________ .
3. Animals can be classified by whether or not they have a(n) ________________ .
4. Invertebrates make up the ________________ animal group on Earth.

What are some invertebrates?

5. The simplest invertebrates are ________________ .
6. Sponges do not have ________________ .
7. Invertebrates that have ________________ on tentacles are called ________________ .
8. Clams, squid, and snails are soft-bodied invertebrates with hard shells and are called ________________ .
9. Sea stars, sea urchins, and sand dollars are spiny-skinned invertebrates, called ________________ .
10. All echinoderms have a support structure inside their bodies, called a(n) ________________ .

Name ______________________ Date ____________

What are arthropods?

11. Invertebrates with jointed legs and body sections are called ________________.

12. Arthropods have a hard outer covering, called a(n) ________________, that protects their bodies and holds in moisture.

How are worms classified?

13. Worms are classified as flatworms, ________________, or ________________ worms.

14. Flatworms have ribbon-like bodies, and some types ________________ inside the bodies of other animals.

15. Roundworms have thin bodies with ________________ ends.

Critical Thinking

16. Why do you think the first way an animal is classified is by whether it is a vertebrate or an invertebrate?

____

____

____

____

____

____

____

Name ______________________ Date ____________

Invertebrates

Use the words in the box to fill in the blanks.

arthropod	echinoderm	exoskeleton	mollusk
cnidarian	endoskeleton	invertebrate	sponge

1. The hard outer covering that protects an invertebrate's body is its ______________________ .

2. A spiny-skinned invertebrate, such as a sea star, is called a(n) ______________________ .

3. A(n) ______________________ is an animal without a backbone.

4. A soft-bodied invertebrate, such as a clam or snail, is called a(n) ______________________ .

5. An invertebrate with jointed legs and a sectioned body is a(n) ______________________ .

6. An internal support structure in an animal is a(n) ______________________ .

7. An invertebrate with stingers at the end of tentacles is a(n) ______________________ .

8. The simplest kind of invertebrate is a(n) ______________________ .

Name ______________________________ Date ____________

Invertebrates

Use the words in the box to fill in the blanks.

arthropods	endoskeleton	mollusks
backbone	exoskeleton	segmented
cnidarians	invertebrates	sponges

Scientists use various traits to classify Earth's many animals. One way to classify animals is as vertebrates or ______________________ . Vertebrates have a(n) ______________________ , and invertebrates do not.

Insects and arachnids are invertebrates called ______________________ and have a hard outer ______________________ . Echinoderms are invertebrates that have a(n) ______________________ inside their bodies. The simplest invertebrates are ______________________ . Other invertebrate groups are ______________________ with stingers and ______________________ with soft bodies protected by hard shells. The final group of invertebrates is worms: flatworms, roundworms, and ______________________ worms. Some kinds of flatworms and roundworms live inside the bodies of other animals.

Name ______________________ Date __________

LESSON
Outline

Vertebrates

Use your textbook to help you fill in the blanks.

What are vertebrates?

1. Vertebrates are animals that have a(n) __________ .
2. Some vertebrates are __________ and maintain their body temperature by breaking down food to make __________ .
3. Some vertebrates, such as fish, amphibians, and reptiles, are __________ and cannot control their body __________ .
4. There are seven classes of vertebrates: mammals, __________, reptiles, birds, and the three classes of __________ .
5. The three classes of fish are jawless fish, cartilaginous fish, and __________ fish.

What are some other vertebrate groups?

6. A vertebrate that spends part of its life in water and part on land is called a(n) __________ .
7. Snakes, lizards, turtles, and crocodiles are __________ . They have tough, dry, scaly __________ that holds in moisture.
8. The only animals that have feathers are __________ . They are also __________ .

Name ______________________ Date ____________

What are mammals?

9. A warm-blooded vertebrate with hair or fur is

a(n) ____________________ .

10. Female mammals produce milk to ____________________ their young.

11. Most mammals give birth to live young. Only a

few ____________________ .

12. Kangaroos, koalas, and opossums carry their young in

____________________ until they are grown.

13. The platypus and spiny anteater are the only mammals that

reproduce by ____________________ .

Critical Thinking

14. Why do you think there are three separate groups of fish instead of one group for all fish?

____

____

____

____

____

____

____

Name Samuel 22 Date ____________

Vertebrates

What am I?

Choose a word from the box below that answers each question, and write the correct word in the space provided.

amphibian	cartilage	reptile	warm-blooded
bird	cold-blooded	vertebrate	

1. ____________ I am a member of the second largest group of animals on Earth. Animals in my group have backbones. What am I?

2. ____________ I can keep my body at one temperature. I do this by breaking down food to make heat energy. What am I?

3. could-blooded I My body temperature changes with the surrounding temperature. What am I?

4. ____________ I spend part of my life in water and part on land. My skin must be kept moist. What am I?

5. reptile Snakes and lizards are part of my group. We live on land and have tough, scaly skin. What am I?

6. ____________ I have scales and feathers and hollow bones that make my body light enough to fly. What am I?

7. ____________ I am rubbery and make up the skeletons in lampreys, sharks, and rays. What am I?

Name ______________________ Date ____________

Vertebrates

Use the words in the box to fill in the blanks.

bony	invertebrates	warm-blooded
cold-blooded	mammals	vertebrates
fur	reptiles	

Invertebrates are the largest group of animals on Earth. The second-largest group is ______________ . Vertebrates have backbones, and ______________ do not.

Some vertebrates keep their bodies at one temperature by eating food to make heat energy. These animals are ______________ and are classified as birds or ______________ . Birds have feathers, and mammals have ______________ or hair. Other vertebrates are ______________ . Cold-blooded animals are classified as jawless fish, cartilaginous fish, ______________ fish, amphibians, or ______________ . The body temperature of cold-blooded vertebrates depends on their surroundings.

Name ______________________________ Date ____________

Gentle Giants

Write About It

Explanatory Writing Find out more about another endangered animal. Write a short explanation of why it is endangered.

Getting Ideas

Select an endangered animal. Use the cause-and-effect chart below. Fill it in as you do research.

Cause	→	Effect
	→	
	→	
	→	
	→	

Planning and Organizing

Here are some sentences that Kristen wrote about lemurs. Circle the part of the sentence that tells the cause. Underline the part that shows the effect.

1. Lemurs are losing their habitat because people cut down trees for farming.
2. Some people hunt lemurs because they are afraid of them.
3. Every year there are fewer lemurs because they are hunted for food.

Name ______________________ Date __________

Revising and Proofreading

Here is part of Kristen's explanation. She made six capitalization mistakes. Find the mistakes and correct them.

Lemurs live on madagascar and the comoro islands. These are islands off the coast of africa. Before humans arrived, there were many species of Lemurs. over time, at least fourteen species became extinct.

Drafting

Write a sentence to begin your explanation. Tell the name of the animal and your main idea about it.

____

____

Now write your explanation. Use a separate piece of paper. Begin with your topic sentence. Include facts and details to explain how the animal became endangered. End by telling what scientists are doing to save this animal.

Revising and Proofreading

Now revise and proofread your writing. Ask yourself:

- ▶ Did I explain how the animal became endangered?
- ▶ Did I tell what scientists are doing to save it?
- ▶ Did I correct all mistakes?

Name ______________________ Date __________

LESSON
Outline

How Animals Change

Use your textbook to help you fill in the blanks.

What are the stages of an animal's life?

1. All animals have a life cycle that follows a pattern of ______________________, growth, ______________________, and death.

2. The life span of an animal can range from a few days to many ______________________.

3. Organisms usually live long enough to reproduce and take care of their ______________________.

What is metamorphosis?

4. The process of ______________________ includes a set of separate and completely different growth stages.

5. Incomplete metamorphosis includes separate ______________________ stages that are not very different. Complete metamorphosis includes growth stages that are ______________________ at every stage.

How do animals reproduce?

6. All animals come from another animal, called a(n) ______________________.

7. Some animals are born ______________________, and some ______________________ from eggs.

Name ____________________ Date __________

8. Budding and regeneration are types of ____________ reproduction.

9. Organisms that reproduce with one parent produce exact copies, or ____________ .

10. In two-parent reproduction, a male sperm cell and a female egg cell combine during ____________ and produce a(n) ____________ .

What is inherited?

11. Traits such as eye color, height, and body color are determined by ____________ before an organism is born.

12. Parents pass on ____________ to their ____________, but other behaviors are learned.

Critical Thinking

13. Which kind of animal do you think would have a longer normal life span: one that had mostly inherited behaviors or one that had mostly learned behaviors? Why?

____

____

____

____

____

____

How Animals Change

What am I?

Choose the letter that matches the word from the box below to answer each question, and write the correct letter in the space provided.

a. clone	**d.** instinct	**g.** life span
b. heredity	**e.** learned behavior	**h.** metamorphosis
c. inherited behavior	**f.** life cycle	

1. ________ I am the stages through which an animal passes, including birth and death. What am I?

2. ________ I am the length of time that an organism is expected to live. What am I?

3. ________ I am the process that gives some animals very different body forms as they grow. What am I?

4. ________ I am the offspring of only one parent. I am an exact copy of my parent. What am I?

5. ________ I control the traits that are passed on from parent to offspring. What am I?

6. ________ I am the behavior with which an organism is born. What am I?

7. ________ I am a behavior that an organism gains from experience. What am I?

8. ________ I am an example of inherited behavior. What am I?

Name ______________________ Date __________

How Animals Change

Use the words from the box to fill in the blanks.

birth	growth	metamorphosis	separate
gradual	life span	produce	

All animals go through stages that make up the life cycle. These stages include ______________, ______________, reproduction, and death. The amount of time an animal is expected to live is called its ______________. An animal is expected to live long enough to ______________ offspring.

The stages of growth can be ______________ or ______________ and different, a process called ______________. The life cycle of every animal begins with birth and ends with death.

Name ____________________ Date __________

Meet Christopher Raxworthy

Read the passage in your textbook. Look for information about the Mantella poison frog and dwarf dead leaf chameleon.

Write About It

Compare and Contrast How does the life cycle of the Mantella poison frog compare to the life cycle of the dwarf dead leaf chameleon?

Compare and Contrast

Fill in the Compare and Contrast graphic organizer. Tell how the frog and the chameleon are alike and how they are different. Then, answer the question in the box above on a separate piece of paper.

Frog	Chameleon	Frog and Chameleon
Its body has vivid colors to warn ____________.	Its body resembles a(n) ____________.	Babies hatch from ____________.
Females lay eggs in ____________ areas.	The animal hides during the day in dead leaves on the ____________.	Frogs and chameleons become ____________ in about ____________.
Eggs hatch when it ____________.	Females lay eggs in ____________.	
Tadpoles move to a nearby ____________.	Eggs hatch in ____________ weeks.	

Name ______________________ Date ____________

Compare and Contrast

Read the paragraph below. Compare and contrast the work of Christopher Raxworthy and the scientists in Madagascar with that of the scientists at the San Diego National Wildlife Refuge.

San Diego National Wildlife Refuge

In the 1990s, the people of San Diego began working with government groups to help protect the environment. A wildlife refuge was created. The goals of the San Diego refuge include preserving endangered species and helping endangered species increase in number. The refuge protects all the wildlife native to the area, not just the endangered species. It also protects the habitats of migratory birds. The refuge provides visitors with opportunities to learn about wildlife.

Write About It

Write a short paragraph in which you compare and contrast the goals of Christopher Raxworthy and the other scientists in Madagascar with those of the scientists at the San Diego Refuge Complex.

____

____

____

____

____

Animal Kingdom

Circle the letter of the best answer.

1. An animal that lives part of its life in water and part of it on land is

a. an amphibian.

b. a reptile.

c. a mammal.

d. a fish.

2. What is an arthropod?

a. an invertebrate with a spiny skin that lives in the ocean

b. an invertebrate that remains anchored to one spot

c. an invertebrate that lives inside the body of another animal

d. an invertebrate with jointed legs and a body divided into sections

3. The only warm-blooded animals with a body covering of feathers are

a. snakes.

b. birds.

c. mammals.

d. fish.

4. One trait that all mammals share is

a. having hair or fur.

b. giving birth to live young.

c. holding young in pouches.

d. being cold-blooded.

5. An organism that is produced by only one parent organism is called

a. an egg.

b. an embryo.

c. a clone.

d. a seed.

6. The passing of traits from parents to their offspring is known as

a. cloning.

b. heredity.

c. instinct.

d. behavior.

Name ______________________ Date ____________

Circle the letter of the best answer.

7. A cold-blooded animal

a. cannot control its body temperature.

b. can control its body temperature.

c. uses the food it eats to make heat energy.

d. has a short life span.

8. What is an instinct?

a. a learned behavior

b. a learned trait

c. an inherited behavior

d. an inherited trait

9. Which of these animals goes through complete metamorphosis?

a. ants and spiders

b. earthworms and damselflies

c. grasshoppers and termites

d. mealworms and butterflies

10. A hard protective outer covering that keeps in moisture is

a. an endoskeleton.

b. an exoskeleton.

c. a backbone.

d. a scale.

11. If an animal's body parts match around a point or central line, that animal has

a. endoskeleton.

b. symmetry.

c. exoskeleton.

d. instinct.

12. Animals are classified as vertebrates if they

a. do not have a backbone.

b. have a backbone.

c. can move.

d. live on land.

Name ______________________ Date ____________

Living Things in Their Environments

Ecosystems

contain living factors known as ____________

Examples of ____________ factors are:

1. ____________
2. ____________
3. microorganisms

can be broken down into six different ____________

The six ____________ are:

1. ____________
2. ____________
3. tropical rain forest
4. ____________
5. ____________
6. desert

go through changes

Change can be caused by:

1. natural events
2. ____________
3. ____________

contain nonliving factors known as ____________

Examples of ____________ factors are:

1. ____________
2. ____________
3. ____________
4. ____________
5. ____________

Name ______________________ Date ____________

Introduction to Ecosystems

Use your textbook to help you fill in the blanks.

What is an ecosystem?

1. All the living and nonliving things in the ______________________ make up a(n) ______________ .
2. Plants, animals, and microorganisms are the living things, or ______________________ , in an environment.
3. Water, rocks, and soil are some of the nonliving things, or ______________________ , in an environment.
4. Ecosystems can be very large or ______________________ .
5. Living and nonliving things in an ecosystem ______________________ on each other to survive.
6. The place in an ecosystem in which each organism lives is that organism's ______________________ .
7. Different ecosystems have ______________________ types of habitats.

What is a food web?

8. Energy passes from one organism to another in a(n) ______________________ .
9. Animals that ______________________ other animals are predators. The animals they eat are prey. Some animals are ______________________ predator and prey.

10. Animals and plants ______________ against each other to obtain food, water, and other things they need. That struggle is called competition.

What are populations and communities?

11. Ecosystems have different ______________ of species.

12. All the populations in an ecosystem make up a(n) ______________.

13. Different ecosystems have different communities of ______________ things.

14. Warm and wet ecosystems usually have larger communities than ______________ and ______________ ecosystems.

Critical Thinking

15. What do you think is the most important factor affecting the size of a community in an ecosystem?

____

____

____

____

____

____

____

Name ______________________ Date ____________

Introduction to Ecosystems

Read each clue. Write the answer in the blank and fill in the crossword puzzle.

Across

1. members of one kind of organism in an ecosystem

____

5. all of the populations in an ecosystem

____

6. every living thing's place to live in an ecosystem

____

8. typical weather pattern in an environment

____

Down

2. the nonliving factors of an ecosystem, such as rocks

____

3. all the living and nonliving things in an environment

____

4. how all food chains in an ecosystem are connected

____

7. the living factors of an ecosystem, such as plants

____

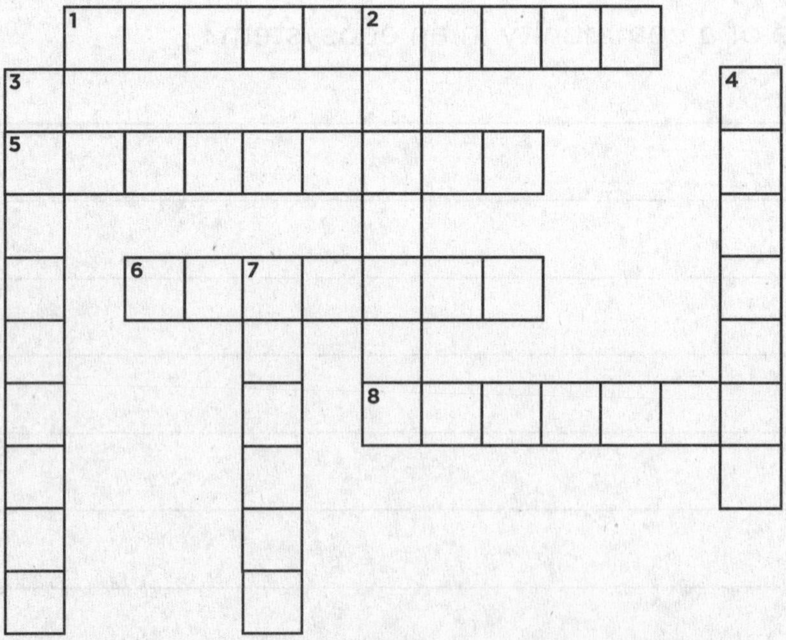

Name ______________________________ Date ____________

Introduction to Ecosystems

Use the words in the box to fill in the blanks.

abiotic factors	dry	moist
biotic factors	ecosystem	small
climates	habitats	

All the living and nonliving things in an area make up the environment. The living things, such as plants and animals, are called ____________________. Nonliving things, such as water and soil, are called ____________________. The biotic and abiotic factors in an environment work together to form a(n) ____________________.

Ecosystems can be large or ____________________. They can also have very different ____________________. Some ecosystems are hot and ____________________, and others are cold and wet. Ecosystems that are warm and ____________________ tend to have more organisms living in them. Different ecosystems have ____________________ that are suited to different types of living things. For example, a desert community is suited to cactuses and lizards.

Name ______________________________ Date ____________

Biomes

Use your textbook to help you fill in the blanks.

What is a biome?

1. A large ecosystem with a unique set of characteristics is called a(n) ________________________ .

2. Some biomes can be found only in certain places on ______________________ , while others can stretch across an entire ________________________ .

What are grasslands and forests?

3. A biome whose plant life includes mostly grasses growing in its ________________________ soil is a(n) ________________________ .

4. During hot, dry summers, ________________________ burn, and this produces rich soil for farming.

5. Oaks and maples in ________________________ forests lose their leaves each year.

6. The ________________________ has three distinct levels where a(n) ________________________ of organisms live.

What are deserts, taiga, and tundra?

7. Cactuses and yucca plants survive in the ________________________ , where the temperature gets as high as ________________________ and as low as ________________________ .

8. Black bears and fir trees live in the ________________________ , the largest biome in the world.

9. The tundra is home to mammals that ____________ or leave during winter and plants that grow close to the frozen ____________ .

Are there water biomes?

10. Earth has two main water ecosystems: ____________ and ____________ .

11. Freshwater ecosystems include lakes, ponds, rivers, ____________ , and some ____________ .

12. Saltwater ecosystems differ by the water's ____________ , and ____________ from shore.

Critical Thinking

13. Why do you think so many different organisms live in the tropical rain forest?

____

____

____

____

____

____

____

____

____

Name ______________________ Date __________

Biomes

Match the correct word to its description by writing its letter in the space provided.

a. biome	**d.** grassland	**g.** tundra
b. deciduous forest	**e.** taiga	
c. desert	**f.** tropical rain forest	

1. ________ This is one of six major ecosystems that has its own special plants, animals, soil, and climate.

2. ________ This biome, such as a prairie, has fertile soil and enough rain for grasses but not enough rain for trees to grow.

3. ________ Many trees in this biome lose their leaves every year in autumn.

4. ________ This biome is located near the equator. It is hot and humid year round. It is home to a large variety of plants and animals.

5. ________ Earth's northern regions are the location of this forest biome. Its plant life includes large numbers of conifers.

6. ________ This hot, dry biome gets little rain and has few varieties of plant and animal life.

7. ________ The ground is frozen year round in this harsh biome.

Biomes

Use the words in the box to fill in the blanks.

biomes	harsh	taiga
characteristics	hot	tropical rain forest
cold	organisms	
deciduous forest	populations	

Earth has six major ecosystems. These ecosystems, also known as ____________________, have their own ____________________, including temperature, precipitation, and soil. Each biome also has a special community made up of different ____________________ of plants and animals.

Three of the biomes, the grassland, ____________________, and ____________________, have a climate suitable to a variety of ____________________. The other three biomes have ____________________ conditions. The ____________________ and tundra have very ____________________ environments. Deserts have very ____________________, dry environments. There are fewer plants and animals in these three biomes.

Name ______________________________ Date ____________

Museum Mail Call

Read the selection from your textbook. Look for information about how building affects an ecosystem. On a separate piece of paper, write the sentences that state facts about the mangrove swamp.

Write About It

Draw Conclusions What might happen to the plants and animals of Florida's wetlands if people continue to build there?

Fill in the Draw Conclusions graphic organizer about the mangrove swamp.

My Prediction	What Happens
Many mangroves are being replaced by stores, ____________, and parking lots.	Cutting down the mangrove trees will change the ____________.
The mangroves are home to many ____________.	Loss of the mangroves will affect the population of the ____________.
Mangrove roots provide shelter for ____________.	Animals will have to find a new habitat, and some species may not ____________.
The mangroves protect the ____________ from wind, waves, and floods.	The coast will not be protected from winds, waves, and ____________.

Reread Tommy's message. If you were one of the museum's scientists, how would Tommy's note help you? What would you and other museum scientists do to keep the mangroves safe? How would you protect the plants and animals that live in the mangroves? Write an informative response to Tommy and answer his question.

TO: Tommy
FROM: American Museum of Natural History
SUBJECT: Save the Mangroves!
Dear Tommy,

LESSON **Outline**

Name ______________________ Date ____________

Animal Adaptations

Use your textbook to help you fill in the blanks.

What are adaptations?

1. Survival is not easy for organisms, because each ecosystem has special ______________.

2. Organisms have traits or ______________ that help them survive in their environments.

3. Physical (body) traits and ______________ are two kinds of adaptations that help animals to survive.

4. Organisms that live in desert ecosystems have adaptations for staying ______________ and saving ______________.

5. The fennec fox has large ears that give off ______________ and thin ______________ that helps it stay cool.

6. Kangaroo rats survive in the desert because they get water from the ______________ they eat.

7. Camels have humps to store fat for ______________, and they have ______________ to walk on sand.

What are some other adaptations of animals?

8. Animals can avoid cold winters by ______________ or by leaving the area until the weather gets warmer.

9. Some animals have adaptations, such as the ______________ on a hedgehog, to protect themselves from ______________ .

10. Some animals ______________ themselves and blend in with the colors and shapes in their environments.

11. Hover flies use ______________ to look like other, more dangerous organisms.

How do animals sense changes?

12. Animals have ______________ systems that let them control their bodies.

13. Invertebrates have a simple nervous system, but the ones in vertebrates are more ______________ .

14. With this system, animals can use their ______________ , such as sight and smell, to learn about their surroundings.

Critical Thinking

15. An animal has large, flat teeth good for chewing tough plants; brown fur; and the ability to run fast. In which biome would these adaptations be useful? Why?

____

____

____

____

____

____

Name ______________________________ Date ____________

Animal Adaptations

Choose a word or words from the box below that completes each statement, and write the correct words in the space provided.

adaptation	hibernate	nervous system	prey
camouflage	mimicry	predators	

1. Some animals have traits that they use to protect themselves from ______________________ .
2. Some organisms "copy" the traits of other living things in their environment. This adaptation is called ______________________ .
3. The brain is an important part of a mammal's ______________________ .
4. Any trait that helps an organism survive in its environment is called a(n) ______________________ .
5. Animals that serve as food for other animals are called ______________________ .
6. The fur of an arctic fox changes color so it can blend into its environment. This adaptation is called ______________________ .
7. Some animals survive the cold winter because they are able to remain completely still for a long period of time, or to ______________________ .

Name ______________________ Date ____________

LESSON
Cloze Activity

Animal Adaptations

Use the words in the box to fill in the blanks.

adaptations	behavior	challenges	different	predators
avoid	camouflage	colors	mimicry	survive

All ecosystems present challenges to the organisms that live there. Living things have different ____________________ that make them better suited to the ____________________ in their environments and help them ____________________ .

Survival in ____________________ environments requires different adaptations. An organism with ____________________ can hide from ____________________ because it blends in with the ____________________ and shapes of its environment. An organism that has ____________________ is copying the physical traits and ____________________ of other organisms that predators usually ____________________ . Different animals have different adaptations and different behaviors, but all of them have the same goal—survival.

LESSON **Outline**

Name ______________________ Date ____________

Plants and Their Surroundings

Use your textbook to help you fill in the blanks.

How do plants respond to their environment?

1. Plants respond to their ____________________ in many different ways.
2. Something in the environment that causes a living thing to respond is called a(n) ____________________.
3. The response of a plant to a stimulus is called ____________________.
4. A plant reacts to a stimulus by changing its ____________________ or ____________________ of growth.
5. Plant stems that grow upward ____________________ a source of light and plant ____________________ that grow toward a source of water are examples of tropisms.
6. Plant roots also grow downward because of the pull of ____________________.
7. The green ____________________ of plants grow ____________________, opposite the pull of gravity.

What are some plant adaptations?

8. Plants have ____________________ that help them ____________________ in different environments.

9. A cactus in the desert has adaptations for saving ______________________, such as spongy tissue inside and a very ______________________, waxy outer skin.

10. Some trees lose their ______________________ every winter because cold weather can ______________________ the leaves.

11. The trees live on ______________________ food until spring, when new leaves grow and the plant makes food again.

Critical Thinking

12. What do you think would happen to trees if their leaves did not fall off before winter?

____

____

____

____

____

____

____

____

____

____

____

Name ______________________ Date __________

Plants and Their Surroundings

Choose a word from the box below that completes each statement, and write the correct word in the space provided.

adaptation	light	tropism	water
energy	stimulus	upward	

1. A tree that loses its leaves in the fall survives during the winter by living on stored food for ______________.

2. A cactus has spongy tissue inside for storage and a very thick, waxy skin on the outside to prevent loss of ______________.

3. A trait that helps a plant survive in its environment is called a(n) ______________.

4. Anything in the environment that causes a plant to react, such as chemicals, heat, gravity, or water, is called a(n) ______________.

5. The reaction of plants to any stimulus is called ______________.

6. Some stimuli that affect plants are heat, gravity, water, and ______________.

7. A plant responds to gravity in two ways: its roots grow downward, and its green stems grow ______________.

Name ______________________ Date ____________

LESSON
Cloze Activity

Plants and Their Surroundings

Use the words in the box to fill in the blanks.

adaptations	leaves	tropisms
direction	light	water
ecosystem	respond	
food	stimulus	

Plants, like animals, have traits that help them survive in their environments. Plants in a desert ____________ have ____________ for storing ____________. Deciduous trees lose their ____________ in the fall. They live on stored ____________ until the leaves grow back in the spring.

Plants cannot move, but they can ____________ to stimuli. All plant responses are called ____________. A plant can react to a(n) ____________ by changing its ____________ or pattern of growth. Plant roots respond to water, and plant stems respond to ____________ sources. Plant roots also respond to the pull of gravity.

Name ______________________ Date ___________

A Field of Sun

Write About It

Descriptive Writing Do some research about another plant. Write a description of how this plant reacts to its environment.

Getting Ideas

First, choose a plant. Write its name in the center circle in the web below. Do some research. Write details you find about this plant in the outer circles.

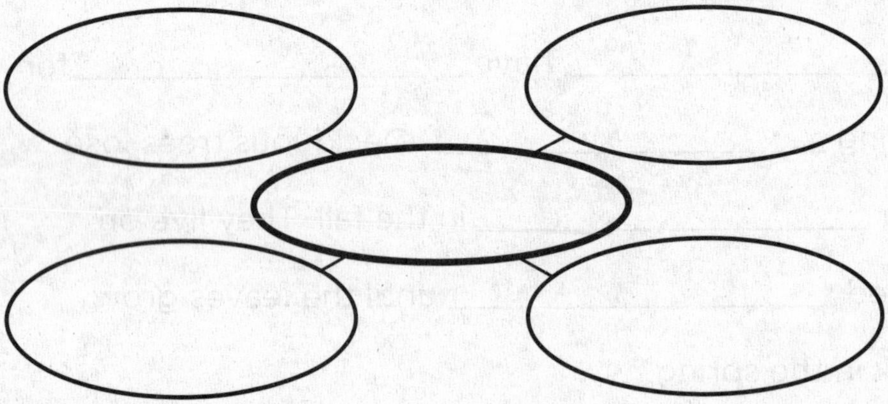

Planning and Organizing

Alberto decided to describe the saguaro cactus. Here are some sentences he wrote. Identify the sense to which the details in the sentence appeal. The five senses are sight, hearing, taste, smell, and touch.

1. ______________ The saguaro cactus has a smooth, waxy skin.

2. ______________ It has pretty white flowers with yellow centers.

3. ______________ The cactus makes a sweet nectar.

Name ______________________ Date ____________

Drafting

Write a sentence to begin your description. Tell what plant you are writing about.

____

Now write your description. Use a separate piece of paper. Begin with the sentence you wrote above. Use vivid details and sensory words to describe the plant.

Revising and Proofreading

Here is part of Alberto's description. He left out some sensory words. Choose words from the box or pick your own. Write them in the blanks.

hot	massive	spiny	white

The saguaro cactus stood alone in the middle of the ______________ desert. Its long ______________ arms seemed to reach for the Sun. Its ______________ stem was about 20 inches in diameter. Its beautiful ______________ flowers waited for the Sun to go down. Then they bloomed.

Now revise and proofread your writing. Ask yourself:

- Did I describe how a plant responds to the Sun?
- Did I include details and sensory words?
- Did I correct all mistakes?

Name ______________________ Date ____________

Changes in Environments

Use your textbook to help you fill in the blanks.

What causes an ecosystem to change?

1. Environments do not remain the same. They are always ________________.
2. Some changes make it difficult for plants and animals to ________________.
3. Some changes are long lasting, such as those caused by a volcano, hurricane, ________________, or fire.
4. Living things can change a(n) ________________ in ways that can be ________________ or harmful.

How do people change ecosystems?

5. Some changes that people make to ecosystems are helpful, and some are ________________.
6. Building roads, homes, and shopping malls affects an ecosystem by destroying the ________________ of other living things.
7. Some examples of how people change ecosystems are ________________, overpopulation, and ________________.

Name ______________________ Date ____________

LESSON
Outline

What happens when ecosystems change?

8. Some living things survive changes by changing their ____________ and habits.

9. An individual organism's response to changes is called a(n) ____________.

10. When an entire kind of organism cannot adapt and most of its members have died, it is ____________.

When no members are left, it is ____________.

How can people prevent extinction?

11. Scientists try to keep animals from becoming endangered or ____________ by ____________ places where they live.

Critical Thinking

12. Why do you think birds and other small animals might move to an alligator hole even if an alligator might eat them?

____

____

____

____

____

____

Name ______________________ Date ____________

Changes in Environments

What am I?

Choose a word from the box below that answers each question, and write the correct letter in the space provided.

a. accommodation	**c.** endangered	**e.** overpopulation
b. deforestation	**d.** extinction	**f.** pollution

1. ________ I am the name for a kind of organism that only has a small number of members left alive and is in danger of dying out. What am I?

2. ________ I make the air, land, or water in an ecosystem dirty and unsafe. What am I?

3. ________ I am what happens when a forest is cut down to make room for roads and buildings. What am I?

4. ________ I am the result of more and more living things moving into an ecosystem, taking up more space, and using more resources. What am I?

5. ________ I am what happens to an entire kind of organism when its last member dies. What am I?

6. ________ I am the ability of some living things to survive changes in an ecosystem by changing their behavior and habits. What am I?

Name ______________________ Date ____________

Changes in Environments

Use the words in the box to fill in the blanks.

accommodation	helpful	pollution
adapt	hurricane	protecting
harmful	natural	short term

Environments are always changing. An ecosystem can be changed by ____________ events, like a volcano, drought, or ____________ . These changes can be ____________ or long lasting. Living things can also affect ecosystems. Swarms of locusts have a(n) ____________ effect, but alligators can have a(n) ____________ effect. People can harm an ecosystem with ____________ , or help it by ____________ its resources.

When ecosystems are changed, organisms survive by changing their habits and behaviors through ____________ . If a type of organism cannot ____________ , its members die out. If all of the members die out, that plant or animal becomes extinct.

Name ______________________ Date __________

Mail Call

In your textbook, read the letter Clara wrote to the museum scientists. Write the sentence that describes the sudden event that caused the change in the chaparral.

____

____

Write the sentences that Clara uses to describe the changes in the chaparral.

1. ____
2. ____
3. ____
4. ____

____

Write About It

Predict Read the letter again. Predict what the chaparral will be like next year. What might happen to the environment if there is a drought? Write your predictions in the form of a paragraph.

Name ______________________ Date ____________

Predict

Complete the graphic organizer below. Given the predictions shown, tell what you think will happen.

Prediction	What Will Happen
Another drought will occur during summer.	
Another wildfire will occur in the chaparral environment next year because of the lack of rain in summer.	
Seeds from monkey flower and scarlet larkspur will burn in the wildfires.	
Fields of wildflowers will grow.	
Shrubs and bushes will grow.	

Now write a paragraph describing what might happen if a drought were to affect the chaparral next year.

____

____

____

____

Name ______________________ Date ____________

Living Things in Their Environments

Circle the letter of the best answer.

1. An animal that blends into the colors and shapes of its environment shows
   - **a.** accommodation.
   - **b.** hibernation.
   - **c.** mimicry.
   - **d.** camouflage.

2. All the pine trees in a forest make up a group of organisms called
   - **a.** a community.
   - **b.** an ecosystem.
   - **c.** a habitat.
   - **d.** a population.

3. Which of the following is NOT a biome?
   - **a.** desert
   - **b.** mountain
   - **c.** tropical rain forest
   - **d.** taiga

4. Animals that struggle for the same resources are involved in
   - **a.** adaptation.
   - **b.** competition.
   - **c.** migration.
   - **d.** protection.

5. Some animals save energy during winter by
   - **a.** hibernating.
   - **b.** accommodating.
   - **c.** stimulating.
   - **d.** camouflaging.

6. Cutting down an entire forest to build roads or buildings is called
   - **a.** accommodation.
   - **b.** adaptation.
   - **c.** deforestation.
   - **d.** deconstruction.

Circle the letter of the best answer.

7. Some organisms look like other, more dangerous organisms, which is called

a. response.

b. mimicry.

c. camouflage.

d. accommodation.

8. Some animals survive a change in their environment by changing their behaviors or habits. This is called

a. accommodation.

b. adaptation.

c. adjustment.

d. acceptance.

9. When all of its members have died, a kind of plant or animal is

a. environmental.

b. endangered.

c. in the ecosystem.

d. extinct.

10. Any harmful substance that enters the air, water, or land can cause

a. overcrowding.

b. pollution.

c. extinction.

d. danger.

11. A food web shows how the organisms in an ecosystem are

a. different sizes and shapes.

b. connected by the need for energy.

c. sharing the same habitats.

d. similar in their adaptations.

12. Which of these biomes has the richest variety of life?

a. deciduous rain forest

b. grassland

c. tropical rain forest

d. tundra

13. Which group of animals has the simplest nervous system?

a. birds

b. fish

c. invertebrates

d. mammals

Name ______________________ Date __________

The Story Goes On

Read the Literature feature in your textbook.

Write About It

Response to Literature The poet brings to life a sequence of events that happens every day in nature. What do you think the poet is describing? Write a story that tells what might happen next.

Name ______________________________ Date ____________

LESSON
Cloze Activity

Earth and Sun

Use the words in the box to fill in the blanks.

axis	plants	seasons	summer
Earth	revolution	Southern	Sun
energy	rotation	stored	sunlight

Earth spins every 24 hours. This ______________________ causes day and night. It is day on the part of Earth facing the ______________________ , and in 12 hours, it will be night.

Earth also completes a(n) ______________________ around the Sun. Because ______________________ is revolving on a tilted ______________________ , there are ______________________ . During the ______________________ , the Sun's rays hit the Earth at steep angles and the light is bright. In winter, ______________________ reaches Earth at a low angle. The seasons in the ______________________ Hemisphere are the opposite to those in the Northern Hemisphere.

The Sun is the source of all ______________________ on Earth. This includes the energy produced by ______________________ and the energy ______________________ in fossil fuels. The Sun also controls much of Earth's weather.

Name ______________________________ Date ____________

Without the Sun

Write About It

Fictional Story Write your own story about what would happen if sunlight could not reach Earth.

Getting Ideas

First

Next

Last

Planning and Organizing

A good story has characters, a setting, and a plot. Justin wrote three notes to plan his story. Write Character next to the note that mainly describes the character. Write Plot next to the note that mainly describes the plot. Write Setting next to the note that mainly describes the setting.

Note 1. ______________________ It is the year 5002, and total darkness has covered Planet Earth.

Note 2. ______________________ Professor Jamison is a scientist. Her specialty is the Sun.

Note 3. ______________________ Professor Jamison and her staff are trying to find out why Earth is suddenly in total darkness.

Name ______________________ Date ___________

Revising and Proofreading

Here are some sentences that Justin wrote. He needs to include descriptive details. Choose a word from the box. Write it on the line.

black	brilliant	chilly	total

At first, there was a hint of darkness. The air became ______________ . Then, suddenly, there was ______________ darkness. The sky had been a ______________ blue. Now it was as ______________ as the darkest ink.

Drafting

Begin your story. Start with an exciting sentence to get the reader interested.

____

____

Continue your story. Use a separate piece of paper. Include details that tell about the main character and the setting. Make sure your story tells what would happen if sunlight didn't reach Earth.

Now revise and proofread your writing. Ask yourself:

- Did I write an interesting beginning, middle, and end?
- Did I describe the characters and the setting?
- Did I correct all mistakes?

LESSON **Outline**

Name ______________________ Date ____________

Earth and Moon

What is the Moon like?

1. Moonlight is reflected light from the ______________.
2. Earth's closest neighbor in space is the ______________.
3. The Moon has ______________ similar to those on Earth but no ______________ and little ______________.
4. Temperatures on the Moon can be both ______________ than any place on Earth.
5. The Moon's surface is covered by ______________ made by ______________.

What are the phases of the Moon?

6. The Moon orbits Earth once every ______________ days.
7. At any given time, the Sun lights ______________ of the Moon.
8. As the Moon orbits Earth, we see different parts of it lit as it cycles through ______________.
9. Earth is between the Moon and the Sun during the ______________ Moon.

What is an eclipse?

10. During a(n) ______________ eclipse, Earth casts a shadow on the Moon.

Name ______________________ Date ____________

11. During a(n) ____________________ eclipse, the Moon casts a shadow on Earth.

12. A solar eclipse happens only when there is a(n) ____________________ .

What causes the tides?

13. The pull of the Moon's gravity causes ____________________ to bulge on opposite sides of Earth. Those bulges cause ____________________ .

14. When the gravity of the Sun and Moon pull in the same direction, tides are higher than normal. These are called ____________________ , and they happen about twice a month.

15. Tides are lower than normal when the Sun and Moon's gravity pull in ____________________ directions. These are ____________________ .

Critical Thinking

16. Which do you think occurs more often, a partial solar eclipse or a total solar eclipse? Explain your reasoning.

____

____

____

____

____

____

LESSON
Vocabulary

Name ______________________ Date ____________

Earth and Moon

Use the words in the box to fill in the blanks.

crater	meteoroids	phases	tides
lunar eclipse	new Moon	solar eclipse	waning Moon

1. Ocean ________________ are caused by the pull of the Moon's gravity on Earth.

2. The apparent shapes of the Moon in the sky are called its ________________ .

3. The Moon casts a shadow on Earth during a(n) ________________ .

4. A hollow pit in the ground is called a(n) ________________ .

5. When the lighted side of the Moon faces away from Earth, it is called a(n) ________________ .

6. Large rocks that fall from space are called ________________ .

7. When less and less of the lighted side of the Moon becomes visible each night, it is a(n) ________________ .

8. Earth casts a shadow on the Moon during a(n) ________________ .

Earth and Moon

Use the words in the box to fill in the blanks.

Earth	high	spring tides
full Moon	new Moon	Sun
gravity	shadow	tides

The Moon orbits Earth once every 29 days. When the Moon and the Sun are on the same side of Earth, the part of the Moon that is in ________________ faces Earth. This phase of the Moon is called the ________________. When the Moon is on the opposite side of ________________ from the Sun, we see the brightly shining ________________.

The Moon's ________________ causes the changes in the levels of the ocean, which we call ________________. When the part of the ocean nearest the Moon bulges, that part of the ocean has ________________ tide. About twice a month, the ________________ and Moon pull on Earth's oceans in the same direction. This causes ________________, which are higher than normal. Neap tides occur about twice a month, too, and bring lower than normal tides.

Name ______________________ Date ____________

The Solar System

What is the solar system?

1. Each planet revolves around the Sun in an orbit shaped like a(n) ____________________ .
2. Newton discovered that the balance between gravity and ____________________ keeps the planets in orbit.
3. In the 1500s, ____________________ proposed that the planets revolve around the Sun.

How do we learn about the solar system?

4. Telescopes use ____________________ or radio waves to view objects in space.
5. Rockets launched by NASA allowed astronauts to explore ____________________ .
6. The United States worked with other countries to build the ____________________ , which can stay in space for a long time.
7. A crewless ship that carries data-recording equipment into space is called a(n) ____________________ .

What are the rocky planets?

8. Earth, Mars, ____________________ , and Venus are closest to the Sun and are called the rocky planets.
9. The atmosphere of Venus is made of ____________________ .

What are the other planets?

10. The four gas giants lie beyond ____________________ .

11. All of these planets are made mostly of hydrogen and ____________________ .

12. The largest planet is ____________________ , and the next largest is ____________________ .

What else is in our solar system?

13. When comets get close to the Sun, they form a(n) ____________________ of gas and dust.

14. Most asteroids lie in a belt between ____________________ and ____________________ .

Critical Thinking

15. What other planet would you like to live on? What do you think would be the hardest thing to get used to?

____

____

____

____

____

____

____

____

LESSON
Vocabulary

Name ____________________ Date __________

The Solar System

What am I?

Choose a word from the word box below that answers each question, and write the correct letter in the space provided.

a. asteroid	**c.** gravity	**e.** meteorite	**g.** solar system
b. comet	**d.** meteor	**f.** planet	**h.** telescope

1. ________ I am the Sun and all of the objects that orbit it. What am I?

2. ________ I am one of the eight largest objects orbiting the Sun. What am I?

3. ________ I am an invisible pulling force that keeps the planets in orbit around the Sun. What am I?

4. ________ I can make distant objects appear to be closer. What am I?

5. ________ I am a chunk of ice mixed with rocks and dust. I travel around the Sun in a long, narrow orbit. What am I?

6. ________ I am made of chunks of rock or metal. I lie in a belt between Mars and Jupiter. What am I?

7. ________ I am a meteoroid that falls into Earth's atmosphere and burns up. What am I?

8. ________ I am a meteoroid that strikes Earth's surface. What am I?

Name ______________________ Date ____________

The Solar System

Use the words in the box to fill in the blanks.

comets	gas giants	Neptune	Venus
Earth	hydrogen	planets	
ellipses	Jupiter	rocky	

The solar system consists of an average star, called the Sun, and all of the objects that revolve around it. These include eight ______________, many moons, and several smaller bodies, such as asteroids and ______________.

The ______________ planets are ______________, Mercury, ______________, and Mars. They are closer to the Sun and are made mostly of rock. The planets known as ______________ include ______________, Saturn, Uranus, and ______________. All of these are made mostly of ______________ and helium. The orbits of the planets are shaped like ______________. Earth is the only planet in our solar system that has what living things need to survive.

Name ______________________ Date __________

To the Moon!

How have scientists explored our solar system? What scientists learn about the Moon may help them explore planets and other solar system objects.

Write About It

Main Idea and Details Reread the introduction and the captions on the time line. Then write a paragraph that explains the main idea and details of this article. Be sure to include facts and examples in your paragraph.

Main Idea and Details

Fill in the Main Idea and Details Chart using information you find in the introduction and captions of the reading feature.

Main Idea	Details

Name ______________________ Date ____________

Planning and Organizing

Answer these questions in more detail.

1. What was the first spacecraft to travel in space, and when was it launched?

____

2. What spacecraft was the first to land a person on the Moon, and when did this happen?

____

____

3. What was the last manned spacecraft to travel to the Moon, and when was it launched?

____

____

Drafting

Explain how people first learned about the far side of the Moon.

____

____

Are scientists still studying the Moon? Why?

____

____

____

____

Name ______________________ Date ____________

The Solar System and Beyond

Circle the letter of the best answer.

1. When the North Pole is tilted toward the Sun, it is

a. summer in the Northern Hemisphere.

b. winter in the Northern Hemisphere.

c. daytime in the Northern Hemisphere.

d. nighttime in the Northern Hemisphere.

2. When Earth is between the Moon and Sun, we see a

a. half Moon.

b. full Moon.

c. new Moon.

d. gibbous Moon.

3. A partial solar eclipse occurs during the

a. full-Moon phase.

b. new-Moon phase.

c. gibbous-Moon phase.

d. half-Moon phase.

4. The largest bodies that orbit the Sun are called

a. asteroids.

b. comets.

c. meteors.

d. planets.

5. The shape of Earth's orbit is

a. a circle.

b. an ellipse.

c. a rectangle.

d. a triangle.

6. The Sun seems to move from east to west each day because of

a. Earth's rotation.

b. the eclipse effect.

c. the Moon's rotation.

d. the Sun's phases.

7. Which of these is NOT a fossil fuel?

a. coal

b. gas

c. oil

d. wood

Name ______________________ Date ____________

CHAPTER
Vocabulary

Circle the letter of the best answer.

8. Space craft that do not carry people but explore other worlds are called

a. astronauts.
b. probes.
c. radio telescopes.
d. rockets.

9. The Moon has more craters than Earth because it has no

a. atmosphere.
b. mountains.
c. plains.
d. water.

10. What is the name for the lowest tides, which occur when the Sun and Moon pull on the oceans in opposite directions?

a. crescent tides
b. gibbous tides
c. neap tides
d. spring tides

11. Which of the following is a chunk of ice mixed with rocks and dust?

a. comet
b. asteroid
c. meteoroid
d. meteorite

12. Which planet has a pole pointed toward the Sun?

a. Saturn
b. Uranus
c. Mars
d. Neptune

13. Besides Earth, which other planet has ice caps?

a. Venus
b. Mars
c. Mercury
d. Uranus

14. Which star is closest to Earth?

a. Sirius
b. Proxima C
c. Ross 154
d. Sun

Name ______________________ Date ______________

Weather and Climate

Complete the concept map about weather and climate. Some parts have been done for you.

Properties of Weather

Temperature: how hot or cold air is

______________ : how much water vapor in air

Air pressure: downward

____

Measuring Weather

Thermometer: measures temperature

______________ : measures air pressure

Hygrometer: measures

____

______________ : shows amount of rainfall

Weather and Climate

Climate

Climate: ______________ of weather over time

______________ : near the equator, warm and humid

______________ : between poles and equator,

four ______________

Weather

Air masses: similar

____

______________ : form where air masses meet

Severe storms:

______________ , and hurricanes

Name ______________________ Date __________

LESSON
Outline

Air and Weather

Use your textbook to help you fill in the blanks.

What is in the air?

1. The blanket of air surrounding Earth is called the ______________ .
2. The atmosphere is made up mostly of ______________ and ______________ .
3. The four layers of Earth's atmosphere, from lowest to highest, are ______________ , ______________ , mesosphere, and thermosphere.
4. All living things are in the ______________ .

What are some properties of weather?

5. The condition of the atmosphere at a given time and place is called ______________ .
6. When you measure how hot or cold something is, you measure its ______________ .
7. Winds start to blow when the air temperature ______________ .
8. A measure of the amount of water vapor in the air is ______________ .
9. Water vapor comes from ocean water that ______________ from a liquid to a gas.

Name ______________________ Date __________

10. As air cools, the air pressure ______________ .

11. Any form of water that falls to Earth is called

______________ .

How can you measure weather?

12. Scientists collect and analyze data from different

______________ to track and predict the weather.

13. To measure rainfall, researchers collect rain in a tube

called a(n) ______________ .

14. A tool used to measure air pressure is called

a(n) ______________ .

Critical Thinking

15. What weather tools do you think are used in the desert, the humid tropical rain forest, and the frozen tundra?

____

____

____

____

____

____

____

____

Name ______________________ Date ____________

Air and Weather

What am I?

Choose a word from the box below that answers each question, and write the correct letter in the space provided.

a. air pressure	**d.** rain gauge	**g.** wind
b. barometer	**e.** temperature	**h.** wind vane
c. humidity	**f.** thermometer	

1. ________ I am the weight of the air above you. What am I?

2. ________ I am moving air. What am I?

3. ________ I can tell you how hot or cold the air is. What am I?

4. ________ I can tell you how much it rained. What am I?

5. ________ I can tell you what the air pressure is. What am I?

6. ________ I point to where the wind is coming from. What am I?

7. ________ I am the amount of water vapor in the air. What am I?

8. ________ I am a measure of how hot or cold something is. What am I?

LESSON
Cloze Activity

Name ______________________ Date __________

Air and Weather

Use the words in the box to fill in the blanks.

air pressure	lowest	thermometer
barometer	predict	troposphere
higher	temperature	weight

Weather is the condition of Earth's atmosphere at any given time and place. All weather takes place in the ____________________ level of the atmosphere, called the ____________________ . Scientists use many tools to help them track and ____________________ the weather. A measure of how hot or cold the air is, or ____________________, is found with a(n) ____________________ .

A measure of the ____________________ of the air pushing down on an area is called ____________________ . It is measured with a(n) ____________________ . Cool air has a(n) ____________________ air pressure than warm air. A difference in air temperature causes the movement of air, or wind.

Name ______________________________ Date ___________

Watching Spring Weather

Write About It

Expository Writing Observe the weather in your area every day for two weeks. Record the temperature, air pressure, precipitation, clouds, and wind speed. Write a newspaper article about the changes you observed.

Getting Ideas

Use the information you recorded to fill out the chart below. Under main idea, write an important idea about the weather. Then write facts and details that support your main idea.

Main Idea	Details

Planning and Organizing

Here are some sentences Zack wrote about the weather in his area. Write "MI" if the sentence tells the main idea. Write "D" if it tells a detail.

1. ______ At first, the temperature was in the 70s.

2. ______ The weather has changed a lot during the last two weeks.

3. ______ There wasn't a cloud in the sky.

Name ______________________ Date __________

Revising and Proofreading

Here are some sentences Zack wrote. Combine each pair of sentences. Use the transition word in parentheses.

1. There has been a big threat of forest fires. It hasn't rained in two weeks. (because)

____

____

2. Brush fires start. Leaves and grass dry out from the wind. (when)

____

3. The weather report said to expect thunderstorms. There is a warm air mass moving through our region. (because)

____

____

Drafting

Write a sentence to begin your article about weather in your area. Tell your main idea about how it changed.

____

____

Now write your article. Use a separate piece of paper. Remember to include specific details such as the amount of rainfall.

Now revise and proofread your writing. Ask yourself:

- ▶ Did I tell a main idea about the weather?
- ▶ Did I include facts and details to back up this idea?
- ▶ Did I correct all mistakes?

Name ______________________ Date ____________

LESSON **Outline**

The Water Cycle

Use your textbook to help you fill in the blanks.

Why does water change state?

1. Water moves from Earth's surface to the ______________ and back again.
2. Water in the gas state is called ______________ .
3. The process during which a liquid slowly changes to a gas is called ______________ . Heat from the ______________ causes ocean water to evaporate.
4. The process during which a gas changes to a liquid is called ______________ . When the air cools, water vapor condenses on objects; for example, ______________ forms on grass.
5. Liquid water becomes a solid when it ______________ .

Where does water go?

6. Earth's water is constantly changing state by moving through the ______________ .
7. When water vapor rises, it cools and ______________ onto a surface.
8. As water vapor condenses in the atmosphere, ______________ form.
9. Rain, snow, sleet, and hail are different forms of ______________ .

LESSON
Outline

Name ______________________ Date ____________

What are some types of clouds?

10. Low, layered clouds are called ____________ clouds.

11. White, puffy ____________ clouds can become thick and dark ____________ clouds that produce precipitation.

12. Thin, wispy clouds high in the sky are called ____________ clouds.

What are other forms of precipitation?

13. In freezing air, bits of ice crystals will fall to the ground as ____________ .

14. Hailstones form inside tall ____________ and are usually the size of peas.

Critical Thinking

15. Describe examples of the water cycle inside your house.

____

____

____

____

____

____

____

Name ________________________ Date ____________

LESSON
Vocabulary

The Water Cycle

Match the correct word to its description by writing its letter in the space provided.

a. condensation	**d.** melting	**g.** snow
b. evaporation	**e.** precipitation	**h.** water cycle
c. freezing	**f.** sleet	**i.** water vapor

1. ________ This is the process that causes a liquid to change into a solid.

2. ________ This is the ongoing movement of water through many different processes and states.

3. ________ These are small drops of rain that freeze in the air before they hit the ground.

4. ________ This is the process of a liquid becoming a gas.

5. ________ These are ice crystals that form in clouds when the air is cold and then fall to Earth.

6. ________ This is any type of water that falls from clouds to Earth.

7. ________ This is the gaseous form of water.

8. ________ This is the process of a gas becoming a liquid.

9. ________ This is the process of a solid becoming a liquid.

Name ______________________ Date ____________

The Water Cycle

Use the words in the box to fill in the blanks.

cirrus	cumulus	stratus
clouds	evaporates	vapor
condenses	precipitation	water cycle

Water moves from Earth to the atmosphere and back again. This path is called the ____________________. Water changes to a gas, or ____________________, from the surface of oceans, lakes, and other places. Water ____________________ rises into the air and cools. Then it ____________________ onto tiny particles of dust and forms ____________________.

There are three main types of clouds. Puffy white clouds are called ____________________ clouds. Low, layered clouds are called ____________________ clouds. Wispy clouds high in the sky are called ____________________ clouds. Eventually, the water in clouds falls back to Earth as ____________________. The different types of precipitation include rain, snow, sleet, and hail.

Name ______________________ Date ____________

LESSON
Outline

Tracking the Weather

Use your textbook to help you fill in the blanks.

What are air masses and fronts?

1. A large region of air with nearly the same temperature and water vapor throughout is called a(n) ____________.

2. Dry air masses form over land, and moist air masses form over ____________. Warm air masses form near the equator, and cold air masses form near the ____________.

3. The boundary between two air masses is a(n) ____________.

4. A warm air mass that overtakes and pushes into a cold air mass is called a(n) ____________.

5. A cold air mass that pushes under a warm air mass is called a(n) ____________.

6. Two air masses that are not moving into each other form a(n) ____________.

What does a weather map show?

7. Weather maps use half circles or triangles to show ____________ and colors to show ____________.

8. Predicting weather conditions is called ____________.

9. In the United States, fronts tend to move from ____________ to ____________.

Name ______________________ Date __________

What are thunderstorms?

10. Thunderstorms develop when warm, moist air

______________________ .

11. Movement of air upward is called a(n) ______________ .

12. Thunderstorms bring ______________ caused by the movement of particles of ice and rain and

______________________ , the sound of air expanding quickly when heated by lightning.

What are tornadoes?

13. Some thunderstorms develop violent wind storms

called ______________________ .

What are hurricanes?

14. Some thunderstorms develop over warm ocean water near

the ______________________ . The can become hurricanes,

with winds ______________________ around the eye at very high speeds and carrying heavy rain.

Critical Thinking

15. Why do you think the weather usually becomes cool and clear after a severe thunderstorm?

____

____

____

____

____

Name ______________________ Date __________

Tracking the Weather

Match the correct word to its description by writing the word in the space provided.

cold	hurricanes	tornadoes
forecast	mass	warm
front	thunderstorm	

1. The boundary between two air masses is called a ______________ .

2. Meteorologists study weather patterns and maps so that they can predict or ______________ the weather.

3. If a front brings stormy weather, then it is a ______________ front.

4. A large region of air with nearly the same temperature and water vapor throughout is an air ______________ .

5. When a ______________ front pushes under cold air, it brings light, steady rain.

6. Although ______________ are very wide storms that form over the ocean, they can also cause severe damage on land.

7. Heavy rain and lightning are signs of a ______________ .

8. Rotating columns of air form ______________ that can reach speeds of 500 km (300 mi) per hour.

Name ______________________ Date ____________

Tracking the Weather

Use the words in the box to fill in the blanks.

air mass	equator	land	poles
cold front	front	oceans	warm front

The weather pattern on the ground depends on what is happening in the air. The body of air that slowly passes over a wide area of water or land is called a(n) ____________________. For example, cold, dry, air masses form over ____________________ and close to the ____________________. Warm, moist air masses form over ____________________ and close to the ____________________.

The place where two different air masses meet is called a(n) ____________________. A cold air mass overtaking and pushing under a warm air mass is called a(n) ____________________. A warm air mass overtaking a cold air mass is called a(n) ____________________. To forecast the weather, scientists locate fronts and track how they are moving.

Name ______________________ Date ____________

Hurricane Season

Read the passage in your textbook. On the lines below, write the information that lets you know when and where hurricanes occur.

____

____

____

Write About It

Fact and Opinion

1. What technologies help scientists study hurricanes?
2. What do you think would happen during a hurricane in your neighborhood?

____

____

____

____

____

____

____

____

____

____

Name ______________________ Date ____________

Fill in the Fact and Opinion graphic organizer. Then answer the questions.

Fact	Opinion
Hurricanes usually happen in the ________________ and northeast ________________ oceans.	The National Hurricane Center in ________________, thinks there will be more hurricanes this year than last year.
There must be certain ________________ for a hurricane to form.	The temperature of the ocean water isn't ________________ enough for a hurricane to form until late June.
Hurricanes are storms that bring violent winds, large ________________, ________________, and lots of ________________.	Violent ________________ may knock down trees, and large ________________ may cause ________________.
Data about hurricanes comes from buoys, ________________, ________________, and supercomputers.	People tell what they ________________ about hurricanes.

1. Why would a prediction be considered an opinion rather than a fact?

____

____

Name ______________________ Date __________

LESSON
Outline

Climate

Use your textbook to help you fill in the blanks.

What is climate?

1. The pattern of seasonal weather that happens in an area year after year is called ______________.

2. Two important factors that define climate are ______________ and ______________.

3. Temperate climates often have four ______________.

4. The types of ______________ that farmers can grow depend on climate.

What determines climate?

5. The thin lines that run across maps are lines of ______________.

6. Latitude is a measure of how far a place is from the ______________, and it increases as you move north or south.

7. The lower the latitude, the ______________ the climate.

8. The temperature differences between low and high latitudes cause ______________.

Name ______________________________ Date ____________

9. Warm air near the equator ______________________ and moves toward the poles; cold air near the poles

______________________ and moves toward the equator.

10. A directed flow of water through the ocean is called

a(n) ______________________.

11. Water heats more slowly and cools more ______________________ than land does.

12. Climates near the ocean are milder than climates

______________________.

How do mountains affect climate?

13. The climate at the base of a mountain is always

______________________ than the climate at the peak.

14. As a(n) ______________________ travels over a mountain,

it dries out. So the ______________________ on one side will be wetter than the climate on the other side.

Critical Thinking

15. What do you think the climate would be like if you lived at the base of a mountain near the ocean?

____

____

____

____

____

Name ______________________ Date ____________

Climate

Match the correct letter with its description by writing its letter in the space provided.

a. altitude	**d.** equator	**g.** mountain
b. climate	**e.** global winds	**h.** ocean current
c. current	**f.** latitude	

1. ________ the characteristic weather of a region over the course of several years

2. ________ a measure of how far a place is from the equator

3. ________ the directed flow of a gas or liquid

4. ________ a formation that can separate two different types of climates

5. ________ a measure of how high a place is above sea level

6. ________ the directed flow of water over long distances through the ocean

7. ________ winds that circulate in the air between the equator and the poles

8. ________ where the latitude is set at zero degrees

Name ____________________ Date __________

Climate

Use the words in the box to fill in the blanks.

altitude	degrees	precipitation
climate	latitude	temperatures
cold	land	tropical

The weather in a particular region can be averaged over a long period of time. This is called the ____________________, and farmers depend on it to grow their crops. Average yearly ____________________ and ____________________ define the climate of a region. Areas at the equator have a(n) ____________________ of zero degrees and have ____________________ climates. Latitude at the North and South poles is 90 ____________________, and these areas have ____________________ climates.

Air temperature decreases with ____________________, so higher areas have cooler climates than lower areas. Water warms and cools more slowly than ____________________ does. This is why areas near the ocean usually have milder climates than inland areas.

Weather and Climate

Circle the letter of the best answer.

1. Which tool is used to measure air pressure?

a. hygrometer

b. anemometer

c. barometer

d. thermometer

2. The most abundant gases in the atmosphere are nitrogen and

a. oxygen.

b. carbon dioxide.

c. water vapor.

d. hydrogen.

3. Which is the lowest layer of the atmosphere?

a. stratosphere

b. thermosphere

c. ionosphere

d. troposphere

4. Humidity is a measure of

a. the weight of the air.

b. the amount of water vapor in the air.

c. precipitation.

d. how hot or cold the air is.

5. The process during which a liquid changes into a gas is called

a. condensation.

b. freezing.

c. evaporation.

d. melting.

6. Dew forms on grass when water vapor from the air

a. condenses.

b. evaporates.

c. melts.

d. freezes.

7. Wispy clouds that form high in the sky are called

a. cumulus clouds.

b. stratus clouds.

c. cumulonimbus clouds.

d. cirrus clouds.

8. An air mass that forms over tropical ocean water will be

a. warm and dry.

b. cold and dry.

c. warm and moist.

d. cold and moist.

Name ____________________ Date ____________

Circle the letter of the best answer.

9. A cold air mass pushing under a warm air mass is called

a. a warm front.
b. a cold front.
c. a stationary front.
d. an occluded front.

10. Fronts in the United States tend to move from

a. west to east.
b. east to west.
c. north to south.
d. south to north.

11. A large storm with an eye at its center is called a

a. tornado.
b. thunderstorm.
c. winter storm.
d. hurricane.

12. Global winds are caused by

a. temperature differences between high and low latitudes.
b. temperature differences between high and low altitudes.
c. ocean currents.
d. mountain ranges.

13. Which of the following will cause a climate to be cooler?

a. lower altitude
b. higher altitude
c. lower latitude
d. ocean current from the equator

14. Where does the latitude measure 0°?

a. North Pole
b. South Pole
c. equator
d. polar current

15. Which of the following is a measure of the weight of air pressing down on an area?

a. air pressure
b. temperature
c. precipitation
d. humidity

Name ______________________ Date ____________

Tornado Tears Through Midwest

From *Time for Kids*

Read the Unit Literature feature in your textbook.

Write About It

Response to Literature What would happen if a tornado struck your community? Write a fictional story. Describe how your community would stay safe. How would it rebuild after the disaster?

Name ____________________ Date __________

Light and Electricity

Complete the concept map about light and electricity. Some parts have been done for you.

Light

Nature and Movement	Refraction	Reflection
part of ______ spectrum travels in ______	can be ______, or refracted, when passing to different ______	colors that ______ surface of object makes ______ work gives objects ______

Electricity

Nature and Movement	Control of Movement	Uses
result of electrical charge; can be ______ similar charges: ______; ______ charges: attract charged particles: ______ in electric current	made easier by ______; ______ by insulators; carried along circuit; made of power source, ______, and load	converted into heat, light, or ______

Name ______________________ Date ____________

LESSON
Outline

Light

Use your textbook to help you fill in the blanks.

What is light?

1. Light is a form of ________________ that travels in ________________ .
2. A tool used to separate white light into different colors is a(n) ________________ .
3. The colors that make up white light are called the ________________ .

How does light travel?

4. Light rays ________________ as they pass from one material to another.
5. Light travels more slowly through ________________ materials.
6. A lens is a tool used to ________________ , or bend, light.
7. A lens that bends light outward, making objects look smaller, is called a(n) ________________ lens. A lens that bends light toward its center, making objects look bigger, is called a(n) ________________ lens.
8. The lens of an eye focuses the image on the ________________ . Optic nerves send signals about the image to the ________________ .

LESSON
Outline

Name ______________________ Date ____________

What is reflection?

9. Reflection occurs when light strikes and then

______________________ a surface.

10. Smooth, shiny surfaces, such as ______________________, reflect the most light.

11. The law of reflection involves ______________________

light rays: the ______________________ ray and the outgoing ray. The angles of both rays

are ______________________.

What can light pass through?

12. Opaque material blocks light, ______________________ material allows light to pass through, and translucent material allows some light to pass through but

______________________ it in different directions.

Critical Thinking

13. The iris of the eye narrows to let less light in through the pupil or widens to let in more light. Which action would it take on a sunny day? What about in the early evening? Why?

____

____

____

____

____

Name ____________________ Date ____________

Light

Match the correct word or words with their descriptions by writing its letter in the space provided.

a. electromagnetic	**d.** reflection	**g.** transparent
b. opaque	**e.** refraction	**h.** visible spectrum
c. prism	**f.** translucent	

1. ________ a tool used to separate white light into all of its colors

2. ________ the spectrum that encompasses all the wavelengths of light

3. ________ the bending of light rays as they pass through different materials

4. ________ all the colors we see that make up white light

5. ________ description of a material through which light cannot pass

6. ________ description of a material through which light can pass

7. ________ description of a material through which light can pass but will be scattered in different directions

8. ________ the property of light in which light rays strike a mirror and bounce off

Name ________________________ Date ____________

Light

Use the words in the box to fill in the blanks.

blocked	reflection	transparent
concave	refraction	two
mirrors	translucent	

Light has certain properties. It passes through some materials and is ____________________ by others. Opaque materials block light, ____________________ materials let some light pass through, and ____________________ materials allow all light to pass through.

The process in which light waves bend as they pass from one transparent material to another is called ____________________. Lenses refract light in different ways. Two kinds of lenses are ____________________ and convex lenses.

Light can also bounce off an object. This is called ____________________. Smooth, shiny surfaces, such as ____________________, reflect the most light. Reflection involves ____________________ light rays: an incoming ray and an outgoing ray. The angles of both rays are equal.

Name ______________________________ Date ____________

LESSON
Outline

Seeing Light and Color

Use your textbook to help you fill in the blanks.

How do you get color from white light?

1. Sir Isaac Newton passed light through a(n) ______________________ and saw all the colors of the rainbow.
2. When he passed the colors through a second prism, the colors were combined again and made ______________________ light.
3. Newton noticed that each color ______________________ at a different angle.
4. We see rainbows because ______________________ in the sky act like a prism and divide white light into colors.

How do colors look in colored light?

5. Objects called ______________________ change the color of an object by absorbing some colors and letting others ______________________ .
6. If you look at an object that is red through a red filter, it will still look red. If you look at it through a(n) green filter, the filter blocks out every color except ______________________ . A red object will look ______________________ because the object can only reflect red light.
7. We see colors because our eyes have special ______________________ that react to colors.

Name ______________________ Date ____________

8. Some of the cells react to red, some to ______________ ,

and some to ______________ .

9. Red, blue, and green are ______________ , and they can be combined to make other colors.

What happens when color is reflected?

10. Objects have colored substances called ______________ that reflect some colors and absorb others.

11. All the colors that are reflected join to give an object

its ______________ .

12. For example, leaves ______________ red and

blue light and ______________ green light. That is why they look green.

13. If an object reflects all colors, the colors join together to

make the object look ______________ .

14. If an object ______________ all the colors, it looks black.

15. Objects that are transparent, like glass, let light

______________ .

Critical Thinking

16. Why would an object change color when it is given a fresh coat of paint?

____

____

____

Name ______________________________ Date ____________

Seeing Light and Color

Match the word or words to their descriptions by writing the letter in the space provided.

a. absorbed	**d.** primary color	**g.** spectrum
b. filter	**e.** prism	**h.** transparent
c. pigment	**f.** reflected	

1. ________ type of light that gives an object its color
2. ________ material that blocks some kinds of light and lets others through
3. ________ type of light that is not reflected in the color of an object
4. ________ band of different colors
5. ________ substance in objects that reacts with light to produce color
6. ________ material that lets all light pass through
7. ________ red, green, or blue
8. ________ object that can be used to split light into different colors

Name ______________________ Date ____________

Seeing Light and Color

Use the words in the box to fill in the blanks.

black	different	pass through	white
color	eyes	primary	
combination	mixed	reflect	

Objects have colors because they have pigments. These substances ______________ a particular color. The light that is reflected gives the object its ______________. Objects have different pigments that each reflect ______________ colors. The color they have is a(n) ______________ of all the reflected colors. Transparent objects do not reflect light but instead let it ______________. Objects look ______________ if they reflect all light. Those that look ______________ absorb all light.

We see colors because our ______________ have cells that react to one of three colors, green, red, and blue. These are called the ______________ colors. They can be ______________ in different combinations to make different colors. If equal amounts of red, blue, and green reach these cells, you will see white.

Name ______________________ Date __________

A Beam of Light

Read the paragraph below.

Surgeons are doctors who perform operations to fix injuries or treat diseases. They can use scalpels—special tools with sharp blades—to cut through skin, muscles, and organs of the human body. Today, surgeons have another tool they can use to do operations. This tool is a beam of light!

This beam of light is called a *laser*. Lasers are very powerful. They can cut through the human body without causing much bleeding.

Lasers were first used to remove birthmarks on children's skin. Today, surgeons also use lasers to treat injuries to the brain, the heart, and many other parts of the body. Lasers are also used to improve people's eyesight.

Write About It

Summarize Read the article again. List the most important information in a chart. Then use the chart to write a summary of the article.

Name ______________________ Date __________

Planning and Organizing

▶ List the most important information from the article in the chart below.

Most Important Information

Drafting

▶ Start by writing a clear statement that describes the main idea of the article.

▶ Write three supporting details.

▶ Read what you have written. Cross out anything that does not directly support the main idea.

▶ Exchange papers with your partner and ask him or her to check your choice of a main idea. Have your partner also check your choice of supporting details.

Summarize Write your summary on a separate piece of paper. Use your own words. Include the main ideas and details you wrote.

Electricity

Use your textbook to help you fill in the blanks.

What is electrical charge?

1. Electrical charge is a(n) ____________________ .

2. Scientists call the two types of electrical charges ____________________ and ____________________ .

3. When positive and negative charges ____________________ , the matter is said to be neutral.

4. Like charges repel or ____________________ each other, but opposite charges ____________________ , or pull toward each other.

5. When two objects touch, ____________________ move between them.

6. Negative charges move more ____________________ than positive charges.

What is static electricity?

7. The buildup of electrical charges on an object is called ____________________ .

8. Rubbing one object against another causes a ____________________ of one kind of charge.

9. When you rub a balloon on wool, negative charges build up in the ____________________ .

Name ______________________ Date ____________

10. When you place the balloon against a wall, it

______________ positive charges in the wall.

Because of that, the balloon ______________ against the wall.

What is an electrical discharge?

11. Lightning is the discharge of ______________ inside a storm cloud.

12. A(n) ______________ is the movement of static electricity from one object to another.

13. When lightning strikes, ______________ in a cloud push down on the negative charges in the ground.

14. The safest place in a lightning storm is ______________.

What are conductors and insulators?

15. Copper and silver are good ______________ because charges flow through them easily.

16. The outside of an electrical wire is covered by a(n)

______________ such as rubber or plastic.

17. The insulator keeps the electricity inside the wire and

______________.

Critical Thinking

18. Suppose you walked on a carpet and built up a charge of static electricity. Would you feel a shock if you touched a plastic cup? Why or why not?

____

____

Name ______________________________ Date ____________

Electricity

Match the correct word or words to their definitions by writing the letter in the space provided.

a. attract	**d.** electrical charge	**g.** repel
b. conductors	**e.** insulators	**h.** static electricity
c. discharge	**f.** neutral	

1. ________ Rubber, plastic, and glass are good examples of these materials.

2. ________ Two objects that both have negative charges will do this to each other.

3. ________ This property of matter has two types, positive and negative.

4. ________ When clothes stick together after coming out of a clothes dryer, they might have this buildup.

5. ________ Copper and other metals are good examples of these materials.

6. ________ Walking across a carpet and then touching something metal can cause this movement of electricity.

7. ________ Objects with a negative charge will do this to objects with a positive charge.

8. ________ Objects that have an equal number of positive and negative particles are said to be this.

Name ______________________ Date ____________

Electricity

Use the words in the box to fill in the blanks.

charged particles	insulators	static electricity
conductors	negative	
electrical charges	positive	

Electricity powers traffic lights, appliances, and computers. There are different kinds of electricity, but all electricity is the result of ____________________ .

There are two types of electrical charges. Scientists call these charges ____________________ and ____________________ . When two objects touch, ____________________ can move from one object to the other.

The buildup of electrical charges is called ____________________ . It is what makes clothes stick together.

Metals such as copper and silver are good ____________________ because they let charges flow through them easily. Rubber, plastic, and glass are examples of good ____________________ . These materials do not let charges flow through them easily.

Name ______________________________ Date ____________

LESSON
Outline

Electric Circuits

Use your textbook to help you fill in the blanks.

What is electric current?

1. Electrical ______________ can be made to flow continuously through materials.
2. A flow of electrical charges is known as a(n) ______________.
3. The path along which electrical charges flow is called a(n) ______________.
4. A complete, unbroken path is called a(n) ______________.
5. Electric current cannot flow in a(n) ______________.
6. A(n) ______________ is a part of a circuit that opens and closes the circuit.
7. An electric circuit begins at a(n) ______________.
8. Current needs to flow through a connector such as ______________.
9. Current reaches a(n) ______________, such as a lamp or a computer that uses the electricity.

What is a series circuit?

10. In a series circuit, all of the electrical charges flow ______________ and along ______________.
11. If any part of a series circuit is removed or broken, the circuit is ______________.

Name ______________________ Date __________

What is a parallel circuit?

12. A parallel circuit is a circuit in which the electric current flows through ________________ .

13. The ________________ of a parallel circuit divide the electric current between them.

What affects electric current?

14. The amount of electric current that can flow through a circuit depends on ________________ and ________________ .

15. Voltage is measured in units called ________________ .

16. Increasing the ________________ of a circuit decreases the flow of electrical charges through it.

17. A(n) ________________ can stop the rest of the circuit from operating properly and can be dangerous.

Critical Thinking

18. Do you think the material inside a light bulb is a conductor or has resistance? Why?

____

____

____

____

____

Name Samuel 22 Date ____________

LESSON
Vocabulary

Electric Circuits

Use the clues to unscramble each of the words. Take the letters that appear in the boxes marked with circles and unscramble the letters for the final message.

Clues

1. a property of matter — **REIGELTCRALCACHE** electric current
2. a flow of electrical charges — **RUTCENR**
3. can build up as static electricity and can be discharged — **GESAHCR**
4. the unbroken path along which an electric current flows — **TIRCIUC**
5. status of a circuit that is complete and unbroken with flowing electric current — **SECDOL**
6. status of a circuit that has breaks or openings in which electric current cannot flow — **NEPO**
7. opens and closes the circuit — **CHTISW**
8. a circuit in which all electrical charges flow in the same direction and along the same path — **SISREE**
9. the strength of a power source that is measured in volts — **EVLOGTA**
10. the ability of a substance to slow down electric current — **CANSETSERI**
11. circuit in which the electric current follows two or more paths that are called branches — **LLLAPREA**

						B			B

Name Samuel 22 ____________________ Date ____________

Electric Circuits

Use the words in the box to fill in the blanks.

charges	electric current	parallel circuit
current	open	series circuit

People depend on electricity to light up rooms and to power televisions and computers. The electricity that people use relies on a(n) ____________________ of electrical charges. A flow of electrical charges is known as a(n) ____________________. Electric currents keep ____________________ moving.

All electrical charges flow in the same direction and along the same path in a(n) ____________________. If any part of a series circuit is removed or broken, the circuit is ____________________. That means the current no longer flows.

A(n) ____________________ is a circuit in which the electric current follows more than one path. If any part of a parallel circuit is removed or broken, the current continues to flow.

Name ______________________ Date ____________

LESSON
Outline

Using Electrical Energy

Use your textbook to help you fill in the blanks.

How is electrical energy used?

1. An incandescent bulb produces ____________ and light.

2. Inside incandescent bulbs is a thin wire called a(n) ____________ that glows when it receives current.

3. A fluorescent bulb uses a(n) ____________ to produce light. It also glows when it receives current.

4. Electrical energy can be converted into ____________.

5. Electric motors change electrical energy into ____________.

How does electrical energy get to your home?

6. Electrical energy is produced in ____________.

7. As it travels, ____________ change the voltage of electric current.

8. Electric current from a power plant enters a(n) ____________ transformer. Electric current leaves the transformer with a strength of about ____________ volts.

9. Before reaching homes, the current must pass through a(n) ____________ transformer to be made weaker.

10. Appliances in a home usually run on ____________ volt circuits.

Name ______________________ Date __________

How can homes use electrical energy safely?

11. Short ______________ can cause electrical fires.

12. A(n) ______________ stops the flow of charges by switching off the current if it gets too high.

13. A short circuit might happen when the ______________ of a wire frays.

14. A(n) ______________ melts and breaks the circuit if the electric current in the circuit gets too high.

15. Plugging too many devices into one circuit can also cause too much current to go through a(n) ______________.

16. Surge ______________ stop the flow if there is too much electric current.

Critical Thinking

17. Is the circuit connecting a power plant and the homes in your neighborhood a series circuit or a parallel circuit? Why?

____

____

____

____

____

____

____

Name ______________________ Date ____________

Using Electrical Energy

Read each clue. Write the answer in the blank and fill in the crossword puzzle.

circuit breaker
filament
fluorescent
fuse
incandescent
transformer

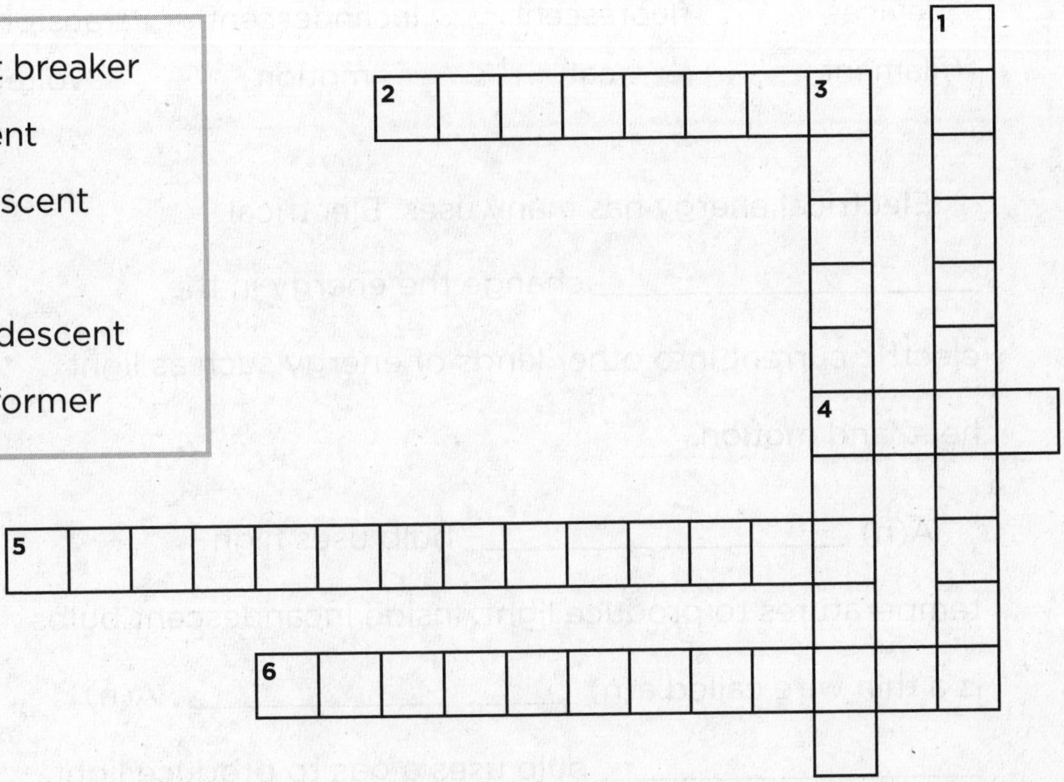

Across

2. a thin wire found in incandescent bulbs

____

4. can melt to break the flow of electric current in a circuit

____

5. can stop the flow of charges by switching off the current

____

6. a bulb that produces light and heat through a glowing wire

____

Down

1. a bulb that uses gas to produce light ________________

3. changes the voltage of electric current

____

LESSON
Cloze Activity

Name ____________________ Date __________

Using Electrical Energy

Use the words in the box to fill in the blanks.

devices	fluorescent	incandescent	transformers
filament	heat	motion	voltage

Electrical energy has many uses. Electrical ____________________ change the energy in the electric current into other kinds of energy such as light, heat, and motion.

A(n) ____________________ bulb uses high temperatures to produce light. Inside incandescent bulbs is a thin wire called a(n) ____________________ . A(n) ____________________ bulb uses a gas to produce light.

Electrical energy can be converted into ____________________ . Electric motors change electrical energy into ____________________ . Electrical energy travels from a power station through wires and ____________________ to a home. Transfomers are used to change the ____________________ of an electric current. Safety devices such as fuses and circuit breakers protect homes and stores from an electric overload.

Name ______________________ Date ____________

Hybrid Power

Read the passage in your textbook. As you read, write down the topic sentence of each paragraph.

Topic sentence:

1. ______________________

2. ______________________

____

3. ______________________

4. ______________________

5. ______________________

Write About It

Summarize Read the article again. How do hybrid cars work? How do hybrid cars help the environment?

1. How do hybrid cars help people?

____

2. How do hybrid cars work?

____

____

3. How does that help the environment?

____

Name ____________________ Date __________

Reread the article. As you read, record the details that support each of the sentences in the Summarize graphic organizer.

Main Idea	Details
Hybrid cars that use ____________ and ____________ energy can lessen our ____________ on gasoline and reduce ____________ pollution.	The gasoline we use is made from oil, a nonrenewable ____________ .
	In a traditional car, the ____________ engine runs all the time.
	Hybrid cars use two power sources: ____________ and ____________ .
	A hybrid car uses less ____________ and switches to a(n) ____________ motor powered by ____________ when the car slows down or comes to a stop.
	The batteries ____________ when the car comes to a stop.
	The gasoline engine in a(n) ____________ car is small and ____________ efficient.

Name ______________________ Date __________

Light and Electricity

Circle the letter of the best answer.

1. The strength of a power source is its

a. charge.

b. discharge.

c. resistance.

d. voltage.

2. A safety device that switches off dangerous currents is a

a. circuit breaker.

b. insulator.

c. resistor.

d. transformer.

3. Charges do not flow easily through

a. conductors.

b. copper wire.

c. insulators.

d. silver.

4. The continuous flow of electrical charges is

a. discharge.

b. electric current.

c. static electricity.

d. voltage.

5. Light is blocked completely by material that is

a. opaque.

b. reflective.

c. translucent.

d. transparent.

6. Which of these is NOT a primary color of light?

a. blue

b. green

c. red

d. yellow

7. You can produce all the colors of the rainbow using a

a. glass.

b. mirror.

c. prism.

d. table.

Name ______________________ Date ____________

Circle the letter of the best answer.

8. The voltage of an electric current can be increased by a(n)

a. fuse.

b. insulator.

c. resistor.

d. transformer.

9. Resistance is the ability of a substance to

a. change the charge of an object.

b. provide power to a circuit.

c. slow down electric current.

d. speed up electric current.

10. Visible light is the part of the electromagnetic spectrum

a. with the shortest wavelength.

b. with the longest wavelength.

c. that travels through space.

d. that we can see.

11. Eyeglasses contain this kind of lens because it bends light inward, making objects larger.

a. concave

b. convex

c. optic

d. reflective

12. Objects in the world have color because they

a. absorb all the Sun's light.

b. reflect some of the Sun's light.

c. give off their own light.

d. glow from making light.

13. Electric current flows through different paths in a(n)

a. fuse.

b. open circuit.

c. parallel circuit.

d. series circuit.

14. The path of electric current is called a

a. circuit.

b. fuse.

c. switch.

d. transformer.

Name ______________________ Date ____________

CHAPTER
Concept Map

Magnetism

E
L
E
C
T
R
O
M
A
G
N
E
T
I
S
M

What causes a magnetic field to be produced around a wire?

____

____

How can an electromagnet be made?

____

____

How many poles do all magnets have?

____

When is a magnetic force stronger? When is it weaker?

____

____

____

What items in your house use electromagnetics?

____

____

LESSON **Outline**

Name ______________________ Date __________

Magnets

Use your textbook to help you fill in the blanks.

What is a magnet?

1. When you bring two magnets together, they will either ______________ or attract each other.

2. A magnet is an object with a(n) ______________.

3. The strongest parts of the magnet are called the ______________.

4. When two magnets are brought together, a north pole and a(n) ______________ attract each other.

5. The magnetic force between two magnets is ______________ when the magnets are far apart.

How do magnets attract?

6. Most magnets are made of ______________.

7. Inside a magnet, the tiny particles are lined up with ______________ facing one direction and south poles facing another.

What is a magnetic field?

8. Magnets point north because they line up with ______________ magnetic field.

9. A(n) ______________ is the area of magnetic force around a magnet.

10. The magnetic field allows a magnet to ____________ an object without even touching it.

11. Much of the inside of Earth is made of ____________ .

12. The iron creates a magnetic field that ____________ our planet.

13. Earth spins on its ____________ , an imaginary line through the center of Earth.

14. The ____________ is a display of lights near the South Pole.

What is a compass?

15. A(n) ____________ is an instrument that uses Earth's magnetic field to help people find directions.

Critical Thinking

16. How does a compass work?

____

____

____

____

____

____

____

____

____

LESSON
Vocabulary

Name ____________________ Date __________

Magnets

Use the words in the box to fill in the blanks.

attract	geographic	magnetite
axis	magnet	poles
compass	magnetic field	

1. Earth's magnetic north pole is near its ____________ North Pole.

2. Earth spins around on a(n) ____________, which is an imaginary line through the center of Earth.

3. A(n) ____________ is any object with magnetic force.

4. A(n) ____________ is the area of magnetic force around a magnet.

5. When two magnets are brought together, the north pole and the south pole ____________ each other.

6. A(n) ____________ is an instrument that uses Earth's magnetic field to find direction.

7. The parts of a magnet where the magnetic force is strongest are called the magnetic ____________.

8. A natural magnet containing iron is ____________.

Name ______________________________ Date ____________

LESSON
Cloze Activity

Magnets

Use the words in the box to fill in the blanks.

magnetite	permanent	push
metal	poles	repel
north	pull	temporary

Magnets come in many shapes and sizes. A magnet that always has a magnetic force is a ____________________ magnet. The strongest part of a magnet is the ____________________ . Unlike poles attract each other and like poles ____________________ each other. The mineral ____________________ is a natural magnet containing iron. When you bring a magnet near certain ____________________ objects such as paper clips, tiny particles in the object will line up. The tiny particles ____________________ and ____________________ in all different directions until they come in contact with a magnet. Then, the tiny particles line up facing the ____________________ pole and the south pole. The paper clip becomes a ____________________ magnet. It can attract other metal objects as well!

LESSON **Outline**

Name ______________________ Date ____________

Electromagnets

Use your textbook to help you fill in the blanks.

What is an electromagnet?

1. When an electric current flows through a wire, it creates a(n) ____________________ around the wire.
2. A(n) ____________________ is a coil of wire wrapped around a core, usually an iron bar.
3. The magnetic field in the coil of wire causes ____________________ inside the metal core to become magnetic.
4. When a current in an electromagnet stops, the metal core is no longer ____________________ .

How does a loudspeaker work?

5. A(n) ____________________ is a device that changes electrical energy into sound.
6. The ____________________ is the part of the loudspeaker that vibrates to create sound.
7. When electric current flows through the electromagnet, it is pushed and pulled by the ____________________ .
8. The movement of the diaphragm is what we hear as ____________________ .

9. A telephone receiver is actually a(n) ______________.

10. The telephone mouthpiece is like a loudspeaker in

______________ .

11. A(n) ______________ is a device that uses a magnet to convert sound into electric signals.

How else are electromagnets used?

12. Electromagnets are often more useful than ordinary

magnets because they can be ______________ .

13. Electromagnets are used in ______________ that increase or decrease the voltage of electric currents.

14. They are also found in many household

______________ , such as doorbells, vacuum cleaners, and dishwashers.

Critical Thinking

15. Why are electromagnets more useful than permanent magnets?

____

____

____

____

____

____

____

Name ______________________ Date ____________

Electromagnets

Match the correct letter with the description.

a. current	**d.** electromagnet	**g.** microphone
b. diaphragm	**e.** generate	
c. electric signals	**f.** loudspeaker	

1. ______ When a friend calls you on the phone, his or her voice is changed into this.

2. ______ This device uses a magnet to convert sound into electrical signals.

3. ______ This part of a loudspeaker vibrates to create sound.

4. ______ This device changes electrical energy into sound.

5. ______ This means to make an electric current.

6. ______ When this is turned off, the electromagnet is no longer magnetic.

7. ______ This is a coil of wire wrapped around a core of iron.

Name ______________________ Date __________

Electromagnets

diaphragm	electromagnet	Michael Faraday
electric current	loudspeaker	microphone
electrical signals	magnetic field	sound

Electromagnets are very useful in our daily lives. In the 1820s, ____________ and Joseph Henry discovered that magnets could generate a(n) ____________. When the current is flowing, it creates a(n) ____________ around the wire. When the current is turned off, the ____________ is no longer magnetic.

A loudspeaker is a device that changes electrical energy into ____________. The ____________ is the part of the loudspeaker that vibrates to create sound. A telephone also has a tiny ____________. A friend's voice on the phone is changed into ____________. The mouthpiece of the phone contains a(n) ____________ that uses a magnet to convert sound into electrical signals. Electromagnets are used in many household appliances and toys.

Name ______________________ Date __________

Magnetism

Circle the letter of the best answer.

1. Magnetic force is strongest at the

a. axis.

b. center.

c. magnetic field.

d. poles.

2. A device that changes sound into electrical signals is a

a. generator.

b. loudspeaker.

c. microphone.

d. motor.

3. Objects with magnetic force are called

a. alternating.

b. fields.

c. generators.

d. magnets.

4. The north and south ends of Earth's axis are Earth's

a. geographic poles.

b. equatorial poles.

c. magnetic poles.

d. electromagnetic poles.

5. A diaphragm makes sound when it

a. becomes magnetic.

b. vibrates.

c. senses light.

d. generates electricity.

Circle the letter of the best answer.

6. To work properly, loudspeakers and microphones need both

a. electricity and magnetism.

b. light and sound.

c. curved and straight magnets.

d. a stereo and a television.

7. Electromagnets are used in

a. compasses.

b. pianos.

c. applliances.

d. door knobs.

8. A magnet can attract or repel another object that enters its

a. alternating current.

b. direct current.

c. pole.

d. magnetic field.

9. A device that changes electrical energy into sound is a

a. turbine.

b. loudspeaker.

c. microphone.

d. motor.

10. An electromagnet is a magnet that

a. attracts any object.

b. can be switched on and off.

c. is permanent.

d. is weak.

11. A compass needle points

a. east.

b. north.

c. south.

d. west.

Name ______________________ Date ____________

Magnetic Migration

From *Ranger Rick*

Read the Unit Literature feature in your textbook.

Write About It

Response to Literature Have you taken a trip to a different place? Where did you go? How did you get there? Write about a trip you have taken. Be sure to include how you figured out the directions.